**Public Administration
Towards Social Governance**

走向社会治理的公共管理

——2013 第八届中德公共管理国际研讨会论文集

尹庆双
唐兴霖 / 主编

社会科学文献出版社
SOCIAL SCIENCES ACADEMIC PRESS (CHINA)

第八届中德公共管理国际研讨会开幕式

第八届中德公共管理国际研讨会全体专家合影

张宗益校长致辞

唐兴霖院长主持开幕式

社会改革与社会政策—2013第八届中德公共管理国际研讨会

尹庆双副校长致闭幕辞

BUSCH 院长在开幕式致辞

德国成都领事馆马晏子副领事致辞

目 录

社会创新：理念、方法与政策

变革社会的社会问题与社会政策

转型期中国的社会冲突与社会管理

中德社会政策比较

中德社会改革与整体社会政策协调

附录

在第八届中德公共管理国际研讨会开幕式上的讲话

张宗益[*]

尊敬的各位嘉宾，老师们、同学们：

上午好！

今天，我们相聚于此，隆重举行"第八届中德公共管理国际研讨会"开幕式，一起探讨中德公共管理理论与实践中的重大问题。在此，我谨代表学校向出席研讨会的各位嘉宾表示热烈的欢迎！向本届国际研讨会的顺利开幕表示热烈的祝贺！

"中德公共管理国际研讨会"由我校与柏林经济政法大学合作创办于2005年，已成为中德两国学者研讨公共管理理论与实践的重要学术平台，但我校与柏林经济政法大学的合作却可以追溯到1986年。27年来，从最初提议的非正式访问到两校师生正式年度互访，从确立与安联保险集团开展合作，到"中德货币政策国际研讨会"等合作研究制度逐步完善，从五所欧、亚大学合作协议的签订到中德学术文化周及公共管理论坛的陆续启动，我校与柏林经济政法大学合作的领域不断拓展，深度持续发展。其中，基于"欧亚链"项目的国际经济与商务硕士研究生联合培养项目已累计为中国人

---

* 张宗益：西南财经大学校长。

民银行、财政部及相关高校培养了近 300 名高级官员和教学骨干，互换的留学生也有 100 多名。可以说，两校的合作既是卓有成效的，也是极富远见的。

各位嘉宾：全球化进一步凸显了国际交流与合作的紧迫性与重要性，以传承和创造知识为使命的高等教育更是如此。可以说，自创办以来，我校就特别强调古今融合、中西贯通。2012 年，我校将办学历史追溯到 1925 年 6 月 3 日，1925 年上海爆发了五卅反帝爱国运动，从当时圣约翰大学脱离出来的部分师生创办了光华大学；1938 年，日本军队炸毁了上海的学校，光华大学内迁到我们此刻相聚的地方继续办学。光华大学时代，当时留学英美的归国留学生中，约有 1/5 在光华大学任教，如胡适、章伯钧、潘光旦、罗隆基、王造时等，光华教师阵容之强在当时上海堪称一流。近年来，我们注重人才评价激励的国际国内竞争因素，按照国际国内公认的第三方学术评价机构〔英文期刊采用 Thomson – ISI 发布的国际公认的 JCR《期刊引证分析报告》（*Journal Citation Reports*）〕发布的学科体系和科研成果评价体系，建立起科学的教师业绩评价体系和激励机制，面向全球延揽人才。目前，学校已有来自哈佛、斯坦福、哥伦比亚、伦敦经济学院等国际知名高校的全职海归博士 180 余名，特聘海外院长 9 人，为我校经济学、管理学等学科带来了新的学术视野、研究范式和前沿理论。学校与 50 多个国家和地区的近 100 所知名大学建立了合作与交流关系；与美国花旗银行、汇丰银行、渣打银行、高盛集团、英国英杰华保险公司等全球金融行业巨头共建多个合作教育机构。2012 年，学校第十二次党代会确立了"建设特色鲜明高水平研究型财经大学"的目标定位，其中，"深度开放"是我们四大核心战略之一。因此，我坚信，无论时光怎么流逝，我校与柏林经济政法大学的友谊之树将万古长青，与国内高水平大学之间的合作与交流还将全面深入推进。

各位嘉宾：当前，无论是中国还是欧美国家，经济社会建设都面临着许多共同的问题，如交通环境、教育改革、社区发展、就业与民生、医疗与社会保障等。加强各国公共管理改革经验和研究成果的交流，创新公共管理理念，探索适应时代要求的治理模式，是各国政府和我们学术界的共同梦想。迄今，"中德公共管理国际研讨会"已举办七届，大家围绕公共管理领域的重大理论与实践问题进行了深入的研讨，也催生了许多相当有见地的成果，有力地促进了公共管理学科的发展和公共管理理论的进步。我期望，本届研讨会能够紧密围绕我们共同关注的新问题、新挑战、新经验展开深度对话，取得理论与实践的新突破。在此，我也盛情邀请与会的各位专家、学者常来我校访问讲学，向西财学子播撒创新社会管理的思想。

最后，预祝"第八届中德公共管理国际研讨会"圆满成功！

谢谢大家！

2013 年 9 月 24 日

走向社会治理的公共管理

——2013 第八届中德公共管理国际研讨会会议综述

尹庆双　唐兴霖　唐代盛

由西南财经大学公共管理学院、德国柏林经济与政法大学，西南财经大学科研处、国际合作交流处共同主办，西南财经大学公共管理学院承办的2013 中德公共管理国际研讨会（第八届）于 2013 年 9 月 24 日~9 月 25 日在成都成功召开。本次会议的主题是"社会改革与社会政策"，来自德国驻成都领事馆、德国柏林经济与政法大学、北京大学、苏州大学、西南财经大学、广西民族大学等中外 60 余名学者就这一主题进行了深入研讨。

社会变革与社会政策是当前经济社会快速发展，特别是在重要战略机遇期和矛盾凸显期相互交织的情况下，社会领域的一系列新情况新问题提出的重要课题。无论是中国还是欧美国家，经济社会建设都面临着许多共同的问题，如交通环境、教育改革、社区发展、就业与民生、医疗与社会保障等。加强各国公共管理改革经验和研究成果的交流，创新公共管理理念，探索适应时代要求的治理模式，是各国政府和学界的共同理想。

本次研讨会围绕"社会创新：理念、方法与政策"，"变革社会的社会问题与社会政策"，"转型期中国的社会冲突与社会管理"，"中德社会政策比较"，"中德社会改革与整体社会政策协调"5 个议题，举行了 2 场主题发言、2 场分组讨论和 1 场专题发言，30 余位专家学者进行了发言，提出了自己的学术见解。

社会创新：理念、方法与政策。北京大学国家研究院博士生导师、旅美学者刘国恩教授作了主题发言，其主要内容是经济转型和国家医疗改革，他认为中国的医疗改革可以成为国家经济转型的推动力量，如果中国政府进行有关国民健康的产业和服务的开发和发展，将成为中国经济结构转变和经济发展的强大动力，可以更好地推动改革和发展；苏州大学政治与公共管理学院院长金太军（长江特聘教授）从文化的角度来研究社会治理问题，他指出中国的意识形态太脆弱，要建构一个包容性的意识形态，多一点信仰的层面，多一点出世的精神来做事情；广西民族大学副校长李珍刚教授对公共管理的框架问题进行了探究，他提出分好类是公共管理的起点和基本方法，并就公共事务分类进行多角度的探讨，提出建立一个关于"公共事务分类"的学科；西北大学公共管理学院席恒教授从有公共管理特色的角度回答了两个问题，一是公共事务的本质和问题，二是合作收益最大化和合作收益分配合理化，他认为合作的障碍是外部的制度条件，并从社会政策的角度对此进行了探讨；上海师范大学政法学院何精华教授从社会物理学的角度就社会创新与社会变革提出了三个观点，一是如果社会治理模式不能及时回应经济社会发展的需求，社会系统就会出现劣质化的倾向，二是社会政策的目的是建立一个以"双改"（一个是改善民生，一个是改善制度）为特征的社会指导模式，三是公众对自己的主体地位、主体价值的自省意识，社会治理创新不是加强管理而是改善制度，通过制度这一游戏规则建立公众的合理预期和正和博弈；内蒙古自治区行政学院徐永平教授研究了中国特色社会主义社会管理体系，他提出社会管理体系是社会建设的重要组成部分，社会利益矛盾应在社会管理制度、体制机制和法律框架内得到有效解决，培育社会和谐关系、实现社会和谐，需要坚实的社会管理制度体系的保障；湖南大学法学院李金龙教授从民生取向的视角研究了中国公共政策的公共性价值，他认为公共政策的公共性具有时空特质，在中国集中体现为公共政策的民生取向，中国当前需要从公共政策制定者的民生观教育、公共政策制定过程的民意反映、民生公共政策的切实执行、公共政策绩效的评估标准等方面进行强化和完善；西南财经大学公共管理学院唐兴霖教授研究了政府治理的政策工具问题，他提出政策工具理论的逻辑在于对各种工具的特性、类型进行研究，在不同分析框架下结合特定情境进行选择与评估，发展并完善政府治理的政策工具理论分析框架的内容，一是发挥工具功能，实现政策效果，二是渗透政治因素，达到预期目的，三是强调制度理性，灵活选择机制；西南财经大学公共管理学院任勤教授研究了德国养老保障服务经验及其对中国的启示，从社会养老保险体系、养老服务体系、老年人护理培训体系、养老保险管理运作体系四个方面全面阐释了德国养老保障服务体系框架，提出中国的养老保障服务体系方面要着力改进覆盖面较低、资金来源不足、基金管理不善、服务方式单一、人力资源短缺等问题；安徽师范大学法学院刘晓峰博士对当代农民的"非制度化政治参与"问题进行了探究，他认为乡土社会治理权力转移与现行政治制度设计不足的矛盾，引发农民在现行制度框架下及更为复杂的外部环境中的理性选择为越级上访、组织化抗争和"弱者的武器"；西南财经大学外事处副处长顾绚博士对美国、日本、新加坡政务服务的特点进行了探究，她提出美、日、新等国家的政务服务已经由管制型政府向服务型政府转变，出现了行政权力分散化、行政职能市场化、行政服务社会化、行政信息电子化等发展趋势，可以在观念、制度、服务和科技等方面为中国政务服务提供基本借鉴；上海行政学院公共管理教研部孙志建博士对中国公共行政研究概念进行了探究，他认为在关于中国公共行政的研究中，有必要倡导一种基于现象聚焦，锁定学科重大理论问题，且以中层概念生产为取向的概念创新。

变革社会的社会问题与社会政策。内蒙古自治区行政学院徐永平教授研究了中国社会的非制度化现象，他认为中国社会存在大量非制度化现象，如何看待和怎样消除这些非制度化现象是中国制度化发展的重要课题，制度化发展、制度化建设是中国社会政治建设和政府管理体制变革的根本所在；西南财经大学公共管理学院章群教授研究了患者权利保障问题，她提出保护患者权利的法理在于生命权是一切权利的基础，中国长期形成的医患关系不平衡表现为就医权、健康权和知情权，药费过高、政府投入不足是医患双方共同关注的主要问题，需要尽快建立患者权利的保障机制；重庆文理学院经管学院田书芹副教授从发展人类学的角度对城市化过程中农村人口空心化治理模式与实现机制进行了探究，她采取了城乡二元分析范式从制度纠偏机制和多中心治理层面提出城镇化过程中农村人口空心化治理模式与政治、经济、社会和文化等制度实现机制；西南财经大学公共管理学院徐程副教授从经济学的视角研究了医药卫生政策与管理问题，她认为中国医药卫生领域中的诸多现实问题迫切需要深入开展卫生经济学评价研究，通过全面系统地评价医药卫生技术和公共卫生服务项目的经济性，有利于有效配置医药卫生资源，提高卫生决策的科学性和透明度；南京大学社会学院社会工作与社会政策系郭未博士对社会性别视角下的中国老年人口失能预期寿命及代际支持问题进行了探究，他的研究发现低龄阶段老年人口的存活子女数不断减少且将持续一段时间，这抵消了老年人口失能预期寿命压缩对照料资源需求的减少，对失能老年人口而言，单纯依靠家庭资源已无法满足养老需求，社区帮扶和养老机构的发展显得尤为重要；中国人民大学公共管理学院欧纯智博士对税收执法行政自由裁量权的合理使用问题进行了探究，他认为自由裁量是税务部门执法人员不可或缺的管理工具，然而在执法人员不能形成正义、效率、效能的行政精神之前，对行政自由裁量的监督还是必要的，自由裁量的边界不是无限的，纳税人的有效参与也会对执法人员正确行使自由裁量起到有效的促进作用。

转型期中国的社会冲突与社会管理。苏州大学政治与公共管理学院院长金太军（长江特聘教授）研究了天津滨海新区的社会治理问题，从社区治理结构、工具和方法三个层面评估社区治理实际成效，总结社区治理发展战略，提炼社会治理的基本思路；宁波大学法学院公共管理系主任赵永红教授研究了社会公益服务枢纽型组织的生长与运作问题，他提出政府、市场和社会是现代社会公益服务不可缺少的参与主体，这是一项跨界合作的事业，中国社会公益服务碎片化问题较为突出，这一跨界合作之间存在着信息不对称的问题，而枢纽型社会组织的生长为解决这一问题提供了可能有效的模式；中国海洋大学法政学院同春芬教授以青岛为例研究了决策型海洋渔业应急管理系统，他提出为适应服务型政府建设和行政体制改革的要求，应建设以应急预案为核心的决策型体系；太原理工大学政法学院公共管理系主任乔运鸿副教授研究了草根NGO与乡村多元共治路径问题，他提出乡村善治离不开草根NGO的参与，应探索从二元治理到多元共治的乡村治理的新道路；西南财经大学公共管理学院冯华副教授对高校志愿者参与志愿服务的动机及激励机制问题进行了探究，将志愿者参与志愿服务的动机创新性划分为传统型、现代型和后现代型，认为志愿者参与动机呈现阶段性发展趋势，并提出认可型、自我发展型、自我愉悦型、全程型和"言利"型等激励机制；四川农业大学余华博士对中国西部地区构建农产品质量安全应急管理"全域联动"机制问题进行了探究，他认为应围绕"三个强化"构建"全域联动"农产品质量安全应急管理机制，围绕"三个推行"推进农产品质量安全应急管理"全域联动"，围绕"三个促进"提高农产品质量安全应急管理"全域联动"效能。

中德社会政策比较。德国柏林经济与政法大学 Gerd Kulke 教授研究了中国社会主义市场经济与德国社会市场经济比较的可能性，他认为从工业化开始国家经济的变革是两个国家的共同点，德国一开始完全依靠市场经济，后来改为运用市场调节和政府的宏观调控相结合的经济体制，中国一开始实行完全的计划经济体制，最后又引入市场经济，中国和德国是存在很多相似性的，具有相互比较和借鉴的可能性；德国柏林经济与政法大学 Dörte Busch 教授研究了德国现行社会政策及其对家庭的影响，他提出德国正面临着与家庭相关的另外的挑战，"家庭"正在迅速而急剧地改变，理想的家庭形式（一对夫妻及两个孩子，最好是一儿一女）已经发生了巨大的改变，现在更多的是单亲家庭、有孩子的未婚夫妻、有孩子的同性夫妻（男男夫妻，女女夫妻），在未来的社会政策中不得不将这些考虑进来；德国柏林经济与政法大学公共管理学院经贸系 ORR Wolfgang Strehl 教授研究了市场经济中的社会政策，他认为市场本身就是最好的社会制度，但尽管如此，现在毫无疑问需要政策，特别是社会政策，政策看起来已成为一个体系的内在要求；德国柏林经济与政法大学 Hans Paul Prümm 教授研究了实现德国社会国家的传统路径，他认为德国定义的这种社会国家不是一个弱的国家，而是一个强大的保护和促进社会公平的社会国家，社会国家是嵌入在与其他相关的国家原则之中，特别是民主原则，因此"社会公平的进步"可以最终以民主的方式推进，并展示了社会国家关于历史选择的不同路径，这些路径相互支持，并形成社会国家的历史文化记忆；德国柏林经济与政法大学 Jochen Breinlinger - O'Reilly 教授研究了德国医疗联盟和医保供应网络问题，他认为公共、私人、慈善医院形成联盟的好处在于：一是设备使用和技术合作中体现协力优势，二是员工、病人的能力和灵活性增加，三是对专家和员工的资格认证和继续教育有积极影响，四是客服系统内的部门界限被认为是一种显著的优势，对垄断机构、大型实体及不灵活性等缺点则可以通过政策干预加以削减；德国柏林经济与政法大学经济学家 Frank Diebel 研究了医疗保健部门中的质量保证问题，他通过德国 ISO 与 KTQ 的对比分析提出，ISO 对医院、医疗实践和医疗服务中心、疗养院、康复设备和应急救援设施而言，不需要像 KTQ 模型那样需要专业的认证流程，这种新的医疗专业标准是否会在德国流行起来还有待观察，但至少它代表了一个良好的开始，即对一个完整的质量和风险管理提出建议，以及一个好的过程绩效现代化的机会；西南财经大学公共管理学院博士生导师邓燕华教授研究了浙江农村少数民族社团及其社会抗争问题，探讨了浙江传统少数民族社团功能的演化及其在少数民族社会抗争中扮演的积极角色，她由此认为组织化的社会抗争在中国是可行的。

中德社会改革与整体社会政策协调。西南财经大学公共管理学院幸强国教授对西部城市财力不均现象进行了政策思考，他提出人均财政收入不均衡问题在西部城市会进一步持续下去，对西部城市现在的基本公共服务形成很大的挑战，基本公共服务得不到有效保障；西南财经大学李筠副教授对失业保险跨行业补贴对就业的影响进行了探究，她寻求了影响国家失业保险计划的内生性政策因素；西南财经大学公共管理学院唐代盛副教授研究了中国劳务派遣员工心理契约特征及其政策含义，他提出，"双雇主性"使得劳务派遣员工的归属感模糊、职业生涯发展不清晰、工作稳定性不强，劳务派遣员工心理契约存在不同程度的破坏，并基于宏观、中观和微观三个层面提出劳务派遣制度的价值取向、政策含义和管理策略；西南财经大学公共管理学院颜吟芳副教授研究了"医院治疗率和溢出效应：所有权有影响吗"这一问题，她提出医院间的空间相关、市场结构和治疗类型变化等因素影响了医疗治疗率和溢出效应；西南财经大学公共管理学院黄硕副教授研究了外商直接投资与中国地区发展问题，她通过扩展的索罗经济增长模型描述了中国地区经济增长模式和条件趋同，并通过控制 FDI 等相关增长变量进一步检验了 FDI 对区域发展的影响，FDI 对中国地区经济发展有很大的帮助；西南财经大学公共管理学院 Gergely Horvath 副教授研究了群落结构对银行挤兑现象的影响，他将群落分为交叠和随机两种类型，通过中介变量探究了挤兑现象发生的概率；重庆文理学院经管学院田书芹副教授研究了统筹城乡发展中新生代农村劳动力开发的价值功能和内容体系问题，她提出社会多元主体对新生代农村劳动力开发具有重要的经济价值、政治价值、社会价值、科技文化价值和哲学价值，要真正实现统筹城乡发展的目标，必须对新生代农村劳动力进行心理开发、生理开发、伦理开发、智力开发、技能开发和环境开发。

"中德公共管理国际研讨会"已成功举办八届，中德学者围绕公共管理领域的重大理论与实践问题进行了深入的研讨，催生了许多相当有见地的成果，有力地促进了中德公共管理学科的发展和公共管理理论的进步。

社会创新：理念、方法与政策

论构建中国特色社会主义社会管理体系

徐永平 *

【摘要】 中国共产党在全面建设小康社会进程中坚持以人为本，加强社会建设，着力构建社会主义和谐社会。社会建设以改善民生为核心，以推进社会公平正义、构建社会和谐为目标，而社会和谐的根本在于利益权利关系的和谐，这就要使社会成员各方的合法权益诉求在社会管理制度、机制和规范中得到积极体现，使各种社会利益矛盾在社会管理制度、体制机制和法律框架内得到有效解决，即培育社会和谐关系实现社会和谐，需要坚实的社会管理制度体系保障。因此，构建社会管理体系是社会建设的重要组成部分。

【关键词】 社会建设；和谐社会；社会体制改革；社会管理体系

一 构建社会管理体系是社会建设的重要组成部分

中国共产党在全面建设小康社会进程中不断推进实践创新、理论创新、制度创新，坚持以人为本，推进社会公平正义，加强社会建设，着力构建社会主义和谐社会。中共十七大以来，中国社会事业取得了重大进步：基本公共服务水平和均等化程度显著提高；教育事业迅速发展，城乡免费义务教育全面实现；社会保障体系建设成效显著，城乡基本养老保险制度全面建立，

---

* 徐永平：内蒙古自治区行政学院教授。

新型社会救助体系基本形成；全民医保基本实现，城乡基本医疗卫生制度初步建立；保障性住房建设加快推进；等等。但社会事业越是发展，越是需要科学合理的社会管理制度体系的支撑。同时，社会建设过程存在的诸多问题依然没有得到充分解决，有些问题甚至出现恶化的趋势。事实证明，这些问题许多是由于社会管理体制机制等制度原因造成的。因此，社会建设一方面要加快解决发展过程中以保障和改善民生为核心的各种社会问题，另一方面要创新完善解决这些问题的制度体系，构建中国特色的社会主义社会管理体系。中共十八大报告明确提出："在改善民生和创新社会管理中加强社会建设。"① 这一论断蕴含着加强社会建设要立足改善民生、创新完善社会管理制度体系"两个维度"，即社会建设核心要围绕这两个方面。一方面要解决关系人民福祉的民生问题；另一方面要解决制约民生发展的体制机制障碍问题，不断提升中国社会管理科学化水平，根本任务之一就是要构建社会管理制度体系。因此，社会建设过程中改善民生与推进社会管理制度改革，构建社会管理体系密切相关。如果说改善民生是社会建设的基本内容建设，那么社会管理制度体系是社会建设的制度建设，二者相互促进，相得益彰。

第一，构建中国特色社会主义社会管理体系是社会建设的应有之义。社会建设包括推进社会管理科学化水平，包含着社会管理制度体系建设。社会建设作为一项复杂的系统工程，包括促进社会事业的发展和社会关系的改善。而社会事业的发展和社会关系的改善与社会管理制度的健全程度密切相关，即社会事业的发展和社会关系的改善最终要靠健全的社会管理制度。同时，我国的社会结构、社会组织形式、社会利益秩序已经发生变化，适应这些变化进行社会管理制度创新尤为重要。罗尔斯说："正义是社会制度的首要价值，正像真理是思想体系的首要价值一样。"② 社会管理制度体系的健全完善是推进社会建设、实现社会正义的根本所在。因此，加强社会建设的任务之一就是要完善社会管理制度体系，从制度上统筹协调各方面的利益关系，实现社会矛盾源头治理，促进社会和谐，从而激发社会凝聚力和创造力。

---

① 胡锦涛：《坚定不移沿着中国特色社会主义道路前进　为全面建成小康社会而奋斗——在中国共产党第十八次全国代表大会上的报告》，中国共产党第十八次全国代表大会，北京，2012。

② 〔美〕约翰·罗尔斯：《正义论》，中国社会科学院出版社，1988，第3页。

第二，社会管理体系的健全完善是巩固发展民生成果的制度基础。改善民生才能奠定社会管理创新的现实基础，但社会管理体系健全完善才能从制度基础上巩固发展民生的成果。中国社会建设从社会管理创新发展的角度看，本身包括基本民生建设、社会管理体系建设和政府社会服务体系建设，而这三项建设相辅相成。基本民生建设直接关系到民众的生存发展问题，社会管理首先要管好公民生存、健康和发展的基本民生事务。创新社会管理要促进民生建设，把保障和改善民生作为创新社会管理政策举措的得失标准，把健全政府社会服务体系作为社会管理创新的重要组成部分，推动政府从行政管制型向服务型转变。

第三，社会建设要从创新社会管理制度、构建社会管理体系上保障公民社会权利的实现。社会管理权作为社会公共资源范畴，社会管理制度安排关系到社会基本结构，直接关系到社会利益分配的公平正义。罗尔斯讲："社会基本结构之所以是正义的主要问题，是因为它的影响十分深刻并自始至终。"① 从现实情况看，城乡、区域发展不协调及各社会阶层间的利益差别明显，昭示我国社会发展不均衡状况并未根本改变，从社会制度上解决公民社会权利均衡发展和实现社会公平正义依然是社会建设要长期面临的问题。因此，创新社会管理就要坚持以人为本，从保障和发展公民社会权利出发，以创新社会管理为契机，通过制度层面的建设，用统筹兼顾的方法协调各社会阶层、利益群体间的权益关系，进一步推进社会管理体制改革，构建社会和谐坚实的社会管理制度体系基础。

二　着力构建中国特色社会主义社会管理体系

加强社会建设要加快推进社会体制改革，要从我国社会结构、社会组织形式、社会利益发生深刻变化出发，构建中国特色社会主义社会管理体系，为此，要着力以下几个方面的工作。

第一，加快形成健全的社会管理体制。社会管理体制是社会管理体系的基础，是社会管理的基本制度，是健全社会管理体系的重中之重。中国传统

---

① 〔美〕约翰·罗尔斯：《正义论》，中国社会科学院出版社，1988，第 7 页。

的社会管理体制存在诸多问题，突出表现在如下方面。

第一，党政不分，直线式威权型管理。其一，自上而下的"塔型"直线管制式和组织威权型管理，使党的领导的政治地位与政府管理职能行政化，形成实际社会管理对社会事务的管制效能。封闭僵化的管制式管理导致日趋庞大的政府管理体系，使社会管理成本急剧飙升。其二，社会管理体系内在弹性不足，自治功能缺失。政府管制式的社会管理方式，更多地以外在性组织的控制方式解决社会问题，忽视了社会管理社会主体协同和公众广泛参与的社会治理特点，面对日趋复杂的社会管理问题只好不断强化管制，而庞大的管制体系又导致社会矛盾的积累集聚，给社会和谐稳定埋下严重隐患。其三，法治缺失，管理章法混乱。社会管理的根本是通过科学合理的规则体系规范社会秩序，而传统管制型社会管理主要依据相关国家政策和行政命令进行，长官意志是管理过程的常有现象，社会管理章法混乱，甚至无章可循。针对传统社会管理体制弊端和社会管理复杂的形势变化，中共十八大报告明确确定社会管理要"加快形成党委领导、政府负责、社会协同、公众参与、法治保障的社会管理体制"，① 这就从党、政府、社会组织和公众四个方面明确了社会管理主体构成及其在社会管理活动中的功能作用，明确了法治是社会管理的根本依据和保障。

中国特色社会主义社会管理体制必须突出党的政治领导地位。中国共产党是中国国家政治体系和社会生活的领导核心，党的各级领导组织起到确定发展方向、规划发展蓝图、统筹全局的功能作用，党员及党的各级基层组织还有组织群众宣传、服务群众和组织协调化解矛盾的功能；政府负责就是要突出政府担负着落实党的社会管理政策方针的行政使命，突出政府在提供服务和公共资源配置中的主体地位，强调政府通过制定实施各项社会政策统筹调节配置社会公共资源，均衡各社会阶层和各社会群体利益，并且为社会提供优质公共产品和公共服务；所谓社会协同就是重视各类社会组织的社会影响力，实现与党和政府的良好互动沟通，使其与党和政府同心同德，通力合作，

---

① 胡锦涛：《坚定不移沿着中国特色社会主义道路前进　为全面建成小康社会而奋斗——在中国共产党第十八次全国代表大会上的报告》，中国共产党第十八次全国代表大会，北京，2012。

协调沟通社会各方面各层次的关系，推进党和政府的各项社会管理工作健康有序、公平效率地进行；公众参与就是要遵循我们党所强调的人民群众当家作主的社会价值取向，尊重群众参与管理社会的权利，充分发挥社会自组织功能，发挥社会力量在社会管理中的积极作用，引导公众自觉维护社会和谐秩序；法治保障就是要把法治精神贯穿于社会管理的体制机制、途径方法等社会管理体系的方方面面，努力提升社会管理过程的法治化、规范化和科学化水平。

第二，加快形成健全完善的基本公共服务体系。我国目前社会公共服务总体水平还比较低，政府公共服务能力及能够提供的公共服务资源有限，而且存在明显配置不公平、不合理现象，特别是城乡差别现象突出。中共十八大报告明确提出要"加快形成政府主导、覆盖城乡、可持续的基本公共服务体系"，[①] 这就强调社会管理要强化政府社会服务职能，着力逐步消除城乡公共服务差距，逐步消除公共服务差别待遇，实现社会发展成果人人共享。中共十八大报告特别强调政府的主导地位，进一步明确政府社会管理的基本服务职责。从理论上讲，社会管理本质上就是为社会提供公共服务，满足社会公共需求，就政府本身而言"管理"就是"服务"。事实上，社会管理的"管理"其实是"管"和"理"职能的具体化，"管"就是要实现政府的社会管理权威职能，通过行使政府社会管理权威职能合理分配公共资源，维护社会正常秩序，实现社会关系的有效整合，而"理"就是要以社情民意为基础，满足各类社会群体的公共服务需求，理顺各种社会关系，促进社会和谐。中共十八大报告还明确指出要"改进政府提供公共服务方式，加强基层社会管理和服务体系建设，增强城乡社区服务功能，强化企事业单位、人民团体在社会管理和服务中的职责，引导社会组织健康有序发展，充分发挥群众参与社会管理的基础作用。完善和创新流动人口和特殊人群管理服务"。[②] 这就更进一步明确了今后社会服务体系建设的着力点。

---

① 胡锦涛：《坚定不移沿着中国特色社会主义道路前进　为全面建成小康社会而奋斗——在中国共产党第十八次全国代表大会上的报告》，中国共产党第十八次全国代表大会，北京，2012。

② 胡锦涛：《坚定不移沿着中国特色社会主义道路前进　为全面建成小康社会而奋斗——在中国共产党第十八次全国代表大会上的报告》，中国共产党第十八次全国代表大会，北京，2012。

第三，加快形成健全完善的社会组织体制。社会组织体制决定社会组织机制，社会管理组织体制的局限性必然要反映到社会管理运作的组织机制方面。因此，健全的社会组织体制是社会管理过程得以顺利进行和取得实效的体制基础。社会管理是一个以政府为主导、由各类社会组织和公众参与的、对整个社会事务运行过程、环节的协调和整合过程，社会管理本身是一种社会组织行为。传统的行政化社会管理的政社不分、权责不明、秩序混乱、社会自治功能缺失现象比较普遍，严重制约和影响了我国社会管理的健康运行。中共十八大报告明确提出要"加快形成政社分开、权责明确、依法自治的现代社会组织体制"。① 政社分开就是要尊重社会管理规律，明确政府与社会组织及公众参与在社会管理运作过程中的不同功能作用，克服传统行政化社会管理体制，增强社会管理活力；权责明确就是要使各类社会管理主体各显其能、各尽其责，积极推进社会管理规范化，提升社会管理内生激励动力，提高社会管理效能；依法自治就是要重视培育和发展各类社会管理组织，积极构建社会管理体系的自治功能，把法治、治理理念引入社会管理组织机制，保障各类社会主体依法积极参与社会管理过程。事实上，各类社会组织在实现社会整合过程中起着沟通政府与社会的桥梁纽带作用，鼓励其积极参与社会管理可以有效减轻政府的社会压力。一定程度上讲，强化社会自组织管理功能建设是建立化解矛盾长效机制的中心环节。广泛有效的社会沟通协调是形成社会内聚力的重要条件，社会管理组织体系没有有效畅通的协同渠道和利益协调组织平台，就会陷于僵化被动的局面。因此，要加快健全社会管理体系的运作组织体制。要健全社会管理体系运作组织体制机制，就要把社会管理体系自治功能完善与政府主导作用相结合，全面改革传统管制性社会管理体系及运作模式，实现社会管理自组织与他组织有机结合的社会化管理运作体制机制，实现科学、高效、法治的社会管理组织运行。

第四，加快健全社会管理机制和完善社会管理方法。社会现象纷繁复杂，社会事件千差万别，社会管理也不可能整齐划一，社会管理过程要卓有

---

① 胡锦涛：《坚定不移沿着中国特色社会主义道路前进　为全面建成小康社会而奋斗——在中国共产党第十八次全国代表大会上的报告》，中国共产党第十八次全国代表大会，北京，2012。

成效，就要加快健全社会管理机制和改进完善社会管理方法。

其一，加快形成社会管理机制。党的十八大报告提出要"加快形成源头治理、动态管理、应急处置相结合的社会管理机制"。"建立健全重大决策社会稳定风险评估机制。"① 首先，加快形成源头治理的社会管理机制。社会管理单纯行政化倾向必然忽视沟通协调的管理功能，在管理机制上形成重事后结果处置、轻源头治理的现象。而事实上，任何社会矛盾的激化都有一个集聚发展的客观过程。社会管理的复杂性、具体性要求做到防患于未然，就要找到矛盾产生形成的源头，从源头治理。从源头治理就要进一步加强和完善党和政府主导的维护群众权益机制，形成科学有效的利益协调机制、诉求表达机制、矛盾调处机制、权益保障机制，统筹协调各方面的利益关系，即统筹协调各方面的利益是源头治理之本。其次，加快形成动态管理的社会管理机制。我国经济社会发展正处于特殊机遇期，社会矛盾活跃期、多发期、易激化的高风险期，这不仅要求增强忧患意识，更要积极化解各类社会矛盾。要认真分析各类社会矛盾的性质和发展态势，将社会矛盾疏导化解在萌芽状态，这就要求社会管理制度设计时要重视健全各种社会矛盾沟通疏导的动态管理机制。再次，加快形成动态管理应急处置社会管理机制。社会突发事件应急管理是指对社会突发事件进行有针对性的管理控制和疏导过程。社会矛盾纷繁复杂，社会矛盾的集聚激化有时会出现不可控因素，引发突发事件。但任何社会矛盾都有一个萌芽发展过程，如果社会管理组织机构善于沟通疏导，积极应对处理潜在的社会矛盾，社会突发事件就会得到有效化解或控制。因此，社会管理组织机构要充分警觉和积极管理控制可能激化的社会矛盾，形成反应灵敏、功能齐全、协调有序、运转高效的动态应急处置管理机制。最后，建立健全重大决策社会稳定风险评估机制。各种社会矛盾的形成有其具体客观原因，要认真研究总结各类社会矛盾形成的原因和矛盾性质、特点和发展态势，要避免社会矛盾发生和激化，就要建立预测和化解社会矛盾的长效机制，预防和杜绝社会突发事件，特

---

① 胡锦涛：《坚定不移沿着中国特色社会主义道路前进　为全面建成小康社会而奋斗——在中国共产党第十八次全国代表大会上的报告》，中国共产党第十八次全国代表大会，北京，2012。

别是要健全重大决策社会稳定风险评估机制。

其二，加快改进完善社会管理的途径和方法。要充分认识到我国目前面临的各类社会矛盾主要是利益矛盾，是人民内部矛盾，是通过沟通协调可以解决的矛盾。目前我国社会管理陷入困境，社会矛盾激化现象增多、群体性事件频发的根本原因，是人民群众的实际权益受到侵害，权益得不到切实维护和保护，人民群众与政府之间缺乏积极有效的利益诉求沟通回应机制，人民群众之间的权益矛盾不仅不能及时得到解决，而且人民群众的诉求表达、利益协调、权益保障机制不畅通，由此导致社会矛盾集聚与加剧。因此，解决矛盾的关键是要切实坚持以人为本的社会管理理念，积极主动寻求解决矛盾、化解矛盾的有效渠道和科学方法。正如中共十八大报告明确提出的，要"正确处理人民内部矛盾，建立健全党和政府主导的维护群众权益机制，完善信访制度，完善人民调解、行政调解、司法调解联动的工作体系"，[①] 这就明确指出了社会管理面对的矛盾的人民性质，即根本问题是如何处理人民内部矛盾，强调社会管理应该选择的途径和方法是建立健全维护群众的权益机制，完善利益矛盾诉求表达的信访制度，完善解决人民利益矛盾的各类调解工作体系，畅通和规范群众诉求表达、利益协调、权益保障渠道，最终实现化解矛盾、解决矛盾、构建社会和谐的目的。

参考文献

胡锦涛：《坚定不移沿着中国特色社会主义道路前进　为全面建成小康社会而奋斗——在中国共产党第十八次全国代表大会上的报告》，中国共产党第十八次全国代表大会，北京，2012。

〔美〕约翰·罗尔斯：《正义论》，中国社会科学院出版社，1988，第3页。

---

① 胡锦涛：《坚定不移沿着中国特色社会主义道路前进　为全面建成小康社会而奋斗——在中国共产党第十八次全国代表大会上的报告》，中国共产党第十八次全国代表大会，北京，2012。

民生取向：我国公共政策公共性价值当下的集中体现

李金龙　杨巧梅[*]

【摘要】公共性是公共政策的本质属性，也是公共政策的核心价值标准。公共政策的公共性具有时空特质，在我国当下集中体现为公共政策的民生取向。公共政策的民生取向在我国已有初步实践，但仍存在诸多不足，亟须从开展对公共政策制定者的民生观教育、公共政策制定过程中真正反映民意、坚持民生公共政策得到切实执行的基本原则、确定合理的公共政策绩效评估的民生标准（权重）等方面进行强化和完善。

【关键词】公共政策；公共性；民生取向

一　公共性：公共政策的核心价值标准

人类社会一般存在两种决策，一是企业（私人）决策，二是政府（公共）决策。所谓公共政策，是指公共权力机关经由政治过程所选择和制订

---

* 李金龙：（1964～），男，土家族，湖南慈利人，法学博士，湖南大学法学院教授，主要研究领域为地方行政制度创新、政治体系变迁与发展等；杨巧梅：（1988～），女，汉族，湖南娄底人，湖南大学法学院硕士研究生。

的为解决公共问题、达成公共目标、实现公共利益的方案。① 从这个意义来说，公共政策是国家公共权力运行的具体体现，也是政府实施公共管理的重要途径与维护公众利益的主要手段。相对于私人利益而言，公共利益是一种共享程度相当高的普遍利益。根据公共选择理论的观点，政府本身就是一个"理性经济人"，它有自己独立的利益，如部门利益和政府工作人员的工资、福利、待遇等，这些都是政府自身利益的体现，因而公共利益并不必然等同于政府利益。公共利益的确定作为一种政策行为，其核心内容是如何有效地平衡公众的利益需求，使尽可能多的公众接受政府的政策选择。担负社会利益的代表者、国家权力的代理者和公共政策的制定与执行者三种职责的政府需要树立一定的理念、确定一定的标准、通过一定的方式来平衡不同的政策诉求和利益达成。从本质上说，最大化地追求公共利益，最广泛地谋求公众的幸福，是政府存在的合法性基础。作为政府的主要产出，以公共利益为出发点与终极目标也因此成为公共政策的必然选择。

公共权力机构在社会授权的基础上解决公共问题、提供公共产品、满足社会公共利益诉求的性质就是公共政策的公共性。② 公共性是公共政策固有的基本属性，它的缺失将可能使公共政策变为某些个人、阶层或团体谋取私利的工具。公共性理论对中国来说是舶来品。哈贝马斯对公共性观念进行了规范化描述，"公共性本身表现为一个独立的领域，即公共领域，它和私人领域是相对立的"。③ 一般来说，"公共性"可以宽泛地理解为所有公民在公共领域无障碍的开放性、在公共领域内公众对公共权力和公共事务的批判性，以及遵循自由、民主、正义原则进行理性商讨所达成的可以促使独立参与者在非强制状态下采取集体理性行动的共识。哈贝马斯所解析的这些特征（即公开性、批判性和理性化），使得公共性观念成为近代思想洪流中一种主要的政治诉求与具有独特价值内涵的政治原则。这种原则主导着公共领域的价值，守护着生活世界的私人价值，审视和批判着公共权力的合法性，旨在建立一个民主、开放和公平的合理社会。所有公共领域的基本价值只有通

---

① 宁骚：《公共政策》，高等教育出版社，2003，第 185 页。
② 张康之：《公共行政中的哲学与伦理》，中国人民大学出版社，2004，第 15 页。
③ 〔德〕哈贝马斯著，曹卫东译《公共领域的结构转型》，学林出版社，1999，第 2 页。

过公共性观念才能得到阐释，并在现实层面得到落实。在一定程度上，公共政策合法性的来源在于公共政策所追求的价值、蕴含的精神与公民社会的基本价值标准之间的趋同程度。因此，规划并影响政府公共政策的基本目标和价值方向，为公共政策的存在和权威提供合法化的依据，成了作为公共政策本质属性的公共性所承担的最大功用。

公共政策是伴随着人类面对日益复杂的公共事务而诞生的公共产品，它是实现公共意志、满足社会需要的公意选择，也是规范、引导社会公众和社群的行动指南或行为准则。因此，公共政策的价值把握是公共政策意识形态的应有之义，其价值含量是衡量公共政策质量的重要指标。公共政策的价值观化与价值观的公共政策化成为推动政治文明和科学发展观的必然趋势。一般来说，公共政策的价值应该包括自由、正义、宽容、民主、平等、效率、秩序、发展等，然而"这些处于政治冲突核心地位的广泛目标与原则，绝不可能还原为一些绝对的标准"，而只是"社会渴求的至关重要的关怀"。①从这种维度来说，公共政策及其执行是否尊重和维护了公民的基本权利、是否通过公共舆论充分体现和汇集了公民的意志、政策过程中是否超越了政府的自利行为与特殊集团利益倾向而考虑更为普遍的社群利益和社会的长远利益，这是判断公共政策是否具有"公共性"及其所具有的程度的基本标准。也就是说，这些单一的价值原则最终需要综合体现在公共政策的"公共性"属性上，也因此决定了"公共性"是衡量公共政策的核心价值标准。

从人类社会长期发展的角度看，人类社会的发展实际上是政府决策的公共性价值不断丰富和发展的历史，即社会生产力发展水平与人民的权利、民主、法制、规则意识不断增强的历史。哈贝马斯在考量人类社会历史时指出，古希腊时代虽然为城邦公民提供了公共空间，但同时限制了很大一部分人的自由参与权力，使得公共性有其名而无其实。及至中世纪封建社会更是以"私"充"公"——最充分的公共性就是最显赫的私人性的展示。只有在近代社会，伴随着现代意义上的公共领域的形成，公共性才得以诞生。结合我国具体国情来看，改革开放30多年来，我国社会主义市场经济得到迅

---

① 〔美〕德博拉·斯通著，顾建光译《政策悖论：政治决策中的艺术》，中国人民大学出版社，2006，第17页。

猛发展，人们的物质文化生活得到极大改善与保障。当代中国的社会变迁过程，是中华民族对人类社会公共价值的自主求索与艰难认定的过程。作为生产力发展水平、市场经济与人权意识达到一定阶段的产物，公共性在我国已有生存与发展的政治、经济、文化土壤，公共性价值能够成为我国公共政策的核心指导原则。

二 我国公共政策公共性价值当下集中体现为民生取向

一般说来，民生概念具有多层次的含义。广义上的民生是指一切同人民生活直接或间接相关的事情。这种界定由于涉及面太大，不易把握和操作，反而容易分散人们对现实中具体民生问题的切身关注，使得民生问题的解决难以同改善民生的具体政策和措施有效统一起来。狭义上的民生是从微观社会层面着眼，它包括民众的基本生存和生活状态、基本发展能力、基本发展机会及基本权益保护的状况等内容。狭义上的民生相对来说比较准确，也更容易把握，基本上同具体层面的民生政策吻合。因此，在政策具体实践和实际生活领域，人们通常使用的是狭义的民生概念。

公共政策的民生取向是公共政策诸多价值中的一种，是民生理念贯穿于公共政策的具体表现形式。依据美国公共政策学者保罗·萨巴蒂尔对公共政策过程的划分（界定问题，并提交给政府，由政府寻求解决的途径；政府组织形成若干备选方案，并选择政策方案；方案得以实施、评估和修正），[①]笔者认为公共政策的民生取向可以界定为这样一种价值观念：在公共政策的制定、执行、评估与监督反馈的整个运行过程中都要以民生问题为导向，营造以民为本的公共政策环境，致力于满足人民生存和发展的物质与精神需要，制定和执行能够切实保障最广大人民根本利益的公共政策。据此，公共政策的公共性要求公共利益至上，而民生取向的公共政策则是追求公共利益的集中表现和具体体现。公共政策的民生取向有利于弘扬顾客导向的"服务型"公共行政文化，有利于构建闪耀着公民理性的公民社会。

---

① 〔美〕保罗·萨巴蒂尔编，彭宗超、钟开斌等译《政策过程理论》，三联书店，2004，第3页。

从应然层面讲，公共政策必须担负起对效率以外的价值的追求。因此，以民生取向为特征的公共性应该是公共政策形成的逻辑起点。偏离了民生取向的公共政策也就是偏离了为公众谋取公共利益的方向，也就违背了公共政策公共性的本质价值。在我国，改善民生是实现执政党根本宗旨的落脚点，是落实科学发展观的关键点，是推动经济社会发展的着力点。与此同时，提升公众的参与水平是实现政策公共性的根本保障。通过改革强化民生价值早已是社会共识，这实际上意味着利益和财富的再调整。调整的可持续性取决于政治安排与民意的契合，这种契合度越高，改革和调整的动力越足。

从现实角度来看，在以构建和谐社会和强调社会管理创新为主要内容的政治统合与社会治理背景下，公共政策的民生取向与公共性具有内在的一致性。一般说来，公共政策的公共性在不同历史时期与不同政治空间内具有丰富甚至迥异的内涵。进入 21 世纪以来，在倡导以人为本，全面、协调、可持续发展的科学发展观的指引下，我国迎来综合国力大幅提升的战略机遇期的同时，也面临着前所未有的巨大挑战。各种关系人民生计的社会问题层出不穷，如食品药品安全、适用住房紧张、教育不公、就业困难等成了困扰普通民众基本生活的主要问题。经济基础决定上层建筑。现实问题的紧迫性使得公共政策的公共性在我国当前尤其表现为公共政策的民生取向。在社会管理工作日益复杂的今天，公共政策的公共性衰减主要体现为公共政策民生取向的偏离，而当前这一给公共领域带来了诸多负面效应的问题，正日益引人关注。"学有所教、劳有所得、病有所医、老有所养、住有所居"，成了我国政府正致力于实现的和谐社会愿景。

需要注意的是，尽管我国古代已有民生思想，但大多是从维护统治阶级的利益出发而进行的考量，如"民为邦本""民贵君轻"，这些思想实际上都是为了更好地治民而不是实实在在地为民众谋利益。当前我们所倡导的公共政策的民生取向要求公共政策的出发点与着眼点都在于解决民众内心最关切的问题，实际上这种理念本身就是一种贴近民众尤其是底层民众的人文关怀，也是一种深入民众迫切现实需求的政策供给。公共政策的公共性通常可以具体化为公平性、公开性与公正性三个维度，① 这从本质上要求公共政策能够秉持公平正义的精神，坚持透明开放的程序，聚合各方利益表达尤其是照顾好弱势群体的利益。民生取向作为一种新的话语符号与民族文化的阐述方式，既是我国公共政策公共性价值的具体体现，也是当前执政者适应市场经济发展与国际"公民社会"蓝图的新政治哲学理念。而政治倾向于民生，不仅关乎民众的财产福利水平和幸福感的提升，实际上也是对经济和社会发展终极意义的完整阐释。

三　强化和完善我国公共政策民生取向的思考

近年来，我国公共政策已经在解决民生问题上取得不少成就，然而，从根本上解决民生问题仍然任重而道远，进一步完善公共政策的民生取向可以从以下方面着手。

（一）开展对公共政策制定者的民生观教育

美国学者罗斯金曾说，"政府选择政策和规划是与国家的广泛目标相一致的。由于资源总是有限的，因此必须建立一个价值的优先顺序"。② 这意味着政策制定主体在选择与出台政策之前，总会有其自身的价值判断，通常来说，与国家利益相一致的方案更容易受到制定主体的价值倾斜。在罗斯金看来，在民主体制下应该有高度的社会整合，这样社会就会容纳其成员的多样性，政治冲突将会是利益取向的，即直接针对问题和政策，而不是基于不同的肤色、种族、宗教、国籍或性别。因此，在一个和谐的民主体制社会中，更多地关注最广大民众的基本生活需求的满足，才是整合与协调社会多元利益的根本出路。对政策制定者进行民生观教育，一方面具有深刻的重要性，因为它是对政策进行价值定位的第一道关。政策制定者的文明素质、生活习惯、思维方式、民生期望在很大程度上影响和制约着民生问题的解决。

---

① 陈潭：《公共性：公共政策分析的一般范式》，《湖南师范大学社会科学学报》2002 年第 31 期，第 46 ~ 50 页。

② 〔美〕米切尔·罗斯金等著，林震等译《政策科学》，华夏出版社，2000，第 44 页。

另一方面，这种无形的教育具有明显的必要性，在意识支配物质的背景下，内化于政策制定者意识深处的价值观决定着其行为的民生取向。

中国特色社会主义民生观主要包括四个层面的内涵：人民群众是主体，即人民群众既是民生建设又是民生成果共享的主体；促进人的全面发展是目标，以人为本，以实现人的价值最大化为归宿；科学发展观是途径，即民生不是无源之水、无本之木，而是在发展基础上构建起来的；公平正义是核心，即打造一个集机会公平、权利公平、过程公平、结果公平于一体的公平社会环境。对公共政策制定者开展民生观教育是一项需要融合技术与艺术的科学活动。首先需要从中华传统文化中提炼出表达了民生思想的经典之作，为中国公共政策的民生取向提供历史积淀上的支持。同时，依据国外先进社会管理理念，吸收引进民生观教育的伦理逻辑。其次，民生观教育要具体化，深入到人们衣食住行的各个方面，落实到关系着民生大计的社会领域。

法国思想家卢梭提出，只有公益才能够按照国家创制的目的——公共的善——来引导国家的发展方向。因为主权不过是公益的执行而已，所以主权就永远不能被转让给其他人或事物。而且，又因为主权不过是一个集体性的事物，所以就只能由他自己来代表自己的意志。① 因此，对公共政策制定者开展民生观教育，必须要在公益的指引下，尊重人民群众的自主意志和共同呼声。

（二） 在公共政策制定过程中真正反映民意

民意是指示各种社会因素所处状态的晴雨表，是衡量一切社会决策效果的试金石。恩格斯曾经指出，人民群众几乎能从本能上感觉到一种生产关系是否适合于生产力，从而表现出欢迎还是反抗的情绪来。② 在公共政策制定过程中反映民意是完善公共政策民生取向的奠基石。

1. 完善人民代表大会制度

完善人大代表制度，要充分发挥人大代表的作用，让人大代表真正成为

---

① 〔法〕卢梭著，施新州译《社会契约论》，北京出版社，2007，第 28 页。
② 喻国明：《序言》，载李彪主编《舆情：山雨欲来——网络热点事件传播的空间结构和实践结构》，人民日报出版社，2011。

人民利益的代表，成为表达民意并保证代表按选民或全体人民的意志行事的重要纽带。"建构好的堡垒，他们不但要设计得好，并且要恰当配备人员。"① 首先要逐步改善人大代表结构，有效整合社会多元利益主体，使人大代表能够切实代表广大选民利益。在未来实践中，应有重点地逐步改变我国人大代表结构上的官员代表与党员代表偏多、社会代表尤其是社会弱势群体代表偏少的主要弊端。其次，要完善对代表的监督机制。加强对代表活动的监督，是推动代表依法行使职权，切实代表民意的重要措施。再次，要完善人大与代表、代表与选民或选举单位之间的联系制度，这是密切人大代表与人民群众的联系，提高人大代表参政、议政能力的长效机制。最后，要逐步实现人大对公共政策进行及时审视与评估，吸纳民意作出相应的修订，这也是执政者把握民生脉搏的重要环节。当前，完善人民代表大会制度更需要注重议题的开放性与民生性。民主的审议过程与程序，需要能呈现与反映出平等的参与机会、不受控制的自由与公开的意见交流等核心价值。公共讨论的过程本身也将产生教育的效果，提高公民的知能，养成公民们重视公益与合作的精神，并扩大公民参与公共事务的兴趣与能力。②

2. 落实听证制度

包括立法听证在内的听证制度是我国近年来政治实践的创造性发展。听证是具有立法权的行政机构为了制定和修改涉及公民利益的法案和政策，支持公众参与立法过程，通过广泛收集立法信息与征集民意，来制定出符合公众利益的法案。听证鼓励受政策影响的利益相关者参与政策制定过程，表达自身的利益偏好，为利益群体参与公共政策制定营造了一个公共空间。听证制度已经成为我国公民表达利益的规范性渠道，是社会主义协商民主的一种重要形式。

作为现代民主社会的重要支柱，听证制度逐渐引入中国公共政策过程，扩大了人们参与公共政策过程的机会。就治理功能而言，个人或利益集团以听证方式参与公共政策过程，实际上赋予了利益相关者了解有关信息并为自

---

① 〔英〕卡尔·波普尔著，杜汝楫、邱仁宗译《历史决定论的贫困》，上海人民出版社，2009，第 124 页。

② 詹中原：《公共政策问题构建过程中的公共性研究》，《公共管理学报》2006 年第 3 期，第 17 页。

己利益辩护的平等权利和均等机会，在对公共权力和政府官员施加某种形式的外部监督和约束的同时，将特殊利益集团活动限制在尽可能狭小的范围内。假定现有制度结构稳定不变，只要在开放从调查、提案、动议、决策到实施的公共议程的基础上，将听证制度嵌入上述公共政策过程的各个环节，仅仅是基于理性经济人的个人选择就能对公共政策过程施加均衡性影响，甚至迫使政府官员超越于自身利益慎用自由裁量权，从而产生意想不到的利益集团治理效果。

然而在具体实践中，听证制度常流于形式、浮于表面，真正的民意并未被吸纳到决策过程中来，导致所谓的民生决定实际上还是经营层的"拍脑袋"决策。要加大听证制度对政策制定的影响，就必须在听证会中大力提倡协商民主精神，将听证会构建为各利益群体或公民进行协商民主的常态化场所；允许和鼓励各利益群体与公民积极参与、大胆发言，充分吸取他们的合理利益需求；提高听证内容和过程的公开透明度，使听证会能够真正对政策制定发挥影响，防止出现听证会走过场的情况。落实好听证制度，将是增强公共政策制定过程民生取向的一个重要补充，也是践行民生价值的一个综合性指标。

（三） 坚持民生公共政策得到切实执行的基本原则

一是计划性原则。政策执行是一个涉及很多因素的系统工程，具有时间上的阶段性、连续性和空间上的协调性，因此要求执行者必须统筹兼顾，有计划、有步骤地进行。这就需要执行者在执行前拟定周密的计划并严格按计划执行政策。

二是忠实性原则。在执行政策的过程中，执行者必须忠实于政策的基本宗旨。执行机构及人员对政策基本精神的理解要准确，不要一知半解或随意解释，甚至为了部门利益蓄意曲解政策的原意。在实际执行过程中，要保证政策不走样、不搞土政策、不搞看关系"下菜碟"。要依据政策执行计划及时有效地落实政策。在执行过程中要善于发现问题，并及时解决问题。

三是创新与灵活性原则。政策执行的环境复杂多变，考虑再周全的政策也不可能完全适应于所有的具体情形。因此，要求政策执行者在把握政策精神实质的基础上，因地制宜，结合具体的执行环境，采取灵活的策略，创造性地执行政策。这里说的灵活性与创造性，指的是为了保证在有效的期限内达成政策目标而在手段和策略上进行的灵活变通，政策目标本身是不允许"灵活"的。

由于公共政策主要是由公职人员这一群体自上而下地实行，始终坚持从民众的利益诉求出发，保障人民群众最为关切的与生活息息相关的各项权益，以民众满意度为指向标，将政策在基层的具体情况自下而上进行反馈、修正，是公共政策执行者需要坚持的一项核心原则，也考验着公职人员作为人民公仆的合格度。

（四）确定合理的公共政策绩效评估的民生标准（权重）

"评估政策制定过程的一个重要方法，就是查看公共精神在该过程里占多大优势。"① 是否坚持了公共责任和顾客至上的理念，以及是否关注了客户满意度与公众参与度，应该成为公共政策评估的指导思想。当前，中国政府职能正悄然发生着转变，未来将越来越重视其所承担的公共责任，同时以公众利益为导向，在进行政策评估的体系中大幅增加有关质量和顾客满意度指标，把提升公众的满意度当作重要的执行绩效的指标。这种改变将打破以往绩效评估的内部性和封闭性，使政府及其政策以更加开放的姿态去吸收公众和服务对象的广泛参与。

为实现加快推进以改善民生为重点的社会建设目标，完成政府确定的更加注重社会建设、着力保障和改善民生的工作任务，应尽快建立包括民生指标在内的政绩考核体系。这个体系不仅要看经济增速和财政收入，还应将该地区低收入家庭或贫困人口的生活能否得到保障、公共卫生能否满足中低收入阶层居民的需求、社会保障所覆盖的广度及生活环境改善程度、政府财政用于改善民生的支出所占份额等纳入考核范围，最终推动各级政府更加关注与重视民生，在保障和改善民生上下功夫、花力气。

在政策绩效评估指标体系方面，要兼顾政策运行（尤其是政策执行）能力、行为和结果，追求过程满意和结果满意，注重效益、效果和公平性，强化民生型政府的核心理念。在标准建设方面，运用定量为主、定性为辅的

---

① 〔美〕史蒂文·凯尔曼著，商正译《制定公共政策》，商务印书馆，1990，第200页。

标准体系，使得绩效评估在实施中具有更为明确的引导作用，同时具有可靠的操作性，为有效完成政策绩效评估提供可度量的标准与具有可行性的考量依据。以满足公众需求为导向的完善的绩效指标和标准体系为政策绩效评估的科学性奠定了基础。在政策执行绩效评估体系的构建过程中需要遵循以下一系列原则：首先是全面性原则，即绩效指标体系的构建要能够体现科学发展观的要求，充分考虑政治、法律、社会、环境、公众协调发展等因素，兼顾效率与公平；其次是可行性原则，即绩效指标体系结构设计合理、表述明确、口径统一，要达到的标准具有明确性、可实现性、可测量性、与目标相关联性、时效性等特征，并与评估过程中的信息采集一致；最后是重点性原则，即绩效指标要少而精，不能面面俱到，要对政策目标的实现具有关键作用。整体而言，政策绩效指标应包括效果、效率、公平性和满意度等相关维度，关注过程评估和结果评估的统一，体现公共政策的民生导向。

在考核方法选择上要多元化，既要有定性评价，也要有定量分析；既要有政府考核，也要由社会评价；既要有干部考核，也要由群众评议，尤其要重视公众的满意度，让广大人民群众评价政府的民生业绩，促进科学民生观的树立。科学指标体系的建立是对整个政策过程及其效果进行评估的基础，蕴含着民生关怀的公共政策绩效评估指标是强化我国公共政策民生取向的必要考量。

参考文献

〔美〕保罗·萨巴蒂尔编，彭宗超、钟开斌等译《政策过程理论》，三联书店，2004，第 3 页。

陈潭：《公共性：公共政策分析的一般范式》，《湖南师范大学社会科学学报》2002年第 31 期，第 46~50 页。

〔美〕德博拉·斯通著，顾建光译《政策悖论：政治决策中的艺术》，中国人民大学出版社，2006，第 17 页。

〔德〕哈贝马斯著，曹卫东译《公共领域的结构转型》，学林出版社，1999，第2 页。

〔英〕卡尔·波普尔著，杜汝楫、邱仁宗译《历史决定论的贫困》，上海人民出版社，2009，第 124 页。

喻国明：《序言部分》，载李彪主编《舆情：山雨欲来——网络热点事件传播的空间结构和实践结构》，人民日报出版社，2011。

〔法〕卢梭著，施新州译《社会契约论》，北京出版社，2007，第 28 页。

〔美〕米切尔·罗斯金等著，林震等译《政策科学》，华夏出版社，2000，第 44 页。

宁骚：《公共政策》，高等教育出版社，2003，第 185 页。

〔美〕史蒂文·凯尔曼著，商正译《制定公共政策》，商务印书馆，1990，第 200 页。

詹中原：《公共政策问题构建过程中的公共性研究》，《公共管理学报》2006 年第 3 期，第 17 页。

张康之：《公共行政中的哲学与伦理》，中国人民大学出版社，2004，第 15 页。

乡土政治变迁一景：
农民"非制度化政治参与"

——来自荃镇的田野调查[*]

刘晓峰[**]

【摘要】 农民非制度化政治参与的逐渐增多，是近几年乡土政治变迁的一个显著特征。其本质是乡土社会治理权力转移与现行政治制度设计不足之间的矛盾，是农民在现有制度框架下及更为复杂的外部环境中的理性选择，在现阶段主要表现为越级上访、组织化抗争和"弱者的武器"三个类型。

【关键词】 乡土政治；政治参与；非制度化

乡土政治在本质上涉及的是有关乡土场域内政治资源的配置问题，其核心是政治权力的分配，也即乡土社会治理权力主体的变迁问题。从纵向上

---

* 基金项目：国家社会科学基金重大项目"中国特色社会主义社会管理体系研究"（11&ZD070）；安徽省教育厅人文社会科学研究一般项目"乡土社会资本与乡镇干部行为研究"（SK2012B196）。本文调研材料来自笔者在2009年8月至2010年4月对山东省荃镇政府做的为期9个月的田野调研。荃镇是中国北方一个典型的农业型乡镇，距其所属县城20多公里，工商业欠发达。对该镇的分析能揭示北方欠发达地区基层政府的一些共性，本研究更普遍的适用性尚待论证。

** 刘晓峰：（1981～），男，山东济宁人，安徽师范大学法学院行政管理教研室主任，讲师，管理学博士，主要研究方向为基层政府、组织行为。

看，国家对底层农民自治权利的强化是最近几年乡土政治变迁的主要内容，直接表现为农民逐渐增强的政治参与冲动和逐渐增多的政治参与行为。但矛盾的是，国家的目的是试图在制度性框架内发展这种政治参与权利，而实际上，这种自下而上的政治参与是"非制度"化的，而更大的问题还在于基层政权缺乏接纳这种"非制度"性政治参与的制度设计，这就给乡镇政府带来了前所未有的压力。本文尝试结合笔者在荃镇政府所做的一项田野调查，分析当下农民的"非制度化政治参与"问题，以更生动的方式呈现乡镇政府所面临的自下而上的政治压力。

一 乡土政治变迁：以社会治理权力为视角

传统乡土场域中，乡土社会治理是"少数人"的游戏，强大的国家权力通过政府延伸至乡村社会，面对强大的国家权力，高度分散的农民个体缺乏适当的制度性利益表达途径，当国家权力或其他社会力量对农民个体的掠夺超过其维持最简单的小农经济再生存底线时，农民则往往付诸"揭竿而起"等不合法的表达方式争取权利，于是，古代中国便始终难以摆脱治乱循环的怪圈，没有哪个封建王朝能实现乡土社会的长治久安。传统乡土社会的上述政治现实，也逐渐养成了传统农民在政治上的高度依附性，马克思曾对这种现象作过生动的分析："小农自己不能代表自己，一定要别人来代表他们。他们的代表一定要同时是他们的主宰，高站在他们上面的权威，是不受限制的政府权力，这种权力保护他们不受其他阶级侵犯，并从上面赐给他们雨水和阳光。所以表现为行政权力支配社会。"

新中国成立之后，国家通过土地改革、合作化和集体化运动，自上而下建立起了人民公社体制，这就从制度上实现了国家政权和乡土社会的高度重合，一方面，公社既是国家政权在乡土社会的延伸，另一方面，公社又是乡土社会自身组织生产和生活的机构，"政权组织经济化，行政活动党务化，管理活动军事化"① 是人民公社的一大特征，笔者认为它在实质上是实现了

---

① 彭勃：《乡村治理：国家介入与体制选择》，中国社会出版社，2002，第103页。

乡村社会的"国家化"，在这一时期，由于"公社控制了对土地等生产资料的所有权，直接具有对全公社范围内经济活动的管理权，对人力和资金的支配权，并且凭借这些权力在流通领域控制了一切生产和生活资料的自由流动和交易"。① 在这种整体性结构下，农民的政治利益表达也被完全国家化了，尽管农村社会表现为一种超稳定结构状态，但这是以农民的政治愿望和诉求被压抑为代价的，国家几乎控制了整个乡土社会的社会生活和农民的个人自由。

改革开放之后，国家通过家庭联产承包责任制使农民获得了土地经营权，农民从经济上获得了一定的自主性，在经济上摆脱了国家的"强控制"，由于生产经营上的自由，农民可以根据自己的情况安排生产活动，再加上市场开放程度的增加，农民外出务工的情况逐渐增多，在这个过程中农民的政治参与意识明显加强，国家也先后出台了一系列提高农民政治利益的政策，农民获得了以村民自治方式从事政治参与的权利。就像马克思所形容的"马铃薯"，处于分割的原子化状态，他们既无力把握风云际会的政治，也无力把握变幻莫测的高度自由的市场经济带来的高风险，这使村民感到了自身的经济脆弱性，同时他们接受政治信息较少、利益渠道狭窄、组织化水平低，这又进一步增加了他们在村级公共事务中的无力感。② 农民在失去了村社共同体保护之后发生了严重分化，大部分农民因为缺乏应付现代社会的资源，在广阔的新天地中成为孤零零的原子。经济资源的缺失与政治地位的低下决定了普通村民在村庄政治中的"棋子"角色。他们在形成自己的政治态度时往往受到村庄精英的裹挟，被动或主动地依附于村庄精英进入村庄政治生活。③

从农民的角度来看，无论在经济发展方面，还是在社会服务方面，遇到的困难都是很多的，应该说这就是农村公共服务的巨大需求空间。但是，农民对自己的这种强烈需求，又普遍缺乏表达。即便他们知道自己的需求，也没有制度化和组织化的渠道表达利益要求，分散的个体化农民根

---

① 周晓虹：《中国农民的政治参与：毛泽东和后毛泽东时代的比较》，《香港社会科学学报》2000 年秋季号。

② 金太军：《村庄治理中三重权力互动的政治社会学分析》，《战略与管理》2002 年第 2 期。

③ 仝志辉、贺雪峰：《村庄权力结构的三层分析》，《中国社会科学》2002 年第 1 期。

本无法与相对而言强大得多的乡镇政府进行讨价还价，处于一种近乎失语的状态。在调查中笔者问及农民"对乡村政府和干部有何要求"时，许多农民的回答是："对于干部没有什么要求，只要他们少收点钱就行了"；更有甚者说道："不敢想干部的什么服务，只要他们少干点坏事就行了。"这种失语状态表明的并不是农民对基层干部和公共服务没有需求，而是农民对乡村政权的失望不满和"沉默的反抗"，展示了基层组织和农民之间的疏离，这种冷漠氛围构成乡村社会常态的紧张关系。从这个角度看，也可以说，乡村冲突主要起因于在新的制度环境下，农民的政治需要得不到满足。[①] 利益是人们参与行动的原始动力，当原有的制度结构出现失衡，农民无法从中获取利益或利益受到损害与威胁时，就会出现非制度的政治参与行为。利益诱致是农民个人或群体自发改变现行规则或秩序以参与政治的动力。[②] 当正式的利益表达和意见输入渠道被堵塞时，非制度化政治输入便成为农民的一种选择。

二 农民"非制度化政治参与"的三种形式

农民非制度化的政治参与是在现有制度框架下及更为复杂的外部环境中的必然选择，这种选择给乡镇政府及其成员造成了前所未有的政治压力，笔者认为当前农民的非制度化参与主要有以下三种形式。

(一) 越级上访

上访也叫信访，是指"公民、法人或者其他组织采用书信、电子邮件、传真、电话、走访等形式，向各级人民政府、县级以上人民政府工作部门（以下简称各级行政机关）反映情况，提出建议、意见或者投诉请求，依法由有关行政机关处理的活动"。[③] 上访是公民表达利益诉求的一种制度性方式和过程，也是政府提高合法性和有效制约基层官僚行为的一种制度设计，

---

① 赵树凯：《乡村治理：组织和冲突》，《战略与管理》2003 年第 6 期。
② 方江山：《非制度政治参与：以转型期中国农民为对象分析》，人民出版社，2000，第85 页。
③ 国务院：《信访条例》，中国法制出版社，2005。

是"国家高度科层化的片面发展和与社会之间联结机制存在断裂的一种修补性措施"。[①] 而所谓"越级上访"则是指"上访人越过所在的基层单位，或者应该处理他提出诉求或反映问题的单位，到他的上一级机关去上访"[②]的行为。由于信访稳定是每一级政府的重要考核项目，另外，领导者也普遍认为，上访所反映的都是自身工作中的不足，是自己的"短处"，因此各级政府都反对"越级上访"，尽管《信访条例》中并未明确禁止"越级上访"。

"信访稳定"是荃镇的中心工作之一，所谓"信访稳定"工作的实质，就是要"减少本级上访，杜绝越级上访、群体访"，从荃镇的文件中我们也能看得出乡镇一级政府对"越级上访"的敏感程度。

镇党委、政府要求各管区、行政村"一把手"务必增强责任意识，树立稳定压倒一切的思想，安排包村干部、村干部切实抓好稳控工作。任务上肩，责任砸死，对可能越级到省进京上访的人员看死盯牢，想尽千方百计，不惜一切努力，坚决杜绝到省进京上访滋事情况的发生。对发生到省进京上访问题情况并产生恶劣影响的管区、村，副科级领导，由县委给予戒勉，年底定为考核不称职等次；村支部书记一律停职检查，村主任不得领取年终奖。同时按年初镇与管区、村签订的《责任状》给予经济处罚。对包案领导、管区总支书记、有关部门负责人、各管区主任、包村干部所负责的上访人发生到省进京上访情况，另扣发两月工资。同时，镇党委安排各管区写了保证书，进一步砸死了责任。[③]

但是，笔者在荃镇了解到，最近几年越级上访的数量不仅没有减少，反而在增加。荃镇的信访办主任就坦言，"基层信访工作越来越难做了"。笔者根据荃镇所提供的信访材料，整理了最近五年本级上访和越级上访的情况（见表1），可以看到越级上访由 2005 年的 13 起 16 人次上升到 2009 年的 21 起 26 人次，总体上访事件和人次也都有增加的趋势。

---

① 应星：《大河移民上访的故事》，三联书店，2001，第 314~327 页。
② 张双山：《正解"越级上访"》，《公民导刊》2006 年第 8 期。
③ 荃镇党政办材料：《2008 年 7 月 22 日荃镇委镇政府向县委、县政府所做的关于信访稳定的工作汇报》。

表 1　荃镇近五年上访情况

时　间	2005 年	2006 年	2007 年	2008 年	2009 年
平级上访	49 起 106 人次	48 起 132 人次	56 起 118 人次	59 起 138 人次	56 起 141 人次
越级上访	13 起 16 人次	13 起 14 人次	15 起 17 人次	18 起 22 人次	21 起 26 人次
总　　计	62 起 122 人次	61 起 146 人次	71 起 135 人次	77 起 160 人次	77 起 167 人次

资料来源：根据荃镇信访办内部材料整理。

　　农民越级上访事件的增多也说明乡镇政府公信力正在衰退，农民对基层干部也表现出越来越强的不信任感，因此他们大多采取直接到省、市政府甚至中央政府上访的方式，以 2008 年荃镇的上访情况为例，共有 9 起 13 人次到市上访，9 起 9 人次到中央上访。这些越级上访多发生在政府重要会议和重要节日期间，因此，每到这些"敏感时期"，乡镇政府就格外"紧张"，荃镇每年年初，在"两会"召开期间都会专门下发通知，并召开会议部署工作，砸死责任，严格奖惩。

　　"春节将至，中央、省、市、县'两会'即将召开，做好这一时期的信访稳定工作，确保不发生越级上访、集体上访和滋事闹事问题，维护社会大局稳定，是当前一项重要政治任务……实行区域负责制，包案领导、相关部门、管区及时了解第一信息，掌握第一资料，分析第一信号，研究第一动向，制定周密可行的严防措施；包村干部作为各村的信访信息联络员，与村支两委主要干部是村级直接责任人；各管区总支书记、管区主任为管区第一责任人……这段时间内，镇带班领导、有关部门、各管区及所辖行政村负责人严格落实监控措施，24 小时不间断监控，手机 24 小时开机，确保人员在位，信息畅通，反应迅速，处理及时。"①

　　荃镇对上访事件的"重视"也使得一些农民逐渐意识到似乎利用上访的手段能更好、更快地解决问题，这也是上访事件逐渐增多的原因之一。甚至还出现了一些农民为了"获取不合法不合理的利益"，利用上访来"要挟"地方政府的情况，荃镇的领导干部把这些人称为"刁民"。笔者在荃镇就曾遇到一个典型案例，荃镇 Y 村 48 岁的村民 CQL 自 2006 年年初便多次到省、市、县上访，② 主

---

① 荃发［2010］4 号《关于做好四级"两会"及春节期间信访稳定工作的通知》。
② 根据访谈及中共荃镇委、荃镇人民政府于 2007 年 2 月 9 日向国家信访局所做的《荃镇 YJD 村村民 CQL 上访问题调查处理情况汇报》等资料整理。

要反映该村村干部违纪问题，荃镇党委政府曾经成立专门调查组，经过调查认为，"其上访目的是撤换掉现任支部书记兼村主任王兆勤，本人想当村干部。其反映的问题基本与事实不符"，并分别于 2006 年 4 月 20 日、6 月 2 日将调查处理结果向上访人进行了答复，2006 年 7 月 20 日、11 月 30 日，S 县信访局、荃镇镇党委政府将调查处理情况还先后两次向省信访局接访一处领导进行了汇报，但是由于 "CQL 性格比较固执，对所有调查处理意见一概不予认可，坚持撤换村干部。在镇、村多方做其思想工作的同时，CQL 又到京上访，给首都的政治社会稳定造成了不良影响"。当时这件事搞得荃镇的领导干部 "焦头烂额，也给正常的政府工作造成了很大影响……有的干部都睡不着觉了……像这种无理上访的人，抓住一个得狠治，不下狠心不行"。①

（二）组织化抗争

目前荃镇农民的非制度化政治参与行为主要还是分散的，并没有组织性，但是有研究表明，目前在很多地方已经出现了农民 "组织化抗争" 的情况，有分析显示 "组织起来抵制地方社区组织的种种非政策甚至非法行为，已经成为农民自觉或不自觉的行动趋向"。② 于建嵘的研究发现，自 1998 年以来，农民对基层政权的抗争实际上已经进入了 "有组织抗争" 或 "以法抗争" 阶段。"农民有组织抗争是以具有一定政治信仰的农民利益代言人为领导核心，通过各种方式建立了相对稳定的非正式社会动员和信息交流网络，以中央或上级政策为依据，以县乡两级政府制定的土政策为抗争对象、以直接动员农民抵制为手段、以宣示和确立农民合法权益或公民权利为目标的一种政治性抗争"。③ 他通过在湖南省 H 县所进行的长达三年多的跟踪调查，详细分析了这种行为的特点、产生原因、过程及所蕴藏的政治风险和改革机遇。

农民的组织化抗争具有以下特点：一是拥有一批意志坚定、具有广泛群

---

① 资料来自访谈资料：20091208ZAG。

② 赵树凯：《矛盾、引导和历史的契机：关于 196 封农民来信的初步分析》，《农民日报》1998 年 1 月 28 日。

③ 于建嵘：《农民有组织抗争及其政治风险》，《战略与管理》2003 年第 3 期。

众基础和动员能力的"农民利益代言人";二是建立了一定规模的组织;三是具有较明确的政治性,抗争的对象是基层干部,抗争的依据是国家法律和党的政策,抗争的形式从上访为主转变为与基层政府直接对抗,抗争的靠山是中央的权威。

农民的组织化抗争是转型期社会冲突的重要表现形式,表明目前我国农村政治体制已面临比较严重的治理性危机,不仅影响到农村的社会稳定和发展,而且在一定程度上制约了国家由传统社会向现代社会的转型。因此,基层政府对这种形式的抗争行为往往采取粗暴压制的方式,但这恰恰进一步激化了干群矛盾,使农村基层政权出现功能性退化。

尽管荃镇并没有发生过这种农民的组织化抗争,但也有抗争组织化的倾向,荃镇在2009年曾经发生过一起南石村15户居民集体越级上访事件,上访所反映的主要问题,一是2005年小麦直补款被挪用买变压器、2006年小麦直补款没有发放;二是"327国道拆迁补偿不知道标准,要求全部发放";三是"村干部四人多占土地200多亩";四是"村干部违反计划生育";五是15户低保户发放低保款不及时。由于上访规模较大,而且是越级上访,于是从县到镇都十分重视,专门组织人员进行核实并及时给予处理:上访人YRM等15人反映问题基本属实。关于2009年度小麦直补款问题县镇财政所会同管区正在入村丈量核实,将按实际情况如实发放到户;关于村干部四人多占土地问题,目前由县纪委牵头,农业局、司法局镇党委政府积极配合,根据《农村土地确权办证实施方案》要求,正在整改中;关于YHE违反计划生育政策问题,镇纪委根据《中国共产党纪律处分条例》已给予YHE撤销支部书记职务处分;关于低保款发放不及时问题,经镇政府民政部门督查,现已全部发放了低保款。以上所有问题查清后,将根据该村党员干部违规违纪情况进行坚决处理。①

这表明,乡镇干部对农民有组织的抗争形式具有强烈的畏惧感,相对于单个农民的抗争,这种形式给乡镇干部造成更大的政治压力,在应对方式上他们会尽量避免粗暴压制,而更倾向于通过合法手段并同群众协商解决,在结果上会倾向于对群众有所"照顾",这些都体现了乡镇干部对这类反抗形

---

① 资料来源于荃发〔2009〕15号《荃镇南石匣村上访案件的调查报告》。

式的畏惧心理。

（三）"弱者的武器"

如果说 "越级上访" 和 "组织化抗争" 是一种公开的、正式的抗争形式的话，那么下面将要讨论的这种抗争形式则涉及那些更为隐蔽和非正式的行为，即农民利用 "弱者的武器" 进行 "日常" 形式的抗争。农民的这种抗争形式是由美国著名社会学家斯科特所提出并进行系统研究的。斯科特在马来西亚一个村庄进行了为期两年（1978～1980）的田野研究，他并没有关注那些在以往研究中占主角的有关农民大规模的、有组织的抗议行为，而是将目光聚焦于那些在现实中更普遍却被研究者所忽视的 "农民反抗的日常形式"。

他认为，"在第三世界，农民很少会在税收、耕作模式、发展政策或繁琐的新法律等问题上去冒险与当局直接对抗；他们更可能通过不合作、偷懒和欺骗去蚕食这些政策。他们宁愿一点一点地挤占土地而不是直接侵占土地；他们选择开小差而不是公开发动兵变，他们宁可小偷小摸也不去抢公共的或私人的粮仓。而一旦农民不再使用这些策略而采取堂吉诃德式的行动，这通常是大规模铤而走险的信号"。[①] 也就是说，农民与国家权力的斗争，往往是以一种更加隐秘的但却更加普遍和温和的方式进行的。

在荃镇，这种利用 "弱者的武器" 所进行的日常抗争也是很常见的，用荃镇领导干部的话来说就是 "老百姓越来越难管了"，"难管" 暗含了一种对农民不合作或对抗行为的无奈情绪。笔者在荃镇调研期间感受到，农民往往表现出对镇政府及村委会的极度不信任感，当镇政府（一般是联合村委会）在乡村开展一些活动时——即便是那些有利于农民利益的活动，他们也并很少积极配合，有时甚至会阻挠活动的开展。笔者曾经参与了一次 S 县 "春季计划生育集中活动"，这是由县计生办联合荃镇政府的一次大活动，县里来了 20 人，镇里有一大半人员都参加了，主要是为了迎接省里的计划生育抽查活动，事先由县乡两级对育龄妇女体检、抚养费征收、长效避孕节育措施落实及超生情况进行筛查摸底，做到 "心中有数"，调查人员按

---

① 詹姆斯·C. 斯科特著，郑广怀等译《弱者的武器》前言，译林出版社，2007，第 3 页。

管区分成八个组，由管区主任和各村的包村干部负责带领检查人员进村进行"拉网式"排查，即每个村都要挨家挨户"入户"进行询问和登记。笔者参加了活动第一天在泉水村的调查，我们一行五人于上午9时到达该村，可奇怪的是，很多住户都大门紧闭，随行的包村干部笑言肯定是谁"走漏了风声"，对那些大门紧锁的人家我们试图通过询问邻居了解情况，可得到的答复却往往是"不知道"，我们还到过一户怀孕9个月的人家调查情况，尽管该户是第一胎合法怀孕，但显然男主人对我们充满了戒心，让我们出示工作证。在调查中笔者深深地体会到，这些日常抗争行为的确为基层工作的开展带来诸多不便，乡镇干部也能感觉到这种无形的压力。

三 结语

农民非制度化政治参与行为的逐渐增多，已经成为近几年乡土政治变迁的一个显著特征。其本质是乡土社会治理权力转移与现有政治制度设计不足之间的矛盾，是农民在现有制度框架下及更为复杂的外部环境中的理性选择。这一变化给基层公共管理者带来了前所未有的挑战，一方面，需要基层公共管理者转变以往对待上述非制度化政治参与行为的态度，以更加灵活智慧的方式加以应对。另一方面，更需要在制度层面上进行改革，疏通正式的利益表达和意见输入渠道。目前，农民正式的利益表达渠道主要有信访、选举人大代表和村民自治，但就当前的情况看，这三种方式还不完善，比如信访制度是典型的计划经济时代的产物，与市场经济和现代民主所强调的程序正义、规则平等原则是相违背的，在农民利益"表达"这一意义上显得捉襟见肘，并且引发了地方政府截访、打压等扭曲行为。地方人大代表应该成为农民利益表达的重要载体，但目前农民代表比例还比较低，并且其人选也多是"乡村能人"，很难真正代表普通农民的利益。而作为农民利益表达最直接渠道的村民自治制度也存在较大的问题，尚不能扮演其应有的政治角色，在基层政治场域中缺乏应有的话语权，村委会成了基层政权的代理人，难以承担其农民表达利益诉求的职能。因此，首先应当完善有关村民自治的制度，特别是议事规则的明确、基层政权与村民自治组织的关系需进一步明确、加强村民自治中的程序法建设等；其次，完善地方人代会制度。尽管

2010 年的选举法修正案规定 "城乡按相同人口比例选举人大代表"，但这不一定能够保证农民代表反映农民诉求。更为关键的是还要进一步规范候选代表的选举过程，保证农民选出真正代表农民利益的人大代表，同时还要完善农民对代表的监督制度。

参考文献

方江山：《非制度政治参与：以转型期中国农民为对象分析》，人民出版社，2000，第 85 页。

金太军：《村庄治理中三重权力互动的政治社会学分析》，《战略与管理》2002 年第 2 期。

彭勃：《乡村治理：国家介入与体制选择》，中国社会出版社，2002，第 103 页。

仝志辉、贺雪峰：《村庄权力结构的三层分析》，《中国社会科学》2002 年第 1 期。

应星：《大河移民上访的故事》，三联书店，2001，第 314 ~ 327 页。

于建嵘：《农民有组织抗争及其政治风险》，《战略与管理》2003 年第 3 期。

詹姆斯·C. 斯科特著，郑广怀等译《弱者的武器》前言，译林出版社，2007，第 3 页。

张双山：《正解 "越级上访"》，《公民导刊》2006 年第 8 期。

赵树凯：《矛盾、引导和历史的契机：关于 196 封农民来信的初步分析》，《农民日报》1998 年 1 月 28 日。

赵树凯：《乡村治理：组织和冲突》，《战略与管理》2003 年第 6 期。

周晓虹：《中国农民的政治参与：毛泽东和后毛泽东时代的比较》，《香港社会科学学报》2000 年秋季号。

借鉴德国经验完善中国养老保障服务体系

任　勤[*]

【摘要】德国是世界上最早建立社会保障制度的国家之一，有着相当规模的养老保障服务体系，本文从社会养老保险体系、养老服务体系、老年人护理培训体系、养老保险管理运作体系四个方面较全面地阐释德国养老保障服务体系框架；探讨德国养老保障服务体系的特点。针对存在的问题，借鉴德国成功经验，提出中国养老保障服务体系提升和完善的政策措施。

【关键词】德国；养老保障；服务体系；中国；借鉴

养老保障服务体系是指整个社会对养老提供各种制度、政策、服务等方面所构成的系统的总称。一个完善的养老保障服务体系应是一个缜密的安全网络，应该包括对老年人的经济支持制度、精神支持制度及服务支持制度。其中，经济支持制度包括社会养老保险制度、社会救济制度、企业补充养老保险制度、个人储蓄制度，以及家庭制度等；精神支持制度包括家庭制度及有关的社区服务制度；而服务支持制度包括家庭、机构和社区服务制度。德国是世界上最早建立社会保障制度的国家之一，有着相对比较完善的社会福利制度，合理借鉴德国养老保障体系建设的成功经验，无疑对我国提升和完

---

　　* 任勤：女，经济学博士，教授，硕士生导师。主要研究领域为公共产品理论与实践、政府经济管理、公共政策分析。

善自身的养老保障体系具有重要的指导意义。

一　德国养老保障服务体系的框架

德国的养老保障服务体系不仅有充足的资金保障和优秀的专业护理人员，更充满了浓厚的人文关怀，为退休老年人提供了一个相当周全的养老保障服务体系，被冠以"最慷慨"养老制度的美誉。

（一）完善的社会养老保险体系

德国的社会养老保险体系由国家强制性的法定养老保险系统、企业养老保险系统和私人自愿养老保险系统三大支柱构成，外加德国护理保险构成了德国的养老资金保障的四大支柱。

第一支柱是法定养老保险。这是德国养老保险制度的主体，在德国社会保障制度中也自成一体，超过80%的从业人员是法定养老保险的成员，这是联邦政府的一种强制险。每一个雇员、企业、团体必须在法律规定下定期投保。投保项目包括：（1）退休金；（2）丧失劳动能力；（3）死亡。目前的缴费比例为雇员工资的19.9%（税前），雇主和雇员各负担50%。当雇员收入低于某一限额时，由雇主单独缴付。法定养老保险每年能获得占当年总支出20%的国家补贴。它采取"转移分摊原则"来进行收缴和支付，即在职雇员交纳的养老保险金用于支付退休雇员的养老金。领取数额是根据退休者退休时的工资和工龄计算，最高限额为退休时工资的75%。目前，退休雇员领取的法定养老金占工资比例平均为53%。第二支柱是企业补充养老保险。德国企业养老保险制度是法定养老保险制度的补充，是一些规模大、经济效益好的企业为激励员工，留住人才而设立的。企业将雇员工资的一定比例投入养老基金中，员工退休后就可从中获益，现在企业养老保险已经成为德国养老保险体系中一个重要的支柱。第三支柱是私人补充养老保险。德国的私人保险是通过个人净收入支付保险费，在退休后领取养老金的一种方式，是一种私人养老手段。其对象主要是医生（如牙医）、药剂师、律师等高工资和高收入群体。21世纪初期，德国法定养老保险、企业养老保险和私人养老保险所支付养老金的比例大约分别为70%、20%和10%，企业养老保险和私人养老保险在整个养老保险体系中所占的比例还相对较低，因此德国政府希望私人养老保险支付的养老金近期可以提高到整个养老金的15%，中远期达到25%～30%的水平，逐渐将企业养老金和私人养老保险从现在的补充地位逐步提升到与法定养老保险相近的支柱地位。[1] 第四支柱是护理保险。[2] 德国法律规定了"护理保险跟从医疗保险的原则"，即所有医疗保险的投保人都要参加护理保险，这是以强制保险的方式要求公民必须参加养老护理保险和储蓄保险资金，在公民未来行动不便的时候，由相关机构的人员提供护理协助，所产生的费用由保险人支付的制度。德国采取了强制性保险，即本国公民必须按照法律规定参加护理保险，它属于社会基本养老保险范畴，从1995年起正式推行。法定护理保险的费用为月毛工资的1.7%，雇主和雇员各承担50%，退休人员的护理保险费由退休人员和养老保险机构共同承担，失业人员保费由劳工局支付。这样通过不同的渠道，将参加法定保险的人员全都纳入养老护理保险中来，扩大了养老护理保险的范围。

养老保险的四大支柱是养老资金筹措的主要来源，分别发挥着正常保障功能、补充保障功能和前瞻性保障功能。此外还有援助计划，对老年人实施各种优惠政策，如减低房租、贷款、住房基金、民间援助、针对老年人的监护法等。

（二）健全的养老服务体系

1. 建立"储存个人服务时间"的制度，解决"人力需求"矛盾

德国政府从人文关怀、社会关爱、全员护理的视角和现实需要出发，切实采取措施，认真着手解决养老保障制度中日益突出的"人力需求"矛盾。推出一项叫作"储存个人服务时间"的制度。凡年满18岁的公民，均可利用公休或节假日义务到老年公寓、老人院和老年病康复中心提供各种护理服务，不拿报酬，但服务时间可随时储存在服务者个人档案中，以备将来自己

---

[1] Hein – Dietrish Steinmeryer, "The Private – Operated Organization of Endowment Insurance Germany", *Social Security Studies* 01（2005）.

[2] 中国保险网：《独具一格的德国法定护理保险》，www. rmic. cn。

需要接受护理服务时，将这些服务时间提取出来免费享用。这项制度深受德国公众欢迎，因为它既避免了年轻公民人力资源的浪费，增强了人们的社会责任感，也为年老和病残公民的自我救助提供了一种选择。在某种意义上，也是"转移支付"原则在人力资源合理分配使用上的具体应用。

2. 多元化的养老方式，满足养老的不同需求

德国老年人主要有五种养老方式：第一种是居家养老，老年人在家中居住，靠政府每月发放的养老金度日，这种形式最普遍。第二种是机构养老，顾名思义，老年人在老年公寓、教会提供的公寓或其他类似的机构生活。第三种是社区养老，正在成为主流。第四种方式是异地养老，包括旅游养老、度假养老、回原居住地养老等。第五种是"以房防老"，即为了养老而购买房子，利用房租来维持自己的退休生活。

3. 独具特色的长期照料服务，解决老年人的后顾之忧

德国的长期照料服务体系比较完善，采用被保险人、保险人（长期照料社会保险机构）和第三方（长期照料服务机构）共同运作的机制。被保险人缴费，享有长期照料服务，保险人负责筹集和管理长期照料社会保险基金，根据法律和服务合同向第三方拨付基金，主要是联邦卫生部、中央长期照料社会保险基金联合会和联邦长期照料服务机构联合会。第三方独立运作，按照法律和服务合同为失能人群提供长期照料服务。德国的长期照料服务机构分为居家服务和机构服务两个层次。至 2007 年共建立服务机构20300 个，包括 10600 个居家服务机构及 9700 个长期照料服务专门机构。据德国卫生部资料，这些机构和设施不仅基本可以满足德国全部失能老年人长期照料的服务需求，而且在实施长期照料社会保险制度以后，服务设施不断改善，服务质量也在逐步提高。德国长期照料服务机构的设施投资费用主要由联邦各州负责，如果在运行时出现不足，不足部分由失能人群共同承担。

4. 大学向老年人开放，精神赡养的重要途径

早在 20 世纪 40 年代，德国的著名心理学家安妮特拉·卡斯腾就认为人们不能在沙发上饮食终日，无所事事地消极被动地度过人生最后二三十年，而应该正视现实，积极地心安理得地走进人生的第三阶段。她最早办起了德国歌德老年大学，招收 65 岁以上的退休男性和 60 岁以上的退休女性，年龄

最大的 86 岁。设置了广泛的专业，有法律、教育、经济、社会、心理、艺术教育、神学等。这些专业和老年人息息相关，符合办学宗旨。20 世纪 70 年代，德国又兴起了"大学向老年人开放"的运动。这些活动丰富了老年人的生活，也成为老年人精神赡养的重要途径。

（三）严格的老年人护理人员培训体系

德国 2003 年正式颁布了老年护理职业法，该法规共分为九个部分，较为详细阐述了老年护理职业从业人员的条件与资质认定的程序，老年护理培训的入学条件与考试的规定，以及相关的培训费用规定。新法律要求养老护理人员要从年轻人培养起。德国护理质量发展网络体系（DNQF），意指使专业的护理人员在护理问题上能够找到标准化的东西。建立这个体系的目的在于，无论在任何地方的护理人员，在实践和专业标准上都能达成共识。DNQF 的工作是通过一个质控委员会来完成的，委员会的成员都是在护理行业从事各项工作的专业人士，委员会的工作涉及护理产业、管理、培训和实习。目前的培训模式是双轨制，对职业护理要培训三年，级别较低的护理辅助仅需要培训一年。这个职业没有年龄的要求，培训完后就可以上岗，当然要达到法定工作年龄。双轨制的培训强调理论与实践相结合，每月有几天要去老人院实习。职业培训的费用由实际用人单位每月支付，而且还要给护理人员一定的费用，也就是说这样的培训不仅是免费的，而且接受培训的护理员在培训期间还可以得到一笔收入。此外还有专门的机构监督护理效果，监督人员按照有关法律实施对护理的监督。德国养老护理员的福利待遇现处于德国中等偏上的水准：一般是每月 3500 欧元。德国老年人护理人员队伍建设稳定发展，1995 年共有 39.4 万从业人员，到 2004 年，从业人员发展到 44.1 万人，其中 90% 为妇女。养老机构的护理人员与被照护老年人的比例规定如下：0 级 1∶7.74；1 级 1∶4.01；2 级 1∶2.5；3 级 1∶1.97，上述标准国家每半年要组织修订一次。

（四）分工明确的养老管理运作体系

德国的养老管理运作分工明确，各司其职。首先，政府负责制定政策，保险业务实行社会化管理。德国联邦政府规定：基本养老保险、失业保险和医疗保险等政策的制定，分别由联邦社会保障部、劳工部和卫生部负责。联邦下属的 16 个州政府除了设有内政、财政、文化、经济、教育、工商、法院等部门外，均专门设有社会保障部。各州政府的社会保障部又设有家庭保障、工作保障、健康保障、社会保障、保障法律制定和办公室 6 个部门。这种专管体制的建立有效地保障了政策制度的高效运行。其次，社会保障实行社会化管理，由专门的社会保险组织负责。这种社会保险组织是独立的社团法人，财务和组织上均独立于政府部门。开展工作时通过董事会和代表大会进行，投保者和雇主每 6 年通过自由的选举产生出代表大会代表，候选人的提名由雇员与雇主协商产生，最多不超过 60 名。董事会由代表大会选举产生，一般有 12 名董事，其主席由董事会选举产生，业务经理由代表大会根据董事会提名选举产生，实行"自我管理"。

二 德国养老保障服务体系的特点

（一）德国养老保险制度覆盖面广，体现共同责任的原则

德国现行养老保险制度主要分为三个层次，第一层次是法定基本养老保险；第二层次为资本市场结合的补充保障，主要由政府支持或税收减免的企业补充养老保险体系（即企业年金）承担；第三层次为其他补充保障，主要由传统的私人养老保险和寿险构成。这三层次责任明确，政府、雇主与雇员在社会保障制度中的责任机制对养老保障基金来源、津贴水平、覆盖范围、制度模式、基金安全及制度效果都产生直接影响，呈现明显的共同责任原则。德国的养老保障覆盖面广，保障主旨就是谋求大众的福利，使全体国民能共享国民经济发展的成果。德国实行的是全员保障原则，其社会保险法的适用范围是全体劳动者，养老保障制度作为其整个社会保障制度的一个重要组成部分，对保障经济的持续、繁荣、健康发展，维护社会安定和谐，倡导公平公正的社会理念，缓解雇佣和社会矛盾，完善其社会法律制度，发挥了巨大的作用。

（二）养老服务体系全面，体现社会互助的原则

德国养老服务体系设计周到全面，还吸收人类社会中互助互济的优良传

统。不仅养老模式多元化，满足不同养老需求，还从人文关怀、社会关爱、康残互助、全员护理的视角和现实出发，为老年人的生活提供保险。特别是为了解决老年护理人员短缺的问题，实施了特殊政策"储存时间"制度，在某种意义上，这种保险模式是"转移支付"原则在人力资源合理分配使用上的具体应用，同时促使全社会尤其是年轻人关爱老年人，服务于老年人，在制度上有了保障。

（三）社会化的养老保险管理，体现自主管理的原则

德国的社会保障由准政府性质的社会保险机构进行自主管理，政府部门并不直接参与。专门的社会保障管理机构有利于管理的专业化和规范化，社会组织的身份也能更好地体现被保障对象的意志，有利于避免政府利益与国民利益的错位。政府除了根据实际情况及时调整政策、制定标准、规范运作、提交法案经联邦或州议会通过施行外，凡是能由社会团体、企业和私人承办的社会保障事项，均按市场经济的规律、规则和方式办理，各司其职，从而节约了资源，降低了成本，提高了效率。

德国的养老保障制度不仅结构严谨，发展完善，而且在其发展进程中，政府主动采取了一些调整和改革措施来适应社会经济的新发展。德国养老保障服务体系在功能定位、经办主体、具体组织方法等方面都具有鲜明的特色，设计科学、结构完善的养老保障服务体系运行多年，总体平稳。

三　德国经验对完善我国养老保障服务体系的启示

我国目前老龄化速度明显加快，现已成为世界上老龄化速度最快的国家之一，但是我国的养老保障服务体系的建设却未能与经济发展同步，甚至远远滞后于国民经济的发展，合理借鉴德国养老保障服务体系建设的成功经验，无疑对我国提升和完善自身的养老保障服务体系具有重要的指导意义。

（一）针对我国养老保险覆盖面窄的问题，建立全国统一的覆盖全体国民的养老保险体系

我国养老保障城乡二元分割，缺乏衔接，且存在严重的城乡失衡。城镇

养老保险以城镇职工为参保对象，农村社会养老保险则以农村居民为参保对象，这样，以户籍为标准，养老保障被分割成城乡二元体系，城镇养老保险的保障水平远高于农村，农村人口则难以进入城镇社会养老保障体系。在德国，任何一个投保人员都具有社会福利号码，并且接受福利的状况不受地区、企业性质的限制。我国也应尽快建立一个没有城乡差距、地区差异的统一福利制度，解决中小企业、个体户、农民等养老保障问题。因此应以体现基金征集同待遇支付相配套、社会统筹与个人账户相结合、权利与义务相对应、公平与效率相联系为原则，建立资金来源多渠道、城镇劳动者全覆盖的养老保障制度，在此基础上，不分城乡、不分区域、不分企业性质及职工身份，将全部从业人员、城镇灵活就业人员、城镇个体劳动者纳入基本养老保险的保障范围。覆盖范围越大，保障程度越高，保障成本越低，扩大社会保险覆盖面，可以提高抗风险能力，增加养老保障基金收入，增强调剂能力，充分发挥社会养老保障的互助互济功能。

（二）针对我国养老保险资金来源不足的问题，建立多层次的养老保险体系

长期以来，我国的养老保障除了依靠家庭外，主要的依靠是国家养老保障，养老资金非常有限。因此借鉴德国经验构建多层次的养老保障体系在有效应对人口老龄化发展方面不失为一种理性和科学的选择。完善的养老保险体系应包含国家基本养老保险、企业补充养老保险、个人储蓄性养老保险和特殊群体附加救济金这四个层次的构建，以满足不同地区、不同经济状况和不同收入水平人员的养老需求。首先，国家基本养老保险应为养老保险的基础保障和重要支柱。要实现我国国家公务员、事业单位工作人员、企业职工三大群体养老保险计发办法方案的统一，并在此基础上针对公务员、事业单位、企业职工的不同性质与特点分别颁布法案，解决各自面临的特殊问题。其次，企业养老保险作为养老保险的补充保障。以企业为主，该层次养老保险由企业和个人共同出资建立，即把原有的个人账户从基本养老保险中分离出来，并将个人账户的个人部分做成实账后，与企业的补充保险合并，合并后的个人账户由企业和个人按新的政策规定缴费，积累储存，构建第二层次的保障。再次，个人储蓄性养老保险作为养老保障的第三层次。

个人储蓄性养老保险可以由居民自愿选择参加。选择参加途径有两种：第一，购买商业养老保险；第二，在银行开办养老储蓄账户。个人储蓄性养老保险统一由政府制定优惠政策，在一定程度上减免税收，提升利率，若参保人提前支取则按正常利率和税率计算支付金额。最后，对特殊群体附加救济金作为救助型养老保障。通过家庭收入调查，对那些真正需要社会提供帮助的高龄人口或特殊贫困人口，以社会救助或低水平的社会养老金的方式为他们提供附加保障。

（三）针对养老保险金管理不善的问题，厘清政府与市场的责任，优化社会保险与商业保险的关系

我国对养老保险资金的管理缺乏相应的法规，资金的收缴、管理和支付等各环节不规范，往往无章可循，再加上社会保障资金由隶属于政府部门的机构负责增值和营运，难免会在运营的过程中掺杂政府部门的行政干预因素。且我国的养老保险制度采取的资金积累模式也意味着数额巨大的资金储备，因此就会出现被挪用或占用的现象。合理界定政府的责任与作用，优化社会保险与商业保险的关系，建立和加强基金的行政监督、社会监督和管理机构的内部监控是十分必要的。首先，明确政府与市场的责任，各自发挥优势作用。从德国的经验看，在养老保障体系中政府中发挥了主导作用，主要体现在四个方面：一是统筹养老保障制度建设，主导养老保障立法、体系框架设计及政策措施制定等方面的工作；二是组织，提供基本养老保险，为尽可能多的国民提供基本生活的收入保障；三是提供一定的财政补贴或税收优惠等方面的政策支持，鼓励或吸引企业及个人为老年生活进行理性规划；四是对基本保险和补充保险进行监督管理，维护受益人的合法权益和市场的稳定可持续。其次，充分发挥市场在资源配置中的基础性作用，基本养老保障之外的各项制度的经营管理应实行完全的市场化作用，充分发挥各类金融机构的服务优势，如银行的账户管理、托管优势，保险业的精算、产品和计划设计、风险管理、年金化发放、资产负债匹配管理优势，基金公司的资本市场投资优势等。社会保险部门应该完全退出补充保险市场，专注于养老救助和社会保险，为全体国民提供最基本的养老保障。

（四）针对我国养老服务方式单一问题，构建多样化的养老模式

与德国多样化的养老方式相比，我国的养老方式还显得比较单一，主要还是以家庭养老为主，而当然这是受我国多年积淀下来的厚重的文化底蕴影响的。按照我国"9073"养老格局，即90%为居家养老，7%为社区养老，3%为机构养老的构想，就是要充分发挥三种养老模式的作用和功能。一是以居家养老为基础，构筑"居家养老"的社会支持系统。独生子女政策的实施，家庭日益小型化、核心化，"空巢家庭"越来越多，家庭养老资源正在萎缩。因此，有必要通过相关的福利政策，构筑"居家养老"的社会支持系统，支持、维护甚至放大家庭养老的功能。二是将"以人为本、依托社区、互助而助"的社区养老作为居家养老的辅助。落实国家"星光计划"：从中央到地方，民政部门把发行福利彩票筹集的福利金的绝大部分用于资助城市社区老年人福利服务设施、活动场所和农村乡镇敬老院的建设，使老年人不出社区就能享受到需要的服务。三是扩大机构养老规模，增加床位，完善设施，适当降低门槛和收费标准，发挥机构提供标准化、高质量的养老服务的功能。

（五）针对老年护理人力资源短缺问题，推广"个人服务时间存储"制度

在一个逐渐进入未富先老的国度，如何就地解决日益突出的护理费用过高与护理需求增大的矛盾、人力资源浪费与人力资源短缺的矛盾，德国的经验值得重视和推广。我国城市大多数是独生子女家庭，而独生子女通常缺乏为他人服务的意识。尽快开设法定护理保险，推广"个人服务时间存储"制度是解决以上短缺矛盾的重要途径。实施护理保险制度，解决老年护理的资金问题，建立志愿者服务"储蓄"制度，解决老年护理和服务人员问题。不断扩大养老护理志愿者队伍，吸引一批有爱心、有能力的年轻人加入养老护理队伍，为养老护理作贡献。对一些参加社区养老护理服务的年轻人，对他们服务的次数和质量以一定形式记录下来，把他们为社会作的贡献"储存"起来，在他们因年老或其他原因需要护理的时候，"支取"他们为护理所作的贡献。志愿者队伍的出现，一方面可解决老人养老的后顾之忧，另一

方面可充实年轻人的生活，还能促进敬老、爱老等社会风尚进步，更为重要的是，它能有效地解决"精神养老"的问题。

参考文献

陈南雁：《德国推进养老保险制度改革的策略研究》，《国际论坛》2008 年第 6 期。

郭琳：《中国养老保障体系变迁中的企业补充养老保险制度研究》，中国金融出版社，2008。

于洪：《外国养老保障制度》，上海财经大学出版社，2005。

俞可：《论德国"大学向老年人开放"运动》，《复旦教育论坛》2013 年第 2 期。

张啸：《德国养老》，中国社会出版社，2010。

钟添生：《中国人口老龄化与养老保障体系探析》，《江西行政学院学报》2009 年第 1 期。

美、日、新政务服务的特点及分析

顾 绚[*]

【摘要】20 世纪 70 年代以来，为了回应财政危机、管理危机和信任危机的影响，传统行政模式逐渐被新公共管理模式取代，开始由管制型政府向服务型政府转变，出现了一系列新的发展趋势。本文选取了在政务服务的提供上具有代表性的三个国家——美国、日本和新加坡，总结出其各自政务服务的特点，并对各自的特点进行了梳理，进而努力寻求能够为我国政府提升政务水平、与国际接轨的有效路径。

【关键词】政府服务；一站式服务；新公共管理

20 世纪 70 年代以来，为了回应财政危机、管理危机和信任危机的影响，美国等发达国家掀起一场顾客导向、市场价值回归的行政改革浪潮，致力于克服政府弊端和提高政府绩效。传统行政模式被新公共管理模式所取代，开始由管制型政府向服务型政府转变，出现行政权力分散化、行政职能市场化、行政服务社会化、行政信息电子化等的发展趋势。本文选取了在政务服务的提供上具有代表性的三个国家——美国、日本和新加坡，总结出其各自政务服务的特点：美国，一站式服务的标杆；日本，坚持法治的持续改革者；新加坡，便民宜商的公共服务模

---

* 顾绚：讲师，西南财经大学劳动经济学博士，美国乔治·梅森大学访问学者。

范，并在此基础上进行分析，以期寻求到能够为我国政府提升政务水平、与国际接轨的有效路径。

一　美、日、新三国政务服务的特点

（一）一站式服务的标杆——美国政务服务

美国的政务服务是以行政服务中心为载体的。美国的行政服务中心建设是一个在创新中不断发展的过程。20 世纪 70 年代，伴随着行政制度改革的深入，美国便出现了类似于行政服务中心的行政服务机构。进入 80 年代之后，在新公共管理运动思潮的主导下，美国出现了以行政服务中心为载体的政府"一站式"服务理念，并提出了"无缝隙政府"[①] 的政府治理模式。

美国行政服务中心是在行政审批制度改革中逐渐形成，以新公共服务理论为理论基础，建立在完备的法制体系上，存在于完善的机构设置之中，并以信息化技术为基础的电子政府为主要内容和推动力，以网络虚拟和机构实体两种形式存在的现代公共行政服务方式之一。整体上来看，美国的"一站式"服务有以下特点。

1. 多样化服务渠道

在"一站式"政府服务机构的实现手段上，美国主要存在 5 种渠道：（1）传统的办公室（楼）渠道。也就是指面对面的柜台式办公。（2）互联网站渠道。即通过互联网构建针对公众的网站。从全球范围来看，目前在"一站式"领域应用最广的渠道是通过互联网。（3）自助服务亭渠道（Kiosk）[②]。这有些类似 ATM 自动取款机，自助服务亭比集中的办公中心要

---

① 无缝隙政府（Seamless Government）指的是政府整合所有的部门、人员和其他资源，以单一的界面为公众提供优质高效的信息和服务。无缝隙政府是要突破传统的部门界线和功能分割的局面，所以也称"无界线政府"。

② Kiosk 源于土耳其语，原意为路边无人看管的书报摊，现引申为一种自助的概念：自助服务机和信息服务亭，提供产品或储存信息及提供媒体展示的自助式服务设备。具体来看，这种自助式服务设备整合了各式软硬件设备，以影片、图片、文字、音乐等多媒体数据库形成互动环境，提供各类产品贩售或是信息服务。

分布得更广泛。美国"Hassle – Free Communities"（无忧社区）① 项目中数以千计的 Kiosks 就很有代表性。（4）电话服务中心渠道（CallCenter）。通过电话来提供各种信息、指导或办理公共服务。这方面，美国的集成电话中心（即 800 政府免费热线）是个典型。（5）移动一站式服务渠道。例如美国拥有一站式服务移动车（Hassle – Free Communities Van），② 这样就能够使政府在紧急状况下把服务送到公民面前。

2. 规范完善的流程

美国"一站式"政府服务机构的建立，一般可分为以下几个阶段。（1）制定战略和明确法律地位。在美国，构建"一站式"政府服务机构已经成为被普遍接受的观念，并有了比较明确的"一站式"发展战略。例如美国在"一站式"服务理念的引导下，先后实行了访问美国计划（Access America Project）、"无忧社区计划"和"第一政府计划"（FirstGov Project）三个"一站式"服务计划，并在管理和预算办公室中专门设立了"信息和管制事务办公室"（Office of Information and Regulatory Affairs，OIRA）作为组织实施的监督领导机构。（2）开展大规模调研以明确服务方向。美国在建设"一站式"政府服务机构时，对公民进行了广泛的调查，看公民们希望得到什么样的公共服务，希望通过什么渠道提供。例如由美国一所大学对公民进行调查，他们试图了解对于公共服务和私营部门的服务，公民更偏好哪种服务渠道，结果发现互联网方式更受青睐，人们希望在单一的一个政府网站上有所有的公共服务。（3）向民众进行宣传。按百姓意愿开展服务之后，还应该让广大民众知晓，了解政府通过哪些渠道、有哪些服务提供给民众，这一点也不可缺少。于是，美国政府往往对所提供的服务进行大规模的

---

① Hassle – Free Communities 意为无忧社区，源于美国政府在 20 世纪初推行的"无忧社区计划"，该计划选取了美国各地的 12 个社区，由联邦政府与州和地方机构合作，以"发展最需要的客户服务"的无缝交付，为公民提供一站式服务。为了惠及所有的公民，政府在超市、商场、公交站等地设立了数以千计的自助服务亭，公民可以通过带有触屏功能的自助服务设备免费获得政府服务。

② Hassle – Free Communities Van 意为一站式服务移动车，相当于车轮上的一站式服务政府，可以为公民提供上门服务，是对固定服务中心和自助服务亭的一种补充。同时，在公民处于危机时，政府可以通过派送 Hassle – Free Communities Van 快速到达灾源地，作为暂时的市民服务中心，援助幸存者。

宣传，例如美国会在网站"推特"（Twitter）上的官方账户公开发布服务内容和细则，以宣传其新的服务内容。（4）不断收集反馈改进意见。在开展了服务之后，国外政府还经常开展调研、咨询，向民众征集意见，以不断改善服务。例如美国的部分州政府会定期进行大规模的客户调查，根据反馈改进服务。

（二）坚持法治的持续改革者——日本政务服务

日本的政务服务改革是一个不断创新发展的过程，主要表现在对规制的改革方面。从20世纪60年代后期开始，日本先后进行了7次行政审批制度改革，到了90年代，面对日益低迷的经济形势，日本政府先后推出了四个规制改革计划，对6000多项规制进行了改革。日本的规制改革是由"规制缓和"向"规制改革"逐渐发展的过程，其改革的重点由"经济性规制领域"逐步向"社会性规制领域"扩展。

90年代中后期以来，日本在规制改革方面实行了一系列的新举措，主要包括：创建"结构改革特区"；引进"市场化试验"制度，将部分由政府垄断的公共服务项目通过政府和民间企业平等竞标的方式委托给在成本和服务质量方面都具有优势的中标者经营；建立更趋科学化，即可以量化规制安全性和经济性的"规制影响分析"评估体系。

1. 创建"结构改革特区"

作为推动规制改革的重要措施，日本政府于2002年4月提出设立"结构改革特区"设想。所谓结构改革特区是指"依据各地方政府自发制定的方案，针对该地区的特点，设立引进特定调控机制的特定区域，并在该区域内实施结构改革"的地区。其目的是：通过在特定区域实施结构改革的成功事例的示范作用，将规制改革推向全国，进而搞活全国的经济。截止到2007年7月底，日本各地已经建立起963个结构改革特区。

2. 引进"市场化试验"制度

为了将规制改革引向深入，2003年12月，日本综合规制改革会议在"关于推进规制改革的第3次答询"中，提出实施"市场化试验"制度的建议。2004年3月，小泉内阁通过了"推进规制改革、民间开放3年计划"，该计划具有两个特点：一是将"推进民间开放"（市场化试验）的观点引入规制改革的计划；二是将改革的重点由经济性规制转向社会性规制。这种在"市场化试验"中由政府委托民间部门提供公共服务的行为即是政府购买公共服务的活动，后来这一活动在专门的法律规范下和专门的机构组织下运行，遵循严格的程序，逐渐形成了政府购买公共服务的制度。从 2005 年开始，小泉内阁对 3 个领域的 8 项事业引入竞争机制，包括：与公共就业相关的领域、与社会保险相关的领域、与刑罚设施相关的领域。具体项目如职业介绍项目、青年职业介绍项目、职业招聘项目、职业培训项目、国民年金保险费征收项目、保险事业促进项目、年金电话咨询项目、刑罚设施相关等项目，通过竞标委托给民间经营。2006 年 5 月，日本国会通过了《关于通过竞争改革公共服务的法律》，以法律形式明确了改革公共服务事业的原则，增强了规制改革的透明度。2006 年 9 月，日本的市场化试验进入正式实施阶段。例如，职业介绍及职业体验等 6 项服务于 2007 年 4 月 1 日向民间公开招标。之后面向驻日外交官的日语进修、文化艺术交流等 7 项事业也将进入招标程序。

3. 建立对新规制的评审机制

日本在推进规制改革的同时，重视加强对新规制出台前及实施中的评估，并对因社会环境变化而失去效力的规制进行修订或取消。政府要求主管部门在制定各种规制时应考虑法律的整合性，规制的必要性、恰当性、排他性及国民的负担等因素，绝不出台无关紧要或妨碍民间企业自由竞争的规制。为使对规制的评估更加趋向科学化，日本引进了被称为"规制影响分析"的评估体系。该体系的评估项目包括规制的内容（规制的目的、必要性）、规制的费用分析（实施规制的行政成本、执行成本、社会成本）、规制的利益分析（规制实施后给企业和国民带来的利益、社会性利益）等内容。如日本总务省规定，今后中央各省厅在制定新规制的同时也承担着对其效果进行事前评价的义务，要尽可能量化规制的安全性和费用，客观分析规制的利弊。

（三）便民宜商的公共服务模范——新加坡政务服务

新加坡由于独特的自身条件——国土面积小、国民人口少、观念开放、服务理念超前，同时具有社会信息化程度高、电子政务发展成效卓著的优势，于是迅速形成了以网络电子服务为主、实体机构服务为辅的行政服务模式。[①] 2012 年 3 月，在联合国发布题为《2012 年联合国电子政务调查报告：面向公众的电子政务》的 2012 年全球电子政务调查。[②] 报告中，新加坡以 0.8474 的电子政务发展指数排在榜单的第 10 位。新加坡电子政务的政务服务变革经历了一个循序渐进的更替性过程，在每个时期相应政务服务新项目的建立也与当时的环境背景、技术支持和人员参与相匹配。

新加坡的电子政府起步于 20 世纪 80 年代初。经过 30 多年的发展，取得了很大的成就。总的来说，新加坡电子政府建设历程可分为以下几个阶段：（1）公民服务计算机化计划（1980～1999 年），这一阶段强调公共服务的效率，主要内容是自动化的公共服务和基本的 IT 基础设施和数据中心的建设。（2）电子政府行动计划（2000～2005 年），这一阶段强调的是公共服务的卓越，主要实现了在线服务的交付，包括了 1600 项电子服务的网上功能的实现。（3）整合化政府 2010 规划（2006～2010 年），这一阶段强调的是一体化政府的整合，主要实现的是政府机构数据、过程及系统的集成，完成了 300 个移动政府服务系统的部署。（4）电子政府 2015 年规划（2011～2015 年），这一阶段强调的是政府私有化的价值创新和经济竞争力，专注于政府内部和外部的协作。经历这样一个长期阶段性的发展，新加坡电子政务已日趋成熟，而每阶段均展开了一系列各具特色的政务服务项目的构建，形成了独具本国特色的政务服务系统。

按照服务对象的不同，新加坡政府将电子服务的功能主要分为面向个人的服务（G2C，Government to Citizens）和面向企业的服务（G2B，Government to Businesses）。

1. 基于个人的服务

新加坡政府向个人用户提供了范围广泛的在线电子服务，个人用户可以通过电子公民门户网站（www. ecitizen. gov. sg）获得每天 24 小时不间断的服务。网站具有"人生周期、顾客导向、一站式服务"的特征，在这里，

---

① 彭博、张锐昕：《新加坡行政服务中心建设的内容、特点和启示》，《电子政务》2012 年第 11 期。

② 《2012 年联合国电子政务调查报告：面向公众的电子政务》，http：//zh. wikipedia. org/wiki/ E% E6% 94% BF% E5% BA% 9C。

政府提供的数百项或各种"套装"居民服务项目大都是以公民需求为导向进行设计的，用户无须知道有关事务是由哪个部门管辖的，只需按程序接受政府服务。

2. 基于企业的服务

通过在线服务，企业不再像往常一样填写烦琐的表格。新加坡政府建立了一套先进的政府电子商务系统（GeBIZ，Government Electronic Business①）。该系统是一个点对点的集成服务平台，本地和国际企业可以登录到该网站查询商业机会或进行电子交易。具体来说，按发展历程来看，新加坡的政务服务主要形成了以下一些便民宜商的经验。

（1）eGAPI②时期。该时期的典型项目，除了之前所述的"eCitizen"社区化和"GeBIZ"的在线化，还有以下内容：①SingPass③是"Singapore Personal Access"的简称，意为"新加坡个人通行证"，在当地又被简称为"新密"，是"宜民"类的服务。推出"SingPass"的目的是让不同的用户利用密码来登录政府的网站，使用各种服务。②TRUST项目在包括新加坡各类节庆日期间都提供其所授权的在新加坡的旅行社的公众最新信息，包括海外或本地信息，即将来临的贸易或消费活动；这些同样作为"宜民"类的服务。

（2）eGAPⅡ④时期。①OBLS⑤（Online Business Licensing Service，意为

---

① 根据新加坡政府 GeBIZ 项目网站（http：//www.gebiz.gov.sg/index_ aboutUs.html）："GeBIZ 是新加坡政府电子采购的一站式门户。所有的公共部门的邀请报价和投标在 GeBIZ 上发布。供应商可以搜索政府采购机会，下载招标文件，并在线提交他们的投标。" GeBIZ 允许任何供应商随时随地访问公共部门。当前，进入 GeBIZ 项目官方网站（http：//www.gebiz.gov.sg），即可进行在线申请，所有申请内容都公开透明，公示于网站中。对使用 GeBIZ 的各种问题，网站有详尽的解答，见 http：//www.faqhome.com/ifaq/spring_ faq_ selected.asp？category=25821。

② eGAPI即 e-Government Action Plan（2000-2003），该计划旨在打造为政府服务的电子化手段。

③ 根据新加坡电子政务网站（http：//www.egov.gov.sg/egov-programmes/programmes-by-citizens/）："SingPass 代表新加坡个人访问，设计它的目的是提供一个身份验证系统来访问所有政府电子商务系统，与政府交易。2003 年 3 月 1 日以后，所有 15 岁及以上的新加坡居民可以申请 SingPass ID/密码，与政府在线进行电子商务。"

④ eGAPⅡ即 e-Government Action Plan Ⅱ（2003-2006），该计划旨在使客户满意，使公众联系。

⑤ 根据新加坡电子政务网站（http：//www.egov.gov.sg/egov-programmes/programmes-by-businesses/obls）："OBLS 项目即 Enterprise One（企业通）服务，该项目允许企业申请、更新和终止一套包括 80 个类别的商业执照，它贯穿了政府相应 17 个部门的在线营业执照签发机构的交易。"

网上商业执照服务）系统。它作为"宜民"项目实现了 30 多个政府部门的业务整合，让企业的申办者通过"一次申请、一次支付"即可直接获得超过 200 项的商业执照申领业务，取得了很大的成功。②Citizen Connect 项目。政府部门旨在持续努力推动电子商务并提供给所有公民，财政部（MOF）、人民协会（PA）和其基层组织启动一个试点社区项目称为"Citizen Connect"。① 这个项目的目的，是提供一种简单方便的方式让公众与政府通过互联网交易。

（3）iGov2010② 时期。①Unique Entity Number③ 项目通过有效的促进非机密信息在基础设施的公共部门机构共享，支持交付更好、更个性化的服务。通过使用统一的 UEN 账号，各种相关事宜交易只需要统一的流程来执行。行政审批流程得到了简化和统一化。②eIACS④（enhanced Immigration Automated Clearance System）项目旨在提升移民系统的效率。超过 300 万的新加坡公民通过自动化的系统进行护照读取流程。

新加坡在 1997 年首次推出移民自动通关系统（IACS）智能令牌和自动化门。该系统可以通过自动化的手段来清除，利用相同的标记，并自动注册用户已经注册 IACS，这大大增加了旅客的数量。与此同时，使用伪造证件检测设备和指纹匹配引擎，确保 eIACS 提供一个安全的自助过关。

（4）eGov2015⑤ 时期。①Cube⑥ 项目是公职人员的协作社交平台，可以交流思想，分享知识和共同努力。该项目旨在推动跨越机构边界的公职人员之间的团队合作和沟通，建立一个更加网络化的公共服务社区，服务全国共享的共同目标。Cube 于 2011 年 12 月进入测试阶段。尽管有一个低调的介

---

① CitizenConnect 于 2005 年在五个社区俱乐部进行了为期一年的行驶示范计划。由于项目的成功，它已经扩展到 27 个新加坡的中心。

② iGov2012 即 iGov2010 Masterplan（2006 - 2010），旨在从整合服务向整合政府转变。

③ Unique Entity Numbe，新加坡电子政府网站（http：//www. egov. gov. sg/egov - programmes/programmes - by - businesses/unique - entity - number - uen）："截至 2009 年 1 月，通过 UEN，所有政府机构采用了在 2009 年 7 月和 UEN 连接，促进过渡到 UEN，UEN 向公共、私人和社会部门机构提供服务。"UEN 网站地址：http：//www. uen. gov. sg。

④ Unique Entity Numbe，新加坡电子政府网站。

⑤ eGov2015 的总体规划（2011 ~ 2015 年），旨在以人为本，丰富顾客的生活。

⑥ Unique Entity Numbe，新加坡电子政府网站：http：//www. egov. gov. sg/egov - programmes/programmes - by - government/cube。

绍，仍有 99 个政府机构的近 3000 名公职人员参与了 Cube 项目。Cube 将在 2013 年 5 月正式启动，正在努力推动其 13 万的公职人员使用。Cube 的用户友好特性和功能包括社交。通过 Cube 这个平台，公职人员可以与来自全国各地的公共服务人员交换想法和共同感兴趣的问题的答案，无论他们处于怎样的地理位置和机构职务位置。全面的搜索功能使得它便于专家级人员和朋友进行在线联系。Cube 的 Wiki 和文件协作功能，使组内成员能够轻松地进行合作和知识共享。②OneInbox① 项目是一个一站式的官方的和值得信赖的平台，代替纸质信件，为个人和企业接收政府的电子函件。根据调查和民意测验的结果，大多数个人和企业宁愿接收电子函件而非纸质信件。它将提供一个值得信赖和有保证的信箱，不受垃圾邮件影响。对那些经常出差或生活在海外的公民，OneInbox 将方便他们随时随地访问信箱与接收政府信函。

二　美日新政务服务的比较分析

由上述论述可知，美国的政务服务发展水平在全球处于领先地位，其"一站式"服务模式发展成熟，在服务渠道的构建和服务流程的设计方面极具参考价值。日本的政务服务发展历史较长，在规制改革方面经验丰富，尤其是日本在 20 世纪初推行的一系列改革新举措，取得了较好成效，提高了政府的行政效能。新加坡的公共服务以其优质的电子政务模式为依托，一直走在亚洲国家前列。

（一）美日新三国政务服务受到无缝隙政府理论、新公共管理理论、新公共服务理论的冲击

美日新三国先后不同程度地受到了无缝隙政府理论、新公共管理理论、新公共服务理论的冲击，均强调从"以政府为中心转变为以社会为中心和

---

①　Unique Entity Numbe，新加坡电子政府网站（http：//www.egov.gov.sg/egov-programmes/programmes-by-citizens/oneinbox）："OneInbox 是一个免费的数字化服务，通过 SingPass 账号进行个人访问。"

以用户、公众和企业为中心"，"从关注效率转向关注公共利益和公共产品的品质"，政府职能也由管制型向服务型转化，"强调服务理念、责任理念、参与理念和人本理念"，其官僚制的行政范式为民主制的行政范式所取代。

由林登提出的"无缝隙政府"理论指出，"无缝隙组织是指可以用流动的、灵活的、弹性的、完整的、透明的、连贯的等词语来形容的组织形态"。其实质上就是要求对现有政府进行无缝隙再造，使之以结果、竞争、顾客为导向。美国的一站式政务服务正是对政府功能的无缝隙整合，使得即使公民申办的事项涉及多个政府主管部门，也能在一个"窗口"办理，真正实现跨部门、跨职能的实时服务体系，进而更方便、更快捷、更直接地为公民提供高质量的公共服务。

从理论和实践中体味新公共管理，这场运动本质上要求对政府流程进行再造和重新设计，以期提高政府公共服务的质量和水平，使政府不拘泥于传统官僚制的繁文缛节，放开手脚进行全面改革，追求服务效率，最大限度地满足顾客不断变化的种种需求。因此，日本政府在规制改革中的不断创新，以及市场化运作方式的引入，都是对新公共管理运动的践行。

20 世纪 90 年代，登哈特夫妇提出了著名的新公共服务理论，以构建新的公共行政范式。"新公共服务是一场基于公共利益、民主治理过程的理想和重新恢复的公民参与运动。"[1] 登哈特认为公共行政官员的职责既不是掌舵，也不是划桨，而是"建立一些明显具有整合力和回应力的公共机构"。[2] 他认为公民权和公共服务比企业家精神更重要。新公共服务理论这一新范式具有宪政主义的渊源，尊崇回应性、代表性和责任，核心在于民主、公民权和公共利益。新加坡政府便民宜商的政务服务的不断创新，事实上是对新公共服务理念的回应。

（二）实现了政治层面的制度创新

美日新三国都是市场经济体制下的民主国家，因此都需要一个开放和平

---

[1] 珍妮特·V.登哈特、罗伯特·B.登哈特：《新公共服务——服务，而不是掌舵》，中国人民大学出版社，2004。

[2] 珍妮特·V.登哈特、罗伯特·B.登哈特：《新公共服务——服务，而不是掌舵》，中国人民大学出版社，2004。

等的政治环境，包括政府信息的公开、政府决策模式的公开及决策过程的民主参与。从信息的公开来看，美国通过一站式服务，多渠道、多层次地为其民众提供各种所需的信息支持；政府决策模式公开的代表则在日本，日本给予其民间部门"市场化实验"的机会，具体参与公共服务的提供过程，使其公众更为了解政府决策的模式；新加坡政府则在完善的政府网络平台上，通过 Cube①，以及 OneInbox 给民众充分表达民意的机会。同时，这三个国家都制定了与信息公开有关的法律，在制度上保证了民众对信息及政策决策的获知权。

（三）实现了行政层面的制度创新

同样，美日新三国因为是市场经济体制下的民主国家，因此无论在其行政的价值、行政范式及行政职能上都有着一定的市场基础和民主基础。行政层面的制度创新目标是解决好政府、社会与市场的关系问题，也即是形成以政府为中心的多元化管理格局的问题。美国、日本、新加坡政府的经验说明，要实现行政目标，创新制度，首先需要行政观念的转变。观念的转变包括两个层次，第一个层次，公众不是政府管理的对象，而应该是政府服务的对象，这是从管制型政府向服务型政府观念的转变；而更重要的是第二个层次观念的转变，公众不应该仅仅是公共服务的顾客，还更应该是公共服务的建议者和参与者，这是治理观念的转变。美国政府的"一站式服务""日本政府的市场化实验"，新加坡政府的公众回应项目，都可以理解为是其行政观念转变的产物。其次，要实现行政目标，创新制度，需要行政流程的优化再造。美国实行三个一站式服务计划，访问"美国计划""无忧社区计划"和"第一政府计划"均通过顶层设计，对所涉及的行政流程进行了优化和重构；日本在通过不断的改革创新，在法制化基础上，实现其政府流程的合理化、科学化。新加坡的"人生之旅 G2C"堪称全球 GPR（政府流程再造）的标杆。

---

① Unique Entity Numbe，新加坡电子政府网站：http://www.egov.gov.sg/egov-programmes/programmes-by-government/cube。

三 各国政务服务的国际比较对我国政府服务的借鉴

以上探讨了美国、日本、新加坡三个国家的政务服务特点，其理论的基础，以及政治层面、行政层面制度创新的相关问题。分析国外政府服务的发展道路，总结和汲取国外先进政务服务经验，其目的是为了结合本地实际进行适当创新，实现从观念引导、制度先行、服务至上、科技支撑的全方位国际接轨。美日新三国的政务服务经验对我国政府服务借鉴主要体现在以下几个"接轨"。

（一）观念接轨：向公众中心的治理理念和顾客导向的服务理念转变

理念决定趋势，趋势创造领先，领先引导潮流。首先就应从理念上加以转变，与国际接轨。西方新公共管理运动倡导公众参与，强调政府对公众需求的回应性并接受公众的监督，视公众为顾客，向其作出承诺并赋予他们参与的权利。在中国，我们的政府治理观念也必须从以政府为中心转变为以公众为中心，破除"官本位"的思想。实现与国际一流政务服务接轨的战略认识上的统一。

（二）制度接轨：进一步提高信息公开程度

完善信息公开制度，规定政务信息公开基本程序和方式，扩大政务信息公开范围。依托政府信息公开化四大支柱：一是以民主政治为前提，宪法赋予人民主权只有通过民主政治建设来实现；二是以法制建设为基础，只有依靠法制的权威性和稳定性才能保证公民知情权的实现；三是以权力监督制约为核心，只有建立对国家权力强有力的监督制约机制，才能使国家权力真正代表并体现民意；四是以加大领导力度为保证，政务公开是对权力的监督和制约，只有领导有力才能使公开顺利进行。

（三）服务接轨：促进流程再造

流程再造要将传统的职能导向工作模式向以流程导向工作模式转变，将中心内的各个已经实现部门内部职能集中化的窗口有机地结合起来，从而使工作流程不断完善，持续提升服务供给质量。政务服务中心可以根据各服务窗口的职能分工，对公众提交的"订单"进行分解，从而形成以"订单"为工作中心的"服务链"，各窗口以订单分配的结果列为考核的主要指标体系，并与绩效管理和薪酬管理挂钩。以提高便捷服务为出发点，减少中间环节，缩短审批时间，以提高服务效能。通过组织结构再造和体制机制创新来巩固和扩大流程再造的成果，提高政府组织的整体运作效能，树立服务型政府的良好形象。

（四）科技接轨：大力发展电子政务

在科技创造领先的现代社会，要充分依靠和发挥高科技信息技术的力量以实现政务服务现代化、国际化的良好效果，尤其是电子政务和全面质量管理的运用。全面质量管理主要是通过对行政审批项目的权限、流程、申报材料、承诺时限、收费标准、存档资料等内容的规范，提高政务服务中心窗口审批工作的可操作性。电子政务可以为流程再造提供信息和网络技术的支持。信息共享是流程再造的基础，通过信息共享，减少一些工作和信息的重复录入，过去传统业务流程中重复和交叉的部分得以精简和整合，以此来划清每个职能部门的职责范围，使进驻政务服务中心的各个审批部门各司其职，而整个行政流程既相互联系又各具内在逻辑。具体来说，就是当政务服务中心接收到企业和公众的服务请求后，中心统一的网络平台根据公众请求问题的性质将工作分解，分配到各审批服务部门操作，各职能部门以统一数据接口为中介，在源头一次捕获每个流程应该采集的信息，并通过电子政务系统的运用，实现信息全方位、全过程共享。更重要的是，通过技术革新，在梳理了业务流程后可以清晰地将工作分解，把传统的串行流程作业转变成并行流程作业，这样不仅可以极大地提高行政效率，而且可以将网络上的相关统计结果作为部门和个人绩效考核的依据，为监控电子政务实施效果奠定基础。

参考文献

彭博、张锐昕：《新加坡行政服务中心建设的内容、特点和启示》，《电子政务》2012 年第 11 期。

珍妮特·V. 登哈特、罗伯特·B. 登哈特：《新公共服务——服务，而不是掌舵》，中国人民大学出版社，2004。

政府治理的政策工具理论研究：
一个文献综述

唐兴霖　吴　天*

【摘要】作为决策者或决策团体所采用的一种行动机制，政策工具承担着实现政策目标、解决政策问题的功能，同时有助于理解政府治理之道。政策工具理论的逻辑在于对各种工具的特性、类型进行研究，在不同分析框架下结合特定情境进行选择与评估。关于政策工具的研究仍需要不断拓展研究范围，挖掘认识深度，发展并完善理论分析框架：发挥工具功能，实现政策效果；渗透政治因素，达到预期目的；强调制度理性，灵活选择机制。

【关键词】政策工具；综述；分析框架；治理

政策工具的研究成为近几年来研究公共政策的一股潮流。作为政府的主要手段，其实践效果反映了政府的执政能力。政府治理有很多方法，受公共管理思想发展和全球化、民主化的影响必然会有不同的选择。政府为什么要选择特定的政策工具？其背后的逻辑基础是什么？如何正确理解"空心化

* 唐兴霖：(1965~)，男，四川仪陇人，西南财经大学公共管理学院院长、博士生导师，主要研究领域为公共管理、公共政策；吴天：(1987~)，男，四川仪陇人，行政管理硕士，中国航空无线电电子研究所，研究方向为行政管理。

国家"的概念并在此背景下完成协作？对于这一理论，"我国尚处于引进分析框架的阶段"，其研究历程比较短暂。① 因此，本文从政策工具的内涵与类型出发，从理解特性的角度对政策工具的选择和评估进行解释，并在此基础上总结出一个分析框架，以便更好地实现政策效果，达到政策目标，减少冲突。

一 政策工具的内涵与分类

政策工具也称政府工具或治理工具。最早明确提出政府工具概念的是胡德，他提出了"一种观察政府的独特而陌生的途径"。② 关于政策工具概念的界定，主要有两种观点：目标手段说和行动机制说。两者之间虽有一定的差异，但都通过不同侧面展现出相同的本质，如行为主体、行动对象和行动结构。

关于目标手段说，Marie – Louise Bemelmans – Videc 等人将政府工具定义为"政府为保证政策效果和防止社会突变而对外界施加力量的一系列手段"。③ 毛寿龙也提出类似的界定，即"政府实现其管理职能的手段"，④ 同时它也是被决策者明确地或者下意识地采用，来实现一个或更多政策目标的手段。⑤

关于行动机制说，学界普遍认同休斯的观点。他认为政策工具是政府"通过某种途径用以调节其自身行为的机制"。⑥ 张璋结合我国的实际情况，提出"政府治理工具是政府为了解决公共问题而采用的可辨别的行动机制"的观点。它可以从本质（政府活动机制）、结构化和可辨别性来理解，它实际上是政府治理行动的一种结构化显现，它"建造"着行动。⑦

政策工具在政府治理过程中有不同的表现形式，因此分类的标准也层出

---

① 黄红华：《政策工具理论的兴起及其在中国的发展》，《社会科学》2010 年第 4 期。

② Christopher C. Hood, *The Tools of Government*（The Macmillan Press Ltd, 1983）.

③ Marie – Louise Bemelmans – Videc, Ray C. Rist, Evert Vedung. Carrots, *Sticks & Sermons, Policy Instruments and Their Evaluation*（Transaction Publishers, 1998）.

④ 毛寿龙：《公共行政学》，九州出版社，2003。

⑤ 顾建光：《公共政策工具研究的意义、基础与层面》，《公共管理学报》2006 年第 3 期。

⑥ 欧文·E. 休斯：《公共管理导论》，中国人民大学出版社，2001。

⑦ 张璋：《理性与制度：政府治理工具的选择》，国家行政学院出版社，2006。

不穷。已有研究的常见分类方法有：根据功能差异将政策工具划分为经济的、法律的和交流的工具，并且每种工具都有其分支；根据政府强制力的程度将其分为自愿性工具（家庭与社群、自愿性组织、私有市场）、强制性工具（管制、补助和直接提供服务）和混合性工具（资讯与劝告、公营事业、征税与使用者付费）；依据目标的差异将其分为激励、学习、符号和规劝、能力建设；按照方向性将其划分成垂直化、水平化和时间序列（chronological）的政策工具；也有学者从类型学角度出发，认为工具的分类必须相互排斥且穷尽涉及的所有领域，故将其分为规制（大棒）、经济手段（胡萝卜）和信息（布道）三类；还有学者以全球化和民主化带来的挑战为依据，将政策工具分为传统的实质性政策工具和过程性政策工具，他们注意到政府开始通过一系列的政策工具间接控制社会行动者，以达到预期政策目标。①

总的来说，现有分类方法存在着一些难以克服的困难：一是目前还没有一个分类方法能够穷尽所有的政策工具；二是由于分类依据和标准的不同，对工具的分类也不同，加之工具的属性不能完全确定，不同情况和假设会产生不同的功能、效果，研究中存在着"灰色地带"；三是将工具静态化，误认为某类政策工具只有固定的功能，而自身的细微变化被忽略。工具随着时间和目的而改变用途的可能性也不在考虑范围之内。

二　政策工具的特性

政策工具的基本特性是工具属性或者说价值属性，一般的文献中都存在着这种技术官僚的倾向。② 首先，所有的政策工具都必须考虑不同社会阶层的利益。其次，成本的考虑可能还不足以促进政策工具的实施，还需考虑政治方面的因素。这种工具悖论的存在使得政策工具目标会发生变化，因此，它具有政治性。③ 再次，现实世界中的政策工具是十分"拥挤"的，不可能

---

① Michael Howlett, "Managing the 'Hollow State': Procedural Policy Instruments and Modern Governance", *Canadian Public Administration* 43 (2000): 4.

② 徐湘林：《后毛时代的精英转换和依附性技术官僚的兴起》，《战略与管理》2001 年第 6 期。

③ Deborah Stone, *Policy Paradox: The Art of Political Decision Making* (W. W. Norton& Company, 2002).

孤立静止地考察其特征，因此具有动态性。最后，政策工具有反作用性，它并不是呆滞的，它有其自身的运行逻辑，甚至反过来重塑公共政策本身，产生意想不到的效果。

最初的政策工具只有"工具"的特性，政府完全可以从"工具箱"中找到适合的政策工具。这里的工具假设能明显体现事物的特征，而且行动者在政策制定过程中，政策工具的"自然属性和他们的特征是一致的"。每一个政策问题都可以被相对明确的方法所描述，从而在工具和问题之间建立联系。① 这种简化了的假设，为理解公共政策提供了强有力的途径，因为它将政策工具的选择简化到技术层面，这也很适合政策问题的本质。

随着管理理念和政治的影响，加之洛伊提出的"政策引起政治，还是政治影响政策"观点影响了后来对政策工具的研究，之前过分草率的简化理解逐渐认识到政治的重要性。② 政策工具并不政治中立，选择不同的政策工具将会产生不同的政治过程和政治结果。更重要的是，政策的政治性影响了最初的政策选择和最后的政策执行。伍德西德通过对政策工具特征的设计或选择的关注，论证了政策工具至少得满足两个要求：选择政策工具的人和受这种政策工具影响最大的人群之间的符合或匹配程度要可以被接受、可以被记录，以及能被公众理解。③

政策工具是高度政治化的，同时也是政治运动意识形态的组成部分。里格林在《政府工具的欧洲经验》中首先描述了欧洲大陆历史上发展起来的各种工具模式，验证了新公共管理对工具选择类型的影响，即"掌舵而不是划桨""授权而不是服务"。然后解释欧洲特有的工具选择模式，从比较视角总结得出结论：公共管理理论的发展对政策工具有着同步的影响，政治意识形态的变化和政策工具的选择是同步进行的。

---

① B. Guy Peters, John Pierre, "Governance without Government? Rethinking Public Administration", *Journal of Public Administration Research and Theory* 8（1998）: 2.

② Theodore J. Lowi. , "Four Systems of Policy, Politics and Choice", *Public Administration Review* 32（1972）.

③ B. 盖伊·彼得斯、弗兰斯·K. M. 冯尼斯潘著，顾建光译《公共政策工具：对公共管理工具的评价》，中国人民大学出版社，2007。

在政府治理的"工具箱"中，每一种工具都有区别于其他的特性。他们不是随意的或临时的，而是一种制度化的行动模式。[①] 同时，政策工具会随着时间的推移、治理对象的改变、政策主体治理理念和策略的变化而发生改变。这也正是目前关于政策工具的研究范式为什么越来越趋于建构主义，也就是说"政策工具在政策系统运行过程中不再起决定性作用"，它和个人价值、社会伦理等主观因素一起构建政策问题。[②]

诱因、价值和工具是政策设计过程中需要考虑的三种基本要素。因此，政策工具就成了政策设计的核心要义，我们需要"对政策工具化的自身效应进行分析"，因为其展现了治理者与被治理者之间关系理论化的过程。每个政策工具都浓缩了社会控制和执行的意义。工具在使用时不仅是技术性的，它们有自己的行动力量，会有三种不同的运行逻辑。[③] 首先是惯性效应，即对外界压力的抵抗。比如在行政改革中，强制性过程的引入或废止并不仅仅是一个关乎效用的问题。政策工具在问题化（problematization）过程中促使不同行动者聚集起来讨论某问题，同时通过改变制度环境等变量影响他们的初衷；其次是对所处理问题的特殊表现，其背后还暗含着某些引起社会关注的现实问题。这种"工具引起的表现"（instrument – engendered representation）是建立在两个特殊基础之上：社会中处理情况种类的描述框架和指标系数的确立；最后是使议题成为需要解决的问题。特定的治理工具为决策者就某种现象提供了一种"因果解释系统"，使得决策者倾向于将该问题纳入公共议程。

政策设计的目标之一就是扩大工具与制度（更重要的是政策问题与工具之间）可能的组合，还需要让选择过程中存在的偏见公之于众。[④] 反过

① Lester M. Salamon, *The Tools of Government：An Introduction to the New Governance* (Oxford University Press, 2002).

② B. 盖伊·彼得斯、弗兰斯·K. M. 冯尼斯潘著，顾建光译《公共政策工具：对公共管理工具的评价》，中国人民大学出版社，2007。

③ Pierre Lascoumes and Patrick LE Gales, "Introduction：Understanding Public Policy Through Its Instrument – From the Nature of Instruments to the Sociology of Public Policy Instrumentation", *Governance：An International Journal of Policy, Administration, and Institution* 20 (2007).

④ Linder, Stephen, Peters, "The Logic of Public Policy Design：Linking Policy Actors and Plausible Instruments", *Knowledge, Technology & Policy* 4 (1/2) (1991).

来，政策工具的选择产生了传统解决方式的新组合，还使标准制定中的利益权衡得到了更多的关注。林德和彼得斯就通过对美国社会规制政策设计的研究，从"权威"视角出发，以行动者和工具为考察维度，得出结论：政策设计与政策制定周期或构建最优模型不同，他需要将各种政策形式与实际要素（偏见、系统过程、价值取向等）相结合。虽然最终得到的只是次优政策，但会产生更好的实施效果。①

国内关于政策工具的研究刚刚起步，且研究者将视野局限在某些特定领域。不同领域政策工具的选择体现出政府治理强烈的针对性。通过梳理这些文献，一方面能够了解政府治理的趋势；另一方面能够归纳总结政策工具理论的框架或模型，扩大其分析和解释政府治理行为的能力，并从实践层面丰富政策工具理论的内涵，从中发现特殊点，为政策工具的选择与具体应用提供基于中国国情的特定环境描述和条件约束。

三　政策工具的选择与评估

公共政策工具的选择研究大多遵从着这样一种逻辑：先对各种工具的特性进行研究，再结合不同的情境进行选择。对工具概念、分类和特性的讨论最终都归结为对工具选择和评估的研究，② 而选择模型大致有以下三种。③

一是政治模型。彼得斯用比较政治学文献中的五个变量，即观点、制度、利益、个体和国际环境，解释了政策工具选择和评估。豪利特和拉米什以政治文化及意识形态为基础，认为"政府不可能拥有全套可用的工具，社会和政治的约束会左右它们的选择"。胡德认为选择政策工具需要考虑政治压力、资源、法律，以及过去工具的失败教训四个因素。林德和彼得斯则认为影响政策工具的选择因素有：一是政策风格和政治文化，二是工具对象的自身特性及和其他组织的联系，三是政策环境，四是决策者的专业知识背

---

① Linder, Stephen, Peters, "The Logic of Public Policy Design: Linking Policy Actors and Plausible Instruments", *Knowledge, Technology & Policy* 4 (1/2) (1991).

② 杨洪刚：《中国环境政策工具的实施效果及其选择研究》，复旦大学博士学位论文，2009。

③ 迈克尔·豪利特、M. 拉米什：《公共政策研究：政策循环与政策子系统》，三联书店，2006。

景、认知等个人偏好因素。①

选举对工具的选择也有显著的影响。特里比尔科克和哈特等人阐述了政客和官僚试图在选择政策工具的过程中，通过他们的决定来精心策划安排政治过程。政客有种很明显的趋势：当面对政策问题时，会逐渐从管制最弱的工具转变到强制性的工具。② 具体来说，首先是信息的提供，比如说自身意愿的大量陈述。然后运用选择性激励的手段，最后建立起带有制裁、许可意味的规制。

二是经济模型。最初对政策工具的分析和选择都集中于理性的、线性的和技术性的研究，特别是在经济政策文献。经济模型的研究者主张从政策工具的工具功能和可操作性角度出发，选择效益较高的工具。萨拉蒙认为在提供公共服务或进行管制时，要降低行动对象所付出的代价，因为当可接受成本超过政策对象可承受的能力范围时，就会产生抵触情绪。许多新古典主义经济学家（哈耶克等）和福利主义经济学家（Esping - Anderson 等）都倾向于选择更能体现公平和成本的政策工具，并将此过程视为一种严格的技术操作：评估备选工具的特征和相对成本，选出能有效克服市场失灵的有针对性的工具。③

经济模型是基于"经济人"的核心假设，从"经济人"的理性角度出发，对政策工具进行选择。它认为政策工具的选择存在于由政治家、官僚和利益集团构成的"铁三角"关系中。④ 每个人都在追求自身利益最大化：政治家通过选择符合选民喜好的政策来获得再次当选的机会；官僚有选择性地挑选那些符合部门利益和自身利益的政策；利益集团则通过选择自己的代理人来间接选择实现自身利益的政策。

三是综合模型。不管政治模型还是经济模型都存在不尽如人意的地方，而综合模型融合了多种标准，对政策工具提出更多包容性和环境匹配性要

---

① 迈克尔·豪利特，M. 拉米什：《公共政策研究：政策循环与政策子系统》，三联书店，2006。

② Doern, Wilson., *Issues In Canadian Public Policy* (Macmillan of Canada, 1974) .

③ 迈克尔·豪利特，M. 拉米什：《公共政策研究：政策循环与政策子系统》，三联书店，2006。

④ B. 盖伊·彼得斯、弗兰斯·K. M. 冯尼斯潘著，顾建光译《公共政策工具：对公共管理工具的评价》，中国人民大学出版社，2007。

求。特恩建立了一个以政策网络为中心，分析影响工具选择和应用的环境背景的综合概念框架。[①] 豪利特和拉米什认为国家计划能力的大小和政策子系统的复杂性两个变量的不同组合可以囊括所有的工具选择模型。前者反映出国家影响社会行动主体组织的能力；后者则是政府在执行政策时，所面对的行动主体数量和类型。

"政策制定既不是理性的，也不是线性的"，首先从情境理解（contextual understanding）的角度出发，在选择政策工具过程中，重要的一点是明确问题是如何界定的。[②] 问题的确定直接影响到政策的回应，从而对政策工具的选择产生差异。其次是找准工具对象，这是经常被忽视的一个方面。政策工具的选择往往考虑了意识形态、政治参与者、财政成本、行政压力、预期收益、时间等因素，但忽视了政策对象的态度、行为、动机和对以往政策的反应。再次是对组织的考虑，执行机构的能力、执行组织的目标、是否有必要成立新组织和政策、组织网络都是工具选择的考虑范围。

政策工具的选择是决策的本质。当问题出现时，政策制定者面临着一系列复杂情形：政治议程的混乱，政策目标的模糊，政治信息的矛盾，社会环境的不全面认识，政治参与者的自大，经济和政治结果的背道而驰，有组织的利益相关者及公共部门官僚能力与职责的不对等。政府作出一项决定或确定改革方向绝不是兴致使然，它必须在找出问题、明确目标的基础上结合多种因素进行考虑，方能找到合适的政策工具，便于政策的执行。

为了使政策工具的选择能够达到更好的政策目标，还需要对其评价标准进行研究。

萨拉蒙在总结政策分析、政策执行和政治科学文献的基础上，一共提出五个评价工具的标准：[③] 一是效能。作为公共行动成功的基本标准，效能测量政策执行能够达到预期目标的程度。但是，测量政府的效能存在困难，不

[①] B. 盖伊·彼得斯、弗兰斯·K. M. 冯尼斯潘著，顾建光译《公共政策工具：对公共管理工具的评价》，中国人民大学出版社，2007。

[②] Marie – Louise Bemelmans – Videc, Ray C. Rist, Evert Vedung Carrots, *Sticks & Sermons*, *Policy Instruments and Their Evaluation* (Transaction Publishers, 1998).

[③] Lester M. Salamon, *The Tools of Government*: *An Introduction to the New Governance* (Oxford University Press, 2002).

仅因为在技术上难以确定精准的指标，还因为对首要目标的争议性。不同工具的效能随着环境的变化也在改变。二是效率。效率平衡了成本和收益之间的关系，一方面关注政府执行的成本，另一方面注意对其他社会行动者所产生的成本影响，以达到节约官僚资源（using bureaucracy sparingly）的目的。[1] 三是公平。公平在这里有两层含义，一种是基本的公平，在所有合格者面前收益与成本的分配是尽可能平均的；另一种与再分配有关，即让那些得不到收益的人也能分配到一定比例的利益。这种再分配是理性公共行为的原则之一，也是政府存在的原因之一，即弥补过去的不公，保证所有人获得平等的机会。四是可执行性。政策工具越复杂，涉及的行动者越多，工具执行起来的难度也就越大。有些理论上被证明可行的政策工具，在实际操作中却因为种种障碍不能执行。这也正是普瑞斯曼和维达夫斯基将可执行性作为项目设计的首要原则的原因。[2] 五是合法性和政治可行性。工具的选择影响着政治可行性和公共行动的合法性。政府工具通过确定谁是行动者、受益者来执行项目。不仅如此，工具的选择还影响着公众对公共行动合法性更广义上的认知。

四 理解政策工具的分析框架

理解政策工具是理解政府治理的途径之一。通过对政策工具理论的内容梳理，笔者发现一些学者都是选取某个具体的点切入，根据需要将相关维度进行必要的组合，以囊括所有的可能性，构建出完整或精致的分析框架。总结并发展一个综合分析框架，能够对公共政策的理解、运用起到一定的作用。

首先，是工具功能的实现。政策工具的目的就是实现政策的目标，关注的是政策产出或政策效果的实现。政策工具有被实践所证明了的有效性，所以能预测大部分的政策效果。反之，政策成败与否就在于是否正确选择了政策工具。这种工具至上的观点建立在"人们可以通过对各种工具逐一进行

---

[1] Christopher Hood，"Using Bureaucracy Sparingly"，*Public Administration* 61 （1983）.

[2] Jeffrey L. Pressman，Aaron B. Wildavsky：*Implementation* （University of California Press，1979）.

经验性研究，理解各种工具及其内在作用机制从而形成一整套理论和选择原则的假设之上"。①

因此，弄清工具的属性与特点是研究的起点，将影响到政策参与者的行为、政策目标群的改变和政策意识的修正。政策工具是否能顺利发挥作用、达到目标，预期和效果之间是否受到其他因素的作用，则是本分析框架的第二步。

其次，是政治因素的渗透。从政策工具的思想发展途径来看，它经历了最开始基于技术层面的工具性研究，到系统地分析政策工具与环境的相互作用，再到政策工具与政策问题的主观构建过程。我们可以看到"工具性"特征的逐渐弱化，而政治因素渗透产生的博弈、政策目标的变动和政策学习要求以渐进调试和综合考虑的方法进行研究，这让我们清楚认识到政策工具的性质，提高所选择的政策工具的满意度。"政策工具设计代表了一种渐进和历史的发展。参与的行动者只能在有限的程度上对发展方向和控制发挥影响。"在政策工具选择中不仅涉及政策工具有效性的问题，同时需要反映政策共同体中盛行的那些价值和道德。②

最后，是对制度理性的强调。公共政策工具的选择是一种理性行为。政策工具是理性的，包含了工具理性、制度理性和价值理性。③ 制度理性作为中介，帮助实现了价值理性，调控了工具理性作用的发挥。他在形式合理性与实质合理性之间，保持了中立。制度理性发挥了协调的作用，三者的协同作用共同驱动着具有形式合理性、实质合理性和制度合理性的集体行动以实现人类的利益。

"政策工具混搭"是当代政府治理的一个突出特点。④ 政策工具的选择应基于多元理性（工具理性、价值理性与制度理性）的原则，与政策环境相适应。同时应该能有利于协调政策目标群体，即政策受众的当前利益、中

---

① 陈振明：《政府工具研究与政府管理方式改进：论作为公共管理学新分支的政府工具研究的兴起、主题和意义》，《中国行政管理》2004 年第 6 期。

② B. 盖伊·彼得斯、弗兰斯·K. M. 冯尼斯潘著，顾建光译《公共政策工具：对公共管理工具的评价》，中国人民大学出版社，2007。

③ 陈振明：《政策工具导论》，北京大学出版社，2007。

④ 孙志建：《政府治理的工具基础：西方政策工具理论的知识学诠释》，《公共行政评论》2011 年第 4 期。

期利益和长远利益。还应具有灵活性，针对某一政策问题是选择使用单一的政策工具，或是综合应用多种政策工具，或是以一种为主其他为辅，取决于对以上三方面的条件要求满足的程度，因为政策工具的性质和效用在实际应用的过程中会受到环境和目标群体变化的影响而有可能发生变化。

参考文献

陈振明：《政策工具导论》，北京大学出版社，2007。

陈振明：《政府工具研究与政府管理方式改进：论作为公共管理学新分支的政府工具研究的兴起、主题和意义》，《中国行政管理》2004 年第 6 期。

顾建光：《公共政策工具研究的意义、基础与层面》，《公共管理学报》2006 年第 3 期。

迈克尔·豪利特，M. 拉米什：《公共政策研究：政策循环与政策子系统》，三联书店，2006。

黄红华：《政策工具理论的兴起及其在中国的发展》，《社会科学》2010 年第 4 期。

毛寿龙：《公共行政学》，九州出版社，2003。

欧文·E. 休斯：《公共管理导论》，中国人民大学出版社，2001。

徐湘林：《后毛时代的精英转换和依附性技术官僚的兴起》，《战略与管理》2001 年第 6 期。

杨洪刚：《中国环境政策工具的实施效果及其选择研究》，复旦大学博士学位论文，2009。

张璋：《理性与制度：政府治理工具的选择》，国家行政学院出版社，2006。

B. 盖伊·彼得斯、弗兰斯·K. M. 冯尼斯潘著，顾建光译《公共政策工具：对公共管理工具的评价》，中国人民大学出版社，2007。

B. Guy Peters, John Pierre, "Governance without Government? Rethinking Public Administration", *Journal of Public Administration Research and Theory* 8 (1998): 2.

Lester M. Salamon, *The Tools of Government: An Introduction to the New Governance* (Oxford University Press, 2002).

Linder, Stephen, Peters, "The Logic of Public Policy Design: Linking Policy Actors and Plausible Instruments", *Knowledge, Technology & Policy* 4 (1/2) (1991).

Michael Howlett, "Managing the 'Hollow State': Procedural Policy Instruments and Modern Governance", *Canadian Public Administration* 43 (2000): 4.

Marie – Louise Bemelmans – Videc, Ray C. Rist, Evert Vedung. Carrots, *Sticks & Sermons*, *Policy Instruments and Their Evaluation* (Transaction Publishers, 1998).

Pierre Lascoumes and Patrick LE Gales, "Introduction: Understanding Public Policy Through Its Instrument – From the Nature of Instruments to the Sociology of Public Policy Instrumentation", *Governance*: *An International Journal of Policy*, *Administration*, *and Institution* 20 (2007).

Jeffrey L. Pressman, Aaron B. Wildavsky: *Implementation* (University of California Press, 1979).

中国公共行政研究概念创新：
一项学科发展新议程

孙志建*

【摘要】"概念"是理论创新与知识增长的基石。扎根于本土社会事实且同国际理论接轨的概念创新，乃是推进中国行政学科蓬勃发展的重要一环。概念创新没有标准的程式。中国行政研究的概念创新亟须汲取国际行政学科发展历程中概念创新的基本经验（譬如现象聚焦、锁定重大理论问题等），遵循概念创新的基本原则（包括精简性、客观性、中立性、开放性、平衡性及情境性等原则）和科学思维（包括"领地"思维、"类型"思维、"类比"思维、"变量"思维、"特质"思维及"关联"思维等），并将概念创新同公共行政的研究方法统筹把握。在关于中国公共行政的研究中，有必要倡导一种基于现象聚焦（尤指"元现象"），锁定学科重大理论问题，且以中层概念生产为取向的概念创新。

【关键词】挽救现象；元现象；概念创新；中层概念；行政学想象力

一　问题的提出

在考察中国地方政府管理时，哈佛大学亚洲研究中心主任托尼·塞奇①

---

* 孙志建：博士，上海行政学院公共管理教研部。研究方向：公共政策理论与组织理论、城市（综合）治理、应急管理、基层治理创新。

① 托尼·赛奇：《盲人摸象：中国地方政府分析》，《中国政治发展》2006年第4期。

坦言："我们迄今所发展的概念工具基本上并不能令人满意。在很大程度上，我们试图将中国经验的销子插入西方理论的洞口。"近几年，中国治理研究领域这种概念工具贫乏的现状，已随着一批研究成果的推出有所改观。形成了诸多颇具影响的概念，包括"选择性政策执行""运动式治理""行政发包制"及基层政府间的"共谋现象"等。然而，中国公共行政学界在此方面的贡献力度还相对薄弱。

"概念"兼有理论和实践价值。一方面，关于政策实践的"有效的判断"以概念使用为先决条件，忽视明确概念的政策讨论是极其危险的。[①] 另一方面，概念不仅是理论的种子，而且还是事实收集、数据承载的工具。[②] 因而，概念创新对行政学的理论建构与知识增长颇具助益。在社会科学中相对成熟的学科，包括社会学[③]、政治学[④]等，对"概念形成"（Concept Formation）问题皆颇为重视。基本经验是：对概念和学科发展关系的审视贯彻于各学科发展周期的各个阶段。然而，在学科成立、转型和成长阶段，对概念创新问题的重视又更具重要性。因此，在中国行政学经历了30年压缩饼干式快速"补课"之后的今日，提出中国公共行政研究概念创新的问题正当其时。

当前，从学科发展的高度倡导在中国公共行政研究中推进概念创新，主要基于以下几点考虑：其一，概念创新乃是尊重行政实践复杂性和生动性的基础。正是基于此，行政学家戴维·J. 法默尔[⑤]称，"我们只能依据某一概念系统，某一视角来看世界"。实际上，尤其是对那些看似"不存在的事物"的分析和测量，学者必须依赖一些基本的概念。譬如，社会"失范"。

---

① 马克斯·韦伯：《社会科学和社会政策中的客观性》，华夏出版社，1999，第202页。

② Giovanni Sartori, "Concept Misformation in Comparative Politics", *The American Political Science Review* 64 (1970): 1033 – 1053.

③ Dumont, Richard G, and William J. Wilson, "Aspects of Concept Formation, Explication, and Theory Construction in Sociology", *American Sociological Review* 32 (1967): 985 – 995.

④ Gerring, John, "What Makes a Concept Good? A Criterial Framework for Understanding Concept Formation in the Social Sciences", *Polity* 31 (1999): 357 – 393. Kalleberg, Arthur, "Concept Formation in Normative and Empirical Studies: Toward Reconciliation in Political Theory", *American Political Science Review* 63 (1969): 26 – 39. Mair, Peter, *Concepts and Concept Formation* (Cambridge University Press, 2008).

⑤ 戴维·J. 法默尔：《公共行政的语言》，中国人民大学出版社，2009，第27页。

其二，概念创新乃是巩固和提升行政学科地位与身份的基础。概念化环节乃是将感性认识上升至"论理的认识"的关键步骤。由此，概念的质量和丰富程度决定了行政学科认知行政实践的理论深度及其限度。最后，概念创新乃是推进国际学术对话的前提。"公共行政研究正在发生的全球化意味着，现在在世界各个角落的学者都需要为发展公共行政知识的概念和理论作出贡献"。①

为了深化和推进中国行政实践的理论研究，建构符合本土经验且同国际接轨的公共行政理论，就当给予"概念创新"足够的重视。在中国行政研究中，关于政策、组织及政府行为等方面的行政现象为之确立了最为直接的事实基础。那么，怎样的现象聚焦更有助于推进中国行政研究的概念创新呢？从学科史的角度考察，中国行政研究概念创新可以从国际行政学科的概念创新中汲取哪些"经验"？在关于中国行政现象的经验研究中，概念创新应当遵循什么原则和概念化思维呢？

二 行政学科发展历程中的概念创新：几项"经验"

作为社会科学的分支学科，行政学源自欧陆而繁荣于北美。伍德罗·威尔逊②《行政学研究》的发表标志着行政学的诞生。细细考究行政学百年历程，不难得出一个基本判断，即概念创新与学科发展休戚相关。一定意义上，概念创新的质量决定了学科的成熟度与发展空间。在评价 20 世纪六七十年代"新公共行政"的理论主张时，学者指出新公共行政尖锐地指出了传统理论框架存在的问题，但没有提出自己的替代方案，这集中体现在"未能大胆地提出积极的新概念或新理论"。由此可见，概念创新的止步，势必影响到学科发展的态势与前景。基于行政学科概念创新的系统检视，可以就概念创新的"经验"作如下总结。

第一，概念创新必须紧扣行政学赖以成立和发展的重大基础理论问题来

---

① 敬乂嘉：《评估中国大陆公共行政研究现状》，《复旦公共行政评论》2009 年第 6 期第 5 辑。
② Woodrow Wilson, "The Study of Administration", *Political Science Quarterly* 2 (1887): 197 - 222.

展开。在行政研究中，为学界诟病的"术语混乱"现象多缘于问题意识的缺乏。概念创新应当是问题导向的，或者至少具有明确的理论主题聚焦。譬如，英国学者金斯莱（Donald J. Kingsley）提出"代表性官僚制"（Representative Bureaucracy）概念，就旨在降低官僚制压制和抵消民主的风险，促进理性官僚制与代议制政府的协调，而这属于行政学科的重大理论问题。另外，帕尔卡斯等[①]提出的"问责俱乐部"（accountability clubs）概念，乃基于 NGO 问责中的"政府问责"与"同行问责"的关系这个基础理论问题。

第二，具有清晰现象聚焦的概念创新更具学术价值和生命力。当概念创新脱离纷繁复杂的行政现象，则意味着脱离经验世界，实属缘木求鱼之举。康德曾言，"没有概念的直觉是盲目的，没有直觉的概念是空洞的"。事实上，行政学领域那些最具影响力的概念——包括"脱耦"（decoupling）、"目标置换"（goal displacement）、"有限理性"（Bounded Rationality）等的形成皆基于明确的现象聚焦和扎实的事实基础。在行政研究的概念创新中强调现象聚焦，不仅有助于避免笼统的、大而化之的讨论；而且，亦可以确保理论研究的连续性。譬如，从"渐进主义"到"间断—均衡理论"、从"渐进调试"到"混合扫描模型"等就是很好的例证。

第三，避免"前无古人，后无来者"式的概念游戏。在概念创新中，"前无古人"意味着概念缺乏基本的理论主题聚焦；而"后无来者"则意味着概念拒绝实证检验或只提出研究问题而不重视研究的跟进。[②] 然而，英美行政学研究概念创新的基本经验显示：不会打靶的公共行政研究（概念创新）不是好研究；不愿意成为靶子的公共行政研究（概念创新）同样不是好研究。换言之，行政研究的概念创新要兼顾可追溯性和可证伪性。"可追溯性"就是要使概念创新聚焦相应的理论主题，或者至少有"靶子"可打；而"可证伪性"则旨在以实证研究检验一项概念创新的科学性，或者至少具备成为"靶子"的潜力。

第四，概念创新乃是行政学想象力的基础、印证与缩影。尽管米尔斯在

---

① Aseem Prakash, Mary Kay Gugerty, "Trust but Verify? Voluntary Regulation Programs in the Nonprofit Sector," *Regulation & Governance* 4（2010）：22 - 47.

② 达勒姆、杰克·雷斌等：《公共行政职业中的五大问题》，中山大学出版社，2006，第1314 页。

言语中表示了对"术语"的警惕，但他仍然承认好的"概念"有助于激发"社会学的想象力"。对公共行政学的想象力而言，情同此理。戴维德·J.法默尔认为，在解放和提升行政学的想象力方面，恰当的"隐喻"使用乃是一种基本策略。美国政策学家约翰·W.金登通过将"溪流"的隐喻引入公共政策研究，提出了"政策溪流"和"多源流模型"的概念和理论框架，极大地丰富了议程设置和政策变迁研究。

第五，批判性的学术对话乃是概念创新的不竭动力。美国行政科学的概念创新，仰赖于一种基于多元学科（和哲学背景）的批判性的学术对话。以"非正式组织"概念的提出为例。在古典行政理论中，组织的有效性取决于对权威的正式结构的精细设计。然而，霍桑实验和1948年巴纳德出版的《经理人员职能》则挑战了这种主导性的解释，二者共同关注到"非正式组织"对组织中成员的工作动机、合作意愿及组织效率的深刻影响。[①] 由此，"非正式组织"便成为组织理论和行政研究中不可或缺的概念。坦率地讲，这种学术辩论恰恰是中国公共行政学所欠缺的。

第六，系统地推进概念创新更加有助于行政学科的发展。粗略划分，行政学领域的概念包括标签性概念、描述性概念、解释性概念、倡议性概念四种类型。[②] 其中，"标签性概念"是对某种领域、事物或活动的分类和命名，其成果多为行政学基本范畴，譬如"公共行政""预算""政策工具""监管政策""新公共行政""新公共管理"及"新公共服务"等。"描述性概念"常常是在现象聚焦中被提炼出来，要比标签性概念更为生动，它是对某种结果状态的描述，在研究设计中主要扮演待解释项或因变量的角色。譬如基层政府的"共谋现象""反直觉效应"现象等。而"解释性概念"往往具有经验事实作为原型或基础，它是对某种原因状态的界定，在研究设计中主要扮演自变量甚至是因果机制的角色。常见的解释性概念包括"脱耦化""目标置换""有限理性""交易成本""路径依赖""偏

---

① 登哈特：《公共组织理论》，中国人民大学出版社，2011，第49页。
② 两种概念分类观点：（1）海伍德（2008）将政治学的概念区分为描述性概念和规范性概念两种；（2）李丹（2010）将社会科学中的概念区分为五种类型，包括集群概念、征兆概念、理论建构、可度量的概念及理想型概念。依据研究目的，本文使用全新的概念类型划分。

好伪装"及"非正式组织"等。相比较而言，"倡议性概念"所刻画的情况在当前往往缺乏经验支撑，它更多扮演规范性的倡导、应然描绘或目标导向的功能。譬如"共产主义""后工业社会"及"政治与行政二分"等。总体上，在行政研究中，概念创新要成体系地推进，兼顾上述概念类型。[1] 然而，在社会科学中，"解释性概念"具有更为深远的价值，也应当成为创新的重点。

三 迈向基于"元现象"的中国行政研究概念创新

可以说，"中国公共行政研究"可视为"关于"中国的公共行政研究。反思中国公共行政的 30 年发展历程，诸多前辈披荆斩棘，筚路蓝缕，在理论引进、学科建设、人才培养及理论创新等方面取得了重要的成绩。30 年后的今天，行政学研究者当有新的历史使命：扎根于中国公共行政实践，运用规范的质性或量化研究方法，就中国治理经验进行深刻的理解、诠释和解释性研究。进而，创造关于中国公共行政的：概念和理论。基于此，营造中国行政学的"想象力"，为行政学的发展贡献"中国元素"。

（一）现象聚焦的层次性与"元现象"

在中国行政的经验研究中，对数据的重视超过了对完整意义上的"现象"的重视，这部分解释了概念创新不足的问题。笔者认为，亟须在"数据"（data）和"现象"（phenomena）之间进行区分。[2] 重数据而轻现象的研究，不仅使得行政学界忽视对现实的总体关照，甚至还出现了以局部替代整体的错误研究。基于此，有必要在关于中国行政的经验研究中掀起一场挽救现象（Saving the phenomena）的知识运动。

---

[1] 两点说明：很多时候，描述性概念和解释性概念的边界是模糊的，正如不同的研究设计中自变量和因变量的位置会调换一样；现实和概念皆具有一定的动态性，曾经的预测性或倡议性概念会变成描述性概念（譬如"后工业社会"）。

[2] James Bogen, James Woodward, "Saving the Phenomena", *The Philosophical Review* 97 （1988）: 303 – 352.

然而，现象聚焦具有其内在的层次性，不同层次的现象聚焦决定了理论建构的方向与空间。可以说，低层次的现象聚焦难以支撑富有洞见的概念创新。在中国行政研究中，从对常规现象的聚焦走向反常现象，从碎片化现象走向"总体性社会现象"，从直观社会事实走向隐藏的社会事实等，将是学者努力的方向。

社会科学经验研究的三种"现象聚焦"

层 次	示例："两个过路人"	说 明
初级层次	研究小组 A 发现："他们一个高，一个矮；一个胖，一个瘦……"	此类研究，学者仅识别出直观的、碎片化的社会事实；对政策和理论皆没有多大价值
中级层次	研究小组 B 发现：你要知道，其中矮的比较聪明，高的比较健谈	通过相对深入的调研（譬如访谈）把握"非直观现象"，这具有政策意义，但理论价值不高
高级层次	研究小组 C 发现：二者之间存在一种"磁场""引力"或"关系模式"（隐藏事实）；或者"矮个子跳高比高个子厉害"（反常现象）；或者"二者的互动方式及其意义赋予"（意义世界）	对"隐藏事实""反常现象""意义世界"及"赋予行动以意义的方式"等社会事实的聚焦乃是产生突破性理论的契机，而且也极有可能提出实质性的政策建议

资料来源：作者自制。

在中国行政实践中，存在诸多尚未引起学界注意的行政现象，而沦为隐藏的事实。很大程度上，社会科学研究的魅力也就体现在对"隐藏的事实"的深度揭示和科学解释上。笔者认为，聚焦"元现象"（meta - phenomena）乃是识别和揭示出隐藏事实的方法之一。在考察中国城市摊贩监管时，笔者首次确认了这种"元现象"理念的重要性。[1] 那么，何为元现象？所谓"元现象"，是指那些能更加准确揭示考察对象或研究主题（譬如"中国城市摊贩监管中的政府行为"）之深层逻辑或本质的全景式、总体性和全局性的社会现象。[2]

在中国行政研究中，"元现象"理念强调不可对行政实践领域的现象

---

[1] 孙志建：《模糊性治理：中国城市政府摊贩监管逻辑研究》，博士学位论文，复旦大学行政管理系，2013。

[2] 譬如，A 组看到了"太阳东升"，B 组观察到了"太阳西落"，C 组则发现了"太阳东升西落"。那么，此处"太阳东升西落"则更加接近笔者所称的"元现象"的理念。

予以碎片化处理。尽可能基于完整现象而发展或搜寻概念框架，而非为了适用理论之目的随意编辑现象。以"间断—平衡模型"（Punctuated - equilibrium model）为例，这个概念致力于解释一个简单的现象，即"政治过程通常由一种稳定和渐进主义逻辑所驱动，但是偶尔也会出现不同于过去的重大变迁"。换言之，此处真正的现象既非"政策稳定"，亦非"政策变迁"，而是二者某种偶然的或比例式的结合。由此而论，"元现象"的理念乃是对行政实践复杂性和行政现象整体性的尊重。而且，对元现象的聚焦和诠释，易于在中国公共行政或公共政策研究中促成概念和理论的创新。

（二）概念创新的基本原则与惯用思维

概念创新需要慎之又慎。为了提高中国公共行政研究概念创新的质量，以下几点原则颇为值得注意。

1. 精简性原则

概念创新也要遵循奥卡姆剃刀（Occam's Razor），即"如无必要，勿增实体"。换言之，倘若学界已经存在类似的概念，就没有必要"新瓶装旧酒"，从而减少不必要的概念生产。

2. 客观性原则

以事实为基础乃是概念化最为关键的原则。这也是本文提倡以"现象聚焦"推进概念创新的缘由。当然，在社会科学中，存在指向未来或应然状态，带有预言性的概念，譬如"政治与行政二分"。然而，即使此类概念也应当确立在某种理论论据或经验的蛛丝马迹之上。

3. 中立性原则

在概念创新上强调中立性乃是坚持客观性原则的必然结果。存在两种意义上的中立性。其一，非中心化。概念的中立性最为符合社会科学的"非中心化"。忽略中立性法则，而将概念置于某种形态的西方中心或本土中心的预设之上，将为概念的使用留下隐患。其二，价值中立。受到逻辑实证主义影响，社会科学研究越来越强调在概念创新中祛除价值判断，尽管这难以完全实现。

4. 开放性原则

概念创新需要处理好"开放性"与"封闭性"的关系。法国思想家布尔迪厄极力批判"建构的太好的概念的'封闭性'"，而倡导一种开放性的概念。在此，"开放性"有两点所指：其一，它是指概念要对经验、现象和事实领域保持敏感性；其二，通过概念的开放性赋予"概念'提示性的'特征"。实际上，在概念建构中允许存在某种程度的开放性，有助于避免造成知识上的僵化，解放公共行政研究的想象力。正如韦伯①所言，对经验研究而言，"选择使用不那么精确的概念"有助于更加亲近经验世界。

5. 情境性原则

概念创新亟须顾及特定的语境，譬如历史的、文化的、知识的及意识形态等。基于此，中国公共行政研究的概念创新过程就既要注重挖掘和开发中国传统资源，又要兼顾当前的文化、学术甚至是政治语境。然而，"情境"具有动态演化特性，概念创新也要遵循这种动态性。正如学者所言，在中国公共行政研究的话语中，有必要从"改革叙事"转向"现代性叙事"。并且认为，"从改革叙事转向现代性叙事，是构建中国公共行政应有的知识求索逻辑"。基于此，关于中国公共行政研究的概念创新就有必要从"改革叙事"向"现代性叙事"转变。而且，提出的概念也亟须在传统与现代、现代性与后现代性的大视野中予以检视。

6. 平衡性原则

这意味着在中国行政研究概念创新中亟须处理好以下几种关系：首先，兼顾经验解释和逻辑世界。② 一个概念越是能够平衡经验事实与形式逻辑、归纳和演绎，则越是能够被视为好的概念。正是在此意义上，中国研究专家欧博文认为，限制使用"按照常规而定制的概念"和分析框架，采取更为分析性的方法，已成为中国治理研究的当务之急。其次，平衡经验事实和理

---

① 马克斯·韦伯：《马克斯·韦伯社会学文集》，人民出版社，2010，第61页。
② 马太·杜甘：《国家的比较：为什么比较，如何比较，拿什么比较》，社会科学文献出版社，2010，第27页。

论主题之间的关系。这是指概念创新既要有其事实基础和现象聚焦，又要锁定相关的理论主题——主题聚焦对准确定位新概念的概念家族颇具助益。①再次，处理好"日常概念"和"科学概念"之间的关系。在中国行政研究中，这就是要处理好实践者的语言（譬如"技巧执法""智慧执法"等）与学术概念之间的关系。前者鲜活而生动，且具有较强的提示性功能，但稍显粗糙，尚不具备参与理论对话的能力。最后，概念创新过程涉及在案例覆盖范围和概念抽象程度之间进行的"妥协"。在关于中国行政研究的概念创新中，有必要重视萨托利所强调的"抽象的阶梯"（ladder of abstraction）理念。"概念越是抽象，则案例的涉及面越广泛；而概念愈发具体，则案例的涉及面愈发狭窄。"质言之，"抽象的阶梯"强调：随着研究问题和研究目的的转换，研究者应当在概念建构中适度寻求概念内涵（connotation）与外延（denotation）的妥协。正是基于此，萨托利特别注重"中层概念"，旨在缓和普遍性理论与情景性分析之间的张力的使用。

深谙上述原则，有助于使学者尽可能少地陷入概念创新的误区。然而，更为操作性的问题在于，如何在中国行政研究中进行概念创新？当然，"创新"是难以标准化的，概念创新亦如此。不过，基于社会科学的综视，我们可以总结和归纳出几种颇具指导意义的概念创新思维。

第一，"领地"思维。在行政学领域，基本概念范畴（譬如"公共行政""公共管理""公共政策"及"治理"等）皆基于领地思维而产生。然而，随着学科的精细化和学科分支的发展，仍然可以沿着"领地"思维推进行政研究的概念创新，譬如，"政策执行""政策工具""政策网络""政策子系统""协作性公共管理"及"跨部门合作"等。如此而论，基于领地思维而发展出来的概念越丰富，标志着学科越发完善、健全和精细。然而，这也是一种不可再生的概念创新方式。学者发现某种"领地"，然后赋予其相应标签。标签一旦被选定，就不再有继续创新的空间。

第二，"类型"思维。在社会科学中，概念类型路径（concept - type approach）乃是进行概念创新的常见思维方法，成果也较为丰硕。譬如，韦

① 譬如"渐进主义"同"混合扫描模型"就属于同类概念，二者皆是关于决策过程的描述或解释。

伯在"克里斯玛型权威""传统权威"和"法理型权威"等权威之间进行的类型区分；涂尔干在"机械团结"和"有机团结"间进行的区分；费孝通对"差序格局"和"团体格局"作出的经典比较；等等。此外，在公共政策研究领域，"构成性政策"（Constituent policy）概念——一种关于游戏规则的形成就是典型地基于这种思维。从功能上讲，基于类型思维形成的概念，具有较强的比较研究价值。

第三，"变量"思维。这是一种基于关键变量的特质而对受其影响的某种行为、活动或现象赋予相应概念的过程。埃里森（Graham T. Allison）提出了"理性行动者模型""组织过程模型"和"政府政治模型"等概念模型。[1] 其中，概念化的要害在于识别出塑造和制约决策的关键变量。理性行动者模型将分析要害放在人和组织的理性能力上；组织过程模型则在更为复杂的组织间关系中考察决策行为；而政府政治模型则尝试在开放系统中将"环境"因素纳入决策过程研究。

第四，"类比"思维。很多时候，概念更多是被借用而非被创造。[2] 在社会科学领域，行政学要比其他学科更具学科交叉的特点。因此，公共行政研究也就更多收编和借用了其他学科的概念范畴。笔者将那种基于类比式创造或概念移植而形成概念的称为"类比"思维下的概念创新。譬如，组织研究中的"熵"（entropy）概念就是源自热力学、控制论及信息论。此外，20世纪中期发展起来的"行政生态学"等诸多概念，也是基于这种"类比"思维而确立起来的。

第五，"特质"思维。本质上，这种思维乃是吉瑞[3]所称的概念建构的共同属性路径（common attributes approach），即通过共性来定义某种行为、现象或活动的做法。既有的诸多公共行政概念的提出，多属于此种类型。譬如"选择性政策执行""整体性治理""模糊性治理"及"运动式治理"等。事实上，在中国公共行政研究中，具有深度的概念创新工作就是要紧扣特定约束条件中的政府行为本质特征、制度建设的特殊道路等。在未来中国

---

[1] 登哈特：《公共组织理论》，中国人民大学出版社，2011，第67页。

[2] 马太·杜甘：《比较社会学》，社会科学文献出版社，2006，第259页。

[3] John Gerring, "What Makes a Concept Good? A Criterial Framework for Understanding Concept Formation in the Social Sciences", *Polity* 31 (1999): 357 – 393.

行政研究中，这将是一种富有前景的概念创新思维和路径。

第六，"关联"思维。在经验性的行政研究中，关联性思维乃是揭示碎片化事实或现象背后行政实践之本质特征的重要方法。简单来讲，函数表达式"$Y = f\,(aX1 + bX2 + cX3 + dX4 + eX5\cdots\cdots)$"很好地说明了关联思维的要义。在关于中国城市摊贩监管中的政府行为研究中，Y 表示"摊贩监管中政府行为的本质属性"；X 表示不同的政府行为，这包括"疏导""暴力执法""柔性执法""监视型管理"等；a、b、c、d、e 等则表示不同种类的政府行为的使用比重、程度和时间等方面的"策略"或"技巧"。可以说，现实是支离破碎的，城市政府在摊贩监管中使用了 X1、X2、X3、X4、X5 和 a、b、c、d、e 等多种政策工具或者监管策略。那么，倘若研究者将"暴力执法"（X1）或"运动式治理"（X2）视为摊贩监管中刻画政府行为的元现象，那么他（她）就无法解释为什么摊贩监管还存在"柔性执法"（X3）、"选择性执法"（X4）或"睁一只眼闭一只眼"（a）的一面等。基于此，笔者认为，足以刻画中国城市摊贩监管中政府行为之本质的元现象为"疏堵结合""时紧时松"及"宽严不一"。[①] 为了揭示出这种元现象背后的政府行为本质，就有必要把握住 X1、X2、X3、X4、X5 及 a、b、c、d、e 等之间的内在关联。基于这种"关联"思维，通过运用扎根理论方法这种质性数据分析技术，笔者最终揭示出了"模糊性治理"这个核心概念。实际上，由此而论，基于"元现象"的概念化工作需要借用"关联"思维（或关系性方法）。

在行政学科发展的早期，领地思维下的概念创新乃是主线。随着行政学学科设置和研究领域的细化，这种领域性的概念、术语或范畴的创新空间越来越小。因此，亟须重视"特质"思维、"类型"思维、"类比"思维及"变量"思维等概念创新的路径。

（三）概念创新与公共行政的研究取向

相较于数据收集方法和数据分析方法，"研究取向"乃是研究方法中最

[①] 孙志建：《模糊性治理：中国城市政府摊贩监管逻辑研究》，博士学位论文，复旦大学国际关系与公共事务学院，2013。

为抽象的层次，它旨在为研究确立稳固的方法论哲学基础。总体上，"研究取向"是对一项社会科学研究的基本性质（譬如经验研究或规范研究，定量研究或质性研究）、目标（描述或解释）、价值取向（实证主义、诠释主义或是批判导向）及本体论或者认识论立场等方面的判断和抉择。在公共行政研究中，不同研究取向对于概念创新的要求大相径庭。

首先，具有显著哲学色彩（譬如现象学、建构主义及后现代主义等）的批判性行政研究具有更为强烈的概念创新动力。这是同哲学的使命——对基本范畴的研究——相统一的。譬如，自 20 世纪 90 年代中期以来，法默尔就致力于将后现代主义引入行政研究，提出"后传统治理"（The Post-traditional Governance）、"反行政"（Anti-administration）等概念，推动了公共行政批判理论的发展。此外，查尔斯·J. 福克斯等①亦尝试利用哲学和社会理论提出"一套词汇和概念集"（包括"公共能量场"的概念），以使话语理论有稳定基础。运用这些概念来解构传统（物化的）概念，后者正将行政学研究的注意力引向官僚结构，而忽视了对行政学实践的真实语境（即"真实的、生动的事件"）和社会互动的聚焦。

其次，秉持质性取向的行政研究更加注重概念创新。这主要是由于质性研究旨在发现问题，并对事实或现象予以比较、分类和概念提炼，而量化研究重在进行实证检验。实际上，"在某些类型的定性研究中，概念的澄清对于资料收集来说相当关键"。当然，这并不否认在量化研究中亦存在概念创新的必要性。然而，鉴于质性研究与量化研究的显著差别，有必要在"概念创新"与"概念化"（conceptualization）之间稍作区分。严格来讲，"概念化"乃是量化研究的操作环节，它试图将模糊的、不精确的观念（概念）转换成结构化科学研究中明确、精确的概念的思维过程。换言之，概念化暗含这样一种转换过程，即"概念化→名义定义→操作定义→现实世界中的测量"。

再次，以事实为基础的归纳研究具有更为强烈的概念创新偏好。当一项行政研究采取了扎根理论方法，也就意味着概念创新不仅是目的，而且也是

---

① 查尔斯·J. 福克斯，休·T. 米勒：《后现代公共行政：话语指向》，中国人民大学出版社，2002，第 75 页。

研究过程的内在需要。扎根理论方法的中心是编码、资料排序和组织的过程。在此过程中，概念、类属和核心范畴被识别和发展出来。在整个研究过程中，概念、概念关系和概念的类属乃是分析的重点。作为分析结果，扎根理论研究将生成一个核心范畴，用以讲述一个完整故事。概念工作越发丰富有效，故事将越发生动有趣，而理论也将更为接近"理性认识"。由此可知，一项旨在推进理论建构（而非理论验证或证伪）的研究取向更倾向于进行概念创新。因为，概念是理论的基础，理论陈述往往产生于概念间的关联。[①]

复次，严谨的比较研究（尤其是大样本）更为依赖于概念创新。在比较研究中，样本量的增加意味着抽象层次的提高。在进行大样本的比较研究时，学者往往引入相对抽象的"概念性分类"，[②] 以求超越简单的描述和事实堆积。在比较研究中，好的概念框架将使得比较研究不仅言之有物（事实），而且言之有据（理论）。在缺乏恰当概念框架的情形下，几乎难以产生一项简洁优美且富有新意的比较分析成果。这是一个基本的事实。正是基于此，比较学家萨托利、杜甘等才如此重视概念、概念建构及概念误建（concept misformation）等。

最后，因果解释性的行政研究较为倚重概念创新。在社会科学中，诸多影响深远的概念产生于解释性研究。譬如，阿伦特在解释纳粹事件时所提出的"平庸的恶"（The Banality of Evil）的概念。进一步讨论，倘若选取"机制性解释"这种因果解释方法，概念创新的重心就落在因果机制之上。譬如，"交易成本"（Transaction Cost）的概念就构成了科斯经济学解释"为什么会存在企业"这个组织与管理现象的核心因果机制。[③] 可以说，没有"交易成本"的概念及其所聚焦的经济现象，科斯经济学就会土崩瓦解。

四　结论与启示

难以揣测，倘若没有"脱耦化""目标置换""渐进主义"及"非正式

---

① 乔纳森·H. 特纳：《社会学理论的结构》，华夏出版社，2006，第7页。
② 雷德曼：《最新比较政治的议题与途径》，韦伯文化国际出版有限公司，2007，第10页。
③ 哈罗德·德姆塞茨：《企业经济学》，中国社会科学出版社，2009，第2页。

组织"等抽象概念，我们如何给予行政实践的生动性和复杂性以基本的尊重。概念创新不仅是行政学理论创新的基础，亦是推进学科发展与繁荣的基础性工作。基于概念创新，我们可以激发和挖掘公共行政实践的"想象"，解放和营造中国公共行政研究的想象力，开放"公共行政的思想实验"。① 进而，促使我们拥有更大的"超越现代主义公共行政理论的可能性"。②

在中国行政研究中，"概念游戏""术语的混乱""概念之间的循环论证"等常常为学者所诟病。也正是基于此，有必要将中国行政研究概念创新确立在既有的"经验"之上，并遵循相关原则和路径。总体上，在中国行政研究中，有必要倡导一种基于现象聚焦（尤指"元现象"），锁定学科重大理论问题，且以中层概念（尤指解释性概念）的生产为取向的概念创新。

笔者认为，在中国行政研究中，学者既要避免成为只重材料（即具体）而忽视新观念（即抽象）的"主题专家"，又要避免与之相反的"说明专家"。③ 概念创新要坚持"从具体到抽象，再从抽象到具体"的循环往复的认识过程。一方面，具体的抽象化。概念创新过程乃是从现象聚焦上升至意义诠释和本质揭示的过程。正如毛泽东所言："概念这种东西已经不是事物的现象，不是事物的各个片面，不是它们的外在联系，而是抓住了事物的本质，事物的全体，事物的内在联系了。"换言之，好的概念创新既要对现象、经验和事实具有敏感性，亦要善于运用理论思维和（形式）逻辑思维透过现象看到行政实践的本质。另一方面，抽象的具体化。它是指从抽象概念到具体现象的经验研究过程。哲学家尼采称，"一切概念都来源于差别物的等同"。④ 然而，在概念的具体使用中，忽略差别性、个体性与特殊性的做法是不足取的。可以说，概念乃是"存在"和"本质"的统一。⑤ 只重本质而忽视存在的多样性，以抽象性消融个体性，以形式逻辑压制经验事

---

① 戴维·约翰·法默尔、宋锦洲：《后现代公共行政理论家法默尔教授专访》，《公共行政评论》2008年第2期。

② 戴维·约翰·法默尔：《公共行政的语言》，中国人民大学出版社，2009，第271页。

③ 马克斯·韦伯：《社会科学和社会政策中的客观性》，华夏出版社，1999，第206页。

④ 尼采：《哲学与真理》，上海社会科学院出版社，1997，第105页。

⑤ 黑格尔：《小逻辑》，商务印书馆，2012，第331页。

实，乃是概念创新的误区。

概念创新是手段，不应当成为目的本身。在中国行政研究中，不可为了概念创新而杜撰概念和术语。与此同时，学界亦亟须谨防"概念拜物教"（the Fetishism of concepts）的倾向。海伍德认为，"当人们把概念当成某种独立于、在一定意义上甚至超越于使用它们的人类的一种具体存在时，'概念拜物教'就产生了。简言之，它把概念视为事物，而不是理解事物的方法"。

此外，固然概念创新不容小觑。但在中国行政研究中，对学科中核心范畴的正本清源也是一项不可忽视的工作。[①] 正如在中国实践中所发生的那样，从"财政"到"公共财政"的书写，不仅仅是措辞上变化，它也引发了公共管理理念和实践的转变。

参考文献

查尔斯·J. 福克斯、休·T. 米勒：《后现代公共行政：话语指向》，中国人民大学出版社，2002，第 104 页。

达勒姆、杰克·雷斌等：《公共行政职业中五大问题》，中山大学出版社，2006，第 1314 页。

戴维·约翰·法默尔：《公共行政的语言》，中国人民大学出版社，2009，第 271 页。

戴维·约翰·法默尔、宋锦洲：《后现代公共行政理论家法默尔教授专访》，《公共行政评论》2008 年第 2 期。

戴维·约翰·法默尔：《公共行政的语言》，中国人民大学出版社，2009，第 27 页。

登哈特：《公共组织理论》，中国人民大学出版社，2011，第 67 页。

丁煌：《发展中的中国政策科学——我国公共政策学科发展的回眸与展望》，《管理世界》2003 年第 2 期。

哈罗德·德姆塞茨：《企业经济学》，中国社会科学出版社，2009，第 2 页。

雷德曼：《最新比较政治的议题与途径》，韦伯文化国际出版有限公司，2007，第 10 页。

---

① 丁煌：《发展中的中国政策科学——我国公共政策学科发展的回眸与展望》，《管理世界》2003 年第 2 期。

黑格尔：《小逻辑》，商务印书馆，2012，第 331 页。

敬乂嘉：《评估中国大陆公共行政研究现状》，《复旦公共行政评论》2009 年第 6 期第 5 辑。

马克斯·韦伯：《马克斯·韦伯社会学文集》，人民出版社，2010，第 61 页。

马克斯·韦伯：《社会科学和社会政策中的客观性》，华夏出版社，1999，第 206 页。

马太·杜甘：《国家的比较：为什么比较，如何比较，拿什么比较》，社会科学文献出版社，2010，第 27 页。

马太·杜甘：《比较社会学》，社会科学文献出版社，2006，第 259 页。

尼采：《哲学与真理》，上海社会科学院出版社，1997，第 105 页。

乔纳森·H. 特纳：《社会学理论的结构》，华夏出版社，2006，第 7 页。

孙志建：《模糊性治理：中国城市政府摊贩监管逻辑研究》，博士学位论文，复旦大学国际关系与公共事务学院，2013。

James Bogen, James Woodward, "Saving the Phenomena," *The Philosophical Review* 97 (1988): 303 – 352.

John Gerring, "What Makes a Concept Good? A Criterial Framework for Understanding Concept Formation in the Social Sciences", *Polity* 31 (1999): 357 – 393.

Aseem Prakash, Mary Kay Gugerty, "Trust but Verify? Voluntary Regulation Programs in the Nonprofit Sector," *Regulation & Governance* 4 (2010): 22 – 47.

Woodrow Wilson, "The Study of Administration", *Political Science Quarterly* 2 (1887): 197 – 222.

变革社会的社会问题与社会政策

社会性别视角下的中国老年人口失能
预期寿命及代际支持[*]

郭 未 陈 卫^{**}

【摘要】基于 2005 年"小普查"及 2010 年"六普"汇总数据，本文利用生命表技术及 Sullivan 法，分析了男、女老年人口失能预期寿命及其差异的变化，同时根据历年的生育率、死亡率和结婚率，利用 SOCSIM 微观模拟数据分析老年人口代际支持资源。分析发现，老年人口失能预期寿命占预期寿命的比重呈缩小趋势，且男性的压缩程度低于女性；与 2005 年相比，2010 年老年人口失能预期寿命在低龄阶段略微增加，而年龄较高阶段则下降；老年人口失能预期寿命的性别差异随年龄的提高而下降，这种差异在 5 年间呈压缩趋势。同时，我们发现，低龄阶段老年人口的存活子女数不断减少且将持续一段时间，这抵消了老年人口失能预期寿命压缩对照料资源需求的减少。未来中国，对失能老年人口，单纯依靠家庭资源已经无法满足养老

---

　*　本研究受 2013 年度教育部人文社会科学研究青年基金项目（13YJC840013）资助。研究论文初稿曾在南京农业大学举行的江苏省首届青年老龄论坛暨第三届研究生老龄论坛报告过，感谢南京大学社会学院陈友华教授、南京师范大学社会发展学院黄润龙教授的有益建议，作者文责自负。

**　第一作者：郭未（1979～），四川南充人，北京大学法学博士，南京大学社会学院社会工作与社会政策系讲师。研究方向：人口健康，社会计量，公共政策。第二作者：陈卫（1964～），浙江杭州人，中国人民大学社会与人口学院教授，博士生导师。研究方向：人口统计学，人口与社会发展。

需求，对此，小区帮扶和养老机构的发展显得尤为重要。

【关键词】 失能预期寿命；代际支持；性别差异；老年人

一 引言

"十二五"期间我国进入第一个老年人口增长高峰，而随着人口老龄化的加剧，老年人对长期照料服务的需求量也在不断增加。但在我国医疗保障体系尚不健全及传统文化背景的影响下，众多地方在大力推行"9073"养老格局，即约90%的老年人实现居家养老，约7%是小区养老，约3%是机构养老。由此看来，居家养老仍是目前和今后较长时间内我国主要的养老模式。据此，我们可以看出，在我国超过90%的老人要依靠家庭提供生活照料和精神慰藉，其亲属，尤其是子女就要承担着照护老人的主要责任。[①] 而根据中国老龄科学研究中心的资料，2010 年，我国失能老年人口为1084.3万人左右，占老年人口的6.05%。[②] 如此庞大的失能老人群体，加之当今中国，生育率下降、人口流动加速、思想文化转变从人口因素和居住倾向两个角度带来家庭的核心化，同时妇女劳动参与率不断提高，极大缩小了老人的家庭照料资源，这与失能老人对照料资源与时间的要求形成更多矛盾。

实际上，我国2005 年1% 人口抽样调查就第一次将"健康状况"纳入国家级的大型人口调查中，可见国家对老年人健康状况的重视。老年人口的健康状况不仅是从个体方面作为生命质量的指南，也是宏观层面社会发展等的重要参考指标。[③] 20 世纪90 年代伊始，我国学者就持续研究老年人口生活质量。[④] 此

---

① 刘婕、楼玮群：《完善上海居家高龄失能老人亲属照顾者的社会支持系统》，《华东师范大学学报（哲学社会科学版）》2012 年第 1 期。

② 张恺悌、孙陆军、牟新渝、王海涛、李明镇：《全国城乡失能老年人状况研究》，《残疾人研究》2011 年第 2 期。

③ 杜鹏、李强：《1994～2004 年中国老年人的生活自理预期寿命及其变化》，《人口研究》2006 年第 5 期。

④ 钟军、陈育德、饶克勤：《健康预期寿命指标计算方法的研究》，《中国人口科学》1996 年第 6 期。邬沧萍、苏苹、陈杰、王岸柳：《有关研究健康老龄化方法论的几点思考》，《中国人口科学》2001 年增刊。曾毅、顾大男、凯·兰德：《健康期望寿命估算方法的拓展及其在中国高龄老人研究中的应用》，《中国人口科学》2007 年第 6 期。曾宪新：《我国老年人口健康状况的综合分析》，《人口与经济》2010 年第 5 期。

外，性别差异是研究老年人口问题尤其是健康状况不可忽略的良好分类指标。男性、女性老年人口的差异体现在多个方面，2010年男性人口平均预期寿命为72.38岁，女性为77.37岁，后者高出前者4.99岁。但是，以往研究发现，女性老年人口更高的预寿命并不代表她们的身体更健康，相反，女性老年人口健康状况并不如男性老年人口，[①] 研究发现我国老年人的预期寿命在增长，但是老年人尤其是女性老年人的自评健康预期寿命却是下降的。杜鹏等的研究发现，健康状况改善的程度低于寿命的延长，相比男性，高龄女性老年人处于劣势。近年来，我国社会经济、医疗水平、养老保险、医疗保障等持续发展与完善，在提高老年人的健康状况中发挥了重要作用，也为老年人健康状况改善提供了良好的保障。但是，男性与女性老年人口的差异仍未消除，这种差异既包括生物方面的预期寿命差异，也包括文化水平、收入状况等社会属性方面的差异。一方面，考虑到失能率、失能老人规模是一个国家和地区制定养老机构、养老床位、养老服务规划的主要依据，也是国家和地区制定社会保障计划的重要依据。[②] 另一方面，考虑到在中国现实条件基础上，承袭传统的家庭养老模式中，代际关系成为其中的一项重要内容，包括经济支持、生活照料和日常服务的互惠及亲情、情感的沟通和慰藉。中国目前缺乏健全的小区服务网络和各种老年性服务机构，步入老年尤其是高龄阶段的人在日常生活中所获得的帮助主要来自子女，代际支持成为最重要的社会支持，子女赡养仍旧是人们进入老年以后的首要选择。所以，在测量代际关系层面，存活子女数量和性别成为影响老人，尤其是失能老人生活及养老状况的重要可测量因素，老人在养老方面更加依赖家人，尤其是儿子起重要作用。[③]

那么，老年人口健康状况的性别差异如何测量？老年人口的失能预期寿命有什么变化？不同年龄组老年人口平均存活子女数、平均存活儿

① 柳玉芝：《关注中国高龄老人中的性别问题——中国高龄老人健康长寿影响因素研究项目简介》，《妇女研究论丛》2001年第4期。王树新、曾宪新：《中国高龄老人自理能力的性别差异》，《中国人口科学》2001年增刊。

② 潘金洪、帅友良等：《中国老年人口失能率及失能规模分析——基于第六次全国人口普查数据》，《南京人口管理干部学院学报》2012年第4期。

③ 刘晶：《子女数对农村高龄老人养老及生活状况的影响》，《中国人口科学》2004年增刊。

子数有什么变化？针对这些问题，本文将首先根据 2005 年 1% 人口抽样调查汇总资料及 2010 年第六次人口普查公布的汇总数据，综合分析性别视角下中国老年人口的健康状况，利用具有所需数据简单、消除年龄结构影响、便于比较的特点而应用广泛的 Sullivan 法[①]计算分性别的老年人口的失能预期寿命，分析性别差异的变动趋势；接下来，利用历史人口学数据，使用 SOCSIM 模拟软件，确定 2005 年和 2010 年不同年龄组老年人平均存活子女数、平均存活儿子数，据此为未来相关老龄政策的制定等提供实证依据。

二　数据与方法

（一）Sullivan 方法

1. 抽样调查及普查数据

首先，在老年人失能预期寿命的分析中，本文使用的资料是来自国家统计局公布的 2005 年 1% 人口抽样调查汇总资料，以及 2010 年第六次人口普查汇总资料。我们以 2005 年人口抽样调查及 2010 年第六次人口普查公布的"分性别，分年龄死亡资料"作为生命表的基础资料，以"分性别，分年龄老年人口健康状况"作为计算老年人口失能预期寿命的基础。2005 年的 1% 人口抽样调查是大型人口抽样调查中第一次涉及调查对象的健康状况，即调查问卷中的"R13"项"身体健康状况"。最新的 2010 年第六次人口普查也第一次在人口普查中涉及老年人口健康状况，即调查问卷中的"R28"项"身体健康状况（60 周岁及以上的人填写）"。这为我们分析老年人口健康预期寿命提供了基础数据。需要特别指出的是，2005 年 1% 人口抽样调查中受访对象的健康状况分为"身体健康"，"基本能保证正常的生活工作"，"不能正常工作或生活不能自理"，"说不准"，我们将前两项合并为"身体能自理"，后两项合并为"身体失能"。在 2010 年第六次普查中将自评健康状况分为"健康"，"基本健康"，"不健康，但生活能自理"，"生活不能自

---

① Sullivan DF, "A Single Index of Mortality and Morbidity", *HSMHA Health Rep* 86 (1971): 347 – 354.

理"四个类别，在分析中，我们将前两项合并为"身体能自理"，后两项合并为"身体失能"两类。其次，2005 年老年人口健康状况汇总资料的年龄分组的最高组为"95 岁及以上"，2010 年为"100 岁及以上"，为便于比较，我们将 2010 年的汇总数据按 2005 年标准重新整理为"95 岁及以上"。

2. Sullivan 法的计算过程

我们借鉴 Sullivan 方法计算老年人口失能预期寿命前，基于 2010 年人口普查数据，利用生命表技术计算 2010 年分性别的 60 岁及以上老年人的人口预期寿命，以此作为后续计算的基础。首先，根据重新分类后的健康状况计算 2010 年 60 岁及以上老年人口"分年龄身体失能比率" π_x，即 x 岁失能的比例：

$$\pi_x = \frac{x \text{ 岁失能人数}}{x \text{ 岁总人口}}$$

然后估算失能生存人年数：

$$L_{x失能} = L_x \times \pi_x$$

其中，L_x 为生命表中的生存人年数；

用生命表计算 T_x 的方法计算累计失能生存人年数：

$$T_{X失能}: T_{X失能} = \sum\nolimits_x^\omega L_{X失能}$$

接下来计算失能预期寿命 YLD：

$$YLD = T_{X失能}/l_x$$

最后计算失能预期寿命的标准误：

$$S（YLD）\approx \frac{1}{l_x^2 \sum\nolimits_x^\omega} = 0L_x^2 \frac{\pi_x（1-\pi_x）}{N_x}$$

其中 N_x 是在年龄 x 岁时失能的人数。

（二）SOCSIM 微观模拟

在分析老年人口的代际支持时，我们从最直接的照料资源分析，即分析不同年龄男性及女性老年人口的存活子女状况。但是根据历次普查及抽样调查的数据，我们很难获得有关子女存活状况的信息。对此，我们根据基本的生命率，使用 Hammel 和 Wachter 发明的 SOCSIM 微观模拟系统方法分析各年龄老年人口子女的存活状况。在 SOCSIM 微观模拟中，我们按照生育率、死亡率和结婚率的不同将模拟分为 10 个阶段。首先我们从新中国成立前 200 年开始模拟，得到新中国成立时的一个具有稳定结构的人口，用于新中国成立后的相关数据模拟。对每个阶段的划分，我们依据其生育水平、死亡水平和结婚水平的变动进行划分，同时各阶段中我们采用时期的平均水平或特定年份的值作为模拟参数，因而，需要历年的生育率、死亡率和结婚率，具体阶段划分及模拟参数的设定如附录中表 1 所示。

SOCSIM 微观模拟结果为模拟时期内所有人口，包括性别、出生时间、死亡时间及子女的信息等，因而通过数据匹配后我们可以分析得到 2005 年和 2010 年男性及女性老年人口平均存活子女状况。在此，我们需要对模拟结果进行检验。图 1 所示为 SOCSIM 微观模拟结果与新中国成立后总共六次的人口普查结果的对比，我们可以看出，模拟结果很理想，因此模拟数据可以用于我们的研究分析之中。

三　结果分析

（一）老年人口失能比例的变化趋势

随着年龄的增长，人们的人体功能退化、健康状况下降。正如图 2 所示，2005 年和 2010 年男性及女性老年人口的失能比例均随年龄的提高而不断上升，这符合人口功能退化的规律。

从时间变动角度分析，我们发现一个有趣的现象，与 2005 年相比，2010 年时年龄较小的老年人口失能比例有较低程度的上升趋势，男性与女性低龄老年人口均是如此。而随着年龄的提高，与 2005 年相比，2010 年老年人口失能比例是下降的，下降幅度随着年龄的提高而增加。

从性别差异视角分析，男性失能比例低于女性，且男性与女性之间的差

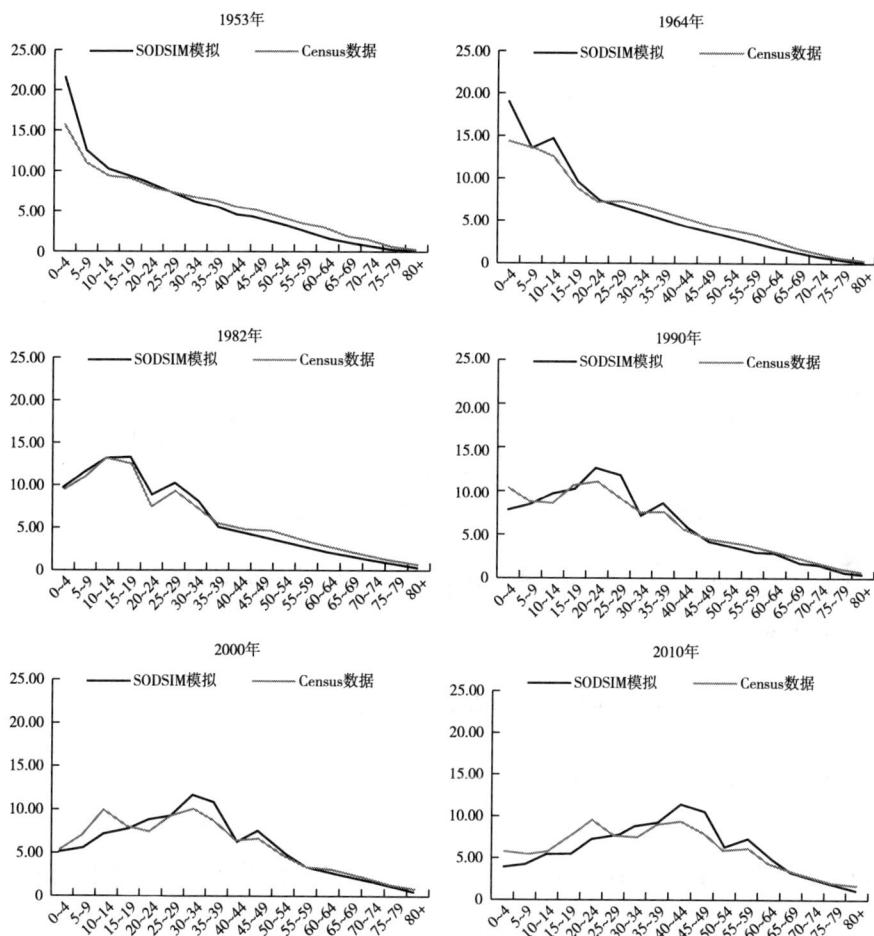

图 1 SOCSIM 微观模拟结果与普查结果对比：人口年龄结构

数据来源：根据历次人口普查汇总数据及 SOCSIM 微观模拟数据整理计算。

异随着年龄的提高而扩大，对 2005 年和 2010 年均是如此。在低龄老年人中，与 2005 年相比，2010 年失能比例的性别差异有所下降，但是在高龄老年人口中，2010 年健康比例的性别差异则高于 2005 年。

一定程度上，老年人口失能比例的下降意味着对照料资源需求的相对减少。但是失能比例的性别差异则说明女性相对男性更长的寿命中，更多的是在失能状况下度过的，因而她们对照料资源需求更多，这恰是将失能比例的性别差异传递到了照料资源需求的性别差异。但是失能比例的性别差异则说明女性在相对男性更长的寿命中，更多的是在失能状况下度过的，因而她们

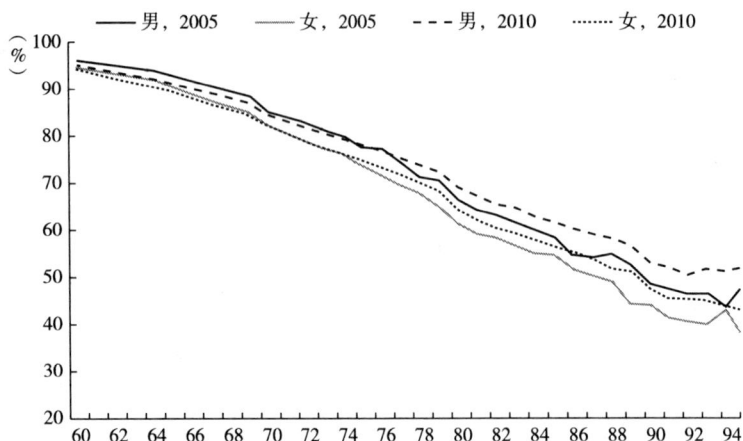

图 2　2005 年、2010 年老年人口失能百分比

资料来源：根据 2005 年 1% 人口抽样调查资料及 2010 年第六次人口普查汇总资料整理计算。

对照料资源需求更多，这恰是将失能比例的性别差异传递到了照料资源需求的性别差异。

（二）老年人口失能预期寿命的性别差异变动

预期寿命是一个标准化指标，可以体现特定人口的健康状况。在预期寿命逐年延长、人口老龄化不断加重的当今中国社会，实际中需要照顾的老年人口的状况、老年人口的照料资源是应对人口老龄化挑战中最需要搞清楚的问题。对此，本文参考 Sullivan 方法，结合失能比例分别计算了 2005 年及 2010 年分性别老年人口的预期寿命及失能预期寿命（具体计算的数据输出请见本文附录中的表 2、表 5）。

老年人的养老问题是目前社会各界关注的重点，但是从实际情况来看，低龄老年人对照料资源要求较少，而高龄老年人口尤其是失能老年人口对照料资源的需求相对较高。为分析老年人口对照料资源的需求，接下来分析老年人口失能预期寿命就显得非常必要了。

图 3 所示为 2005 年和 2010 年分性别老年人口失能预期寿命。与 2005 年相比，2010 年 65 岁及以下女性老年人口失能预期寿命略有上升，但是 65 岁以上则有所下降；而男性老年人口失能预期寿命在 70 岁以下呈略微上升的趋势，在 70 岁及以上开始下降，但是下降幅度略低于女性。从性别差异

的角度分析，女性预期寿命高于男性的同时，其失能预期寿命也高于男性。一方面，老年人口失能预期寿命的性别差异随年龄的提高而下降，另一方面，由于女性相比男性较高的下降幅度，2010 年老年人口失能预期寿命的性别差异较 2005 年呈压缩趋势。

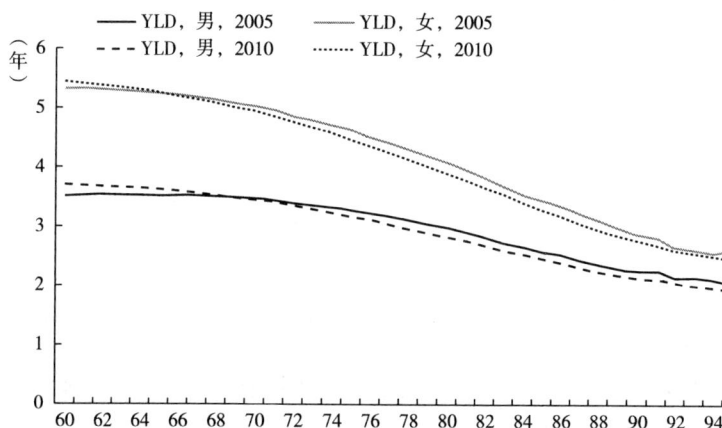

图 3　2005～2010 年老年人口失能预期寿命的变动

数据来源：根据 2005 年 1% 人口抽样调查资料及 2010 年第六次人口普查汇总资料整理计算。

图 4 所示为老年人口失能预期寿命占预期寿命比值（YLD/LE）的变化趋势。从图 4 中我们可以看出，中国老年人口失能预期寿命在余寿中的比值处于压缩状态，这一现象符合 Fries（1980、1989、2003）[①] 提出的"功能缺损的压缩理论"（a compression of morbidity），即随着医疗卫生等的发展，死亡率降低后带来的是残障率的下降，老年人口失能预期寿命不仅在绝对量上有所减少，同时占预期寿命的比重也缩小了。从性别差异角度分析发现，男性的压缩程度远低于女性。

老年人口失能预期寿命的下降及失能预期寿命占预期寿命比重的下降，是老年人口健康状况改善的结果，也说明在老年人口预期寿命逐年增长的当

---

① Fries JF, "Aging, Natural Death and the Compression of Morbidity", *The New England Journal of Medicine* 303（1980）：130－134. Fries JF, Green LW, Levine S, *Health Promotion and the Compression of Morbidity*（Lancet, 1989）, pp. 481－483.
Fries JF, "Measuring and Monitoring Success in Compressing Morbidity," *Annals of Internal Medicine* 139（2003）：455－459.

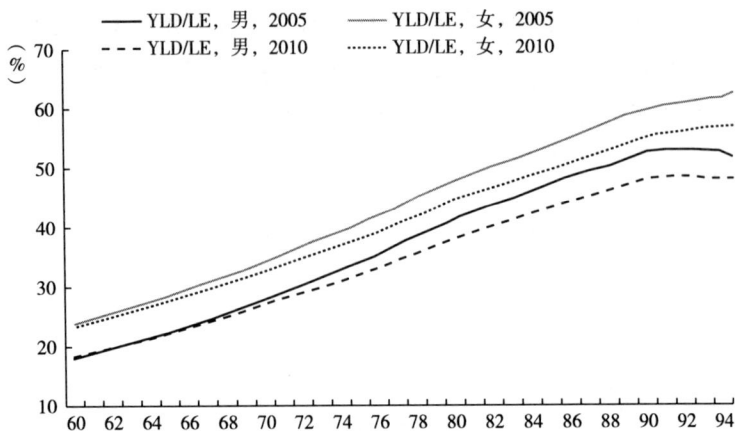

图4 2005～2010年老年人口失能预期寿命占余寿比重
（DFLE/LE）的变动

资料来源：根据2005年1%人口抽样调查资料及2010年第六次人口普查汇总资料整理计算。

下中国，对老年人个体而言，他们在延长的预期寿命中需要人照料的实际客观需求却是压缩的，即对照料资源的需求是减少的。

（三）老年人口代际支持资源的变动

从前文的分析中我们发现，老年人口预期寿命延长的过程中，失能预期寿命有所减少，这在实际意义层面而言，也就是对照料资源的需求会有所减少。这对老年人口日益增多、养老问题日益严重的当今中国社会而言是一个"喜讯"。但是，在前文分析得出老年人口预期寿命延长中反而由于健康状况的改善而对照料资源的需求有所减少的前提下，我们需要进一步思考老年人口的照料资源是如何变化的？这里，我们从老年人口最直接的照料资源，即子女存活状况的角度进行分析。在老人，尤其是高龄老人养老代际支持方面，一些高龄老人隔代居住并由孙辈承担经济及照料责任，在此本文没有对孙辈状况进行分析，这将在未来的研究中进一步开展。

图5所示为老年人口最直接的照料资源状况，即老年人口子女存活状况。从平均存活子女数看，2010年74岁及以上女性老年人口、75岁及以上男性老年人口的平均存活子女数在2005年有所提高。在当下中国，尤其是仍旧存在养儿防老传统观念的背景下，儿子存活状况对老年人口的养老更

加重要，因而接下来我们对老年人口的平均存活儿子数进行分析，结果发现其与平均存活子女数的变动趋势是一致的。于当下而言，这无疑是一个喜讯，老年人口余寿中处于不健康状态的时间压缩，同时其最直接的照料资源又是上升的，两相交汇，说明2010年老年人口的照料负担相比2005年有所减小。

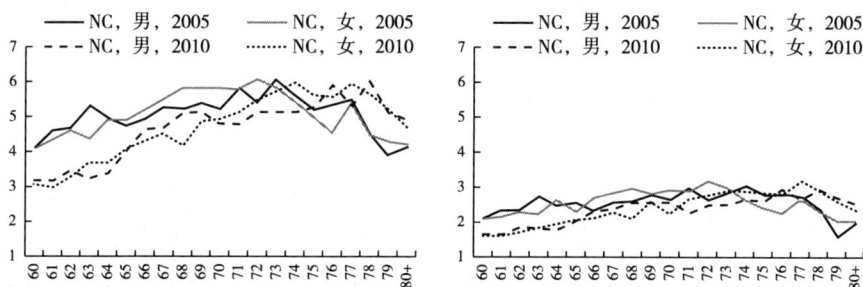

图5　2005年、2010年老年人口平均存活子女数状况

资料来源：根据SOCSIM微观模拟资料结果匹配并计算得到。

但是，我们的分析也发现一个问题，低龄组老年人口平均存活子女数则有较大的减少，而且随着生育水平的不断下降，人们的存活子女数仍会持续下降一段时间，随着这些老年人口逐年进入高龄老年队列，他们的健康状态一天天下降，但是其照料资源却也呈现减少趋势，这对未来的养老而言当然是一个很大的预警信号。

四　结论与讨论

社会、经济、医疗、卫生的快速发展改善了中国老年人口的健康状况，根据我们的计量分析，中国老年人口预期寿命延长的同时，失能预期寿命则减少。这对仍旧以家庭养老为主的当今中国而言，无疑是一个喜讯，在总体层面，这大大减轻了家人尤其是子女对老年人口的照料。特别的，我们的计量结果还发现，对75岁以上的老年人口而言，失能预期寿命缩减，但是他们的平均存活子女数、平均存活儿子数却提高了，这无疑也减轻了当下高龄老人家庭的养老负担。

但是，我们的计量分析也发现，对当下中国低龄老年人口而言，

2010年失能预期寿命比2005年有所提高，这可以反映出他们对照料的需求更大。同时，受计划生育政策的影响，中国人口生育水平有较大幅度的下降，按照SOCSIM模拟的结果，对低龄组老年人口而言，与2005年相比，其2010年平均存活子女数均有较大幅度下降，这些低龄老人随着时间的推移，会进入高龄阶段，这无疑对未来中国的养老形成一个巨大挑战。我们在为老年人口健康状况改善感到高兴的同时，不能忽略未来老人尤其是高龄老人的直接照料资源不断减少这个趋势：考虑到中国已经出现并不断强化的高龄老龄化现状，进入高龄期、失能状态的老年人口的绝对量会随之扩大，而未来不远的时期内，他们的平均存活子女数，尤其是作为主要养老资源的平均存活儿子数的不断减少，这样一种趋势在未来的交汇，不得不引发我们对中国未来养老负担的思考。

失能老人最需要生活照料、长期护理、精神关爱，他们应该是养老机构的主要服务对象。诸如德国、日本、新加坡等许多发达国家已经把失能老人照料作为一项重要的国家层面的公共政策问题加以研究，他们通过技术、政策、制度、市场手段来实施政策。[1] 放眼未来，中国无子女、无配偶老人的照料问题，独生子女家庭失能老人的照料问题，城乡贫困失能老人的照料问题会更加严峻和突出，[2] 而根据我们的计量分析结果，中国老年人口平均存活子女数、平均存活儿子数不断下降，这对失能老年人口而言，意味着单纯依靠家庭资源已经无法满足其养老需求，对此，小区帮扶和养老机构的发展显得尤为重要。但如何进行小区帮扶、如何发展养老机构、如何提高养老机构对失能老人的接纳能力、如何引导老年人口对机构养老的接纳是当下政府和相关政策机构应优先考虑的问题。

① 潘金洪、帅友良等：《中国老年人口失能率及失能规模分析——基于第六次全国人口普查数据》，《南京人口管理干部学院学报》2012年第4期。

② 潘金洪：《江苏省独生子女数量测算及其风险分析》，《扬州大学学报》2007年第1期。

附录：

表 1　SOCSIM 微观模拟阶段划分及率的设置

阶　段	时　期	生育率	死亡率	结婚率
第 I 阶段	1750 年~1949 年	1929 年~1931 年	1929 年~1932 年	1929 年~1933 年
第 II 阶段	1950 年~1958 年	1950 年~1958 年	1953 年~1964 年	1963 年
第 III 阶段	1959 年~1961 年	1959 年~1961 年	1953 年~1965 年	1963 年
第 IV 阶段	1962 年~1971 年	1962 年~1971 年	1964 年~1990 年	1963 年
第 V 阶段	1972 年~1979 年	1972 年~1979 年	1964 年~1983 年	1979 年
第 VI 阶段	1980 年~1989 年	1980 年~1989 年	1988 年	1979 年
第 VII 阶段	1990 年~1999 年	1990 年~1999 年	1990 年~2000 年	1995 年
第 VIII 阶段	2000 年~2009 年	2000 年~2009 年	2000 年~2010 年	2005 年
第 IX 阶段	2010 年	2010 年	2010 年	2010 年
第 X 阶段	2011 年~2150 年	2010 年	2010 年	2010 年

表 2　2005 年老年人口的生活自理预期寿命（男性）

年龄 x	l_x	nL_x	π_x	$L_{x失能}$	$T_{x失能}$	YLD	e_x	YLD/e_x（%）
60	84494	83984	0.03920	3292	297089	3.52	19.48	18.05
65	78636	77864	0.07205	5610	276680	3.52	15.74	22.35
70	69818	68664	0.14855	10200	241715	3.46	12.39	27.94
75	57212	55717	0.22349	12452	186487	3.26	9.54	34.17
80	41404	39673	0.33442	13267	123260	2.98	7.19	41.40
85	24594	22948	0.41369	9493	63155	2.57	5.42	47.38
90	10952	9820	0.51397	5047	24599	2.25	4.27	52.60
95 +	3481	13724	0.51481	7065	7065	2.03	3.94	51.52

资料来源：根据 2005 年 1% 人口抽样调查汇总资料整理计算。

注：l_x 为 x 岁的存活人数；L_x 为 x 岁存活人年数；π_x 为 x 年龄的失能比例；

$L_{x失能}$ 为 x 岁失能的存活人年数；$T_{x失能}$ 为累计失能的存活人年数；

YLD 为失能预期寿命；e_x 为 x 岁预期寿命；

其中，此处的 YLD，e_x，YLD/e_x 所呈报的数据是在计算基础上保留两位小数。

表3 2005年老年人口的生活自理预期寿命（女性）

年龄 x	l_x	nL_x	π_x	$L_{x失能}$	$T_{x失能}$	YLD	e_x	$LE_{x失能}/e_x$（%）
60	90650	90308	0.05151	4652	482725	5.33	22.45	23.72
65	86662	86150	0.09561	8236	454014	5.24	18.36	28.53
70	80341	79496	0.17790	14142	402736	5.01	14.59	34.36
75	70368	69112	0.26475	18297	323337	4.59	11.28	40.74
80	55817	54106	0.38507	20835	227258	4.07	8.54	47.68
85	37699	35804	0.45417	16261	129333	3.43	6.40	53.60
90	20403	18741	0.56102	10514	58188	2.85	4.78	59.66
95+	7359	30798	0.63053	19419	19419	2.64	4.18	63.13

资料来源：根据2005年1%人口抽样调查汇总资料整理计算。

表4 2010年老年人口的生活自理预期寿命（男性）

年龄 x	l_x	nL_x	π_x	$L_{x失能}$	$T_{x失能}$	YLD	e_x	YLD/e_x（%）
60	87621	87148	0.04777	4163	323697	3.69	20.04	18.44
65	82004	81287	0.08843	7188	296653	3.62	16.23	22.29
70	73672	72537	0.15496	11241	254388	3.45	12.76	27.06
75	61125	59619	0.21870	13039	193242	3.16	9.84	32.12
80	45180	43291	0.30892	13373	127750	2.83	7.41	38.18
85	27204	25553	0.38315	9791	66754	2.45	5.67	43.27
90	12682	11517	0.46862	5397	27172	2.14	4.46	48.07
95+	4300	17174	0.48028	8248	8248	1.92	3.99	48.03

资料来源：根据2010年第六次人口普查汇总资料整理计算。

表5 2010年老年人口的生活自理预期寿命（女性）

年龄 x	l_x	nL_x	π_x	$L_{x失能}$	$T_{x失能}$	YLD	e_x	YLD/e_x（%）
60	93309	93026	0.05665	5270	506275	5.43	23.14	20.26
65	89817	89340	0.10614	9483	471202	5.25	18.93	24.01
70	84096	83270	0.18067	15044	414174	4.93	15.04	28.54
75	74401	73182	0.25141	18399	330679	4.44	11.65	33.34
80	60367	58512	0.35615	20839	234884	3.89	8.74	38.98
85	41294	39354	0.43540	17135	135672	3.29	6.61	43.68
90	2683	20978	0.52120	10934	62652	2.76	5.01	48.11
95+	8911	38156	0.57105	21789	21789	2.45	4.28	48.05

资料来源：根据2010年第六次人口普查汇总资料整理计算。

参考文献

陈卫、杜夏：《中国高龄老人养老与生活状况的影响因素——对子女数量和性别作用的检验》，《中国人口科学》2002 年第 6 期。

杜鹏、李强：《1994～2004 年中国老年人的生活自理预期寿命及其变化》，《人口研究》2006 年第 5 期。

杜鹏、武超：《中国老年人的生活自理能力状况与变化》，《人口研究》2006 年第 1 期。

杜鹏、伊密、张鹏、曲嘉瑶、丁志宏：《北京市"健康老人"研究》，《人口与经济》2007 年第 2 期。

杜鹏、尹尚菁：《中国老年人残疾与生活不能自理状况比较研究》，《残疾人研究》2011 年第 2 期。

李强、汤哲：《多状态生命表法在老年人健康预期寿命研究中的应用》，《中国人口科学》2002 年第 6 期。

刘婕、楼玮群：《完善上海居家高龄失能老人亲属照顾者的社会支持系统》，《华东师范大学学报（哲学社会科学版）》2012 年第 1 期。

刘晶：《子女数对农村高龄老人养老及生活状况的影响》，《中国人口科学》2004 年增刊。

柳玉芝：《关注中国高龄老人中的性别问题——中国高龄老人健康长寿影响因素研究项目简介》，《妇女研究论丛》2001 年第 4 期。

潘金洪：《江苏省独生子女数量测算及其风险分析》，《扬州大学学报》2007 年第 1 期。

潘金洪、帅友良等：《中国老年人口失能率及失能规模分析——基于第六次全国人口普查数据》，《南京人口管理干部学院学报》2012 年第 4 期。

汤哲：《北京市老年人健康预期寿命及其变化》，《中华流行病学杂志》2005 年第 12 期。

汤哲等：《北京市不同社会经济状况老年人的预期寿命和健康预期寿命》，《中国临床康复》2004 年第 30 期。

王德文、叶文振：《中国老年人健康状况的性别差异及其影响因素》，《妇女研究论丛》2006 年第 4 期。

王树新、曾宪新：《中国高龄老人自理能力的性别差异》，《中国人口科学》2001 年增刊。

邬沧萍：《提高对老年人生活质量的科学认识》，《人口研究》2002 年第 5 期。

邬沧萍、苏苹、陈杰、王岸柳：《有关研究健康老龄化方法论的几点思考》，《中国人口科学》2001 年增刊。

曾宪新：《我国老年人口健康状况的综合分析》，《人口与经济》2010 年第 5 期。

曾毅等：《中国 1998 年健康长寿调查及高龄老人生活自理期望寿命》，《中国人口科学》2001 年第 3 期。

曾毅、顾大男、凯·兰德：《健康期望寿命估算方法的拓展及其在中国高龄老人中研究中的应用》，《中国人口科学》2007 年第 6 期。

曾毅、柳玉芝、萧振禹、张纯元：《中国高龄老人的社会经济与健康状况》，《中国人口科学》2004 年增刊。

张恺悌、孙陆军、牟新渝、王海涛、李明镇：《全国城乡失能老年人状况研究》，《残疾人研究》2011 年第 2 期。

张文娟、杜鹏：《中国老年人健康预期寿命变化的地区差异：扩张还是压缩?》，《人口研究》2009 年第 5 期。

钟军、陈育德、饶克勤：《健康预期寿命指标计算方法的研究》，《中国人口科学》1996 年第 6 期。

E. A. Hammel, K. W. Wachter and C. K. McDaniel, *The Kin of the Aged in A. D.* 2000. *The Chickens Come Home to Roost*", *Ageing*：*Social Change* (Academic Press, 1987), pp. 11 – 39.

K. W. Wachter, *Kin Models and Simulation*, in J. Bongaarts, T. Burch and K. Wachter (eds.), *Family Demography. Methods and Applications* (Oxford University Press, 1987).

Thomas K. Burch, Kenneth W. Wachter (eds.), *Family Demography*：*Methods and Applications* (Clarendon Press, 1987).

Fries JF, "Measuring and Monitoring Success in Compressing Morbidity", *Annals of Internal Medicine* 139 (2003)：455 – 459.

Fries JF, Green LW, Levine S, *Health Promotion and the Compression of Morbidity*, (Lancet, 1989), pp. 481 – 483.

Fries JF, "Aging, Natural Death and the Compression of Morbidity", *The New England Journal of Medicine* 303 (1980)：130 – 134.

Sullivan DF, "A Single Index of Mortality and Morbidity", *HSMHA Health Rep* 86 (1971)：347 – 354.

城镇化过程中农村人口空心化治理模式与实现机制研究

——发展人类学的解读[*]

田书芹　王东强　宋凡金[**]

【摘要】城镇化进程中许多农村出现了人口空心化现象，农村人口数量的减少和人口结构的失衡，极大地影响了社会主义新农村建设的进程。在发展人类学看来，城镇化进程中农村人口空心化内涵有显性结构和隐性结构、良性发展和恶性发展之分。因此，要从根本上解决农村人口空心化问题，必须在发展人类学视域下对现行的农村人口空心化治理方式进行反思，采取城乡二元分析范式，从制度纠偏机制和多中心治理层面提出城镇化过程中农村人口空心化治理模式与政治、经济、社会和文化等制度的实现机制。

【关键词】城镇化；农村空心化；治理模式；实现机制；发展人类学

---

* 基金项目：本文是国家社科基金西部项目"西部新生代农村劳动力开发实证研究"（批准号：12XRK004；主持人：田书芹）和教育部人文社科规划基金项目"西部地区城镇化过程中农村空心化治理模式与实现机制研究"（批准号：13YJA630075；主持人：宋凡金）的阶段成果。

** 1. 田书芹：（1982.7～），女，汉，山东滨州人，西南财经大学公共管理学院在读博士，重庆文理学院经管学院副教授，研究方向为劳动经济学、人力资源管理与开发等；2. 通讯作者：王东强，（1981.11～），男，汉，山东菏泽人，重庆文理学院旅游学院副教授，博士，研究方向为农村人力资源管理与开发等；3. 宋凡金：（1958.12～），男，汉，山东邹城人，重庆文理学院公共管理学院教授，研究方向为公共管理等。

党的十八大报告在论及"三农"问题时指出,"解决好农业农村农民问题是全党工作的重中之重,城乡发展一体化是解决'三农'问题的根本途径"。① 统筹城乡发展,坚持走中国特色新型城镇化道路,是解决"三农"问题的必然选择和有效途径。进入 21 世纪以来,我国已进入快速城镇化阶段,在城乡经济社会发展和农民收入增加的同时,许多农村出现了人口空心化现象,农村人口数量的减少和人口结构的失衡,极大地影响了社会主义新农村建设的进程。在反思农村人口空心化的现实治理路径基础上,我们发现其实现机制,更需要判断、确认和分析城镇化进程中政治、经济、社会和文化等制度与当地农业、农村、农民发展的关联程度,并自下而上地获取关于治理农村人口空心化的知识和经验。因此,要从根本上解决"三农"问题,实现统筹城乡协调发展,必须从发展人类学角度对农村人口空心化治理方式进行反思,采取城乡二元分析范式从制度纠偏机制和多中心治理层面提出城镇化过程中农村人口空心化治理的政治、经济、社会和文化等制度实现机制,从而进一步完善农村人口空心化治理政策体系。

一 农村人口空心化内涵的发展人类学解读

对农村人口空心化概念的界定和内涵的阐释,大多数是从地理学、人口学、经济学和社会学等传统学科进行解读。譬如,钟勇提出农村人口空心化是指随着农村劳动力外流,在农村的留守人口大多是老人、妇女和儿童,即俗称的 703861 部队。曾学龙提出农村人口空心化是指随着农村贫困地区的青壮年劳动力向东南沿海发达地区转移造成了流出地经济萎缩、人才流失和乡村缺乏活力等现象。刘彦随指出农村空心化特征包括农村青壮年劳动力大量外出,留居人口呈老龄化、贫困化趋势,人口、资金等要素流向城市,引起农村经济的衰退和社会结构的变革。对农村人口空心化比较经典的界定是周祝平教授,他在 2008 年撰文指出农村人口空心化是指"农村青壮年劳动

---

① 胡锦涛:《坚定不移沿着中国特色社会主义道路前进 为全面建成小康社会而奋斗——在中国共产党第十八次全国代表大会上的报告》,新华社,2012 年 11 月 8 日。

力大量流入城市，导致农村人口下降和农村青壮年人口比例下降，农村剩下的人口大多数是老人、妇女和儿童"。① 目前，学界对农村人口的空心化还没有一个统一的界定，但是对城镇化过程中的农村人口空心化问题研究，必须回到这样一个主题上来，即"城镇化是谁的城镇化，农村的发展靠谁，统筹城乡发展的目的是为了谁"。因此，基于发展人类学的视角，我们认为，农村人口空心化概念可以这样界定，即在城镇化过程中，随着农村青年劳动力向城镇转移，引起农村人口数量减少和人口结构失衡，进而导致农村人才流失、资金外移、土地抛荒、农业萎缩、基层组织涣散、社会问题重重等一系列问题的一种现象。

第一，从城镇化过程看，农村人口空心化有显性结构和隐性结构之分。根据发展人类学的核心思想，发展就是要以人为本，要注重农村劳动力人力资本的投入，关注职业发展潜力的提升，不能仅仅关注当前人力资源的数量；要关注农村地区的实际情况和村落文化诉求，实现城乡可持续发展。因此，在部分农村地区，农村人口结构呈现显性为主，可能是青壮年农村劳动力大幅度减少，农村留守人口以老年劳动力、女性劳动力和 16 岁非适龄劳动力为主。但也有可能在部分地区，由于当地教育观念受到普遍重视，人力资本投入意识浓厚，学龄儿童和适龄青年劳动力流向城镇的求学人口占了较大比例，或者由于女性主义在当地受到普遍推崇而导致女性劳动力大量外出城镇就业，使得女性劳动力占了较大比例。但这只是农村人口空心化的隐性表现或者特殊情况，并不能否认农村人口空心化的合理性。

第二，从城镇化结果看，农村人口空心化有良性发展和恶性发展之分。在发展人类学看来，城镇化目的的根本意义在于推进城市现代化的进程中保障社会民生，改善人们的生活，提高人们的福利。因此，在城镇化过程中，我们要看农村青年劳动力转移以后农村当地区域的发展情况，如果流出地剩余的农村人口不仅能够维持农村正常的生活和生产，而且土地可以部分集中进行规模经营，提高了农业生产率，那么就没有形成实质意义上的空心化。当然，如果农村人口结构、家庭结构和就业结构等诸多方面发生的改变导致正常的农业生产活动无法维持，农村留守人口的社会照料成为负担，农村社会日

---

① 周祝平：《中国农村人口空心化及其挑战》，《人口研究》2008 年第 2 期。

益分化等一系列问题接踵而至，甚至形成农村劳动力转移——农村经济社会发展滞后——农村劳动力再转移的恶性循环，这才是真正意义上的空心化。

二　国内外城镇化过程中农村人口空心化治理的发展人类学反思

第一，国外发达国家农村人口空心化治理模式比较成熟，渗透了发展人类学的主要思想，积累了丰富的实践经验。譬如，韩国"新村运动"或农村综合开发是以村庄聚落改造载体，实施乡村土地整理、农村环境改造以及农业基础设施建设，并通过农村特产品开发和观光农业项目建设吸引农村劳动力在本地就业和生活。韩国"新村运动"的成功经验渗透了该国政府利用发展人类学知识，通过土地整理、交通建设和农业改革等手段改变农村生产生活环境，增进农民福祉的发展理念。日本在农村人口空心化治理方面则是根据乡村发展实际，实施村庄合并，然后政府提供优质公共服务；遵循文化多元化要求，发展农村休闲文化旅游，开发富有地域特色的土特产品，振兴农村经济，稳定农村社会。显然，日本政府不仅关注农村人口空心化本身，更关注乡村地区发展实际情况，尊重文化多样性，将本土文化与农村空心化治理相联系来破解农村地区的发展问题。英国治理农村人口空心化则是以中心村为重点，调动当地农村居民共同参与改善中心村生产、生活条件，吸引农村居民向中心村集中。英国的经验表明，应用发展人类学的理论与方法，强调农民社区居民的广泛参与，才能使得统筹城乡发展的基本价值，如公平原则、平等原则、民主原则等得以伸张和实现。

第二，国内在农村人口空心化治理方面也进行了理论研究和实践探索。从理论研究看，很多学者主要从经济学、行政学、管理学、地理学等角度提出了农村人口空心化的调控机制。从治理实践来看，不少地区也采取了大力发展乡镇企业和第三产业、统筹推进户籍制度改革、推进土地适度规模化经营、创新农业产业化经营模式、改善农村留守儿童的教育环境、健全农村留守老人的社会保障体系等诸多举措。但这些理论思考和现实策略往往忽视了农村人口空心化是统筹城乡经济社会发展所必然经历的阶段；为改变农村人口空心化的种种问题，一些机构采纳了以城镇化为基础的发展战略，忽略农村本土化战略对发展所起的作用。对于农村人口空心化治理"堵"多"疏"少，头痛医头、脚痛医脚，缺乏对农村人口空心化治理的系统思考和整体规划；农村人口空心化治理举措往往过分强调政府的行政取向，忽视了民生导向、居民参与、权力有效配置和乡村本地发展的实际，无法有效统筹城乡资源机制与管理制度。

实际上，在我国城镇化进程中，由于中国农村发展在长期城乡二元结构背景下的矛盾激化与问题积淀，当前的农村空心化问题要远比其他国家更复杂、更严重。[①] 国内外农村人口空心化治理的鲜明对比表明，第一，城镇化过程直接导致了农村人口空心化问题，破解农村人口空心化带来的种种问题的关键还在于农村居民的发展问题。第二，由于现有的城市化水平对农村人口的吸纳能力是有限的，治理农村人口空心化的根本不是单纯依靠城镇化可以解决的，而是应该立足乡村发展，靠农村自身的发展来解决。第三，我们只有在发展人类学视野下判断、确认和分析城镇化进程中政治、经济、社会和文化等制度与当地农业、农村、农民发展的关联程度，并自下而上地动员农村居民的广泛参与才能获取关于治理农村人口空心化的知识和经验。第四，农村人口空心化治理对策研究不能局限于特定组织范围内，或只是针对某些个体的利益而设计。在城镇化的实践过程中随着社会经济的不断发展，农村人口空心化问题成为多个主体共同的责任，其治理体系更是一个系统的复杂工程。因此必须从发展人类学角度采取城乡二元分析范式，从制度纠偏机制和多中心治理层面提出城镇化进程中农村人口空心化治理的政治、经济、社会和文化等制度实现机制，才能提高农村人口空心化治理的针对性和实效性。

三 发展人类学视域下农村人口空心化治理模式及实现机制

（一）农村人口空心化治理模式

1. 农村城镇化模式

如上所述，城市化不仅对农村劳动力的吸纳能力是有限的，而且单纯的

---

① 刘彦随、刘玉、翟荣新：《中国农村空心化的地理学研究与整治实践》，《地理学报》2009年第10期。

城市化也带来了诸如住房拥挤、交通堵塞、就业冲击和社会治安等种种问题。正如 J. P. 梅森所讲，"都市化在某些情况下是国家发展的关键性因素，但也可能是落后的标志"。① 那么从这个意义上讲，发展城镇绝对不能以荒废农村为代价，不能忽视农村人口对便利生活和安全保障的需求。根据发展人类学的观点，农村人口空心化的一个重要缘由就是城乡之间公共资源供给和配置的巨大差异，只要消除城乡二元结构，农村劳动力转移带来的问题完全可以在农村来解决。因此，推进农村城镇化模式，实施发展干预机制（主要是交通、卫生、信息、安全和社会保障等制度优化设计），使各种要素不断在农村城镇集聚，千方百计保障农村民生，提高农民福利生活水平，才是治理农村人口空心化的根本出路。此模式有三个重要内容：一是要选择人口数量多、规模大、交通便利和硬件基础较好的中心村，以此推进小城镇建设，并不断采取多种措施吸引周围村民来小城镇创业、居住。二是推进城乡一体化制度建设。消除城乡二元制度差别，统一城乡之间的教育、就业、医疗卫生、信息安全和社会保障等制度，真正实现农村留守人口"少有所教、壮有所用、老有所养、病有所医、贫有所保"。三是完善农村基础设施和公共服务平台建设。推进农村城镇化模式，各级政府以投资、贴息和补助等方式，加大资金投入用于小城镇特别是中心建制镇的交通、体育健身、供水供电、公共文化等公用基础设施建设，并完善就业、医疗、教育、电子政务等公共服务平台，硬件和软件相结合不断吸引更多的农村居民进入小城镇。在农村城镇化过程中，只有农村城镇与大中城市共同消弭城乡二元结构，推进城乡经济社会文化和生态共同持续协调发展，真正实现城乡一体化，才能逐步形成人口聚集、产业发展、市场扩大的良性互动机制，增强小城镇吸纳农村人口、带动农村发展的能力，进而从根本上治理农村人口空心化带来的弊病。

2. 本土化就地转移模式

早在 20 世纪 60 年代末 70 年代初，美国发展经济学家托达罗通过模型建构提出，城乡间预期收入的差异是决定农村劳动力迁移的重要原因。从这

---

① J. P. 梅森著，祝华译《世界快速都市化中的发展人类学》，《国外社会科学》1992 年第 3 期。

个意义上讲，城乡收入差距是造成农村劳动力向城镇流动进而产生农村人口空心化的重要促发因素。基于此，我们是否可以得出这样的结论，只要增加农村青年劳动力在当地就业的收入水平，不断减少社会生活成本和在城市就业的机会成本，那么就可以促使农村青年劳动力更加关注农村社会建设与农业发展，破解照料农村留守老人和儿童的后顾之忧。根据发展人类学观点，我们可以立足于农村发展实际情况，推进本土化就地转移模式，充分利用现有资源，倡导农村劳动力的内部消化和就地转移，实地解决或缓解发展项目中因人口结构失衡或者人口断裂所引起的社会、政治和经济问题，探索利用本土特色提高发展项目实施效果的可能性。[①] 此模式主要包括三个内容：一是当地政府结合本地经济发展战略制定农村人力资源可持续开发战略，有计划、有步骤地实施人力资源开发策略，对当地农民进行各种技能培训，提高农村劳动力的整体素质。二是农村劳动力开发与本地区特定的自然资源、经济资源，尤其是农业产业特色相结合，革新转移就业理念，利用特定的本土资源，以市场为导向，发展特色农业，根据特色农业需要的技能，对当地农民进行培训，形成本土化人才。三是利用特色农业和高素质的本土人才倡导农村劳动力在当地就业和内部消化。通过制定和实施优惠的农村实用人才激励政策，减少或避免人才闲置和人才浪费，真正把农村人力资源开发与当地特色资源紧密结合起来，打造农村人才聚集和发展的平台，吸引部分高层次人才，留住现有的人才，培养新型乡土人才，并在此基础上进行合理的农村劳动力内部配置，有效地推动当地农村经济的发展，进而解决农村人口空心化问题。

3. 农村社区化模式

随着农村劳动力大量向城市转移，一方面村民之间、村民与村之间的关系越来越淡漠，加之村委会基层组织的涣散导致农村内部凝聚力降低，农村发展进一步失去了活力。另一方面，分散的村落空间布局和传统一家一户的土地经营模式制约了农村经济的进一步发展。结果，农村土地抛荒、农业萎缩、留守人口养老、医疗、教育、社会问题等一系列问题出现也就成为必然。发展人类学主张，采取一种积极参与与介入的态度来实现农村参与式发

---

① 杨小柳：《发展研究：人类学的历程》，《社会学研究》2007 年第 4 期。

展。"一些地方发展项目采用了参与和赋权这两种理论和方法，结果表明当社区和社区成员参与发展项目的计划和决策过程、被授权管理和控制他们自己的资源和未来时，平等发展最有可能实现。"① 借鉴这一思想，我们可以通过整合村庄扩大规模，建立农村社区，健全农村社区基层组织，强化城乡公共服务均等化，从而破除城乡二元结构，加快城乡一体化发展，创新农村人口空心化治理模式。农村社区化模式主要包括三个方面的内容：一是并村构建新型农村社区。根据发展人类学的观点，发展要遵循农村本土文化的多样性。因此，推行村庄合并，要充分考虑村庄现有规模和发展水平，又要充分考虑地缘关系、历史沿革、风俗习惯、自然条件等因素。山东德州在农村社区化过程中坚持因村制宜、分类指导，探索出 7 种合并模式，即农村社区整合型、城中村改造聚合型、强村带动型、产业联结型、自然村恢复型、邻近村合并型和村企结合型。② 二是健全农村社区理事会。坚持发展人类学所主张的参与原则，吸纳党员、团员、产业大户和经营能人共同组建农村社区理事会；明确社区理事会赋权原则、议事规则和决策程序，完善理事会的分工负责制度、集中办公制度、党组织生活制度、村务公开制度、民主评议制度，充分发挥农村理事会在凝心聚气、资源整合、互帮互助、信息沟通等方面的社区领导作用，为实现社区发展、解决农村人口空心化问题提供了组织保障。三是强化城乡公共服务均等化。以农村社区为轴心，合理布局农村产业结构，将水、电、气、暖基础设施和生活购物、医疗教育等服务设施全部纳入农村社区规划，强化农村社区的凝聚作用。同步推进城乡就业、医疗、健身、文化、娱乐服务设施建设，增强社区服务和社会保障功能。农村社区化模式不仅节约了土地等资源，为推进土地规模化经营，实现农业的专业化、产业化、机械化提供了空间，而且强化了社区公共服务能力，提高了社区的承载力和吸引力，探索出了一条农村人口空心化治理的新路子。

---

① Peter D. Little, 2005, "Anthropology and Development", in Satish Kedia and John Van Willigen (eds.) *Applied Anthropology*: *Domains of Application*, Westport, CT,: praeger, 转引自陈刚《发展人类学视野中的文化生态旅游开发》，《广西民族研究》2009 年第 3 期。

② 德州市委组织部：《农村社区化建设的"德州模式"》，http://www.dzdj.gov.cn/n852217/n85228，最后访问日期：2010 年 12 月 13 日。

（二）农村人口空心化治理的实现机制

根据发展人类学的核心思想和主要观点，创新农村人口空心化治理模式确实可以为破解"三农"问题提供可行的路径选择。但要真正实现统筹城乡协调发展，必须在发展人类学视域下采取城乡二元分析范式，从制度纠偏机制和多中心治理层面，探讨城镇化过程中农村人口空心化治理的政治、经济、社会和文化等制度的实现机制。

1. 乡土文化诉求实现机制

发展人类学强调尊重乡土文化的多样性，认为只有尊重某一个特定地区历史所形成的社会文化知识，才有可能实现农村的可持续发展。正如Agrawal 所说："乡土知识是独立的、具有显著的地域特色、存在于其持有人的生活之中，因此尝试归纳出其本质、隔离、归档、转化将是一件很困难的事情。"① 在治理农村人口空心化的过程中，我们必须完善乡土文化诉求实现机制，因为其反映了当地人的要求，并存在于当地人的生活中。一是要树立尊重乡土文化的意识。面对城镇化过程中农村乡土文化边缘化的趋势，我们必须重新认识乡土文化在维持自然生态系统平衡和地方可持续发展等方面的作用和地位。二是实现农村人口生育的灵活变通机制。譬如，在城镇化过程中，边远山区、民族地区、贫困地区大量农村劳动力转移使得老年人口缺乏照料，同时农村人口计划生育政策的长期执行，使得独生子女将无力很好地照料留守老人。因此，尊重这些地区多子多福的生育文化观念，当地农村人口生育政策可以适当调整为"提倡一胎，允许二胎，杜绝三胎"，从而解决农村人口数量减少和留守老人照料等问题。三是健全农民工回乡创业机制。为了实现外出农民工的"恋乡"情怀，可以从政策扶持机制、人力资本投入机制、立体化培训机制、资源整合机制等方面鼓励农民工回乡创业，提升农民工返乡创业能力，不仅有利于解决农村富余劳动力就业难的问题，解决留守老人、农村留守儿童等问题，为新农村建设提供了必要的人才支持，还有利于农村产业结构的调整，促进城乡统筹发展。

---

① 刘金龙：《发展人类学视角中的传统知识及其对发展实践的启示》，《中国农业大学学报（社会科学版）》2007 年第 2 期。

2. 自下而上参与式社会发展机制

在发展人类学看来，发展城镇化的目的不是掠夺农村土地资源或者占领农村广阔的市场，而是为了帮助农村地区的人们摆脱贫困，提高农村居民的生活水平。因此，在城镇化过程中，尤其是在统筹城乡权力资源、土地资源、人力资源的过程中和推进农村城镇化模式、本土化转移就业模式和农村社区化模式方面，一定充分考虑当地的自身资源和传统文化，倡导自下而上的参与式社会发展机制。一是赋权模式和参与机制。赋权是发展人类学研究发展的重要理论与方法，农村人口空心化治理就是要通过制度设计而实现农村权利让渡和转移，同时又通过农村居民的参与权力和监督权力，最终回归和服务于农村居民的权利。赋权与社区参与概念相连接，真正的社区参与实践至少要具备下列特征：详细透明的决策过程；高比例的社区居民参与率；高程度的有意义的当地参与；公平和有效的程序；高程度的当地所有权和管理权。① 统筹城乡发展的实践证明，农村本身的发展必须要充分进行社会动员，通过自下而上的方式让当地农村居民积极参与。譬如，小城镇规划、中心村规划和社区规划，都要进行大力社会宣传，尊重居民的知情权和参与权，动员当地农村居民参与区域交通、住房、旅游、教育、医疗等规划和决策的制定过程，依据公平合理的程序，广泛听取他们的想法和对规划建设的态度，做好论证和反馈工作，把好的建设性意见反映在规划中。同时在规划决策和规划执行过程中，充分吸纳农村居民参与，让他们具有真正的决策权和监管权，从而减少他们对各类规划的反感情绪，保障规划的正确和顺利实施。二是农村人口空心化多中心治理机制。农村人口空心化是一个复杂问题，牵涉政府、企业、社区、居民的多方利益关系，其治理离不开各种利益相关者的全面投入或参与。农村人口空心化多中心治理机制有以下四个特征：治理不是一整套规则，也不是一种活动，而是一个过程；治理过程的基础不是控制，而是协调；治理既涉及公共部门，也包括私人部门；治理不是一种正式的制度，而是持续的互动。② 结合城镇化过程的具体实践，农村人

---

① Peter D. Little, 2005, "Anthropology and Development", in Satish Kedia and John Van Willigen (eds.) *Applied Anthropology: Domains of Application*, Westport, CT,: praeger, 转引自陈刚《发展人类学视野中的文化生态旅游开发》，《广西民族研究》2009 年第 3 期。

② 岳春宇：《如何理解全球治理理论中的"治理"》，《河北省社会主义学院学报》2008 年第 1 期。

口空心化治理应该从政府、居民、企业、社区组织及其他社会组织等不同主体的关联性入手，探寻农村人口空心化多中心治理机制，从而切实保证农村人口空心化治理的实效性，提高城乡经济社会发展统筹水平。

3. 统筹城乡政治经济制度纠偏机制

发展人类学沿革至今，一直强调人类在发展中处于中心地位，包括发展的目的是实现人类的全面发展，发展的方式要注重居民全面参与。同时主张要尊重地区的多元文化和发展实际，反对在发展实践和研究中把当地的普通人民及其文化边缘化。在城镇化过程中，户籍制度改革是一个改变城乡二元结构的重要突破口，其不仅是一个涉及土地调整、资源配置的经济问题，更是一个涉及身份变革和社会稳定的政治问题。但在统筹城乡实践中，我们在户籍制度改革过程中出现了强迫转户、一哄而上、一转了之、照抄照搬等诸多偏差，使得农村人口空心化问题日益严重。因此借鉴发展人类学理论和方法，必须对户籍制度改革进行纠偏。一是因地制宜、坚持自愿、循序渐进推进户籍制度改革。国务院办公厅 2012 年 2 月下发的《国务院办公厅关于积极稳妥推进户籍管理制度改革的通知》明确指出部分地方户改的乱象，"有的地方不顾当地经济社会发展实际情况，片面追求城镇规模城镇化速度；有的地方不分城市类别不顾城市综合承载能力，一味放宽落户城市的条件；有的地方擅自突破国家政策，损害群众切身利益"。[①] 因此，户籍制度改革必须根据各地实际情况，充分考虑本地的城市公共资源规模和结构，合理衡量城市综合承载能力；完全尊重农民本人的意愿，不得强制或变相强制收回宅基地和承包的耕地、林地、草地；循序渐进推进户籍制度改革，逐步推开居住证制度和放宽落户标准，明确农民城镇落户后获得权益的内容及先后次序。二是抓住户籍制度的根本，统筹户籍制度改革配套措施。户籍改革的根本就是必须剥除掉户籍之上的利益依附关系，将户籍制度管理回归其社会性职能，因此应将户籍制度由户籍管理向身份管理转变。同时要统筹户籍制度改革配套措施，首先是在国家立法层面应尽快出台户籍法及相关配套立法，

---

① 国务院办公厅：《国务院办公厅关于积极稳妥推进户籍管理制度改革的通知》，国办发〔2011〕9 号，http://www.gov.cn/zwgk/2012 – 02/23/content_ 2075082.htm，最后访问日期：2012 年 4 月 23 日。

以保障公民迁移自由并明确户籍转变的程序、权利、义务等具体内容。其次是完善政府政绩绿色评价机制，减少经济建设在政绩考核中的比重，强化社会公平类、环境保护类、民生保障类指标考核。再者是完善城乡社会保障制度。加大中央财政转移支付力度，把农民、农民工、城镇职工和城市市民等社保政策对象纳入统一财政支付体系建设，推进社会保障制度在区域之间的有效衔接。

参考文献

胡锦涛：《坚定不移沿着中国特色社会主义道路前进　为全面建成小康社会而奋斗——在中国共产党第十八次全国代表大会上的报告》，新华社，2012 年 11 月 8 日。

刘金龙：《发展人类学视角中的传统知识及其对发展实践的启示》，《中国农业大学学报（社会科学版）》2007 年第 2 期。

刘彦随、刘玉、翟荣新：《中国农村空心化的地理学研究与整治实践》，《地理学报》2009 年第 10 期。

杨小柳：《发展研究：人类学的历程》，《社会学研究》2007 年第 4 期。

岳春宇：《如何理解全球治理理论中的"治理"》，《河北省社会主义学院学报》2008 年第 1 期。

周祝平：《中国农村人口空心化及其挑战》，《人口研究》2008 年第 2 期。

J. P. 梅森著，祝华译《世界快速都市化中的发展人类学》，《国外社会科学》1992 年第 3 期。

论行政自由裁量权的合理使用

——以北京地税王纪平落马案为例分析

欧纯智*

【摘要】 尽管当今征管机制被赋予了必要的自由裁量权，但是该权利一直被滥用，对税务行政自由裁量的使用及存废争议极大。本文以北京市地税局原局长王纪平贪腐落马为例，分析并肯定了公务人员应该拥有必要的自由裁量权，强调了行政裁量权的责任，呼唤建立必要的纳税人监督机制和参与机制。

【关键词】 自由裁量；滥用；公共行政精神；纳税人参与

一　导言

税务部门扮演的角色、自由裁量的范围及对纳税人的影响一直是舆论关注的焦点。税务执法人员在日常执法活动中"收"与"不收"、"罚"与"不罚"、"作为"与"不作为"之间的弹性调节范围极大，也就是我们常说的税收自由裁量，而这正是企业争相贿赂税务执法人员的最重要原因。近来，无论媒体还是学界，对"行政自由裁量"呈一边倒的批判态度，似乎官员渎职和行政权的滥用都是"行政自由裁量"惹的祸。面对这种情况，

---

* 欧纯智：中国人民大学博士生。

政策制定者们一直试图寻求变革，以削减税收执法者的决策空间。甚至有学者提出严格控权的主张，收回执法人员的自由裁量权。这种对"自由裁量权"的误解或偏见与现代国家对公共行政的要求是相悖的。① 还有一些研究者认为，一定程度的自由裁量权是可以接受的，② 如果这种自由裁量权不够合意，就应该设法为纳税人提供公平、有效的政府服务。③ 纵观我国现行税收法律，只有较少的税种有独立的法律，增值税作为我国最大的财政收入来源，至今还是以《中华人民共和国增值税暂行条例》示人。由于征纳的权利和义务没有被清晰界定，导致纳税人和税务机关呈现不平等的关系，纳税人缺乏足够的法律武器保护自己，税收机关的自由裁量权被滥用，以致为国聚财的光荣事业陷入正义危机。但是，法律制度的缺位并不是执法者侵占纳税人利益的理由，法律制度的缺位是自由裁量滥用的必要而非充分条件，法律制度之外仍有很多因素制约执法者对自由裁量的使用。可以肯定的是，适当的税收自由裁量是必要的、不可或缺的，简单武断地取消税务机关执法人员的自由裁量权无异于因噎废食。

二　研究问题

关于行政自由裁量权（Discretion）的定义有很多种，《布莱克维尔政治学百科全书》是这样定义的：当政府官员要贯彻法律时，他具有在各种方案之间进行选择的自由。④ Henry Campbell Blak 将其定义为"法官和公务人员享有的，在他们认为适合的情况下作为或不作为的选择权"。⑤ 他作为人类的意识和行为方式受个人价值取向、判断能力和道德的影响。中国学者王

① 杨建顺：《应以"行政裁量"取代"行政自由裁量"》，《北京日报》2007 年 8 月 16 日第 18 版。
② 〔美〕乔治·弗雷德里克森、张成福等：《公共行政的精神》，中国人民大学出版社，2003，第 91 页。
③ Moore, S. T, "The Theory of Street‒Level Bureaucracy", *Administration & Society* 19（1987）: 74‒94.
④ 〔美〕戴维·米勒、韦农·波格丹诺、邓正来主编《布莱克维尔政治学百科全书》，中国政法大学出版社，2002，第 216 页。
⑤ Henry Campbell Blak, *Black's Law Dictionary*（6 edition）, St. Paul, Minn. West Publishing Co 1990: 476.

名扬①、余凌云②将其定义为："自由裁量是指行政机关对于所作出的决定具有很大的自由。"因此，国家权力在具体实践当中经过自由裁量的演绎或多或少会带有人治及特权的色彩。从学理的传统来讲，当今执法人员的行为模式有别于韦伯的传统理性官僚模型，然而，自由裁量也可以被视为必要的创新、战略思维、灵活性的理性回应。③ 为了避免基层人员的无所适从，基层部门应该尽量减少专业性较强的工作的复杂程度及不必要的歧义，复杂和歧义往往是导致自由裁量的隐患。执法人员拥有了解基层具体情况及公众需求的优势，他们据此解释法规并因地制宜地作出决定。由此可见，自由裁量是必不可少并且可以得到有效控制的。

官员滥用自由裁量权绝不仅仅出现在税务部门，也并不是只出现在税务行政审批环节，只不过在该环节自由裁量滥用问题比较突出而已。行政审批衍生出的行政垄断，人为地阻止其他竞争者的进入，并以此获得更多的优惠，这时行政审批的结果就是造成更大的资源浪费，造成低效率，④而行政垄断与自由裁量滥用从来都是相伴而生的。新中国成立以来，法律、法规、规章制度随着政治经济改革正逐步趋于完善，然而，令人遗憾的是，贪腐官员的数量、贪腐的金额、贪腐的形式、贪腐给国家造成的损失呈逐年上升的趋势。在我国社会主义经济建设过程中，尤其是1978年改革开放以后，我们取得了巨大的成绩，社会稳定，人民安康，但也有那么一些害群之马，道德堕落，贪腐成性。腐败在我们今天最突出的表现形式是贿赂犯罪，如图1、图2所示。⑤ 而今，日益猖獗的贪污贿赂犯罪不仅严重地阻碍了中国经济的发展，而且还从某种程度上削弱了党和政府的威信与公信力。

我们看到，我国官员贪腐数额及人数在2002年开始回落，而2002年正是我国进行行政审批制度改革的初始之年，行政审批制度改革限制了执法人

① 王名扬：《美国行政法》，中国法治出版社，1995，第545页。

② 余凌云：《行政自由裁量论》，中国人民公安大学出版社，2005，第23~38页。

③ Maupin, J. R., "Control, Effciency, and the Street – Level Bureaucrat", *Journal of Public Administration Research and Theory* 3 (1993):335 – 357.

④ 唐兴霖：《国家与社会之间》，社会科学文献出版社，2013，第39页。

⑤ 图1、图2的数据来源：杨灿明、赵福军《行政腐败的宏观经济学分析》，《经济研究》2004年第9期。

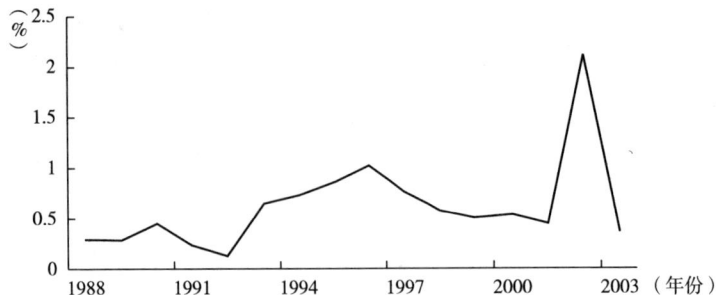

图 1　受贿金额占 GDP 比例

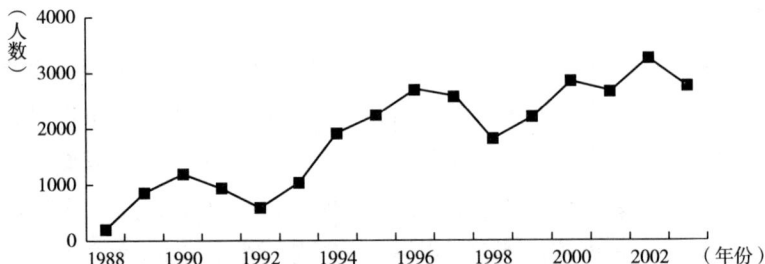

图 2　中国县处级以上受贿人数

数据来源：杨灿明、赵福军《行政腐败的宏观经济学分析》，《经济研究》2004 年第 9 期。

员的自由裁量滥用，从而遏制了执法人员贪腐，行政审批制度改革初见成效。

三　税收执法自由裁量滥用的案例白描

北京地税局原局长王纪平落马案，反映了税务执法人员在行使自由裁量权的时候，突破道德底线和法律界限，将手中的自由裁量权当成自由执法权，在面对利益诱惑的时候倒向了金钱的怀抱。[①]

继北京市原副巡视员任依娜、市地税票证中心原主任刁维列、市地税计财处原副处长彭英斌落马后，2001 年 9 月，王纪平到市地税局担任局长后，着手倡导税控机改革，将手写发票升级为机打发票，大力推动税务系统信息

---

① 孙思娅、王鹏昊：《北京地税局长贪污千万被诉，部下情妇举报落马》，《京华时报》，http://news.qq.com/a/20111010/000070.htm，最后访问时间：2011 年 12 月 20 日。

化进程，更好地防止偷税漏税。这原本是件好事，但是，王纪平也在利用税控机的招投标，以权谋私。他插手税控机的生产商、销售商及税务代理商的选定事宜，左右招投标结果，令与其关联的公司中标。据检方指控，王纪平的贪污发生在 2002 年至 2004 年 10 月，当时正值北京市地方税务局向浪潮电子信息产业股份有限公司购买税控机期间，这是北京市首次推行税控机，浪潮公司是 6 家中标的生产商之一。由王纪平授意促成钰林天元公司成为浪潮电子信息产业公司授权的唯一税控机经销商，钰林天元公司的法人代表是赵耘，曾是王纪平的情妇。检方称，王纪平还促成市地税局信息中心与北京钰林天元科贸有限公司共同出资，成立了北京恒信恒安科技有限责任公司，并逐步将此公司交由赵耘实际控制。北京恒信恒安公司成立于 2002 年 6 月，注册资金 100 万元，市地税局信息中心原主任杨玉杰为该公司的首任法人代表。2004 年 10 月，该信息中心将北京恒信恒安公司的所有股权转让给钰林公司。此后，钰林公司又将北京恒信恒安公司的 80 万元资产转让给赵耘，法人代表也随之变更为赵耘。检方指控，此后税控密码器唯一经销商——钰林公司将税控密码器加价后出售给北京恒信恒安公司，从而使得王纪平和赵耘将加价款 1047 万余元非法占有。据了解，北京钰林天元科贸有限公司代理税控密码机的销售后，2002 年和 2003 年的营业额分别是 2613.37 万元和 3101.44 万元。而北京恒信恒安公司建立之初，该公司即中标市地方税务局的安全外包业务。所谓"安全外包"，是负责安装税控机的安全卡（也叫密码器）。因为税控机在最初买来后，并不能直接投入使用。在使用前，必须先行安装一部密码器，北京恒信恒安公司承担的安全外包服务业务，一方面是安装这些密码器，另一方面是负责解锁，如果由于误操作导致税控机上锁，必须要到北京恒信恒安公司解锁。承揽此项业务，使得北京恒信恒安公司从 2003 年起，每年的营业额均超过 2000 万元。

据指控，2002 年至 2009 年，王纪平单独或伙同其亲属，利用担任市地税局局长之便，为他人在工程承揽、产品采购、工作调动等方面提供帮助，先后多次收受山东浪潮商用系统公司及创意未来建筑装饰设计工程有限公司负责人钟小春等单位及个人的款物共计价值 435 万余元。市地税局原党组书记兼局长王纪平因涉嫌贪污 1047 万元、受贿 435 万元被查处。

我们知道，在王纪平推行税控密码器的年代，使用税控机器是税务行政审批准入的必备条件。王纪平作为北京市地税一把手凭借职务特权,在缺乏有效监管的情况下,巧妙地把税控密码器绑定到税控机上,搭着金税工程的班车大肆敛财。王纪平利用手中的权力乱作为,将自己实际控制的税控密码器强行绑定到税务行政审批当中。

四　行政自由裁量之争

自由裁量在一定程度上滋生腐败这一不争的事实一直以来广受诟病。众所周知,税收执法人员游走在法律、道德的边缘而能独善其身的不二法宝正是税收自由裁量权。令人遗憾的是,自由裁量是如此不受欢迎,却一直如影随形相伴在我们的生活左右,甚至古希腊先哲亚里士多德在强调依法统治的同时,也不得不承认自由裁量的必要。[①] 在日常的征管实践当中,有时为了填补政策的空白,有时是因为碰到需要专业解读的特殊政策,税收执法人员被赋予一定的行政裁量自主权,这样可以根据具体情况酌情决定如何执行税法。但令人遗憾的是,自由裁量在实践中还是被"自由"使用得过了头。

(一) 行政自由裁量权的正义之争

一切有权力的人都会滥用权力,这是亘古不变的真理,[②] 无限的自由裁量权比起其他统治手段对正义更加具有残酷的破坏性。[③] 从权力的本质分析,只有当执法人员做到"权尽其用"的时候,他才会善罢甘休,[④] 税收的强制性使其具有行政专断的趋势,自由裁量的问题比其他领域更为凸显。因为自由裁量导致的腐败使得政策制定部门痛下决心缩小自由裁量的范围,然而这并不是有效减少公务人员贪污腐败的灵丹妙药。权衡取舍"自由裁量"与"贪腐",对立法者来说充满了挑战。因为价值观的差异,税务执法人员可能就"是什么"和"应该是什么"存有较大分歧。所以说,自由裁量从来都不是单纯的制度问题。

---

① 〔古希腊〕亚里士多德:《政治学》,商务印书馆,1964,第168~171页。
② 〔法〕孟德斯鸠:《论法的精神》(上册),商务印书馆,1997,第4页。
③ 〔美〕伯纳德·施瓦茨:《行政法》,群众出版社,1986,第567页。
④ 〔英〕哈耶克:《自由秩序原理》,三联书店,1997,第72页。

行政自由裁量最早可以追溯到古希腊的柏拉图与亚里士多德。两位先哲对自由裁量持对立的观点，柏拉图不赞成行政自由裁量，而他的学生亚里士多德赞成行政自由裁量。要探讨自由裁量，首先要从二者的正义观谈起。

经济和效率的提法无疑是柏拉图的无奈之举，对付专治、腐败、低效政府的最直接办法就是建立一个关心效率和经济的管理型政府。然而，经济和效率不是万能的灵药，不能涵盖公共行政的所有诉求。由于每个人所处的社会地位不同，经济状况不同，如果不遵循社会公平的理念，不考虑政策实施的分配效果，不给予公务人员一定的自由裁量以纠正法律的普遍性所带来的不公正，公共行政可能就会忽视公民的合法利益。

行政自由裁量之柏拉图与亚里士多德的正义之争

	柏拉图《理想国》①	亚里士多德《尼各马科伦理学》②
正义观	国家中每一阶层都应该各司职、人尽其才、不相僭越	公正是一切德性的总汇，公正自身是一种完全的德性
正义的划分	将正义分为两类：个人正义和城邦正义	将正义分为三种：分配正义、矫正正义和交易正义
统治	人类只能最大限度地接近正义，不可能实现完全正义	不主张个人的宰治，而是允许法律的宰治
行政自由裁量权的存废观点及原因	并不需要行政自由裁量权 公务人员能够中立地使用法律	需要行政自由裁量权
公务人员	公务人员简单明确地使用法律；将"正义"作为解释法律的标准是凡人不具备的能力，公务人员亦是凡人	公务人员在使用法律的过程中阐释法律；有一点值得注意，阐释法律如果不考虑公平，就会导致非正义
理论与实践	重视理论	重视实践
公务人员应遵循的价值	公务人员应当遵循制定的法律，做到一视同仁；他们所需要的指导原则仅仅是中立、效率和经济原则	公务人员应当遵循公平原则；强调公务人员对公众的责任，避免中立；公平优于合理合法

① 〔古希腊〕柏拉图：《理想国》，光明日报出版社，2006，第139~163页。
② 〔古希腊〕亚里士多德：《尼各马科伦理学》，中国人民大学出版社，2003，第92~117页。

从上表我们看到，柏拉图倾向于公务人员应当简单地按照其字面含义解释法律，亚里士多德则倾向于公务人员应当依照法律的精神和公平来解释法律。如果柏拉图是正确的，一旦公务人员突破法律的界限来解释法律，我们可以拿出什么样的公认标准来限制公务人员的行为？如果亚里士多德是对的，那么又由谁来制定公正的标准，所制定的标准不具有普适性怎么办？① 这些问题正是现代国家基层官僚使用自由裁量权所面临的问题。

王纪平案折射出的表面问题看起来似乎是权力不受监控、权力过大、"自由"得过头，似乎应该减小，甚至应该取消自由裁量权。然而，问题的关键并不在于自由裁量的存废或是大小。一个缺乏行政责任的公务人员即使拥有再小的自由裁量权力，如果其权力不能得到有效控制，他还是会"自由"而不受约束地使用裁量权。

（二）行政自由裁量的责任之争

税务机关工作人员除了自然人的天然属性以外，还有其特殊的社会属性——税务机关的代理人。如果说，为了维持人类和平的秩序，先哲们提出对人类的天性自由加以束缚的话，那么，没有道理不对这些税务干部的天性给予后天的校正。王纪平因个人利益而背叛了国家利益，在他的各项犯罪活动中，可能所用的方式不同，造成的影响不同，但是，最终都是滥用国家赋予其的权力，将敛财的具体事宜强行嫁接到税务行政审批当中，官商勾结并最终走上不归的道路。

行政国家的出现，使公共行政缺乏相应的责任保障机制的问题在实践中暴露出来，当执法人员拥有自由裁量的权力却不必承担相应的责任时，就将整个国家拖入失控的境地。当权力与责任的关系出现失衡的时候，如果我们要保存权力，就应当加强责任追究，从而使掌握裁量权的行政官员能够负责任地行使手中的权力。

那么，对行使自由裁量权的公务人员来说，怎样才算是负责任的行使了

---

① 〔美〕乔治·弗雷德里克森，张成福等：《公共行政的精神》，中国人民大学出版社，2003，第 91 页。

裁量权呢？盐野宏[①]是从司法审查的角度来理解裁量问题的。他认为裁量问题涉及事实认定、要件认定、行为选择三个方面。他在承认裁量的合理性的同时认为存在着"裁量领域扩张"的趋势，表现在程序选择和时间选择阶段。在对行政自由裁量权的控制方面，除了法院对"裁量权之逸脱与滥用的统治"以外，还存在着"程序的统治"，他强调了行政裁量的法律责任。高斯和弗雷德里克森认为行政官员需要承担两种责任，一种是技术责任，一种是政治责任。技术责任反映的是公务人员赖以生存的客观条件，公务人员必须具备一定的专业技能为公众服务。政治责任是一种主观责任，政治上再忠诚也不能转化为专业上的胜任，二者对技术责任给予了更高的肯定。芬纳认为对公务人员的控制应该从两个方面着手，一个是外部控制，一个是内部控制。来自立法机构的外部控制是一种政治责任，而来自内心的是道德控制，是道德责任。[②]

这样一来，我们至少有四个责任维度来看待行政自由裁量：法律维度、技术维度、政治维度和道德维度。实际上，我们不能简单地说哪一种责任维度更重要，它们因具体情况的不同而调整顺序：当公众对程序正当有更高需求的时候，法律责任是首要责任；当社会对行政效率有更高需求的时候，技术责任就被排在了前面；当公众对社会正义有更高需求的时候，政治责任就是最重要的参考维度；道德是当事人的良心，没有道德就没有真正的内心愧疚。

王纪平贪腐落马案给我们以深刻的启示，行使公共权力的公务人员应该具有行政责任，如果他在上述落马的案件中能够遵守工作程序，具备其职位所要求的综合工作能力，能够以正常的心态利用手中的权力，公正无私地做好本职工作，并且每件工作都可以回应良心的拷问，那么王纪平永远都会是人民的好公仆。

五　建立健全税收自由裁量权的正确行使机制

纳税人监督是税务行政机关外部监督的一种主要形式，然而，纳税人监

---

① 〔日〕盐野宏：《行政法》，月旦出版股份有限公司，1996，第111页。
② 张康之，张乾友：《公共行政的概念》，中国社会科学出版社，2013，第197页。

督的功能至今尚未得到充分发挥。为此，需要进一步完善纳税人监督机制。此外，在很大程度上，可以将更多的纳税人参与吸收到税收立法与执法的过程中。这样，纳税人参与的合法性会进一步提升税收自由裁量的正确使用水平，使征纳双方的权力和义务更对等。征管体制的有效运作需要纳税人的支持与配合。成熟而广泛的纳税人参与不仅可以丰富、充实征管体制的内涵，强化征税机关的公共责任，而且还可以提升纳税服务的品质，推进并保证公共利益的实现。纳税人参与是纳税人权利的运用，是一种权利的再分配，使目前在征管体制、税收优惠、减免退税等活动中尚无法发出声音的纳税人，其意愿在未来能有计划地被政策制定者列入考虑的范围。纳税人参与是在税制的执行和管理方面，税务机关可以更快、更好地回应纳税人的需求，并使纳税人能以更直接的方式参与征纳事务。因此，纳税人参与就是纳税人通过一定的参与渠道，参与或影响税务机关税收政策或征管机制的行动过程。我国的纳税人监督、参与也将是一个持续、渐进的过程，最终将能真正制约税务机关的执法行为，限制执法人员的自由裁量滥用。

六 结论

在中国社会经历经济转型的今天，法律、法规的不健全造成的制度漏洞使这些手握重权的公务人员有了可乘之机，然而最为重要的是他们至今没有正确认识权力及权力的来源与运用，"官本位"的思想根植于个人价值观。自由裁量是公务人员不可或缺的管理工具，然而在执法人员不能担负起相应的行政责任以前，对行政自由裁量的监督和纳税人的有效参与还是必要的。

参考文献

哈耶克：《自由秩序原理》，三联书店，1997，第72页。

柏拉图：《理想国》，光明日报出版社，2006，第139~163页。

伯纳德·施瓦茨：《行政法》，群众出版社，1986，第567页。

戴维·米勒、韦农·波格丹诺、邓正来主编《布莱克维尔政治学百科全书》，中国政法大学出版社，2002，第216页。

孟德斯鸠：《论法的精神》（上册），商务印书馆，1997，第 4 页。

乔治·弗雷德里克森：《公共行政的精神》，中国人民大学出版社，2003，第 91 页。

唐兴霖：《国家与社会之间》，社会科学文献出版社，2013，第 39 页。

王名扬：《美国行政法》，中国法治出版社，1995，第 545 页。

亚里士多德：《尼各马科伦理学》，中国人民大学出版社，2003，第 92~117 页。

亚里士多德：《政治学》，商务印书馆，1964，第 168~171 页。

盐野宏：《行政法》，月旦出版股份有限公司，1996，第 111 页。

杨建顺：《应以"行政裁量"取代"行政自由裁量"》，《北京日报》2007 年 8 月 16 日第 18 版。

余凌云：《行政自由裁量论》，中国人民公安大学出版社，2005，第 23~38 页。

张康之、张乾友：《公共行政的概念》，中国社会科学出版社，2013，第 197 页。

Henry Campbell Blak, *Black's Law Dictionary* (6th edition), St. Paul, Minn. West Publishing Co (1990)：476.

Maupin, J. R. , "Control, Effciency, and the Street – Level bureaucrat", *Journal of Public Administration Research and Theory* 3 (1993)：335 – 357.

Moore, S. T. , "The Theory of Street – Level Bureaucracy", *Administration & Society* 19 (1987)：74 – 94.

患者权利保障实证研究

章　群　黄　文[*]

【摘要】在现代社会，伴随着患者自主决定权意识的不断增强，患者越来越多地要求参与到医疗过程中，患者的医疗权利也随之不断地发展。本文从医患关系入手，分析了我国患者权利保护的历史发展和现有法律规定，在此基础上针对成都市某医院的患者进行了问卷调查，对患者权利保护制度的运行状况和现有问题进行分析，就进一步完善我国患者权利保护的重点进行了探讨。

【关键词】医患关系；患者权利；患者权利保护

现代社会，保护患者权利成为全世界共同的主题，其法理在于生命权是一切权利的基础，是人最基本的权利。患者权利涉及不同的领域，如社会学、医学、法学等学科中都有关于患者权利的界定，其中法学分支学科中宪法、民法等不同位阶的法律也从不同的角度对患者权利予以规定。

在现实的医患关系中，患者权利的应然与实然状态差距过大。现代社会太过重视医学技术的发展，以致忽视了对医学伦理的提升和强化，在医疗活动中，出现了大量侵犯患者权利的事情，医患冲突伴随着医疗技术的进步在

---

　*　章群：女，教授、博士生导师，西南财经大学公共管理学院党总支书记。黄文：男，西南财经大学法学院博士研究生。

逐步升级。

一是伴随医事法律、特别是医疗事故损害赔偿法律制度的逐步完善，加之法律中介组织的发展和患者权利相关法律知识的普及，医患双方已经可以利用法律的平台，通过法律途径主张自己的权利，患者维权意识明显增强。二是医方管理服务水平仍有提升空间。医患纠纷并不一定是源于医方业务知识缺乏、技术水平不高或设备条件不好，也有相当一部分是源于医方管理松懈、制度不完善、后勤工作不能保障医疗需求等。同时，医院迫于舆论的压力，以及对依法解决纠纷的经验与能力的不足，使一些本无过失、协商解决的纠纷都是以医院赔钱为条件，破坏了医患关系的平衡。

综上，医疗体制改革中，构建和谐医患关系，既要重视保护医疗过程中医生的权利，也要重视患者权利的保障。特别在我国长期形成的医患关系不平衡的格局之下，开展患者权利保障研究，明确患者权利的应然内容，了解患者权利保护的现实状态及其问题，进而有针对性地提出患者权利的保障机制，就具有十分重要的现实意义。

一 中国患者权利保护立法现状

我国自 1982 年卫生部颁布《医院工作制度》以来，先后通过部门规章、行政法规、地方性法规与规章、法律等方式对患者权利作出了规定，基本已做到有法可依。其中较为重要的法律渊源有：1982 年，中华人民共和国卫生部颁布了《医院工作制度》；1994 年，中华人民共和国国务院又颁布实施了《医疗机构管理条例》；1999 年，全国人大常委会颁布了《中华人民共和国执业医师法》；2002 年，中华人民共和国卫生部、国家中医药管理局共同颁布的《病历书写基本规范（试行）》；2002 年，中华人民共和国国务院颁布了《医疗事故处理条例》；2009 年，全国人大通过了我国目前为止关于患者知情同意权效力最高的法律《中华人民共和国侵权责任法》（以下简称《责任法》），该法对医疗侵权责任专设了一个章节。《责任法》的通过，具有重要的意义，它标志着我国患者权利制度进入了一个新的发展阶段。这部法律在为我国患者的各项权利制度搭建了一个基本框架的同时，也为医疗纠纷得以依法解决、平衡患者与医方矛盾提供了制度保障和法律依据。

国内关于处理医患关系维护患者权利的法律属性，概括起来共有以下四种学说：① "公益说"。该观点认为，医疗机构属于非营利性机构，不是一般意义上的经营者，医疗服务价格是由政府严格限制的。② "医疗合同说"。此学说为我国目前大部分学者所认同。此观点认为，合同为双方当事人以发生债之关系为目的相互为对立之意思表示。患者到医院按规定支付医疗费用，医院接诊，表示同意为其提供医疗服务，就达成医疗服务合同关系，即患者挂号行为属合同法中的要约行为，医疗机构发给挂号单是承诺行为。如果医院没有提供与医学科学技术水平相应的医疗服务，当属违约行为。而且，医疗合同属于非典型合同（即无名合同）的一种，法律没有对其名称和规则加以相应的明确规定。③ "侵权行为说"。该说认为，医疗卫生事业属于社会福利事业，医疗单位与患者之间并不存在平等的合同关系，医务人员职责职权建立在法律或有关规章的基础上，而不是当事人约定的结果，医务人员的责任亦不得依约定而免除，所以医疗单位与患者之间并不存在合同关系，医务人员过失造成患者身体上的损害，即构成侵权行为。而且因侵权产生的赔偿范围包括金钱赔偿、精神损害赔偿等，较违约责任范围更宽，有利于加强对受害人的保护。另外，如果受害人对医疗单位有债务，如欠医疗费、住院费等，则提起侵权之诉较为有利，因为根据民法原理，侵权行为人不得以其对受害人的侵权与其因侵权所生之债务相抵消。虽然，医患之间存在某种协议，但医患关系及由这种关系所产生的相应义务并不完全取决于合同法原理，由此产生的纠纷适用侵权行为法。④ "医疗消费说"。这主要是法学界人士，如江平、刘俊海、邱仁宗的观点。即认为患者到医院就诊是一种 "接受服务" 的行为，医院从事的是 "提供服务" 的行为，从而医患关系是一种消费者和经营者的关系。

随着我国改革开放的不断深入和发展，人们越来越注重法律意识，近几年，医疗纠纷不断增多，有资料统计，从1997年开始，医疗纠纷平均以每年翻一番的速度发展。患者的权利和医护人员的义务是个相对立的概念。医护人员是如何看待患者权利的，有学者已对相关问题进行了调查，以下表1、表2显示了调查的结果。

表1　医护人员主观上对患者权利保护的认知情况①

调查项目	正确人数	认知率（%）
1. 是否认为患者对自己所患疾病的性质、严重程度、治疗情况及愈后有知情的权利？	186	100
2. 是否愿意让患者打印收费清单或复印病历等？	186	100
3. 是否愿意让患者了解某些检查、治疗的危害或毒副作用？	176	94.62
4. 是否愿意让患者参与到其诊疗活动过程中？	124	66.67
5. 是否愿意让患者指定医护人员为其诊治？	158	84.95
6. 是否愿意为患者了解其所患的疾病作更多的解释？	178	95.70
7. 是否愿意为艾滋病患者进行各种诊疗活动？	90	48.39

注：1~7个调查项目回答"是"为正确选项（调查总人数为186人）。

资料来源：王桂杰，林士军，刘雪梅《医护人员对患者权利的保护情况调查分析》，《医学与哲学》2005年6月第26卷第6期总第289期。

表2　医护人员客观上对患者权利保护的情况②

调查项目	有保护人数	保护率（%）
1. 对患者的贫富、亲疏、地位高低等是否能做到一视同仁？	182	97.85
2. 是否歧视过患病的犯人或精神病人？	94	50.54
3. 你认为患者有权对其所患疾病及治疗、愈后了解吗？	153	82.26
4. 实习医护人员在临床实践过程中，是否征得过患者同意才进行各项操作的？	38	20.43
5. 是否有过在非工作场合谈论病人的隐私？	158	84.95
6. 在为患者检查治疗过程中，是否注意到保护患者的个人隐私？	163	87.63
7. 你认为患者的自由选择权是否得到了很好的保护？	139	74.73
8. 你认为患者的隐私权是否得到保护？	145	77.96

注：调查项目中，第1、第3、第4、第6、第7、第8项回答"是"，第2、第5项回答"否"为对患者权利有保护（调查总人数为186人）。

资料来源：王桂杰，林士军，刘雪梅《医护人员对患者权利的保护情况调查分析》，《医学与哲学》2005年6月第26卷第6期总第289期。

---

① 王桂杰，林士军，刘雪梅：《医护人员对患者权利的保护情况调查分析》，《医学与哲学》2005年6月第26卷第6期。
② 王桂杰，林士军，刘雪梅：《医护人员对患者权利的保护情况调查分析》，《医学与哲学》2005年6月第26卷第6期。

二 患者权利保障情况实证研究
——基于成都市的样本分析

本文采用问卷调查的方式对所研究问题进行实证数据的采集及分析。患者问卷包括甄别性问题 3 个、背景问题 4 个，分别为被访者户籍所在地、本市居住时间、年龄、性别、学历、职业状况及月收入几个方面，主问卷部分包括客观题与主观题共 31 个，主要包括满意度、权利保障现状、法律意识及医患关系几个维度。对问卷的分析采用描述性统计的方法，就所关注的各个维度进行频率分析，分别采用单一因素分析、单一因素对比分析及交叉因素分析等。发放患者问卷 260 份，回收 248 份，其中有效问卷 210 份；医疗工作者问卷 130 份，回收 113 份，其中有效问卷 94 份。

（一）就医前

对一个地区的医疗服务进行评价的一个关键指标是可及性，这也是保障患者权利、生命健康权及医疗照顾权的首要前提。图 1 表明，被调查者中有 80% 的人表示自己或家人需要就医时，可以直接到意向的医疗机构就诊。图 2 表明，当问及造成去意向医疗机构就医困难的原因时，高额的医疗费用、长时间的候诊，以及交通不便利等，成为目前人们就医难的主要原

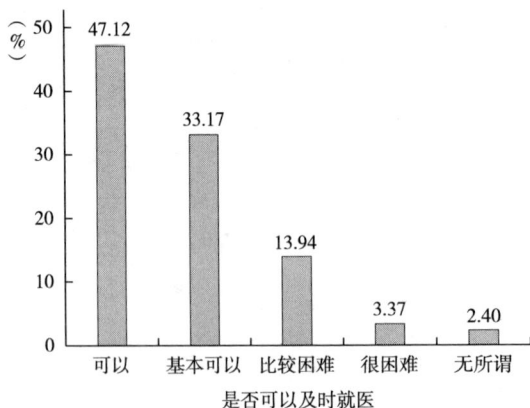

图 1　是否可以及时就医

因。并且选择医疗费用较高导致就医难的被访者表示，医疗费用高的主要原因是要价高（32 人），其次是检查费用高（27 人）。

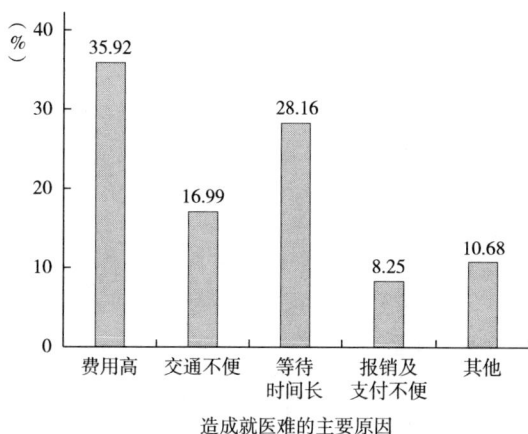

造成就医难的主要原因

图 2　造成就医难的原因

从图 3 和图 4 来看，就医前，患者会在医疗机构之间进行一次选择。本文的调研结果表明，患者就医前，最为关注的首先是医疗机构的医疗技术，这占到被访者的 50% 以上，其次是就医的费用和服务态度，分别各占五分之一的比重。根据患者对医疗结果的预期，我们可以将患者分为高预期、一般预期和没有预期三个类别，其中超过一半的被调查者表示对本次就医有较高的治愈期望，超过 80% 的被访者表示对治愈存在预期。通过分析可知，对

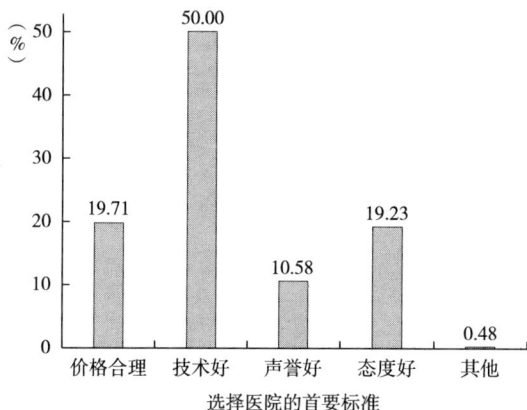

选择医院的首要标准

图 3　选择医院的标准

医疗这样的特殊服务，患者普遍抱有较高的预期，但由于医疗本身所具有的不确定性，这种预期可能单方面地成为加剧医患之间矛盾的一个隐含因素。

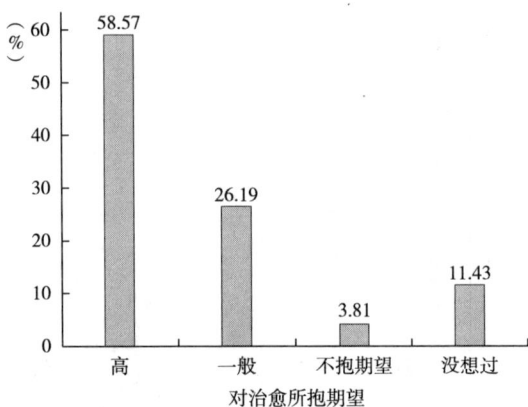

图4　人们对治愈所抱的期望

（二）就医中

患者的尊严是患者权利中的一项重要内容。图5显示，在被调查的患者中，接近80%的患者表示在过去一年的就医经历中，没有感受到来自医疗机构对自身尊严的侵犯，但是需要注意的是20%多的被调查者有过类似经历，并且在这部分被访者中，这种对尊严的侵犯主要来自医生（16人）和护士（15人）。

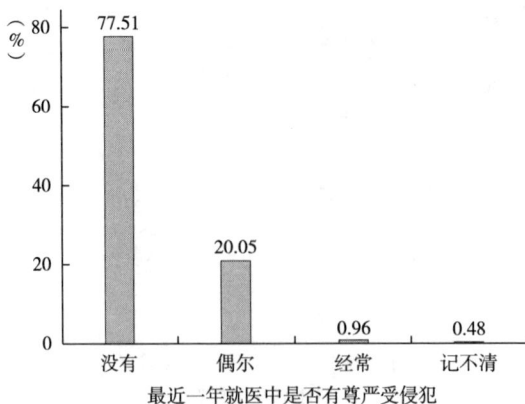

图5　患者就医时尊严是否受侵犯

图 6 和图 7 体现的是患者是否有自主权，即自我决定权，包括患者自己决定及丧失决定能力时的权利。通过调查，发现接近三分之一的受访者表示在自己或家人的就医过程中，从未参与相关决策，且绝大多数的被访者表示在最近一年的就医经历中，对不合理的质量方案没有提出任何反对意见。对自身就医情况缺乏了解，是医疗服务中信息不对称的主要表现，也是产生医患矛盾的主要原因。

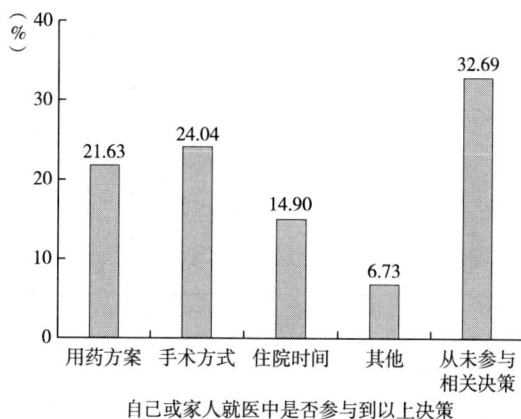

图 6　患者在就医过程中是否参与决策

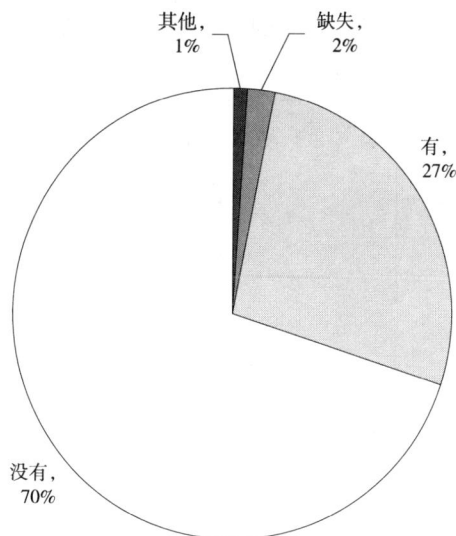

图 7　患者是否对不合理的就医方案提出反对

知情权作为患者的一项基本权利，是指患者有知悉自己的病情、治疗措施、医疗风险、医疗费用和医方基本情况、技术水平及其他医疗信息的权利。图8表明，在被访者中，虽然有超过50%的被访者表示对自己的病情、诊断及检查情况清楚了解，但是仍有超过三分之一的被访者对自己的病情等不清楚，接近一半的人在最近一次检查中，并不清楚每一项检查的目的，分析结果符合我们的一般认知。

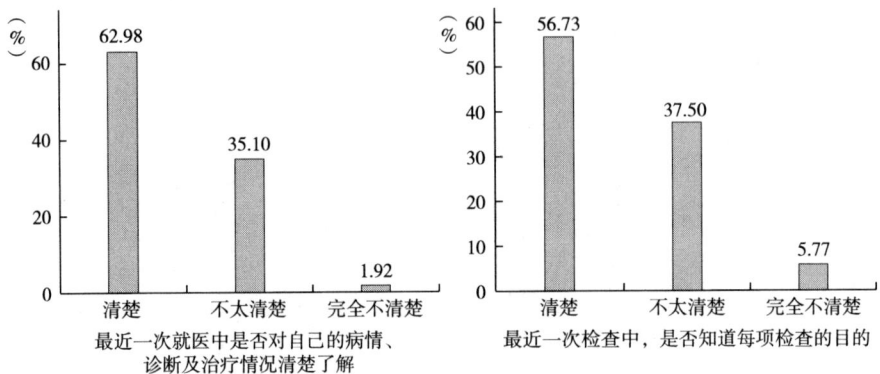

图8　患者对自身病情及检查目的是否清楚

在隐私权方面，图9表明，近70%的受访者表示自己的相关信息并未被医疗机构泄露，同时有三分之一的患者表示自己的个人信息被医疗机构泄露，或者并不清楚是否被泄露。

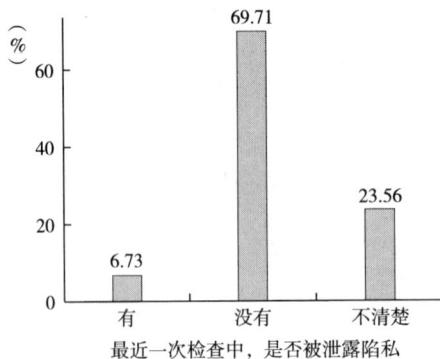

图9　患者是否被医院泄露隐私

148

（三）满意度

图 10 表明，在患者就医满意度调查中，超过 70% 的受访者表示满意或者比较满意，在导致满意的原因中，认为是医护人员态度的有 92 人，认为是诊疗效果的有 46 人；导致不满意的主要原因则是医疗费用。

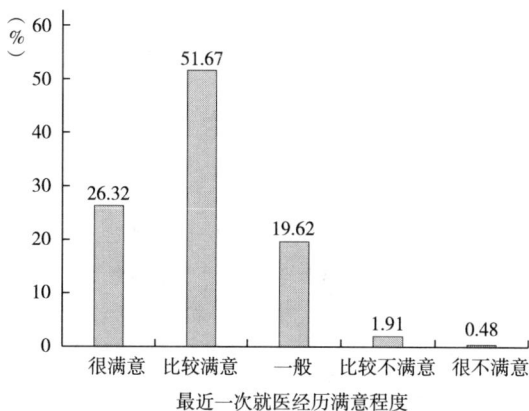

图 10　患者对最近就医的满意程度

（四）法律意识

图 11 显示，有近 80% 的被访者表示在医疗机构就医时会留意对方是否具有合法医师资格，这表示大多数人对自身的权利和人身安全有较高的关注和警惕。并且超过 80% 的受访者表示会妥善保管就医记录。

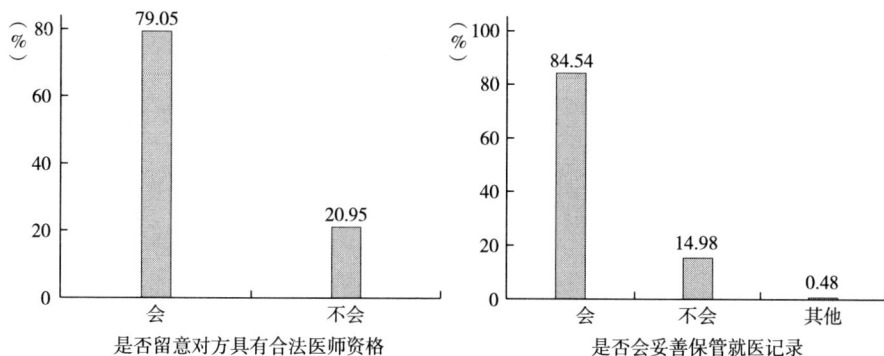

图 11　患者是否留意医生的合法医师资格

图 12 显示，虽然大多数人有保护自我的意识，但是被调查者中大约一半的人都不知道在医疗事故处理中适用"举证倒置"，表明大多数人缺乏对保护自己权利的相关法律知识的了解。

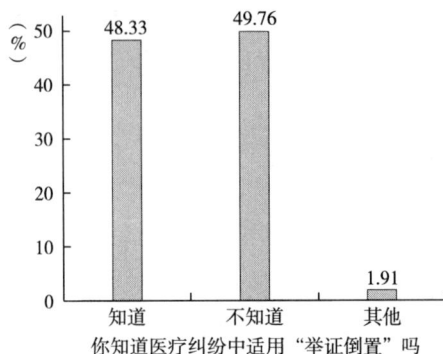

图 12　患者是否清楚"举证倒置"

图 13 显示，当患者与医院产生医疗纠纷时，被调查者中有 26.83% 表示会诉诸法律手段，46.83% 表示会向相关部门投诉，22.93% 表示会直接与医生协调处理。当得知自身信息被医院泄露，隐私权受到侵犯时，只有 30% 的受访者表示会采取法律手段保护自己的利益，且有接近 20% 的人表示多一事不如少一事。

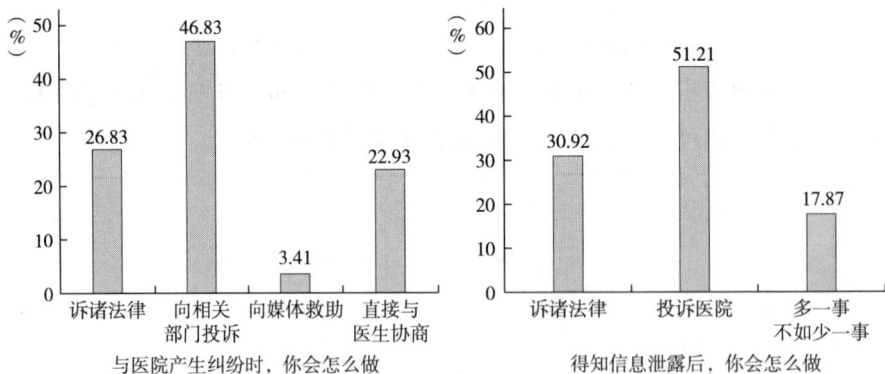

图 13　与医院产生纠纷或发现信息泄露后患者的反应

三　结论

本文将实施调研得到的患者的问卷进行了整理、分析，分别采用了单因素分析、交叉因素分析及对比分析的方法。基本思路遵循患者单因素分析（包括就医过程分析、满意度分析、法律意识分析及医疗改革方面的分析），交叉因素分析（包括性别、年龄、收入、职业等对满意度、参与度的影响），患者－医生对比分析（医患关系定位、满意度、医患关系及医疗改革等相关问题）。实证分析的主要发现有：就医难的主要问题是医疗费用较高及等待时间太长，这会影响患者的就医权与健康权；在诊疗过程中，存在患者的基本权利受到侵害的状况，例如尊严、隐私，特别是患者对自身病情的知情权、诊疗过程的自主权在实际诊疗过程中没有得到应有的重视，集中反映为"不反对、不参与"，即对诊疗决策和检查一般不反对，一般也不参与的状况；性别、年龄和收入对患者的满意度、参与度没有明显的影响；药费过高，政府投入不足仍然是医患双方共同关注的主要问题。

参考文献

邓娟：《论知情同意权中医师的说明义务》，《前沿》2006 年第 8 期。

顾肃：《自由主义的基本理念》，中央编译出版社，2003。

胡永庆：《知情同意理论中医生说明义务的构成》，《法律科学》2005 年第 1 期。

黄丁全：《医事法》，中国政法大学出版社，2003。

侯雪梅：《患者的权利理论探微与实务指南》，知识产权出版社，2005。

李步云：《人权法学》，高等教育出版社，2005。

柳经纬、李茂年：《医患关系法论》，中信出版社，2002。

王利明：《人格权法新论》，吉林人民出版社，1994。

吴雪松、张萌：《知情同意权中的哥德巴赫猜想——知情权与患者认知能之间的冲突》，《医学与哲学》2003 年第 1 期。

张敏智、朱凤春编著《病人权利概论》，大连出版社，2001。

赵同刚主编《卫生法立法研究：卫生法课题汇编》，法律出版社，2003。

郑学宝、李大平：《患者知情同意权》，《法律与医学杂志》2004 年第 4 期。

病人的权利课题组：《病人的权利研究报告（下）》，《中国卫生法制》2001 年第 5 期。

运用经济学评价指导医药卫生政策与管理

徐　程*

【摘要】我国医药卫生领域中的诸多现实社会问题迫切需要我们深入开展卫生经济学评价研究。通过全面系统地评价医药卫生技术和公共卫生服务项目的经济性，合理地制定报销、定价和监督机制，有利于有效配置医药卫生资源，提高卫生决策的科学性和透明度，降低腐败，促进社会的安定与和谐，也有利于促进具有中国特色的医药卫生事业的发展。

【关键词】统筹基金；腐败；医药卫生体系；医疗保险；定价机制；传统中医药

一　现实意义

全球医疗费用不断增长刺激各国思考如何有效合理地配置有限的医药卫生资源来满足本国人民的卫生需求。1993 年澳大利亚率先出台经济学评价指南以来，全球已有三十多个国家先后制定了官方的经济学评价指南或非官方的经济学评价参考，指导药品、医疗器械、诊断技术和治疗方法等医药卫

---

* 徐程：女，博士，1971 年 7 月出生，现为西南财经大学公共管理学院副教授，北京大学光华管理学院卫生经济与管理研究院高级学者。主要从事医药卫生政策和经济学评价的研究和教学工作。曾任美国纽约理工大学管理学院卫生经济与管理学助理教授。

生干预的成本与健康产出的经济学评估，用于临床实践及制定药品报销目录、药品价格、新药评审及公共卫生政策等。随着我国医药卫生体制改革的推进，我国面临的现实社会问题也迫切需要深入开展卫生经济学评价研究，指导政府和医务人员的决策与管理。

首先，以卫生经济学评价为依据，筛选具有成本效益的优良技术和服务项目，为政府部门科学合理地制定医保报销和补偿政策，制定药品和服务项目价格，以及临床合理用药等提供依据，保障医药卫生资源的有效配置。目前，中国基本医疗保障制度基本实现了全民覆盖，保障范围不断扩大，报销水平也在逐步提高。随着新医改各项制度改革的推进，在实际运行中诸多问题也随之而来。主要表现为：医疗需求释放带来的卫生费用的快速增长；过度的医疗消费导致一些省市和地区的城镇职工医疗保险统筹基金出现当年负增长的现象。随着我国人口老龄化趋势迅速扩大和慢性病等问题的迅速蔓延，这种现象如不能得到有效控制和及时调整，将直接威胁整个医疗保障制度的可持续性发展乃至新医改的顺利推进。

其次，经济学评价能够为政府提供循证决策的依据，提高卫生决策的科学性和透明度，有利于减少腐败，促进社会的安定与和谐。2013 年 7 月爆出的葛兰素史克的行贿受贿事件，只是药品行业价格扭曲的冰山一角。由于我国医药卫生服务的定价和监管机制不健全，导致各层机构和个人滥用职权，以公谋私，损害广大患者的利益。同时，由于医药卫生服务的定价不合理，也导致医务人员的利益得不到保障，医患矛盾等问题加剧。

最后，以卫生经济学评价为依据，有利于发展我国的中医药产业。前沿的经济学评价理论和实践证明，仅仅依靠基于临床严格控制条件下的随机临床研究实验（RCT）评价医药卫生的价值是片面和有限的，需要从多方面的临床实际数据、循证医学的经验证据及模型构建来跟踪和分析医药诊疗技术的长期疗效和成本。长期以来，我国传统医学虽然有着上千年临床使用的记载和数据，但是由于缺乏 RCT 的评价研究，其安全性和有效性一直受到质疑，阻碍了其发展。因此，以传统医学理论为基础，结合国外前沿的经济学评价研究，建立和完善经济学评价体系，开展系统的经济学评价，有利于充分发挥中医药"简便廉验"的优势，促进我国医药卫生事业的发展。

二 机遇与挑战

我国新一轮医药卫生体制改革已经历时 4 年。其间，运用卫生经济学评价来指导公共政策和卫生事业管理备受关注。2009 年 4 月 6 日，国家公布的《中共中央国务院关于深化医药卫生体制改革的意见》（中发［2009］6号）提出"建立科学合理的医药价格形成机制"及"对新药和专利药品逐步实行定价前药物经济性评价制度"。国家发改委 2010 年新修订的《药品价格管理办法（征求意见稿）》（2010 年 6 月 1 日）也明确提出由于"可替代药品治疗费用差异较大的，可以以对照药品价格为基础，参考药物经济性评价结果进行调整"。但是，由于经济学评价研究的范围广泛，数据来源千差万别，研究方法日益复杂，现实中决策者的行为受到各种条件的制约。因此，具体实施和开展这些意见和建议，还面临诸多挑战。除了我国的政治和决策体系等复杂的国情外，卫生经济学评价本身在方法上存在很多问题。

近年虽然国内外有关经济学评价的研究日益增多，但争议也很多，阻碍了其广泛的应用。虽然以生命质量调整年（QALY）为健康产出的测量目前应用广泛，但缺乏对健康产出的价值判断，很难被决策者利用。另外，用于测量效用指标的测量工具不同产生的 QALY 差异很大，测量人群和折旧率的选择等对研究结果的影响很大。虽大量研究集中于对研究方法的分析和改进，以便更准确测量成本和健康产出，如对多中心研究的测量，成本效果接受曲线、不确定性、贴现及健康产出评估工具的改进等，但尚无法解决根本问题。相关决策模型无法充分考虑决策的复杂性，且有局限性。如结构假设，证据运用、数据采样，以及参数间的相互关系，尤其是健康的产出关系和相互间作用。如何评价多种干预相结合、动态变化的经济学评价还很少见。

目前大部分的经济学评价研究主要针对新技术进行评价，而对市场上已有产品未给予足够的重视。2009 年奥巴马政府斥资 11 亿美元开展医药卫生的疗效比较研究。这些研究除了强调应用真实世界数据，开展观察性研究设计的评价方法来筛选临床有效的治疗手段外，还提出异质性患者群的价值不同及动态变化等问题。而传统的计量和决策分析模型评估方法通常无法解决这种异质性和系统复杂的动态关联。

三 未来发展方向

（一）进一步与传统和现代经济学相结合

理论上，深入探索医药卫生干预给个人和社会带来的价值的评判标准。还需将经济学评价与卫生经济学研究中有关患者就医行为和医务人员诊疗行为对卫生服务的成本和产出的影响分析有机结合，深入研究探讨社会选择及个体优化决策的相互关系，以便指导如何整合从研究患者、医务人员及健康人群等多方位的成本与产出分析。只有设计合理的制度，使医生、患者和社会角度的成本和利益趋同，在真正意义上开展、整合、评价和应用经济学评价证据，才能更好地指导医药卫生决策，建立公平有效的医药卫生体系。

（二）评估方法和测量工具也有待完善和创新

近年有关 CBA 的研究开始增多。越来越多的研究也开始应用离散选择模型（DCE）来测量健康偏好及价值判断，对 CEA 与 CBA 的共同发展与融合具有一定的促进作用。传统决策模型存在很多问题，因此可以探索应用复杂系统研究中的建模和仿真等方法来研究医药卫生领域复杂系统的动态规律，深入分析医药卫生干预措施的成本－产出路径。通过合理充分地整合现实世界的数据，具体分析比较成本变化因素中哪些是由价格因素导致，哪些由疗程和效果导致；分析比较生命质量变化因素中哪些因患者偏好不同，哪些由疗程和效果导致。

（三）需要找到使用评估证据的突破点

临床经济学评估通常在确认服务项目具有效力和效果后开展才更有意义。因为我们需要把应该做（有效力和效果）的事情做得更好（有效率），使其物有所值。但目前无论是发达国家还是我国，并非所有上市药品和干预手段都用 RCT 开展过效力和效果研究。因此，根据现实情况开展其经济评价仍有重要价值。在我国，有关中医药的临床疗效尚不清楚，是否可用该研究的思路和方法开展经济学评估，剔除经济效果较差的项目后，再对有优势和潜力的品种和项目进行深入的效力研究，从开展经济学分析入手的价值值得深入探讨。

四　我国糖尿病用药的经济学评价的研究框架

有研究表明，2008 年全球有 3.47 亿人患有糖尿病。据 WHO 预测，到 2030 年糖尿病将成为第七位主要死因。国际糖尿病联盟（IDF）的报告指出，仅 2012 年全球因治疗糖尿病及其并发症的医疗费用已达 4710 亿美元。我国糖尿病患病率处于世界最高，2008 年糖尿病患病率已达 9.7%。最新的研究显示，2010 年我国糖尿病患病率已达 11.6%，而且糖尿病前期患病率竟高于 50%。相关的费用也一直处于增长之中，从 1993 年的 22.16 亿元上升至 2007 年的 2000 亿元，卫生总费用占比也从 1993 年的 1.96% 上升至 2007 年的 18.2%。这些惊人的数字表明仅糖尿病就消耗了大量的医药卫生经济资源。但是，这些资源的消耗中哪些是物有所值？哪些是资源的浪费？如何更有效地配置卫生资源？

为了回答以上问题，我们以我国中西医临床用药为核心，以实际发生大样本的保险报销和临床用药数据为基础，深入分析我国糖尿病的临床实际用药的成本和产出，包括与药品不良反应及有效性相关的费用和健康产出。本研究通过建立和运用复杂系统仿真模型，探索从复杂系统的理论和视角，解决传统经济学评价中面临的临床用药的动态关联和变化的相关问题。

该研究以分析成都市、天津市和南通市 2007~2012 年的基本医疗保险报销的数据、卫生统计数据（卫生资源、疾病发生率、死亡率等），中国糖尿病药物经济学研究的数据，以及样本医院的电子病历为主，结合专家咨询访谈和循证医学的方法开展实证研究，应用 Vensim 和 Anylogic 仿真软件对系统动力学模型和基于代理人模型进行建模和仿真。

首先，通过专家访谈和文献查询，参考循证医学证据，建立多角度反馈循环图，提出临床用药和疾病发展过程的评价参数。包括自然疾病转归的动态参数，如糖化血红蛋白（HbA）和血糖的指标与出现糖尿病的时间，病程的发展变化，以及心脑血管病、肾病、眼病、足病等并发症的动态阶段发展。也包括药物对 HbA1c（或血糖）的变化贡献度，在一定用药模式的情况下，干预效果和时间关系可以有标准的函数关系，或者定性关系。

其次，运用多渠道数据分析用药人群、疾病诊断、药品的价格（包括单一使用西药、单一使用中药、中西药联合使用）、数量、门诊、住院费用等各项诊疗费用明细等信息，结合专家意见和逻辑，进行系统模型仿真分析不同用药路径规律及相关的短期和长期的成本和产出。具体包括根据性别、年龄和疾病种类及严重程度等聚类，通过散点分析与聚类分析，建立几个子系统模块分析不同人群用药的成本与产出，将这些模块集成到仿真环境中。

最后，通过专家咨询，根据验证结果和专家及政策制订者的建议，对模型进行修正，全面估算不同临床用药的长期成本和产出。制定医保报销目录等药物政策中的成本产出评价的新框架。筛选临床用药的优势品种，淘汰劣势品种，为政府部门制定药品报销目录、药品定价、临床合理用药等提供依据，也将通过开展科学合理的经济学评估，促进我国中医药产业的发展。

参考文献

李明辉、刘国恩：《中药药物经济学评价的医药与特点》，《中国药物经济学》2009年第 3 期。

Michael F. Drummond 著，李士雪等译《卫生保健项目经济学评价方法》，人民卫生出版社，2008。

吴晶、孙利华、刘国恩：《中国药物经济学学科发展现状》，《中国药物经济学》2008 年第 6 期。

中华医学会糖尿病学分会：《中国 2 型糖尿病防治指南》摘要，北京大学医学出版社，2010。

中国药物经济学评价指南课题组：《中国药物经济学评价指南》，《中国药物经济学》2011 年第 3 期。

Chandra A. Jena, J. Skinner, "The Pragmatist's Guide to Comparative Effectiveness Research", *The Journal of Economic Perspectives* 25（2011）：27 – 46.

Gary Hirsch, C. Sherry Immediato, "Microworlds and Generic Structures as Resources for Integrating Care and Improving Health", *System Dynamics Review* 15（1999）：315 – 30.

J. B. Homer, G. B. Hirsch, "System Dynamics Modeling for Public Health: Background and Opportunities", *American Journal of Public Health* 96 (2006): 452 – 58.

Mark J. Sculpher, Karl Claxton, Mike Drummond, Chris McCabe, "Whither Trial – Based Economic Evaluation for Health Care Decision Making?", *The Journal of Health Economics* 15 (2006): 677 – 87.

M. ChWeinstein, "Recent Developments in Decision – Analytic Modeling for Economic Evaluation", *Pharmacoeconomics* 24 (2006): 1043 – 53.

Xu Y, et al, "Prevalence and Control of Diabetes in Chinese Adults", *The Journal of American Medical Association* 310 (2013): 948 – 59.

Yang W, et al, "Prevalence of Diabetes among Men and Women in China", *The New England Journal of Medicine* 362 (2010): 1090 – 101.

转型期中国的社会冲突与社会管理

草根 NGO 与乡村多元共治路径的构建

乔运鸿　刘　璐*

【摘要】本文对山西蒲韩乡村社区的性质进行了界定，探析了草根 NGO 参与社区乡村治理的乡村多元共治道路，同时提出了当前乡村治理中面临的困境。笔者认为，乡村善治离不开草根 NGO 的参与，应探索从二元治理到多元共治的乡村治理的新道路。

【关键词】草根；NGO；乡村治理；多元共治

乡村社会的善治是和谐社会建设的重要组成部分。中国农村近 30 多年取得的历史性进步，村民自治制度及村委会体制功不可没。但乡村的治理是复杂而艰巨的一项系统改造工程，它需要动员各种力量和积极因素的参与而形成合力，特别是需要唤起作为乡村建设的主体力量的广大村民的主动参与。当今乡村治理的体制层面的"供需矛盾"，不仅不能很好地回应基层民众的多元化需求，制约了乡村社会的发展，同时也加速了转型期村庄社区组织结构和功能的分化。广大的乡村社区组织正面临着新的重组、整合和再造，以满足农民的自治需求和农村社区的全面发展。毫无疑问，开展草根 NGO 组织成为乡村治理的一项重要课题。

* 乔运鸿：男，山西运城人，太原理工大学政法学院，副教授，公共管理系主任。
刘璐：女，山西运城人，太原理工大学思想政治理论教学研究部，硕士研究生。

一 概念及性质的界定

（一）NGO 的概念界定

NGO 并非中文固有的词汇，最早见于 1945 年签署的联合国宪章，① 一般认为，现代意义上的 NGO 出现于第二次世界大战前后。② NGO 的英文原文为 non - governmental organization，直译为"非政府组织"。国外也较多地采用"第三部门""非营利组织"（简称 NPO）、"社区"的说法。国际社会对这种社会组织的关注大致始于 20 世纪 80 年代末。90 年代初开始有学者关注中国的类似组织。关于 NGO 的定义，较为流行的是美国约翰·霍普金斯大学莱斯特·萨拉蒙（Lester Salamon）教授提出的 5 个特征法。即将具有以下 5 个特征的组织界定为 NGO：（1）组织性；（2）非政府性；（3）非营利性；（4）自治性；（5）志愿性。在上述 5 个特性中，非政府性和非营利性被公认为 NGO 的基本特征。

西方学者大多是从宏观上满足了第三部门的发展对理论的需求，清晰地界定了第三部门与政府的边界与范围。具有代表性的理论有：福利国家理论③、政府失灵/市场失灵理论④、合约失灵理论⑤、志愿失灵理论⑥。这些理论更多地集中在对城镇非政府部门身上，较少涉及乡村的非政府组织。对第三部门的实践，理论家对民主的关注也多于对第三部门自治的关注。因此，学术上表现为对非政府组织的缘起、资金来源、与政府关系等投入较大热情，而对其提供服务、内部管理和监督等关注较少。这种关注视角的偏

---

① 在 1945 年 6 月签署的该宪章的第 71 条款中有如下的记述：联合国授权经社理事会"为那些与该理事会所管理的事务有关的非政府组织进行磋商作出适当安排"。

② 1942 年英国 OXFAM 的诞生，被视为 NGO 出现的标志。

③ 福利国家理论主张国家应该成为所有社会服务的唯一提供者，即使在概念上也未给非政府组织一定的发展空间。

④ 政府失灵/市场失灵理论将第三部门的存在视为弥补政府和市场在提供集体物品时的不足，主要是为了克服"搭便车"问题和"集体行动的困境"。

⑤ 合约失灵理论认为某些服务的提供者和购买者并不是直接对接的，消费者并没有足够的信息约束营利企业的逐利行为。因此，第三方部门可以承担起这项"委托 - 代理"的职责。

⑥ 志愿失灵理论，第三部门也会由于慈善不足、慈善的特殊主义、家长式慈善作风和慈善的业余主义等原因出现失灵。

差，导致了对第三部门的发展及供给公共服务形成了不同的政策建议。

（二）社区性质及特点

笔者实地调研的是一个由乡村精英主导、村民自主参与、全方位进行乡村改造和治理实践、集经济合作和公共服务为一体、跨乡镇的内生式新型农村社区组织，它的"新"表现在以下两个方面。

1. 综合性

表现之一，社区社员融会员、顾客、所有者、惠顾者四种身份为一身。蒲韩乡村社区社员是寨子科技中心的部分顾客，对他们购买化肥农药时有一定的优惠。社区用赚来的资金购置学习资料、聘请专家为社员提供各方面的培训，以此为途径将利益返回大家。

表现之二，社区从物质文明和精神文明两个方面发展农民。组织为农民提供的服务不仅在一定程度上能够满足农民的致富需求，而且社区通过多种形式的辩论、演讲等学习活动来提高农民自身的思想道德素质和科学文化素质。

2. 内生式

表现之一，它是自下而上内生的村民组织，制度允许的边界内，组织领导者的选举、组织成员的人事变更、组织决策的制定、执行和监督都不受政府和其他行为主体的干涉。表现之二，组织自筹经费、自我管理、自我服务，在乡村治理中已经作出突出的贡献，正朝着村民共同的愿景迈进。

二 农民协会的乡村治道

（一）农民协会发展历程

图 1 概括了蒲州农民协会的发展历程。经过 16 年的发展，社区从单一的仅提供农资销售服务变为集经济、教育、文化、娱乐、社会公益服务等多功能为一体的组织。

1. 技术培训

1998 年，协会发起人郑冰是一名乡村小学教师，空闲时帮忙打理她

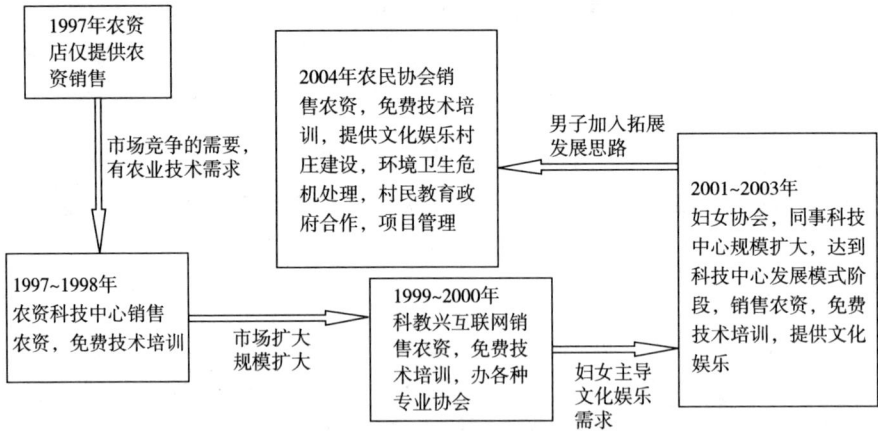

图1 蒲州农民协会发展历程

丈夫谢富政开设的农资店。她发现多数农民购买化肥农药时，不太了解农业技术和实际生产需要而盲目购买。于是她邀请农技专家为村民讲课，通过"妇女"路线来动员村民参加技术培训。2000年成立了科教兴互联网。

2. 文娱活动

2001年，经常聚集在一起的妇女们产生了一起跳舞增加娱乐生活的想法，便成立了妇女协会。利用农业技术培训在周围几十个村庄打下的群众基础，跳舞活动逐渐扩大到三十多个村，活跃了当地妇女们的文化生活，极大地改变了妇女的精神面貌。

另外，社区还发动大家搞辩论赛和学习小组。辩论的主题是发生在村民身边的小事，比如婆媳关系、生男还是生女好。农闲时节，村民们定期进行集体学习，学习内容包括农业技术、农业政策、家庭教育等。这些学习形式不仅打破了一些农村的陈旧观念，更重要的是锻炼了农民的逻辑思维，培养了大家的集体议事能力。

3. 合作经济

经济实体是支撑协会发展的基础。在一次外出考察学习后，协会的骨干们意识到集体经济的效益，萌生了集中村民土地共同经营生态种植的想法。现成立有诸如核桃、棉花、花椒等各种类型的专业合作社，帮助和引导农民参与市场活动，共同抵御市场风险。同时，协会会员参与协会的有机作物项目,实现有机农产品的统购统销,提高农民收益。

4. 公共事务

在妇联推荐下,郑冰赴北京参加了专为农家女设置的培训班,使得成立农民协会的理念开始在她的思想中萌芽。农民协会成立后的第一件大事是组织大家修路和治理卫生环境。寨子村以前是土路,到处是垃圾,下雨天泥泞肮脏不堪。由于各种原因村委无法有效行使公共服务的职责,为了解决道路和卫生问题,平时参与文娱活动的积极分子们成立了生态家园理事会,挨家挨户发传单动员各家修理自家门前的一段路,公共路段则由理事会出钱修理。巷道治理工作只用了 70 天就全部完成,仅花费 3 万元。为了发挥协会在农村治理中的更大作用,2004 年,在当地政府支持下,这个组织正式注册为永济市蒲州镇农民协会,成为法律实体,经费来源主要是郑冰夫妇农资店的利润。

(二)农民协会的村治路径

社区并非主流的农民自治组织,它在曲折的发展历程中走出了一条适合自己的乡村治理道路。

1. 恢复而非改造

社区是要恢复农作物的“原生态”,并非对农作物的全新改造。协会中的有机联合社主要负责引导村民种植绿色无公害的棉花、花椒、苹果等农作物;青年农场负责引导村民种植绿色无公害的蔬菜、花卉,实现农村的原生态。

2. 公益而非营利

协会的主要宗旨是建立一个幸福的家园,其经济实体版块主要是为公共服务版块提供财政支持。社区社员并不计较自己工资的多少,他们更注重的是对农村的建设自己贡献了多大力量。

3. 立足自力更生

协会对外界的支持一直持谨慎态度。郑冰认为接受外界的支持并不利于社区的发展:一是轻易获得太多资助容易滋生依赖情绪,很可能降低自己的工作能力;二是获得外界的资助之后往往会受资助方的掣肘,有时资助方和协会理念并不符合,协会的决策会陷入尴尬境地。

（三）农民协会的村治功效

蒲韩乡村社区是参与乡村治理的典范。具体而言，主要有六个方面的村治功效。

1. 打破单一的行政治理格局，形成多元化的社区治理体系

中国目前的乡村治理结构主要为"乡派村治"，但囿于村两委的行政化倾向、自治性不强、参与度不高、"委托－代理"困境及财权和事权错位等，乡村社区产生了诸多累积性矛盾。"草根"社区组织可以有效拓展村民参与空间，形成多元治理格局，化解基层矛盾，促进乡村和谐。

2. 把农民组织起来应对市场风险，改变我国农业基础薄弱的局面

蒲韩乡村社区设立农业专业合作社，把"原子化"农民组织起来共同应对市场风险，克服家庭联产承包责任制的制度缺陷，避免食利者的盘剥，这是农村经济最有效的出路。

3. 破解乡村社区基本公共服务供给不足问题

无论是在基本公共服务供给数量还是供给质量上，乡村都与城市存在较大差距，农村教育、文化、医疗、村庄环境等社会事业发展缓慢，不能满足农村社区的发展需求。"草根"社区组织以其公益性、自主性和自治性，可以在一定程度上弥补政府和市场在农村基本公共服务供给上的双重失灵。

4. 整合乡村社区人才资源匮乏问题

在市场经济和城镇化双重冲击下，农村社区日趋"原子化""分散化"和"空巢化"。同时囿于现行体制，农村向城市单向度的人才输送机制导致乡村社区发展力量不足，人才匮乏，既有资源亦得不到有效利用。"草根"社区组织在动员能力、运行主体等方面具有比较优势，可充分发挥内部机制整合，以弥补外部整合不足的困境。

5. 破解乡村社区自治发展制度供给缺位

目前由于没有真正以农民为主体、代表农民利益和诉求的组织，致使农民的基本权利得不到切实的保护，合法权益也屡遭侵犯。诸如土地纠纷、子女入学、农民工工资等问题严重拷问着现有的制度安排。"草根"社区组织在增强农民主体地位，维护农民合法权益方面可发挥较大的作用，从而化解村民自治需求增加与制度供给不足的矛盾。

6. 破解农村政治危机

在市场经济体制下，村委会起联结国家与社会、政府与村民的纽带作用，是体制内有合法权威的村民自治组织。但在民主实践过程中"贿选""权力寻租""委托－代理风险"等严重透支着政府治理的合法性，酿成政治危机。而"草根"组织发展是时代潮流和历史所趋，若能有效整合村两委和"草根"组织，促进其优势互补，可重拾村民与政府的纽带作用，恢复和强化政府的公信力和政治合法性。

三　当前农民协会面临的乡村治理困境

（一）体制内合法性的挑战

1. 法律上对新的非政府组织的成立设置了较高的门槛

非政府组织一般要求实行双挂靠制度，但政府部门一般不愿意"找事上身"，使得协会建设面临着"政治门槛、资金门槛、类型门槛"的限制，致使其注册困难，大多数以"黑户"的身份游荡于乡村社会中。这些不确定性和不安全感严重阻碍了协会的发展。目前蒲韩乡村社区的民政注册名称为蒲州镇果品协会，然而其业务范围远远不局限于果品的统购统销。造成这种局面的主要原因是体制内对该类非政府组织的限制。

2. 与村委关系协调困难

草根 NGO 的兴起大多缘于村委会在一定程度上无法满足农民的自治需求，因而它似乎与生俱来就与村两委"势不两立"。二者不可调和的矛盾首先体现于精英争夺和群众争夺。同时，在血缘、地缘、亲缘和业缘关系影响下，自治组织会产生分裂，蜕变为局部化的组织平台。其次，突出体现在社区公共事务中相互拆台。例如村两委截留或是拒绝自上而下输入的资源，自治组织号召会员抵制村两委合理化活动，社区公共事业的发展和公共服务的供给沦为政治斗争的筹码。自治组织与村两委的矛盾斗争从根本上损害了普通村民的基本利益。

（二）外部知识、资金、人员输入过剩

伴随着知识精英群体、基金会组织、其他 NGO 及政府部门与自治组织

的联系不断加强，知识、资金、人员输入也日益强化。首先是知识输入过剩，导致组织领导者功能性丧失。最显性化的形式是顾问制，知识精英直接或间接地把握着组织的话语权。通过改革组织的发展模式、管理体制植入自己的学术思想。最终组织的发展呈现两种态势：一是组织成为知识精英的试验品，二是组织领导者与知识精英在博弈中达成妥协，组织成为二者实现他们捆绑利益的工具。其次是资金输入过剩，导致组织产生资金供给路径依赖。外部资金供给带有一定的目的性或是附加条件，对组织而言是一种"有选择性的激励"。再次，人员输入过剩，导致本土会员出现"搭便车"现象。外部 NGO 多以交流的名义派遣或是委托志愿者加入自治组织，这些志愿者一般接受过专业培训，理论素养和实践能力较强，但负面效应使组织自身成员主体性下降、坐享其成。

（三）组织内部的挑战

首先，各部门职能定位不清。社区现有 18 个部门，虽然每个部门有自己的组织机构，但每个社员的职责没有明确的划分，造成事、责、权不统一的局面。其次，社区的企业化倾向。社区中无论大事小事，郑冰都亲力亲为，容易形成专制的领导方式，社区可能形成一人把持的局面。最后，组织有成员家族式内卷化趋势。蒲韩乡村社区社员大部分是中老年妇女，文化水平不高，大部分社员间都有宗族关系。这一缺陷限制了多样化的人力资源的融入。若成员的老龄化倾向及宗族化趋势难以很快改变，就会造成组织发展的内生动力流失。因此，协会未来的发展应该优化其成员的性别结构、知识结构，克服过高同质性，走多元化之路。

四　构建多元共治的乡村道路

（一）传统的二元乡村治理模型

传统二元的乡村治理模型中，治理主体是基层政府和村两委。基层政府在村治中扮演着主导者的角色，负责政策的制定、执行和监督。在制度操作中，政府承担着乡村社会维稳、基本公共服务供给、发展民主政治等全方位的事务。村委会在法理上是村民自治的组织，实践中却是官僚体制在农村的延伸或是代理者。原本作为民选代表的村委成员被行政吸纳为体制的一部分，承担着大量的来自官僚体制的行政性事务。村委会与基层政府在长期的互动中形成了稳定的"委托－代理"机制，基层政府通过这一机制可以较为有效地管理乡村社会，分担来自上级政府下达的事务，应对体制内的各种绩效考核；村委会在"委托－代理"机制的庇护下弥补了选举合法性低的不足，被动地进行乡村治理活动。传统模型中，村民被排斥在村庄治理边界之外，他们是村庄治理的"搭便车"者和公共服务的消费者。这种角色定位，导致村民没有足够的话语权和宽广的空间参与到村治中。

（二）构建多元乡村治理模型

基于草根 NGO 组织在乡村治理中面临着自身无法克服的困境及传统乡村治理模型的弊端，此处构建多元共治模型，如图 2。

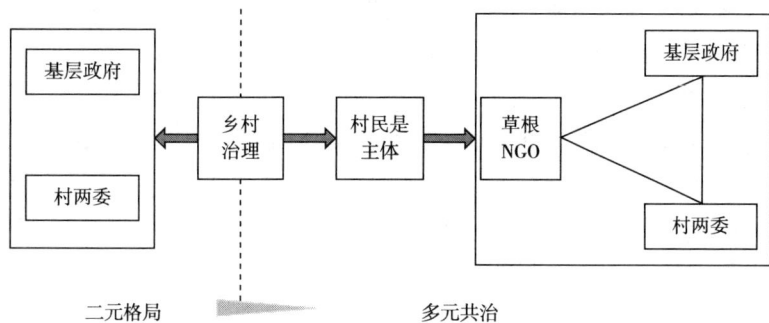

图 2　乡村治理模型

在此模型中，乡村草根 NGO 作为一个新兴的力量加入村庄治理中，而且成为村庄治理的主体，在公共服务、经济事务、村庄建设等方面承担政策制定、政策执行及执行监督的角色。基层政府则瘦身为一个协助者，对NGO 进行帮助、指导和监督，协调不同的 NGO 之间的矛盾冲突和利益分配。同时，NGO 从政府那里获得部分体制的合法性，从而克服自身的体制性障碍。村委会仍然承担着政府摊派的大量行政性事务，如计生、土地资源管理、乡村秩序等，并运用国家分配的资源进行村庄基础设施建设，对村民进行意识形态教育。村委与 NGO 的关系为：村委帮助 NGO 制定决策，并实施监督；NGO 则为村委理解村民需求，解释公众意愿。在新型治理模型中，村民成为治理的主体，成为公共服务的提供者而非消费者，其参与村庄治理的途径是参加草根 NGO 或是村两委，在其中扮演着政策制定、执行和监督的角色。

参考文献

曹锦清：《黄河边的中国》，上海文艺出版社，2000，第 73 页。

曹锦清、张乐天、陈中亚：《当代浙北乡村的社会文化变迁》，上海远东出版社，2001。

迪尔凯姆：《社会学研究方法论》，华夏出版社，1998。

费孝通：《江村经济——中国农民的生活》，商务印书馆，2001。

冯梅：《探索新农村道路的蒲州镇农协》，《女村官》2007 年 7 月 1 日。

贺雪峰：《取消农业税对国家与农民关系的影响》，《开发研究》2007 年第 1 期。

贺雪峰：《缺乏分层与缺失记忆村庄的权力结构》，《社会学研究》2001 年第 2 期。

胡亚柱：《郑冰和她的农民协会实践》，《中国乡村发现》2007 年 1 月 17 日：http：//www. zgxcfx. com/Article_ Show. asp？ ArticleID = 2165。

黄大金：《中国乡村社区治理研究》，博士学位论文，湖南农业大学农学系，2010，第 6 页。

黄宗智：《华北的小农经济与社会变迁》，中华书局，2000。

金太军：《村庄治理中三重权力互动的政治社会学分析》，《战略与管理》2002 年第 2 期。

刘老石：《农民需要新"农会"》，《中国改革·农村版》2000 年第 3 期。

卢福营：《村级治理下的村民公共参与》，《国家行政学院学报》2002 年第 3 期。

陆学艺：《走出"城乡分治、一国两策"的困境》，《读书》2000 年第 5 期。

蔺雪春：《当代中国村民自治以来的乡村治理模式研究述评》，《中国农村观察》2006 年第 1 期。

倪晓峰：《从精英主导型社区整合到半契约型社区整合》，中山大学出版社，2011。

乔运鸿：《乡村治理中的村庄精英角色分析》，《中国行政管理》2012 年第 10 期。

任小平：《永济市蒲州镇果品协会调研报告》，《综合农协》2012 年第 1 期。

苏力：《法治及其本土资源》，中国政法大学出版社，1996。

王红丽、孙彩凤：《农民协会发展刍议》，《北京农业职业学院学报》2007 年第 2 期。

温铁军：《中国农村基本经济制度研究》，中国经济出版社，2000。

王蕙、李尚红：《对我国农村家庭联产承包责任制消极效应的若干思考》，《湖北经济学院学报》2008 年第 1 期。

王凯、鹿泉、梁漱溟：《乡村成人教育思想及其启示》，《继续教育研究》2008 年第 6 期。

王铭铭：《社区的历程》，天津人民出版社，1997。

王铭铭、王斯福编《乡土社会的秩序、公正与权威》，中国政法大学出版社，1999。

吴毅：《村治变迁中的秩序与权威》，中国社会科学出版社，2003。

徐祥临：《关于重建农村合作经济组织的思考》，《农村合作经济经营管理》2001 年第 1 期。

徐翼：《中国需要自己的农民协会》，《中华工商时报》2006 年 10 月 24 日第 4 版。

徐勇：《脆弱的小农能支撑得起一个农村的现代化体系吗?》，《三农中国》总第 2 辑，湖北人民出版社，2004。

徐勇：《当前中国农村研究方法论问题的反思》，《河北学刊》2006 年第 2 期。

徐勇：《建构"以农民为主体，让农民得实惠"的乡村治理机制》，《理论学刊》2007 年第 4 期。

徐勇：《农村微观组织再造与社区自我整合》，《河南社会科学》2006 年第 5 期。

杨帅、温铁军：《农民组织化的困境与破解》，《人民论坛》2011 年第 10 期。

阎云翔：《私人生活的变革》，上海书店出版社，2006。

于国丽：《建国初期农民协会的积极作用对重建农民协会的启示》，《安徽农业科学》2009 年第 8 期。

于建嵘：《农村治理的问题与对策》，《中国政法大学学报》2008 年第 4 期。

于建嵘：《让农民组织起来——我们的试验和思考》，《东南学术》2007 年第 1 期。

于建嵘：《农会组织与建设新农村》，《中国农村观察》2006 年第 2 期。

张成福、党秀云：《公共管理学》，中国人民大学出版社，2007。

张德瑞：《论我国农民自治组织建设的困境与出路》，《中共福建省委党校学报》2007 年第 6 期。

张德瑞：《农会组织不是"洪水猛兽"》，《安徽农业科学》2010 年第 8 期。

张静：《基层政权——乡村制度诸问题》，浙江人民出版社，2000。

张乐天：《告别理想——人民公社制度研究》，上海人民出版社，2005。

张晓山：《中国乡村社区的组织发展》，《国家行政学院报》2001 年第 1 期。

赵晓峰：《寨子村新农村建设的成功之路》，《中国乡村发现》2007 年第 2 期。

〔美〕杜赞奇：《文化、权力与国家——1900～1942 年的华北农村》，江苏人民出版社，1995。

〔美〕莱斯特·M. 萨拉蒙：《公共服务中的伙伴》，商务印书馆，2008。

〔美〕西摩·马丁·利普塞特：《政治人——政治的社会基础》，上海人民出版社，1997，第 180～190 页。

中共中央文献研究室：《建国以来重要文献选编》，中央文献出版社，1988。

社会公益服务枢纽型组织的
生长与运作研究

——以宁波市公益服务促进中心为例

赵永红　赖兆飞 *

【摘要】现代公益事业不只是政府所需承担的责任，更是社会赋予每一个社会成员的共同义务。政府、市场和社会是现代社会公益服务不可缺少的参与主体，这是一项跨界合作的事业。但是由于目前社会公益服务体系发展不成熟，制度不健全，社会公益服务碎片化问题较为突出，这种跨界合作之间存在着信息不对称的问题，主体之间缺乏有效的沟通和互动的平台。而枢纽型社会组织的生长为解决这一问题提供了可能有效的模式。本文将以宁波市公益服务促进中心为例，从该组织的生长背景、生长过程、运作过程和运作效果等方面对社会公益服务枢纽型组织的生长和运作展开深入的研究，并得出相关的结论。

【关键词】社会公益服务；枢纽型组织；生长；运作

目前，我国各级政府把越来越多的目光聚焦在社会建设与社会管理创新

---

* 赵永红：男，1971 年 3 月生，宁波大学法学院公共管理系副教授，主要从事议会政治与中国基层社会治理研究。赖兆飞：宁波大学法学院学生。

工作上，社会创新理念不断加强。社会的不断成熟也使社会释放着各种各样的活力，为社会发挥自我调节和自我发展的作用提供了足够的空间。这一变化在社会公益服务领域有了充分的体现。社会公益服务枢纽型组织的出现进一步满足了社会公益的多样化需求，使公益参与主体之间实现跨界合作成为一种可能。它在一定程度上解决了社会公益服务碎片化的问题，为公益参与主体提供了交流和信息共享平台。同时，公益资源也能通过这一平台进行整合从而释放出更大的能量。宁波市在社会公益服务领域的成功实践也证明，社会公益服务枢纽型组织具有广阔的发展空间，在未来，这种"枢纽式"的运作模式是值得推广和复制的。

一 问题的提出及枢纽型社会组织的引入

公民社会和治理理论的出现及应用使政府与社会的界限变得更加清晰，这两个治理主体在现代公益事业中逐渐建立了合作伙伴关系。[①] 尤其是社会在公益服务领域发挥的作用越来越大，它承担了更多的原本属于政府的公共管理和服务的职能。这正是我国在社会管理和创新理念指导下社会走向成熟与进一步发展的表现。但总体上来说，政府与社会的这种合作尚处于探索和初级阶段，社会公益服务在发展过程中也面临着诸多的问题。正是出于对这些问题的思考、探索和实践，枢纽型社会组织应运而生。枢纽型社会组织的出现为公益服务的发展带来了更多的活力和空间。

（一）社会公益服务的三大主体：政府、市场和社会

社会功能的日益增强，使现代社会公益事业呈现新的发展趋势，即提供社会公益服务的主体不断增加，其提供公益服务的空间得到拓展。现代社会的公益事业，不仅是政府履行公共服务和管理职能的具体体现，它也随着市场的成熟和社会力量的增强而不断融入市场和社会这两个公益服务主体当中。政府、市场和社会根据自身的性质和特点，依托自身掌握的不同资源，

---

① 李红娟：《我国非政府组织提供社会公益的问题及对策研究》，硕士学位论文，中国海洋大学行政管理系，2008。

在公益事业中发挥着不同的作用。

首先是政府。政府本身具有社会管理和公共服务职能，在这一职能的范畴内，极大的一部分包含在了公益事业当中。而作为传统的提供公益服务的主体，政府利用财政资源直接生产公益产品，提供公益服务，满足普遍性的公益需求，同时也依靠行政行为来管理市场和社会在公益事业中的参与。

其次是市场。改革开放之后，市场在我国社会主义建设事业的各个领域都发挥着重要的作用。在公益服务领域，市场的理念也逐渐被引入并得以运用。以市场化模式运作，借助市场的竞争性和自主性提供多元化、高质量的公益产品，这是市场参与公益事业的主要方式。

最后是社会。"小政府，大社会"的理念逐渐在我国的政府改革进程中凸显出来，从政府职能中剥离出来的许多公共服务职能转移到社会管理中，而这种管理模式强调社会的自我组织和自我调节。同时，"大社会"也正在主动承担起政府无法涉及的社会事务，现代社会已经在公益服务领域确立了不可替代的地位。无论是在政府部门注册的民间社会组织，还是未经注册而由社会公民以个人形式发起和组织的草根社会组织，都为公益事业带来了新的活力和发展契机。

（二）社会公益服务发展过程中的问题——社会公益服务碎片化

市场和社会的参与为公益事业的发展打开了新局面，许多政府职责不能涉及和覆盖的公益服务被纳入市场和社会的参与范畴当中。但是市场与社会的加入尚未能解决社会公益服务领域存在的一些问题。

第一，政府、市场和社会三个主体在提供公益服务过程中存在各自的难题。政府在社会管理方面放权之后，在公益服务领域仍旧依靠大量财力的支持，生产和提供单一的公益产品；市场虽然能够承受一部分的公益服务，提供一些形式多样的公益产品，但是由于市场存在必然的利益追求，而大部分公益服务存在市场太小、投入成本高的特点，使市场无法挑起公益事业的"大梁"；社会通过社会组织等形式可以提供多样化的公益服务，满足日益趋向个性化的公益需求，同时也不需要计较成本与利润，但是爆发式增长的社会组织在管理方面相对混乱，"官办"色彩较浓的社会组织在实际运作中表现出了越来越多的依附性与依赖性特征，越来越"官"化。[①] 草根社会组织往往难以被主流因素所接受，它们在实际运作中受到各方面因素的排斥，在"草根化"的同时也遭遇了更多的发展困境。[②]

第二，政府、市场和社会三个主体之间缺乏有效的互动与合作。尽管公益事业在政府、市场和社会三大主体之间已经建立了一定的联系，并且也出现了多样化的公益服务形式，但是由于这种联系的建立较为薄弱，这种跨界之间的联系尚未实现有效的合作。公益服务参与主体所提供的服务质量远远没有跟上参与主体数量增加的脚步。主体之间各自为政，缺乏有效的信息沟通和交流，公益服务形式重复率高；公益资源大量投入，却收效甚微，造成资源浪费；更多的公益服务也只是以"捐款捐物""献爱心"等公益活动形式为主的短期行为，缺乏长效机制。

第三，企业和公民个人的公益意愿缺乏有效的表达平台。社会的进步使公民个人更注重人生价值的实现及个人意愿的表达，更多的人希望为公益事业出一份力，许多特殊的能满足个性化公益需求的活动方式也来源于社会公众。但是在实践过程中，他们往往因缺乏足够的资源和有效的平台，只能通过零散的志愿服务来参与公益事业，难以为公益需求群体提供更多的帮助。而对那些拥有足够的资源和有意于公益事业的企业来说，它们缺乏的是将现有的公益资源转化为公益服务、为那些具有公益需求的群体提供服务的行之有效的途径。

总的来说，社会公益服务在发展过程中的问题就是社会公益服务碎片化的问题，即社会公益服务供需信息不对称，公益服务提供主体之间缺乏信息交换和资源整合的平台。因此，社会公益服务的进一步发展需要成熟的服务体系和健全的管理制度，同时也需要在政府、市场和社会之间，以及公益服务供给方和需求方之间建立桥梁和纽带，为公益服务的提供者和所有参与者提供有效的平台，从而使公益服务取得实际的社会效益和社会价值。

（三）枢纽型社会组织的引入：形式和特点

面对上述社会公益服务在发展过程中出现的问题，我们需要思考的是如

---

① 崔玉开：《"枢纽型"社会组织：背景、概念与意义》，《甘肃理论学刊》2010 年第 5 期。
② 崔玉开：《"枢纽型"社会组织：背景、概念与意义》，《甘肃理论学刊》2010 年第 5 期。

何建立起一个有效的平台，在政府、市场和社会之间建立桥梁和纽带，以加强三者之间的联系，从而真正实现公益事业的跨界互动与合作。同时将这一平台提供给公益服务的供给方和需求方，通过这个平台对现有的公益资源进行有机整合，挖掘潜在的公益力量和资源，实现公益服务所有参与者的价值，达到公益服务的社会效益最大化。枢纽型社会组织的出现，为解决上述难题提供了有效的参考，同时也在实践中逐渐成为社会公益服务发展的有效措施。

1. 枢纽型社会组织的生长及其概念

枢纽型社会组织首次被提出是在北京市出台的关于构建"枢纽型"社会组织工作体系的相关文件中。[①] 这一新思路改变了由政府相关部门担任各类社会组织的业务指导单位的现状，充分发挥了枢纽型社会组织的积极作用。[②] 事实上，上海在2003年便提出"枢纽式管理"的模式并付诸探索与实践。而北京市的实践则开始于2009年，北京市先后在2010年、2011年共认定了27家市级枢纽型社会组织。它们的出现覆盖了北京全市85%的社会组织服务管理工作，之后，上海、天津、广东等地纷纷成立枢纽型社会组织，发挥其在社会组织管理中的作用。

由于枢纽型社会组织在理论上是一个新概念，在实践中是一个新模式，在学术界尚没有对它明确的理论界定。目前较为官方的概念来自2008年北京市的一份政府文件，它对枢纽型社会组织的定义是：枢纽型社会组织是指由负责社会建设的有关部门认定，在对同类别、同性质、同领域社会组织的发展、服务、管理工作中，在政治上发挥桥梁纽带作用、在业务上处于龙头地位、在管理上承担业务主管职能的联合性社会组织。[③] 之后，枢纽型社会组织逐渐被社会各界所认同，并在各地方有了深入的实践和发展。

2. 枢纽型社会组织的形式和特点

枢纽型社会组织在最初的理论和实践中，是在社会建设领域，对社会组

---

① 卢建、杨沛龙、马兴永：《北京市构建社会组织"枢纽型"工作体系的实践与策略》，《社团管理研究》2011年第9期。

② 颜小钗：《"枢纽型"社会组织：置疑声中前行》，《中国社会工作》2010年第136期。

③ 资料来源于北京市社会工委《关于构建市级"枢纽型"社会组织工作体系的暂行办法》，2008。

织进行有效管理的一种形式。目前，枢纽型社会组织的生长具有多样化的形式，其中包括社会组织促进会、基层的社会组织联合会、行业性质的社会组织联合体及服务中心等。①

虽然枢纽型社会组织在形式上呈现多样化，但是它有一个最大的特点，即它本身是社会组织的一种，却能够实现其他社会组织的自我调节和管理。在传统的政府行政体系中，社会组织是其中的一部分，是政府在提供公共服务和管理中的有力助手，因此社会组织的运作充斥着行政色彩。而枢纽型社会组织的出现，改变了社会组织的运行环境和运作机制，使它们成为依靠有机整合机制而联系在一起的独立而又互助合作的团体，行政等级制度在这类团体中逐渐减弱直至消失。这种有机整合机制就是枢纽型社会组织本身的特点。

因此，枢纽型社会组织为社会组织的发展、社会建设及社会自我管理带来了新的模式和参考，在这种模式的影响下，社会组织可以发挥更大的活力，同时也为社会公益服务的发展带来新的契机和空间。

二　社会公益服务枢纽型组织的生长

"枢纽型"的运作和管理方式能够为社会公益服务提供更多的发展空间，能够为公益事业注入更多的力量。它的主要功能在于，能够实现社会公益服务的跨界合作，对现有的呈现"碎片化""零散性"的公益服务进行有机整合，提高社会公益服务的社会效益和公益事业的影响力，切实地解决社会上存在的一些政府所提供的服务无法覆盖的层面的问题。

可以说，在社会建设和社会管理层面，枢纽型社会组织是一个值得深入探索和实践的模式。而在枢纽型社会组织概念出现以来，经济较为发达且社会相对成熟的地区已经在结合当地社会组织建设和管理的基础上进行了深入的实践。除了北京、上海等地区之外，宁波市也已经开始了枢纽型社会组织在地方的实践，并将重点切入在社会公益服务领域。宁波市公益服务促进中心的成立就是典型的对社会公益服务进行"枢纽式"运作和管理的实践。

---

① 高成运：《社会组织管理改革四题》，《社团管理研究》2011 年第 12 期。

（一）宁波市公益服务促进中心的生长背景

宁波市公益服务促进中心的成立不是偶然的，而是在新的时代特征下，宁波市为实现社会建设和社会管理创新的目标而在社会转型框架内的一种探索和实践，也是其社会发展相对成熟的体现。在社会公益需求增加，现有的社会组织运作和管理模式难以满足这种需求的情况下，通过整合公益资源，提高公益服务效益就成为宁波市在社会建设和社会管理创新过程中的重要内容。因此，宁波市公益服务促进中心的生长有其特定时代下的制度和政策背景，同时也是宁波市在探索新公益模式过程中的大胆实践。

1. 制度与政策背景

宁波市公益服务促进中心的生长有其特定的制度与政策背景，主要体现在国家和宁波两个层面。

一方面，近年来我国政府越来越认识到，依靠传统的政府一手抓的社会治理模式已经不能满足社会发展的需求，政府要改善"行政效率低下，行政成本过高"的尴尬局面，就必须加快职能转变，加快社会建设和社会管理创新，突出社会自我建设和管理的功能。可以说，"小政府，大社会"的格局目前在我国已现雏形，这种格局的出现为社会组织的进一步发展提供了更广阔的制度空间。

另一方面，作为全国、全省社会管理创新综合试点城市，宁波的社会建设工作在全国一直名列前茅。[①] 宁波市在社会管理创新中的实践涉及交通事故纠纷处理、提供各类便民服务等方面，宁波已经形成了具有宁波特色的新型社会管理体系，并为社会组织的进一步发展提供了更多的政策支持。在公益服务领域，宁波市实施的《关于公益类社会组织直接登记的若干意见》，意味着宁波市的公益类社会组织可以实现直接登记，这一政策大大降低了这类组织的准入门槛，免去成立之初的找"挂靠单位"之苦，这在浙江省是首例，在全国也鲜有城市出台同类政策。

2. 新公益实践背景

随着社会组织数量的爆发式增长，传统的政府行政管理手段已经难以适

---

① 蒋炜宁：《宁波推进社会管理创新工作全力解答时代命题》，中国宁波网：http://news.cnnb.com.cn/system/2011/12/06/007170599.shtml，最后访问时间：2012 年 2 月 6 日。

应现实发展的需要。尤其在公益服务领域，社会进步带来的更多的多样化公益需求与名目繁多的社会组织难以实现有效合理的对接。而枢纽型社会组织则为公益服务的发展提供了新的实践模式，也为政府和社会在公益服务领域的融合搭建了良好的平台。

近年来，宁波市在探索新公益模式过程中进行了充分的实践，宁波市枢纽型社会组织在助力社会组织满足居民需求方面作出了很大的贡献。新公益实践已经成为宁波市公益服务发展的一种潮流，宁波市公益服务促进中心在这样的新理念中应运而生。

（二）宁波市公益服务促进中心的生长过程

宁波市公益服务促进中心成立于 2012 年 7 月，它是由宁波市民政局主管，宁波市社会组织促进会和浙江大学公民社会研究中心共同主办的为公益参与者提供全方位专业服务的非营利性机构。① 宁波市公益服务促进中心作为枢纽型社会组织在宁波的实践，它的生长并不是一蹴而就的，而是宁波市在社会组织建设过程中，经过多年的探索和实践，积累了宝贵经验之后在公益服务领域的又一大胆实践，它也是宁波市在社会管理创新工作中的亮点。

事实上，宁波市在社会管理创新方面的工作可谓亮点纷呈。早在 2001年，宁波市海曙区政府就成立了"81890"求助服务中心，宁波市民可以通过电话、短信和网站等多种渠道无偿获取全方位服务信息。而在公益服务和社会组织管理领域，宁波市公益服务促进中心并非宁波市第一个枢纽型社会组织。2010 年年底，宁波市海曙区政府成立了"海曙区社会组织服务中心"，它是浙江省的首个枢纽型社会组织。这一枢纽型组织成为满足人们公益需求的助推器，为宁波在市一级成立枢纽型社会组织提供了重要的借鉴意义，也为宁波市公益服务促进中心的生长提供了"肥沃的土壤"。

同时，一种由政府出资为社会公益需求者进行服务投资的方式在地方兴起，这种方式就是公益创投。它的运作类似于企业的"孵化"和风险投资，

---

① 宁波市公益服务促进中心官方网站"公益群"：http：//www. nbgy. org. cn/，最后访问日期：2012 年 5 月 3 日。

由政府出资，对基层社会组织的公益项目、公益活动给予专项支持或扶持。① 根据宁波市民政局的数据，2011 年宁波市出资 800 多万元用于扶持近 300 家社会组织实施公益项目。② 公益创投模式又为宁波市公益服务促进中心生长之后的运作提供了借鉴。随后，宁波市民政部门与多所高校相关机构合作，对筹建宁波市公益服务促进中心进行充分的可行性调研和论证，试图以中心为纽带，在公益服务领域建立起一个专业化、系统化的公益服务供给机制，将政府、市场和社会等公益主体联系起来，形成一个新的公益产业链。

宁波市公益服务促进中心的生长过程是一个理论和实践互为给养、共同作用的过程。它的生长得到了政府部门和社会各界的关注和支持。从设想到成立，政府部门的组织协调、高校科研机构的调研论证、媒体舆论的宣传及相关社会组织的经验指导都是宁波市公益服务促进中心生长过程中的重要助力和推手，它的生长也是社会协同作用的结果。

三　社会公益服务枢纽型组织的运作

宁波市公益服务促进中心作为宁波市一级的社会公益服务枢纽型组织，它将公益参与主体紧密地联系起来，在公益服务领域实现社会协同。同时，它也为社会组织的发展提供了制度和管理模式的参考。传统的社会组织从生长到运作都带有强烈的行政色彩，由政府通过行政手段进行管理。而宁波市公益服务促进中心则打破了社会组织行政化运作的方式，以项目化运作的方式，将公益服务以公益项目的形式展现并实施。而在公益项目的运作过程中，宁波市公益服务促进中心则引入市场竞争机制，将公益项目进行公开招投标，并将评估机制和激励机制纳入公益项目实施的路线图之中。

（一）宁波市公益服务促进中心职能

宁波市公益服务促进中心是一个专业化的具有公益性的综合有机体，作

---

① 郑黎：《政府观念转变宁波："公益创投"大踏步前进》，《瞭望新闻周刊》，2012 年 4 月 9 日。

② 王芳、易鹤等：《我市打造全新公益服务模式》，《宁波日报》2012 年 5 月 23 日。

为社会公益服务的纽带和平台，它的职能就是为每一个公益参与主体提供服务，形成一条全新的公益产业链，其中包括公益需求者、公益资助者和公益生产者。同时，宁波市公益服务促进中心作为社会公益服务的支点和助力器，也为宁波市社会组织的发展输出制度和管理，孵化和扶持社会组织的发展，培育更多专业化的公益人才。具体来看，宁波市公益服务促进中心的职能主要体现在以下几个方面。

1. 收集公益需求，整理公益项目，建立公益项目库

宁波市公益服务促进中心是一个公益项目"水库"，它将公益需求者的需求以项目的形式加以收集并整理，建立起一个庞大的项目库。政府公共服务计划、企业公益资助方案及社会组织甚至个人的公益慈善项目都可以由宁波市公益服务促进中心经过专业化的项目设计纳入公益项目库中。这一职能在一定程度上解决了公益服务碎片化的问题，同时也为部分个性化的公益需求的满足提供了可能。

2. 共享公益信息，整合公益资源，推进公益项目的实施

作为一个公益服务平台，宁波市公益服务促进中心将公益信息进行公开共享，让全社会都能了解公益需求，并为每一个参与主体提供合理的公益服务参与渠道。而作为公益项目"大超市"，宁波市公益服务促进中心将创造性地建立起以公益服务为交易产品的市场，让社会财富和资本通过这一渠道流入社会公益服务领域，为每一个公益参与主体创造更好的条件。[①] 同时，它也使来自政府、市场、企业、社会组织和个人的公益资源互为营养和补充，实现公益资源最大化的整合和配置，使各个公益服务主体的公益资助能够实现最大化的价值。

3. 输出公益服务，同时对公益项目实施效果进行评估和激励

宁波市公益服务促进中心被认购的公益项目都将得以完善和实施。这一过程就是输出公益服务的过程，也是公益意愿和需求被加工成高质量的公益产品反馈给公益需求者的过程。而通过竞争机制以招投标的形式经过项目设计形成的公益服务生产出的公益产品不仅可以多样化，也能够提高公益服务的质量和水平。在项目实施过程中，公益资源得到充分利用，公益需求得到

---

① 许义平：《新理念、新公益》，《公益群》2012 年 6 月第 1 期，创刊词。

满足。公益项目的实施的最终效果将经过专业团队的评估，评估结果将被反馈给每一个公益参与主体，宁波市公益服务促进中心对实施效果的较好的项目进行一定的激励，由此完成了整个公益产业链的周期性运作，公益资源进入再循环利用，整个公益市场也将随之转动起来，使公益服务真正达到全社会协同的状态。

4. 孵化和扶持社会组织的发展，输出制度和管理，培育出专业的公益服务人才[①]

随着社会的进步，社会公益需求呈现个性化、精细化的特点。而现有的社会组织往往难以满足这些公益需求。对宁波市公益服务促进中心来说，一方面它可以利用自身优势和资源为特殊公益需求小群体孵化出能够满足这些小群体需求的社会组织，为其提供社会动员和参与主体；另一方面通过项目合作的方式扶持社会组织中的"弱势"，使之能够在公益事业中发挥更大的作用。同时在此过程中对这些社会组织输出有效的制度和管理。而通过孵化和扶持社会组织的发展及新公益的实践，宁波市公益服务促进中心也能够培育和成就一批新公益的专业人才。

5. 为公益志愿者提供志愿服务平台，宣传新公益理念，加强公益经验的交流和分享

宁波市公益服务促进中心在为政府部门和社会公益团体服务的同时，也为公益志愿者们提供了参与公益服务的机会和空间。每一个对公益服务有意愿的个体都可以加入公益服务的队伍中来，参与公益项目的实施。这也是宣传新公益理念的重要途径，宁波市公益服务促进中心希望能通过志愿者服务平台，加强公益经验的交流与分享，让更多的人了解公益，参与公益，动员全社会的公益力量为社会公益事业添砖加瓦。

（二）宁波市公益服务促进中心的公益项目运作流程

通过对宁波市公益服务促进中心运作职能的了解，项目化运作贯穿公益服务的始终，这也正是其创新和独特之处。宁波市公益服务促进中心作为一个公益服务平台，通过"公益创投"的方式，充分利用项目这一载体，通

---

① 张宝娟：《公益性社会组织培育发展研究》，《社团管理研究》2012 年第 3 期。

过项目征集、项目设计、项目发布、项目资助、项目招标、项目实施、项目评估和项目激励等这一条完整的流程完成公益项目的实施。① 而在这一过程中，政府、媒体、企业、社会组织、高校等各个不同的公益参与主体参与其中，在项目运作的不同阶段发挥不同的作用。

下图为宁波市公益服务促进中心的公益项目实施路线图，通过该图可以清晰地了解到宁波市公益服务促进中心的公益项目运作流程及项目实施的参与主体。根据宁波市公益服务促进中心的职能，从项目征集到项目激励的八个步骤中，我们可以将公益项目的实施主要分为三个阶段。

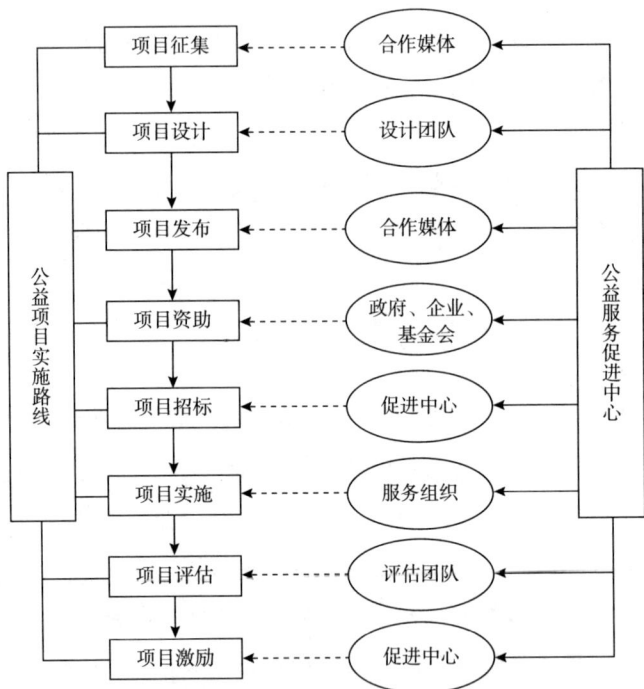

宁波市公益服务促进中心的公益项目实施路线图

资料来源：宁波市公益服务促进中心"公益群"官方网站，http：//www. nbgy. org. cn/。

第一阶段：项目征集、项目设计和项目发布。项目征集主要通过媒体进行公开征集，大到政府部门的公共服务计划、社会组织的慈善项目，小到个

① 宁波政府相关网站：http：//www. baidu. com/link？url＝kmMZG。

人或小团体形式的志愿服务都可以作为公益项目汇集到宁波市公益服务促进中心。项目设计则是由专门的设计团队将每一个征集到的公益计划、慈善项目和志愿服务等都以具体可执行的项目的形式加以设计优化，以确保项目的可行性。而这一设计团队主要由政府部门、合作媒体、社会组织、高校等成员组成。经过设计优化的公益项目通过媒体向社会进行发布，吸引有能力实施这些公益项目的主体前来认购实施。

第二阶段：项目资助和项目招标。经过设计优化及发布之后的公益项目将面向全社会进行公开项目招标，具有公益资源和公益项目实施能力的主体可以通过投标的方式认购公益项目。这些主体包括政府部门、基金会等社会组织及企业等能够提供公益项目资助的资助方。这一环节也是公益项目得以实施的重要步骤。

第三阶段：项目实施、项目评估和项目激励。被认购的公益项目由认购项目的公益投资者联合其他服务组织按照项目计划实施。宁波市公益服务促进中心在此过程中对项目的实施情况进行跟踪，对活动的开展提供相关指导，并在项目实施完成后，由评估团队对实施效果进行评估和反馈，根据评估结果对公益项目实施方通过增加项目资助和投入等方式进行激励，以提高公益项目的实施效率，使公益项目能够在实施过程中发挥最大的社会价值，产生最大的社会效益。

总体而言，公益项目在从项目征集到项目激励这一完整的运作流程中，宁波市公益服务促进中心既是项目实施的组织者，也是参与主体的服务者。在这样的公益服务平台和网络中，各个公益参与主体在公益项目实施过程中既分工明确又紧密合作，整个项目运作呈现信息公开化、资源透明化、服务专业化等特点，极大提高了公益资源的利用效率，更好地满足了差异化的公益服务需求。

（三）宁波市公益服务促进中心的运作效果

从筹建生长到运作至今，宁波市公益服务促进中心得到了政府部门与社会各界的广泛关注和支持。虽然它的运作时间并不长，但是从实际的运作效果来看，它的运作已经取得良好的社会效益，也在公益服务领域打造了一个枢纽型社会组织的实践典范。

第一，宁波市公益服务促进中心的运作广泛传播了新公益理念和公益文化，引导和调动更多的社会力量共同参与社会公益事业。经过大力的宣传和实际的运作，越来越多的人了解了新公益理念，动员了更多的人以自己的方式支持公益服务事业的发展。公益项目库中的许多项目被企业和一些社会组织认购并实施，部分项目进入评估阶段，也有越来越多的人成为宁波市公益服务促进中心的注册志愿者，主动参与到公益项目的实施。宁波市公益服务促进中心已经成为公益服务领域的"81890"。

第二，宁波市公益服务促进中心通过公益项目运作，将物质转化为服务，在一定程度上缓解了公益事业中的"服务贫困"现象，并提高了公益资源的利用率。在宁波这样的爱心城市，有许多具有社会责任感的企业希望在公益事业中有所作为。而部分慈善组织的信任危机导致企业对直接的捐款捐物抱有谨慎态度；企业自己举办的公益活动又收效甚微。而如今，宁波市公益服务促进中心可以为企业量身定制公益项目，将企业的物质输出转化为服务输出，引起了企业的极大兴趣。目前迪信通的大型"助工济困"公益活动、恒源祥的"恒爱行动"等都是通过公益项目的形式向社会提供公益服务。

第三，宁波市公益服务促进中心直接或间接地扶持了宁波市爱心小团体等公益类"草根"组织的发展，为它们提供了广阔的发展空间。这些"草根"组织往往是由爱心人士自行发起、以满足部分群体公益需求的小团体。宁波市公益服务促进中心将这些"草根"组织汇集在一起，让这些爱心力量有一个"家"，通过项目合作等方式使它们参与公益服务，帮助其壮大组织力量，充分发挥其在社会公益服务事业中的积极作用，提升社会服务能力，体现其社会价值。

另外，宁波市公益服务促进中心也为社会公益服务枢纽型组织在宁波其他县市区及全国其他地区的生长提供了实践经验。在它的影响下，更多类似的社会协同体将成为社会管理创新的重要角色，在社会建设领域发挥重要的作用。

四 社会公益服务枢纽型组织在发展中应注意的问题

社会公益服务枢纽型组织是在我国社会建设的背景下出现的，它具有重大的理论和实践意义，在社会公益服务领域具有创新性。但它仍处于探索阶段，也存在许多需要不断完善的地方和尚待解决的普遍性问题。

（一）社会公益服务枢纽型组织与政府部门的互动关系问题

社会公益服务枢纽型组织如何淡化对作为公益服务"枢纽网络"一部分的政府的依赖，如何确保组织运作的独立性，又能合理地获取政府资源、始终与政府保持合作关系，成为一个值得深思的问题。宁波市公益服务促进中心是在政府部门主导下、借助社会土壤生长的社会组织，定位好与政府部门的关系是充分发挥其作用的关键所在。而作为主管单位，宁波市民政局也应在给予公益资源支持的前提下赋予它充分的运作自由，减少行政干预，发挥其积极性和主动性。

（二）社会公益服务枢纽型组织与其他社会组织的互动关系问题

社会公益服务枢纽型组织也是一种社会组织，而作为"枢纽"，如何确定与其他社会组织的管理边界与管理权限，[①] 如何在确保社会组织自身活力的同时激发其更大的发展潜力，这些都是社会公益服务枢纽型组织运作是否有效的关键因素。宁波市公益服务促进中心在发展过程中应以整合其他社会组织的公益资源，汇聚公益力量，为公益服务主体提供服务为主，以为其他"弱势"公益组织输出管理为重。

（三）社会公益服务枢纽型组织的自身建设问题

目前承担着"枢纽"功能的社会组织在一定程度上仍具有浓厚的行政化色彩，在具有优势的同时，也存在着行政化带来的弊端。如何提高工作人员的素质，保持对社会公益需求的敏感度，都直接关系到社会公益服务枢纽型组织能否充分发挥其社会功能的重要因素。宁波市公益服务促进中心较为"年轻"，其生长和运作的时间并不长，许多问题尚未凸显出来，要提供高质量的服务和高水平的管理就应加强自身建设，就要通过不断的探索和实践，建立公益服务的长效机制和可行的制度作为保障，使其能够真正成为公

---

① 崔玉开：《"枢纽型"社会组织：背景、概念与意义》，《甘肃理论学刊》2010 年第 5 期。

益服务领域不可或缺的载体。

只有把握好这些问题，处理好公益服务参与主体间的关系和自身建设问题，社会公益服务枢纽型组织才能充分激发自身的潜能，更好地满足社会公益需求，体现其存在的价值和意义，并在公益服务事业中越走越远。

五　结语

通过对社会公益服务枢纽型组织的生长和运作的研究，我们可以得出，社会公益服务枢纽型社会组织能够较为有效地解决公益服务碎片化、主体跨界合作信息不对称等问题，它汇聚了公益服务需求、公益服务资助、公益服务生产等多方的公益服务力量，激发了社会公益服务的活力。虽然社会公益服务枢纽型组织的发展仍处于探索和完善阶段，同样存在一些亟待解决的问题，但可以说，它具有广阔的发展空间，像宁波市公益服务促进中心这样的社会公益服务枢纽型组织的运作模式是值得推广的，是可复制的有效模式。

本文通过对枢纽型社会组织的了解，对社会公益服务枢纽型组织的生长与运作展开研究，并试以宁波市在这一方面的探索和实践为例进行论述。在研究过程中，宁波市公益服务促进中心作为社会公益服务枢纽型组织的实践模式，它的生长背景、生长过程、运作及其效果都为我们了解这类组织的发展提供了诸多有用信息，为我们了解和认识枢纽型社会组织提供了参考，它也是公益实践过程中公益组织建设的有益探索和实践。但是由于研究水平和写作水平有限，虽然在文中介绍了社会公益服务枢纽型组织的生长与运作的情况，但只是管中窥豹，认识是浅显的，了解是初步的，对社会公益服务枢纽型组织的生长与运作仍有许多问题未能涉及，比如枢纽型社会组织的生长规律研究，如何建立起公益服务的长效机制及如何确保这类组织的生命力和创新力等，希望以后能有机会继续深入研究。

参考文献

崔玉开：《"枢纽型"社会组织：背景、概念与意义》，《甘肃理论学刊》2010 年第5 期。

张宝娟:《公益性社会组织培育发展研究》,《社团管理研究》2012 年第 3 期。

许义平:《新理念、新公益》,《公益群》2012 年 6 月第 1 期,创刊词。

郑黎:《宁波"公益创投"的公共服务》,《瞭望》2012。

王芳、易鹤等:《我市打造全新公益服务模式》,《宁波日报》2012 年 5 月 23 日。

李红娟:《我国非政府组织提供社会公益的问题及对策研究》,硕士学位论文,中国海洋大学行政管理系,2008。

卢建、杨沛龙、马兴永:《北京市构建社会组织"枢纽型"工作体系的实践与策略》,《社团管理研究》2011 年第 9 期。

颜小钗:《"枢纽型"社会组织:置疑声中前行》,《中国社会工作》2010 年第 136 期。

高成运:《社会组织管理改革四题》,《社团管理研究》2011 年第 12 期。

蒋炜宁:《宁波推进社会管理创新工作全力解答时代命题》,中国宁波网:http://news. cnnb. com. cn/system/2011/12/06/007170599. shtml,最后访问时间:2012 年 2 月 6 日。

天津滨海新区的社区治理

金太军[*]

【摘要】 本文选取"泰达模式""新港经验""寨上做法""胜利特色""中新生态城模式"五个典型案例，采用嵌入性多案例比较的方法，从社区治理结构、工具和方法三个层面评估社区治理实践成效，总结社区治理发展战略，凝炼社区治理的基本思路。

【关键词】 经济开发区；天津滨海新区；社会管理；社区治理

社区是社会管理的落脚点，社区治理的优化与创新，关系到社会管理的发展和社会公共服务的实现。滨海新区"立足实际、率先发展、不断创新"，社区治理呈现"百花齐放"的态势，形成了"泰达模式""新港经验"等具有全国意义的社区治理典范。

天津市滨海新区位于天津东部临海地带，全区规划面积 2270 平方公里，海岸线 153 公里，下辖 27 个街镇、360 个居村，常住人口 251 万。近年来，滨海新区经济持续保持强劲发展势头，地区生产总值连续五年跨过五个千亿元台阶，2012 年达到 7205 亿元。滨海新区既包括塘沽、汉沽、大港等老城区，还包括经济技术开发区、高新区、商务区、经济区等功能区，还有旅游

---

 * 金太军：男，1963 年 6 月生，安徽全椒人，现任苏州大学校学位委员会、学术委员会委员，政治与公共管理学院院长。

区、保税港区及生态城等中外合作区,① 行政区与经济区混杂、新城区与老城市叠加，社会管理中既要解决新问题，又要面对老问题，因此，社会管理的经验也更有可行性、可学习性和可推广性。在本文中，我们重点剖析滨海新区的社区治理、社会组织建设、流动人口管理、劳资矛盾治理等方面的基本做法和成功经验。下面，简单说明一下本文的研究路径。

本文聚焦滨海新区的社会管理创新，采用案例研究的方法来分析。因为社会管理是一个现实性极强、又极其复杂的问题，属于"发生在当代但无法对相关因素进行控制的事件"，所以适合采用案例研究方法。② 为了提升结论的说服力和经验的可信性，我们将典型案例剖析和多案例比较综合运用。为避免案例研究由"归纳"分析变为"列举"分析，我们采用了两种方法：一是选择典型案例。我们遵循两个指标：实践成效显著和社会影响度高。衡量的标准是上级政府的肯定和新闻舆论的关注度。二是多案例比较时采取逐项复制的原则，例如"社区治理"部分，为了让案例研究的结果具有更高程度的确定性，我们进行了五个逐项复制，选取"泰达模式""新港经验""寨上做法""胜利特色""中新生态城模式"五个典型案例。

所选案例资料来自四种途径：一是调研中搜集的政府部门的相关政策法规、制度细则等，如《滨海民政（2011 年资料汇编）》《滨海新区社区居委会业务工作使用文件汇编》；二是相关政府或部门的报告文件、宣传材料及政府网站相关的工作报道，比如《构筑社区治理共同体创建现代宜居新社区》《新滨海、新塘沽》；三是国内平面媒体和网络媒体的相关报道和评论，如《"十大员"带来和谐风——天津滨海新区胜利街探索基层管理模式》③；四是相关政府部门领导、工作人员和社区组织负责人的访谈资料。

---

① 滨海新区建成区包括塘沽、汉沽、大港、经济技术开发区、天津港保税、高新、生态城、东疆港、旅游区、中心商务区、临港经济区、轻纺经济区、北塘经济区、中心渔港和天津港。参见天津市滨海新区统计局《2012 天津滨海新区统计年鉴》，中国统计出版社，2012。

② 罗伯特·K. 殷：《案例研究：设计与方法》，重庆大学出版社，2010，第 13 页。

③ 武自然：《"十大员"带来和谐风——天津滨海新区胜利街探索基层管理模式》，《经济日报》2012 年 4 月 17 日第 14 版。

一　分析框架

"社区"由德国社会学家 F. 滕尼斯于 1881 年首次用于社会学，① 中文"社区"由费孝通于 20 世纪 30 年代在《二十年来之中国社区研究》一文中从英文"Community"翻译而来，现在的社区已经成为学术界和政策界的通用概念，它一般涵盖三个层面：行动体系、互动场域和关系网络。"治理"一词最早于 1989 年由世界银行用于政治发展研究，描述发展中国家的政治状况；1995 年，全球治理委员会发表题为《我们的全球伙伴关系》研究报告，其中将治理界定为：治理是各种公共的或私人的个人和机构管理其共同事物的诸多方式的总和。俞可平提出了善治（良好的治理）的六个要素：合法性、透明性、责任性、法治、回应、有效。② 由此可见，治理和善治强调了治理的主体、治理的方式、治理的规则和治理的能力。这说明"社区治理"是一个复合概念，它强调在一定的场域内由发生各种社会关系、具有心理认同感的公共的或私人的个人和机构组成的行动体系来管理共同事务、提供公共服务。根据上面的界定，我们可以将"社区治理"解构为四个维度：社区治理结构、社区治理工具、社区治理方法和社区发展战略，这四部分及其逻辑联系构成本章案例分析的框架体系。

社区治理结构，是社区治理主体及其行为模式和互动关系，其基本构成要素包括社区党组织、社区组织、社区社会组织、基层政府、公民等，这些治理主体之间围绕社区公共事务和社区公共服务展开互动，缔结各种关系网络，构成了社区治理结构。

社区治理工具，是社区治理主体为了解决社区事务问题、实现社区发展目标而采用的具体手段和方式。社区治理工具的选择影响社区治理的绩效和社区治理的目标。

---

① 德文 Gemeinschaft，滕尼斯在《社区和社会》（1887 年）中比较分析了 Gemeinschaft 和 Gesellschaft（一般译为社会）；美国社会学家罗密斯第一次将滕尼斯的书译为英文，*Community and Society*（社区和社会），"Community"一词由此产生。参见娄成武，孙萍《社区管理》，高等教育出版社，2003，第 1 页。

② 俞可平主编《治理和善治》，社会科学文献出版社，2000，第 1~12 页。

社区治理方法，是社区治理主体借助治理工具为提供社区公共服务、满足居民需要而选择的路径及展开的程序和步骤。

社区发展战略，由社区治理结构、社区治理工具和社区治理方法共同构成。它是社区将目标转化为现实的路径，具体来讲就是社区治理主体在一定的治理情境中借助一定的治理工具、运用一定的治理方法满足社区居民需要、提供社区公共服务的方案和对策。

这四个方面是社区治理的基本构成要素，涵盖了社区治理的环境、主体、行为、过程和策略，从静态和动态两个层面对社区治理进行立体式剖析，这也构成了案例分析的框架体系。

二　案例的比较分析

下文将从社区治理结构、社区治理工具和社区治理方法三个层面对五个案例进行比较分析，据此总结滨海新区社区治理的发展战略。

（一）社区治理结构的比较

这五个案例中的社区治理结构虽然各具特色，但是又存在着一个共同点，即多元协作。

"泰达模式"中的社区治理结构是社区治理"共同体"。党组织是"共同体"的核心和基石，总揽全局协调社会关系；政府是"共同体"的主导者，制定政策法规，合理配置各类资源；居民是"共同体"的核心，是社区各项公共事务的发起者、参与者和监督者，居民参与是治理动力，居民满意度是衡量治理的标准；社区组织是"共同体"的纽带，提升社区居民的归属感，增强社区凝聚力，强化社区自治功能；社会组织是"共同体"的细胞，承接政府和社区组织委托事务，培育社区民间组织。

"新港经验"的社区治理结构是"3721"城市社区组织体系。"3"是指三个基本实体工作机构，即一个社区党委、一个社区居委会、一个社区工作站（"一委一居一站"）。"7"指7个专业工作委员会（"七专委"），即社区共建和协调委员会、社区治保和人民调解委员会、社区公共事业发展委员会、社区福利委员会、社区民情委员会、社区公共环境管理委员会、青年妇女儿童工作委员会。"2"指两会，即居民会议（居民代表）和社区民情会议。"1"是指"一个交叉任职的制度机制"（"一机制"），即建立社区党组班子、社区居委会、业主委员会交叉任职，居民小组、楼院门栋长、社区志愿者等民主选举产生。

"寨上做法"的社区治理结构以"共建参与多元化""居站分设"为基本架构。所谓"共建参与多元化"，指党建工作合力共抓，社区事务协力共管，社区环境通力共建，社区事务戮力共办，发展成果群力共享的"五力"并举共建格局。"居站分设"激发基层组织的推动力，推进管理重心下移，公共服务延伸，居务管理自治进小区、进楼门、进家庭。

"胜利特色"通过"结对共建"构筑起社区治理结构。包括六个层面：一是干群帮扶结对，二是党内互助结对，三是街企共建，四是军民共建，五是代表、委员与社区共建，六是监管单位与社区共建。

中新生态城按照"生态细胞－生态社区－生态片区"的三级居住模式响应规划了"生态细胞中心－生态社区中心－城市（次）中心"三级社区服务结构，其中，社区服务的重点在生态社区层面。

通过以上的社区治理结构比较（见表1），我们可以看出一些共同特征：一是治理主体呈现多元异质性，"多元主体"的内涵不仅仅包括社区党组织、社区居委会、社区工作站，还包括社会组织、企业、机关单位与公民等不同性质的治理主体。二是多元主体之间是一种协作关系。虽然，"多元主体"性质类型各不相同、利益诉求各不相同，但是在治理结构中角色清晰、定位明确、功能互补，"多元主体"在协作中"多而不乱"，通过各种联系纽带来缔结各种协作关系，实现"多元主体"中的协作治理。

表1　社区治理结构比较

典型案例 比较指标	泰达模式	新港经验	寨上做法	胜利特色	中新生态城模式
社区治理结构	社区治理"共同体"	"3721"城市社区组织体系	"共建参与多元化""居站分设"	结对共建	"生态细胞中心—生态社区中心—城市（次）中心"三级社区服务结构

（二）社区治理工具的比较

这五个案例中，"泰达模式""新港经验""寨上做法"的社区治理工具相似，都运用了网格化管理和网络技术。网格管理的本质是区域责任制，基本做法是将社区"分片包块"，每一位社区工作人员负责一块"责任区"的管理和服务。网格化管理实现了社区的规范化管理和精细化管理，例如"寨上做法"的"划格结网""一格七员"，七种力量进网格，即"网格党支部书记、网格管理员、网格助理员、网格警员、网格督导员、网格消防员和网格司法力量"，实现工作机制、社区资源和管理手段在"网格"的整合。网络技术在滨海新区的社区治理中得到了广泛的应用，效果显著。基本做法围绕社区居民需求，整合社区服务资源，运用信息化手段开展社区管理服务工作。例如泰达的"数字社区管理信息系统""泰达城市网"。

在社区治理工具中，"胜利特色"和"中新生态城模式"极具特点。"胜利特色"的核心是"十大员"和社区文化平台。"十大员"的基本做法是"分片包块"，按每 260～300 户为一片，片区设督导员、管理员、治安员、教练员、保健员、保洁员、助理员、宣传员、调解员、信息员十大岗位，并结合社区实际和居民需求，"量身定做"岗位职责。它本质上是网格化管理的一种创新，创新点在于挖掘社会资源、调动社会力量，充分发挥社区社会组织和社区志愿者在社区治理中的作用。据调研观察，社会组织已经成为胜利街重要的群众力量，社会组织的成员在社区担当着"十大员"岗位，发挥示范和带动作用，引领周围群众积极参与社区日常管理与服务。社区文化平台在胜利街道的社区治理中也发挥着重要的作用，基本做法是大力发展社区文体组织，搭建社区文化交流平台，"坚持月月有主题，场场有特色的文化发展原则"，以重大节日为依托，广泛开展各类演出、展示、义卖等公益活动；大力推进文化单元建设，实现一个社区一个特色，一个楼门一个主题。社区文化建设有利于居民走出家门、融入社区，增强社区凝聚力，提升社区归属感和心理认同。中新生态城的关键是"社区中心"，"社区中心"是承载生态城社区服务的重要平台和核心节点。整个生态城建设 10 个"社区中心"，综合运用公益服务和商业服务等方式，为社区居民提供医疗卫生、教育文化体育、养老服务、社区公共服务、社区生化服务、社区商业服务等多元化服务项目。

就治理工具来看，网格化管理和网络技术得到了普遍的应用；社区管理和服务"走进"居民，效果显著；鼓励和引导居民参与社区治理，让居民融入社区亟待加强（见表2）。

表2 社区治理工具比较

典型案例 比较指标	泰达模式	新港经验	寨上做法	胜利特色	中新生态城
社区治理工具	网格责任制、"数字社区管理系统"和"泰达城市网"	"网格坐标管理"和社区动态协调机制、"民情110综合管理信息系统"	"一网多格、一格多员、全员参与""数字社区'三通'服务"	"十大员"、社区文化平台	社区中心

（三） 社区治理方法的比较

在社区治理方法层面存在两种思路：一是"提供什么社区服务"，二是"如何提供社区服务"。

第一种思路"提供什么社区服务"，例如"泰达模式"中的需求类型化和"寨上做法"中的"一站七园"。"泰达模式"以社区居民需求多元化为出发点和落脚点，综合分析居民需求和各类社区问题，编制《社区管理与服务手册》，将社区事务分为投诉管理、公共服务、公益服务、社会服务四大类，对314项具体社区事务制定标准化流程。"寨上做法"将服务对象的基本需求和社区提供的公共服务细化为七个功能片区：健乐园、康乐园、百乐园、福乐园、同乐园、民乐园、和乐园，分别对应社区卫生服务站、全民健身服务站、便民服务中心、社区养老服务站、社区文化活动中心、多功能大厅及综治信访服务站。

第二种思路"如何提供社区服务"，例如"新港经验"中服务功能全面化、胜利街道的共同治理和中新生态城的公共服务市场化。新港街道推出"一口式、全业务"服务，每个社区工作人员都能熟悉掌握社区承担的每项业务流程，能够办理每项业务；社区工作人员实行错时工作制，与居民的休息时间对接。胜利街道通过共同治理，把服务下沉到"片区"，充分发挥结对共建单位、社区社会组织和"十大员"的作用，鼓励和引导居民参与社区事务、实现自我管理。中新生态城积极规范政府购买公共服务的行为，探索形成了"政府承担、定向委托、合同管理、评估兑现"的政府提供公共服务方式，在购买公共服务时明确范围和项目、明确工作职责、明确操作程序、明确项目购买方式、明确评估方式。

在这五个案例中，两种治理方法都有体现，只是侧重点略有不同（见表3）。

表3　社区治理方法比较

典型案例 比较指标	泰达模式	新港经验	寨上做法	胜利特色	中新生态城
社区治理方法	需求 类型化	服务功能 全面化	"一站七园"	共同治理	公共服务 市场化

社区治理方法的这两种思路说明目前社区居民的需要呈现多元化格局，需要多元化说明社区居民需求差别不断扩大，造成了居民的诉求内容和诉求关系日益分化，这要求街道和社区必须对日益多元的利益诉求意愿作出积极回应，这对政府的社区管理能力提出了新的要求。为了适应这一形势的需要，基层政府一方面积极提升自身的治理能力；一方面向社会和市场放权，下沉管理和服务职能，由社区社会组织、社区企业、社区志愿者等来承接这部分职能，实现多元化的社区公共服务。

（四）社区发展战略的总结

一般意义上，政府是行政核心，拥有对社区主要的管理权。但是，从天津滨海新区的社区治理中体现出一种新的战略："以服务来实施管理。"具体来说包括三层内涵：第一，重构基层政府社会管理职能，政府向社会和市场放权；第二，大力发展社区社会组织，提升社区自治能力，以承接政府下放的权力和下沉的职能；第三，创新社区治理结构，引导社会力量和市场力量参与社区管理，提升政府与社会的合作能力。五个案例都体现了社区治理这一发展思路。例如"泰达模式"中，运用专业化社会工作方法提升社区服务居民水平，通过提高居民组织化程度增强社区自治能力；胜利街道通过"结对共建、共同治理"来提高政府与社会的合作能力；"寨上做法"采用"居站分设""一站七园"来重构政府社会管理职能；新港街道和中新生态城通过政府购买公共服务来发展社会组织。

三　经验总结

通过上面五个案例的比较分析，我们大致勾勒了滨海新区社区治理的基本轮廓（见表4），滨海新区社区治理的基本思路为：发展社区社会力量，提升社区自治能力，实现社区善治，建设"大社区、强社区、好社区"。具体包括三个方面的内容：

表4　滨海新区社区治理典型案例的比较

典型案例 比较指标	泰达模式	新港经验	寨上做法	胜利街道	中新生态城
社区治理结构	社区治理"共同体"	"3721"城市社区组织体系	"共建参与多元化""居站分设"	结对共建	"生态细胞中心—生态社区中心—城市（次）中心"三级社区服务结构
社区治理工具	网格责任制、"数字社区管理系统"和"泰达城市网"	"网格坐标管理"和街道社区动态协调机制、"民情110综合管理信息系统"	"一网多格、一格多员、全员参与""数字社区'三通'服务"	"十大员"管理、社区文化平台	社区中心
社区治理方法	需求类型化	服务功能全面化	"五和"社区建设	共同治理	公共服务市场化
社区发展战略	重构基层政府社会管理职能，政府向社会和市场放权；大力发展社区社会组织，提升社区自治能力，以承接政府下放的权力和下移的职能；创新社区治理结构，引导社会力量和市场力量参与社区管理，提升政府与社会的合作能力				

（一）完善社区治理结构，构建社区协同治理体制，建设"大社区"

滨海新区的社区治理通过完善社区治理结构，形成了极具区域特色和借鉴意义的协同治理体制。党的十八大报告强调"加快形成党委领导、政府负责、社会协同、公众参与、法治保障的社会管理体制"，关键是要理顺政府与社会之间的关系，实现两者的和谐互动。滨海新区的社区治理体制作出了成功的解读和有益的探索。它以基层党组织为核心，以基层政府为主导，以社区居民为主体，以社区居委会和社区服务中心（站）为依托，以社区社会组织和社区志愿者为纽带，凝聚社会各方力量，构建了社区的协同治理体制。例如"泰达模式"中的社区治理"共同体"，"新港经验"的"3721"城市社区组织体系，"寨上做法"的"两委一站一会""居站分设"，"胜利特色"的"结对共建""共同治理"等，都是这一协同治理体制的典型代表。同时，积极培育新的、多元化的社会组织，加快社区社会组织建设，完善社区自治组织体系。例如寨上街道按照"三社联动"模式（社区、社区工作者和社会公益组织），完善社会组织保障；发挥街道社会组织联合会的作用，依托社区服务中心，建立社会组织孵化器，积极探索社会组织建设和培育的新模式。

（二）优化社区治理工具，搭建社区信息技术平台，建设"强社区"

滨海新区在社区治理中积极优化社区治理工具，充分发挥网络和通信等信息资源功能，通过社区信息网络，建设"数字社区"，一方面搭建了社区服务信息平台，提高了社区治理的效率。例如寨上街道的"三通""数字社区"，在便民服务"一键通、一线通、一点通"的基础上，实现了居委会博客、社区贴吧、网上警务室、民情邮箱、服务热线及 IT 服务便民小超市全覆盖，建设了信息透明、直接对话、平等沟通的网上社区，在社区管理者与居民之间搭起了信息平台。一方面信息技术运用社区事务和社工绩效评估，搭建了社区居民与政府的沟通交流平台，实现了政府与居民的互动，加强了社区居民对社区管理者的监督。例如泰达的"数字化社区系统"中开发的"社区单一事件评价系统"，实现了对社区专业工作队伍的绩效考核。系统按照社区事务难易程度、与居民利益关切度、社会服务效益的不同而赋予不同的权重打分原则，实现了社区工作的量化。大力发展社区志愿者队伍，创新公共服务载体，积累社会资本。

（三） 创新社区治理方法，以居民需求为导向，建设"好社区"

创新社区治理方法，以居民需求为导向，就是从社区的实际情况出发，把解决各类社区成员尤其是大多数居民群众的实际需要放在第一位，把解决社区群众普遍关心的热点、难点问题作为社区治理工作的出发点。例如新港街道针对辖区老旧房集中、老龄化程度较高的特点，一方面开办助老餐厅、设立日间照料室，一方面大力建设老年文艺团队队伍，实现"老有所养、老有所为、老有所乐"。"泰达模式"根据社区居民的需求和社区的热点问题，将社区事务分为非市场化服务和市场化服务两大类，开发设计了两个系统，即侧重于非市场化服务的数字社区系统和侧重于市场化服务的泰达城市网系统。泰达城市网可以使社区居民足不出户享受网上缴费、浏览数字图书馆、调阅家庭健康档案、"B2C"物流配送等服务，有效满足了居民的公共需求、社会需求和商务需求。

总而言之，滨海新区通过完善社区治理结构、优化社区治理工具、创新社区治理方法，提出了社区发展的新战略，这一战略明确了经济开发区社区治理的未来发展方向。这不是偶然发生的，而是由社会需求和政府能力决定的。面对转型社会的常态问题和风险社会的非常态问题，各种挑战和应对挑战的方式也比以往更加纷繁复杂。单一的政府统管机制已经不能满足快速变革的社会需求，尤其不适宜处理常常要超越组织边界的问题。多元主体的利益诉求和参与欲求日益高涨，政府不再是唯一的社会管理者和公共产品的提供者。这要求变革原有的"政府包揽式"社区管理模式，发展社区社会力量，提升社区自治能力，实现社区善治，建设"大社区、强社区、好社区"。

参考文献

罗伯特·K. 殷：《案例研究：设计与方法》，重庆大学出版社，2010，第 13 页。

俞可平主编《治理和善治》，社会科学文献出版社，2000，第 1~12 页。

高校志愿者参与志愿服务的动机及激励机制分析

——基于 20 名访谈者的质性研究

冯　华*

【摘要】本文通过对 20 名高校志愿者访谈资料的整理，在 ERG 需求理论的基础上，将志愿者参与志愿服务的动机创新性地划分为传统型、现代型、后现代型三类，认为志愿者参与动机呈阶段性发展的趋势。本文提出了认可型、自我发展型、自我愉悦型、全程型及"言利"型五种激励机制，实现志愿者需求与公益组织的优化匹配，提高志愿者参与志愿服务的持续性和效率。

【关键词】志愿者；动机；激励；ERG 需求理论

一　问题的提出

首先，随着志愿服务事业的不断发展，国内的志愿者组织开始认识到，过分强调志愿者参与志愿服务的意义和重要性，有时使志愿者精神激励过

---

*　冯华：西南财经大学副教授，社会工作师，主要研究方向为应用社会学、社会工作、志愿者管理。

重，导致志愿者出现过度的紧张与焦虑，同时造成精力和热情过早消耗而无法胜任或坚持完成自己的工作。

其次，国内对志愿者的激励，主要来源于志愿服务的组织机构，如对志愿者的物质保障、表彰奖励、联谊活动等，基本都是志愿服务机构在主导，政府在其中也发挥了积极的作用。但是对志愿服务缺乏整体及全面性的推广及配合，导致人们往往只停留于表面认知层面，没有适当及足够的途径参与，因而欠缺了一股投入参与的动机及实际行动。①

最后，目前所有的志愿者激励都是为了完成服务活动。志愿服务机构开展志愿服务活动和志愿者参与志愿服务活动的一个共同基础，是基于志愿服务项目这样一个公共平台。但由于中国开展志愿服务时间不长，在项目的可持续开展上还很欠缺，临时性或一次性项目较多，对志愿者的激励也主要集中在完成所从事的志愿服务任务上，使得志愿者的激励仅仅停留在最初级的目标上，没有持续的完整的全程激励机制。

目前国内绝大多数关于志愿者参与志愿服务的动机研究所采用的资料收集方法都是结构式问卷调查法，而采用深度访谈等质的研究方法来探寻志愿者参与动机的研究还属罕见。结构式问卷调查法的所有关于动机的各种答案都是研究者事先拟定好的。而被调查者，除了在研究者事先列出的那些封闭式的答案范围内作出选择外，别无他法。因此，这一方法常常漏掉许多被访者实际存在的真实动机。

为了弥补国内在志愿者参与动机研究方面的不足，本研究将采用质性研究方法中的访谈法（Interview），对志愿者参与志愿活动的动机作些探索性的研究。试图探寻：志愿者参与志愿活动的具体动机到底有哪些？他们的参与动机可分为哪几种主要类型？在不同的参与阶段，他们的参与动机有无变化？即进入时的初始阶段的参与动机，与进入后的持续阶段的参与动机是否不同？本研究改变以往研究中的问卷型粗放调查方式，结合 ERG 理论的三大需求层次，对志愿者参与动机进行科学的划分和符合发展需求的划分，从而制定合理有效的激励机制，以有效激励志愿者参与公共事务，优化公共资源配置，提高人力资源利用率。

---

① 谭建光、凌冲、朱莉玲：《现代都市志愿者心态分析》，《中国青年研究》2005 年第 1 期。

二 基于 ERG 理论的志愿者参与动机划分

（一）ERG 需要理论

克雷顿·阿尔德弗尔（Clayton Alderfer）在马斯洛的需要层次理论的基础上，进行了更接近实际经验的研究，于 1969 年提出了一种新的"人本主义"需要理论。阿尔德弗尔认为，人们共存在三种核心的需要，即生存（Existence）的需要、相互关系（Relatedness）的需要和成长发展（Growth）的需要，因而这一理论被称为"ERG"理论。[①]

第一种需要是人们基本的物质生存需要，它包括马斯洛提出的生理和安全需要。第二种需要是相互关系的需要，即指人们对保持重要的人际关系的要求。这种社会和地位的需要的满足是在与其他需要相互作用中达成的，它们与马斯洛的社会需要和自尊需要分类中的外在部分是相对应的。最后，阿尔德弗尔把成长发展的需要独立出来作为第三种需要，它表示个人谋求发展的内在愿望，包括马斯洛的自尊需要分类中的内在部分和自我实现层次中所包含的特征。

除了用三种需要替代了五种需要以外，与马斯洛的需要层次理论不同的是，阿尔德弗尔的"ERG"理论还表明：人在同一时间可能有不止一种需要起作用；如果较高层次需要的满足受到抑制的话，那么人们对较低层次的需要的渴望会变得更加强烈。

马斯洛的需要层次是一种刚性的阶梯式上升结构，即认为较低层次的需要必须在较高层次的需要满足之前得到充分的满足，二者具有不可逆性。而相反的是，"ERG"理论并不认为各类需要层次是刚性结构，比如说，即使一个人的生存和相互关系需要尚未得到完全满足，他仍然可以为成长发展的需要工作，而且这三种需要可以同时起作用。

志愿者活动是基于个人意愿的活动，主要依靠个人的内在驱动力执行。从访谈结果来看，以"责任感"为轴心的传统型动机所占比例已经开始慢

[①] 全国社会工作者职业水平考试教材编写组《社会工作者综合能力》，中国社会出版社，2010，第 49 页。

慢下降，更多的人是倾向于相互关系的需要和发展的需要参与志愿者活动。ERG 理论对人际关系需要和发展需要的强调正好与现存的志愿者动机发展趋势相符合，有利于志愿者动机研究的科学划分。

（二）志愿者参与动机类型分析

在质性研究中，"本土概念"（Native Concept）主要是指被研究者在口头表达中反复使用的一些概念，它们是"经常使用的、用来表达他们自己看世界的方式的概念"。[①] 所以，本土概念实际上蕴含了一个人看世界的视角，质性研究正是通过研究一个人或一个群体是怎么观看世界的，然后来解释这个人或群体的心理和行为方式。在对访谈资料的整理中，15 名受访者都提及和使用了很多"本土概念"，如"责任感""帮助别人或为他人服务""做些对社会有益或有意义的事情""专业实践""锻炼能力""扩大交往圈""丰富生活""寻机会找个兼职""好奇""兴趣""好玩""快乐"等。

结合 ERG 理论的生存需要、相互关系需要和发展需要三个需要层次的内容和所有访谈者使用的本土概念，笔者将志愿者的参与动机划分为三个主要类属概念，即"责任感""发展"和"快乐"。除"发展"概念是笔者根据实际情况建构出的一个概念之外，其余两个概念都是受访者使用的"本土概念"。

"责任感""发展"和"快乐"这三个概念便构成了志愿者参与动机类属分析当中的三个主类属，而在每一个主类属或主要类型的下面，都包含若干个相关的分类属，比如在"责任感"下面有"帮助别人或为他人服务""做些对社会有益或有意义的事情"等；在"发展"下面有"专业实践""锻炼能力""扩大交往圈""丰富生活"等；在"快乐"下面有"好奇""新奇""兴趣""玩玩""开心"等。以下将对志愿者参与动机的三个主要类属或主要类型及其所包含的相关分类属作些具体分析。

1. 动机类型一：以"责任感"为轴心的传统型动机

基于责任感而参与志愿活动，是一种典型的传统型参与动机。人们在满

---

① 陈向明：《质的研究方法与社会科学研究》，教育科学出版社，2000，第 284 页。

足了自己基本的生存需要之后，对相互关系的需要激发了人们的责任感，责任感成了人们参与社会事务的原始出发点。

在被访问者中，提到这一动机的有 10 人。很多人都非常具体地表达了这一参与动机：他们认为，作为一个公民，有义务和责任帮助别人或为他人服务，有义务和责任做些对社会有益的事情。

W 同学说：我一直觉得自己是一个有爱心的人，我觉得就是看到现在社会上有很多不和谐的现象。大家其实生活在一个社会中，就应该互相帮助，这样我们的社会才能变得更好。我想通过志愿者的活动，把自己的能量传递给更多的人。志愿者工作是没有利的，不是功利性的，这样才能更体现出我们人与人之间的互相关怀，将爱和温暖传递给更多的人。

C 同学说：我父母本家是农村，他们经常把自己的幸福更多地分享给别的孩子，我受他们影响，大学后参加志愿者，觉得不仅可以自己去服务，还可以号召更多的人参与到其中来。

2. 动机类型二：以"发展"为轴心的现代性动机

现代性的一大特点是工具理性在人们的世俗生活当中占据极其重要的地位。体现在个体价值层面就是，社会中的个人往往将自我发展或成就动机作为个人的核心价值。随着人们自我意识的觉醒和在西方文化的引导下，很多中国青年的自我发展需要渐渐凸显。在 20 个访谈对象中，以"发展"为轴心的具体参与动机有 10 种，提到这一类参与动机的有 13 人。

（1）获得专业相关的实践机会

由于他们参与的这类志愿活动类似于专业实践，因此，他们把它看成一种跟专业实习有关联的机会。

H 同学说：其实我刚刚开始做志愿者不是很专业的，很迷茫。只是随着我们学院社会部的志愿者队去敬老院帮助老人，后来去校团委的志愿者总队，接触的都是组织。他们接触 NGO 的专业组织比较多，自己也在里面学习，我的兴趣也是在管理方面。……大学只是小部分而已。想以后有机会的话，就去外面更广的活动。

（2）锻炼能力

Y 同学说：有想过找其他更好的工作，最早我是利用寒假时间在这儿待过一个月。后来大三的时候学校实习，我就在这儿实习了一年（不以赚钱为目的），为的是锻炼自己，那个时候我向学校申请到这边来。

（3）扩大交往圈

B同学说：大学第一次进入的团体就是红会，当时并没有想说要做公益活动或是志愿者，但是红会的活动都是志愿者方面的活动，感觉红会的活动跟其他组织的活动很不一样，红会的活动是完全出于自愿的，和其他组织很强的功利性是不一样的。尤其是在活动过程中，你接触到的人，他们的目的都是很单纯的，可能会偏向美好一些。通过红会认识的朋友可能比其他朋友还要珍贵。

（4）接触了解与适应社会

D同学说：大一的时候在学生会做，大二在青协，我认为青协和学生会氛围不一样，觉得青协更轻松自主性更强，到过学生会后，觉得不适合我，而在青协能有更多的机会，学生会官方性很强，有更多任务。青协有很多社会上的活动，服务对象更广。

3. 动机类型三：以"快乐"为轴心的后现代动机

在后现代化（或晚期现代化、反思现代化）阶段，人们开始对早期现代化阶段的古典现代性进行反思，已充分认识到古典现代性，尤其是工具理性的局限性。因此，不再以成就动机和个人发展为核心价值，而是以快乐和幸福为个体所追求的核心价值。

访谈发现，以"快乐"为轴心的具体参与动机共有11种，除"快乐"外，还有5种具体动机，提到这一类参与动机的共有10人，具体情况如下。

J同学说：当时是一个很偶然的机会，当时在校团委工作，作为内部志愿者参加了"挑战杯"的一个会议，那次会议之后对志愿者有了一些了解，也看了陆浩他们写的一些文章，就竞选了学院青协。其实大一的时候我做的志愿者活动也不是很多，大概是老大比较看好我吧，就找我谈话让我做了队长。大二做队长，做的活动比较多，感触也比较多，觉得做志愿者是一件很快乐的事儿。

A同学说：第一次接触公益是汶川地震的时候，最早接触的时候是小时候读到了宋庆龄基金会。后来接触是跟家庭环境有关，我的母亲是援外的，接触得就比较多。后来被汶川地震感动，我本身在学琴，就写了一首歌《爱在进行时》，联合其他歌曲在青海做了一次义演。后来加入了学校的红十字会，接触的资源就更多了，有一些志愿者项目。

（三）参与动机的过程化分析

访谈中有一个意外惊喜，有些被访者在陈述自己的参与动机时，对其做了阶段性划分。从他们的叙述来看，个体的参与动机不是静态不变的，而是处于变动之中。而这一演变的过程大体可以分为两个阶段：进入时的初始参与阶段和进入后的持续参与阶段。两个阶段的参与动机，即进入时的"初始参与动机"和进入后的"持续参与动机"存在很大的不同。

阿尔德弗尔的"ERG"理论并不认为各类需要层次是刚性结构，比如说，即使一个人的生存和相互关系需要尚未得到完全满足，他仍然可以为成长发展的需要工作，而且这三种需要可以同时起作用。这也证明了志愿者参与动机的动态变化符合人本性的需要，对未来的志愿者激励机制的完整性和全程性有更高的要求。

Z同学说：其实我在高中的时候很少涉及这方面的活动，主要是大一刚刚开学的时候戴小红帽的志愿者姐姐从头到尾向我们介绍学校。那时候正好通识学院在招学生会，当时我报的就是青年志愿者那个部门，然后表现不好就被刷了，之后就一直想做志愿者。大二时进了金融青协，刚刚进去的时候没有志愿者的感觉，而且相当忙，还有学生会的工作。这学期我就退出了学生会，因为我想做好专门的志愿者。可以说，从头到尾这学期我们是忙翻了的。慢慢地坚持下来，真的觉得很有意义，包括下学期我仍然想留在青协。大三了能坚持就坚持，而且可以带下面的同学，毕竟他们也需要我们的帮助。

三 基于志愿者参与动机的激励机制探究

（一）社会支持型认可机制

"认可"是对责任感为轴心的传统动机者最大的激励。被责任感驱动的志愿者，他们自己的意识里面已经潜移默化有了公众事务的意识。对他们而言，参与志愿活动是为了完成自己的使命，对自己负责。因此，试图让志愿服务变得更有乐趣和挑战性，或增加部分激励物质，都不如给予志愿者简单的认可。

认可的成本虽然很小，却让志愿者建立起了自尊。为了激励志愿者，志愿者组织通常可以表扬志愿者的成就，让志愿者的行为得到社会的肯定。很小的认可可以有重大的意义，认可就是最大的激励。给予志愿者情感上的认可是志愿者活动持续性的有效保证。活动中真心的赞美、交代任务时强调重要性、活动结束之后的表彰都将有效地激励志愿者，使之获得情感上的愉悦。

（二）"言利"型激励机制

志愿服务较发达的国家大都这样认为：志愿服务是非营利服务，但非营利、不索取并不意味着一无所获。对志愿者的激励，不仅注重精神上的鼓励，而且还可以有物质上的激励，甚至金钱上的回报。

现在很多组织都会设置"时间银行"作为志愿者考核的依据之一，同样这也可以作为志愿者获得物质回报的机制。适当的物质回报有利于志愿者行为的可持续性，同时也可以促进公共资源的公平分配。

为志愿者制定6个月到2年的"服役期"，期满后可得到相应的奖学金（但不能以现金形式支取，仅用于缴纳学费），而且可以获得相关领域的优先实习机会等。志愿服务是可以有报酬的，只不过这些报酬的兑现需要使用特殊的形式。这些规定，可以体现出对志愿者的激励作用，即通过"言利"而"言励"。这些措施不仅是一种对志愿者作出社会贡献的认可方式，也是一种动员更多的社会公众参与到志愿服务中来的激励方式。

（三）自我发展型激励机制

自我发展型激励主要是通过志愿活动为志愿者提供职业岗位之外的锻炼机会，根据志愿者面试时的能力培训要求，安排志愿者的工作任务和工作岗位。特别是一些青少年志愿者，从初期参与社会服务的实际操作，到参与策划、组织各种志愿活动，再到对新志愿者进行指导、培训，不知不觉中就成了有领袖才能的资深志愿者。如果将这些新培养的能力用到职业生活中，相信志愿者的职业生涯就会越来越丰富与成功。

为了留住志愿者骨干分子，组织就必须要想方设法多设计出能为志愿者提升素质、发展自我的活动项目，以此激励保持并扩大志愿者人力资源存量。尝试通过增加工作的复杂性，将相关联的工作任务组合起来，使之成为一种新的、内容更多的工作任务，以增加志愿者工作技能的多样性；扩大对志愿者的授权范围，增强志愿者工作的自主控制能力，让志愿者单独负责有独立意义的某一任务或者项目，以强化志愿者的主人翁责任感，以最大限度地获得自我实现的成就感。志愿者自己参与获得的成就感不仅能够满足志愿者的能力诉求，而且为组织培养继承者。

（四） 自我愉悦型激励机制

志愿者的自我愉悦机制，是指学会在志愿服务中寻找快乐，或者善于将忧愁情绪转化，获得愉悦的体验。只有快乐的志愿者才能够长期坚持进行志愿服务，因为他们不仅有付出，也有收获。

推动志愿者开展志愿服务的是奉献精神，但是维系志愿者长期坚持志愿服务的则是快乐激励。虽然，责任、事业心、热情、慈善心等对志愿者的影响很大，但是对志愿者特别是青少年，在激情、好奇过后就需要快乐激励机制。这就需要组织想方设法让志愿者在服务中体验快乐、享受愉悦。如组织每天都要保持感激的心，对志愿者有所关怀，记下志愿者的点滴闪光点，并适时加以表扬；安排志愿者与组织管理者及服务对象共同参与联谊活动，由接受服务对象以各种方式对志愿者的服务表示感谢等。快乐愉悦的志愿者活动体验对志愿者的激励将有很大的发展空间。通过组织的完整事前准备、活动安排的合理有效和活动内容的趣味性，增强志愿者的快乐体验，将有效增强志愿者的持续服务时间。

（五） 全程型激励机制

全程型激励机制，即从招募就开始激励。组织需要确定"以志愿者为中心"的理念，从项目设计到招募培训，从组织实施到效果评估，都把志愿者的权益和感受放在重要位置。例如在招募培训中，看重志愿者的反馈；在效果评估中，把志愿者的感受作为必需的评估内容。对志愿者的激励也是一样，从志愿者的招募就开始进行，具体可以通过以下四个措施，实现全程激励。

1. 目标激励

对志愿者在新人培训中进行"目标激励"：将组织的长远目标、中期目标和近期目标让志愿者了解，并及时告知志愿者所参与项目的阶段性目标实现情况，使志愿者了解发展进程，了解自己在目标的实现过程中应起到的作用。

2. 工作激励

在志愿者服务前进行"工作激励"：工作本身就是志愿者寻求的目的，最忌讳的是志愿者加入后无事可做，给志愿者合适的工作岗位，让他们尽快参与到工作当中，也是对志愿者的激励。

3. 参与激励

注重志愿者在服务中的"参与激励"：畅通的沟通渠道，平等的对话制度，营造民主化的氛围，给志愿者体现自我价值的机会，体现组织决策的公正性，这样能更大地激发志愿者的积极性，形成组织的归属感、认同感，进一步满足志愿者自我实现的需要。

4. 荣誉激励

最后是对志愿者进行"荣誉激励"：荣誉是众人或组织对个体或群体的正面评价，是满足人们自尊需要、激发人们奋力进取的重要手段，从人的需求来看，人人都需要肯定和荣誉。在项目结束后，给予志愿者精神上的成就和认可，往往足以支撑志愿者作出更多的"牺牲"。事实证明，这种自始至终的激励深度大，效果更长久。

参考文献

陈向明：《质的研究方法与社会科学研究》，教育科学出版社，2000，第 284 页。

全国社会工作者职业水平考试教材编写组：《社会工作者综合能力》，中国社会出版社，2010，第 49 页。

谭建光、凌冲、朱莉玲：《现代都市志愿者心态分析》，《中国青年研究》2005 年第 1 期。

对中国西部地区构建农产品质量安全应急
管理"全域联动"机制的探讨*

余　华　漆雁斌　严玉宝　吴　华　陈迪钦　费　洋**

【摘要】农产品质量安全问题是影响国家经济社会发展的战略问题，关系可持续发展，关系人民群众切身利益。保障西部地区农产品质量安全事关国家经济安全、生态安全、人民健康和社会稳定。妥善处置农产品质量安全应急事件是维护农产品质量安全的重要内容。本文结合我国西部地区实际情况，通过分析提出西部地区构建农产品质量安全应急管理"全域联动"机制的对策建议，着力围绕"三个强化"，构建"全域联动"农产品质量安全应急管理机制；围绕"三个推行"，扎实推进农产品质量安全应急管理"全域联动"；围绕"三个促进"，不断提高农产品质量安全应急管理"全域联动"效能。

【关键词】农产品；质量安全；应急管理；机制；探讨

* 项目来源：国家质检总局科技计划项目"出口猪肉应对技术性贸易壁垒的措施研究"；四川省 2012 年重点科技自筹项目（编号：2012ZRZ014、2012SZZ030）；四川出入境检验检疫局 2013 年度科技项目（编号：SK201314）。

** 余华：(1978 年 8 月~)，男，汉族，四川人，四川农业大学博士研究生，已公开发表论文多篇。
漆雁斌：(1969 年 10 月~)，男，汉族，四川人，四川农业大学教授，博士生导师，已公开发表论文多篇。

农产品是一个民族生存发展的重要基础，是一个国家繁荣富强的基本保障。农产品的安全问题不仅关系国民生存与健康，更是衡量一个国家社会经济发展程度和人民生活水平的重要指标。近年来，我国农产品质量安全监管力度不断加强，监管投入不断增加，应急管理机制不断构建，但是"三鹿奶粉""苏丹红""瘦肉精"等农产品质量安全应急突发事件仍有发生，使人们对农产品质量安全的关注度进一步提高，同时也使人们对农产品质量安全的信任度大大降低。

一　前言

中国西部地区幅员辽阔，西部地区面积占全国国土总面积的57%以上，人口占全国总人口数的近四分之一，是少数民族集聚区域。处理好我国西部地区农产品质量安全问题对保障和维护全国农产品质量安全工作具有重要的意义。针对当前农产品质量安全事件时有发生、影响因素多样、危害后果叠加、易扩散难控制等特点，我国西部地区各级地方政府要紧密结合区域实际，积极探索农产品质量安全应急管理新路子，充分整合社会力量和公共资源，着力构建"全域一体、上下联动、左右协调、社会参与"的"全域联动"农产品质量安全应急管理机制，提升西部地区区域农产品质量安全突发事件应急管理能力和水平。

二　围绕"三个强化"，构建"全域联动"农产品质量安全应急管理机制

（一）强化农产品质量安全应急指挥

西部地区各级地方政府要根据农产品质量安全应急管理工作实际需要，组建本地区农产品质量安全应急管理委员会，将区域内农业、畜牧、质监、工商等相关政府部门统一纳入农产品质量安全应急管理指挥调度系统，负责全区域内农产品质量安全应急事件处置的统一领导、统一指挥。农产品质量安全应急管理委员会主任兼任突发事件处置指挥长，办公室设在地方政府应

急办公室，负责统一领导、指挥协调一般性农产品质量安全应急突发事件处置和较大级别以上的农产品质量安全应急突发事件的先期处置工作。

（二）强化农产品质量安全应急执行

西部地区地方政府农产品质量安全应急管理委员会下面可以根据工作需要，分别设置事件处理、事件调查、对外协调、信息宣传、物资保障、教育培训、监督检查等专项应急指挥小组，负责受理地区范围内农产品质量安全应急突发事件的处置，主要执行处置一般性农产品质量安全应急突发事件处置和较大级别以上的农产品质量安全应急突发事件的先期处置。同时，将农业、畜牧、质监、工商等相关政府部门纳入农产品质量安全应急联动系统，在各自职责范围内负责应急联动处置工作，承担该地区全域联动执行职责。

（三）强化农产品质量安全应急保障

各级地方政府要在开展风险分析、充分论证的基础上，按照优先保障应急装备的原则，保障农产品质量安全事故应急处理所需设施、设备和物资储备，提供应急处置资金，所需经费影单列入同级人民政府财政预算。特别是要充分发挥现代信息化技术平台的作用，进一步完善农产品质量安全应急管理保障体系。

三　围绕"三个推行"，扎实推进农产品质量安全应急管理"全域联动"

（一）推行农产品质量安全信息"全域联搜"

西部地区各级地方政府要针对实际工作情况，以"家园或村社＋网络"的模式，建立起农产品质量安全管理单元，在家园或村社网格内的单位、小区（院落）、社区（村组）、市场（商店或超市）、宾馆（酒店）、企业（工厂）等组织机构中选配农产品质量安全信息员。以家园或村社为单元组成农产品质量安全信息小组，信息小组以小区（院落）、楼栋、街路等为网格配备农产品质量安全信息员，组成农产品质量安全信息网络，实现农产品质量安全信息联合搜集。当农产品质量安全信息发出时，有关部门或单位即可在第一时间内将农产品质量安全突发事件信息垂直上报当地地方政府值班部门，由值班部门负责认真核实、甄别、整理并经过政府相关领导审核后上报上级政府，从而确保农产品质量安全信息迅速、无误传递。

（二）推行农产品质量安全风险"全域联防"

保障安全重在防患于未然，始治于未现。为了切实加强对西部地区地方政府辖区内农产品质量安全风险管理和控制，各级地方政府要按照"质量是基础、安全是底线"的原则要求，牢固树立"保安全就是保民生"的理念和"底线"意识，充分运用"底线思维"的方法，加强对危机、风险、底线的重视和防范，认真计算风险，估算可能出现的最坏情况，不断完善农产品质量安全风险防范体系，提高农产品质量安全风险防范处置能力，守住安全底线，保障西部地区农产品质量安全。具体来看，西部地区各级地方政府要按照县（区）、部门、镇（街道）、村（社区）四级分别建立定期排查、定向排查和联合排查制度，坚持做到每月定期查农产品质量安全隐患，重大活动、敏感时期定向查苗头，特殊时期联合查要害，全面掌握辖区内相关行业、领域的风险隐患。同时，要建立健全"一月一台账""一月一通报"的工作机制。对排查出的农产品质量安全隐患，要详细登记类型、责任领导和责任人、形成原因、整改措施、整改时限等基本内容。对确定的重大农产品质量安全隐患，要开展分级挂牌督办，切实做到整改措施、责任、资金、时限、预案落实到位，每月对整改落实情况进行通报。

（三）推行农产品质量安全应急处置"全域联包"

为了确保农产品质量安全应急处置工作落到实处、收到实效，西部地区各级地方政府可探索建立"政府农产品质量安全应急委包指挥、政府分管领导包督促、政府应急办包协调、责任部门包调处化解、专业部门包应急处置、联防力量包稳控、信访工作人员包接访"的模式，推进实施农产品质量安全应急处置"全域联包"。在日常工作中，要组织建立以"分级设防、分类预警、分案包处、分层明责"为主要内容的"四分"工作机制，确保农产品质量安全日常应急处置工作落到实处、收到实效。具体来讲，"分级设防"就是在西部地区地方政府辖区内建立县（区）、部门或镇乡（街道）、村（社区）、居民小组四级联动的农产品质量安全应急网络体系。"分类预警"就是在西部地区地方政府辖区内，按照农产品质量安全应急突发事件风险等级划分为红色预警、黄色预警、橙色预警，进行区分应急处置。"分案包处"就是在西部地区地方政府辖区内，针对不同类型的农产品质量安全应急事件，认真落实"五包"责任制。"分层明责"就是在西部地区地方政府辖区内，按照分类管理、分级负责、属地管理的原则，对各级领导、相关责任部门和个人分别明确工作职责。

四 围绕"三个促进"，不断提高农产品质量安全应急管理"全域联动"效能

（一）促进农产品质量安全应急资源的整合

整合资源对切实做好西部地区农产品质量安全应急管理至关重要。西部地区各级地方政府要根据各地实际需要，不断建立健全和完善农产品质量安全应急管理平台，有效整合有关农产品质量安全应急管理的社会资源，真正确保农产品质量安全专家、人员及时到位，以及检验检测设施、设备等应急处置资源动态管理的有效链接，切实做到人员管理"一点就通"、物资设施设备"一查就明"，从而充分发挥值班值守、信息汇总、调度指挥、事态跟踪、决策会商和总结分析等农产品质量安全应急管理作用。

（二）促进农产品质量安全应急工作合力的聚集

西部地区各级地方政府要通过整合各部门各单位农产品质量安全应急管理资源、信息和队伍，依托地方政府值班室，着力解决农产品质量安全应急管理工作中容易出现的条款分割、多头指挥等突出问题，从而实现地方政府的统一协调和有关部门的分类管理有机结合，切实做到综合性与专业性有机互补，职责分工明晰，管理协调有序。同时，充分发挥现代化的信息、通信、计算机、控制与指挥系统的作用，使地方政府各级领导能快速获取有关农产品质量安全信息，帮助地方政府领导作出正确、科学、快速的决策部署。

（三）促进农产品质量安全应急处置效率的提升

提升应急处置效率是积极、妥善应对农产品质量安全事件的重要因素。西部地区各级地方政府要依托当地政府值班室值班电话，涵盖政府行政服务的受理终端，切实解决推诿扯皮、办事拖拉等损害群众切身利益、严重影响政府形象的问题，实现应对农产品质量安全事件"统一接案、联合处置"，着力转变以往农产品质量安全应急管理的"联而不动"为现在的"灵敏高效"。

五 结语

"民以食为天，食以安为先"。农产品质量安全问题事关千家万户和子孙后代的健康，是一项民生工程、系统工程。搞好西部地区农产品质量安全工作是一项长期而又艰巨的任务，其中任何一个环节出现问题，都有可能功亏一篑，其中农产品质量安全应急管理就是其中极其重要的一个环节。我们相信，只要西部地区各级政府和社会各界对此项工作高度重视和广泛参与，经过一段时间的努力，我国西部地区农产品质量安全应急管理"全域联动"机制一定能够建成并充分发挥作用，切实保障西部地区农产品质量安全，从而实现好、维护好、发展好最广大人民的根本利益。

参考文献

方佳、李玉萍：《发达国家农产品质量安全体系状况及其对我国的启示》，《世界热带农业信息》2008 年第 1 期。

房宁：《农产品质量安全突发事件中的媒体沟通管理研究》，《农产品质量与安全》2012 年第 2 期。

冯忠泽、万靓军、田莉：《建立农产品质量安全市场准入机制的原则及措施分析》，《中国农学通报》2007 年第 23 期。

康升云、刘晶晶、胡川：《我国农产品质量安全问题成因探析》，《农业与技术》2008 年第 28 期。

钱建平、杨信廷、刘学馨:《农产品快速图形化追溯系统构建》,《农业工程学报》2011 年第 3 期。

钱永忠、王芳:《我国农产品质量安全存在问题及成因分析》,《农业经济》2008 年第 2 期。

秦文远、张丽丽:《加强农业标准化建设提高农产品质量安全水平》,《现代农业科技》2007 年第 19 期。

王为民:《我国农产品质量安全突发事件的特点、成因与对策分析》,《农产品质量与安全》2011 年第 1 期。

杨信廷、钱建平、孙传恒等:《蔬菜安全生产管理及质量追溯系统设计与实现》,《农业工程学报》2008 年第 24 期。

牛艳、王晓菁、吴燕:《农产品质量安全管理长效机制的探讨研究》,《安徽农学通报》2007 年第 13 期。

决策型海洋渔业应急管理系统的
研究和设计

——以青岛为例

同春芬　徐　阳[*]

【摘要】青岛市海洋渔业应急管理部门的现有系统为执行型系统，偏向指挥调度功能，存在决策能力低、缺乏公众沟通功能及功能重叠等问题。为提高政府的工作能力，适应服务型政府建设和行政体制改革的要求，应建设以应急预案为核心的决策型系统。考虑到系统的处理能力、工作范围及所处理事件的性质，强调了重点突出、易集成性和较强的安全性三点设计原则，进而从体系架构、业务流程及组成和工作流程方面对系统进行了基本的设计。最后重点指出了系统建设在改革措施推行、现有系统整合和建设人员素质上应具备的条件和面临的困难。

【关键词】应急管理；决策型系统；信息系统

一　引言

近年来，青岛市发生了 2008 年浒苔灾害、2010 年胶州湾海冰灾害等数

---

* 同春芬：1963 年出生，中国海洋大学法政学院公共管理系系主任，社会学教授、博士，硕士研究生导师，中国农村社会学会常务理事。主要从事海洋社会学、城乡社会学研究。

次重大的海洋渔业突发事件，造成了较大损失。在历次事件中，海洋渔业应急管理部门在处理能力和公众沟通等方面难尽人意，工作面临严峻形势；而在 2013 年 3 月 10 日公布的《国务院机构改革与职能转变方案》中提出整合现国家海洋局及其中国海监、公安部边防海警、农业部中国渔政、海关总署海上缉私警察的队伍和职责，重新组建国家海洋局，① 海洋渔业部门改革的步伐明显加快。工作的形势和部门的改革必然会触发对功能完善、集中统一的新型海洋渔业应急管理系统的需求，高效的决策型海洋渔业应急管理系统（以下简称决策型系统）能够最大限度地满足此需求。本文在对我国应急预案和类似系统研究的基础上，提出了对青岛市海洋渔业应急管理体系的改进建议，并依此对决策型系统进行了基本的体系架构和流程设计，以期为相关人员的下一步研究提供借鉴。

二 青岛市决策型系统建设的背景分析

海洋渔业应急管理系统是海洋渔业部门为应对海洋渔业自然灾害、事故灾难、公共卫生事件、社会安全事件等突发事件而建立的信息系统，依据核心功能和用户的不同类型，可分为执行型系统和决策型系统两类。② 执行型系统的核心功能是指挥调度，主要用户是海洋渔业应急管理部门的系统管理人员，其处理事件的类型一般是规模较小或中等的突发事件，如渔船碰撞、小范围水体污染等；而决策型系统的核心功能是评估决策，主要用户是海洋渔业应急指挥中心统计分析部门的工作人员和相关领导，其处理事件的类型一般是重大突发事件，如风暴潮、大范围溢油等，以及规模、发展势态不明朗的突发事件。

当前，青岛市海洋渔业应急管理部门已建有多个执行型系统，如渔政海监调度指挥系统、海事局海上船舶交通管理系统、海警 GPS 辅助指挥系统等，部分部门内部甚至存在多套不同品牌的该类系统，多数系统具备较为齐

---

① 马凯：《国务院发布机构改革和职能转变方案》，新华网：http://news.xinhuanet.com/politics/2013 – 03/10/c_ 114969788. htm，最后访问时间：2013 年 5 月 10 日。
② 刘志东、马龙：《应急指挥信息系统设计》，电子工业出版社，2009。

全的指挥调度功能，但功能重叠现象严重；与此同时，尚未建立决策型系统，其部分功能分散于现有系统中。经过分析发现，青岛市现有系统存在三点问题。

第一，多数系统欠缺对重大或不明海洋渔业突发事件的决策能力。青岛市海洋渔业应急管理部门的系统管理人员在处理规模较小的突发事件时，依靠对工作的熟悉和以往的经验，往往能够完成任务。但是，现有系统的招标是由各部门独立进行，往往只注重对各自工作的支持，偏向于指挥调度功能，而欠缺对海洋渔业应急管理工作整体方向的把握，缺乏评估决策功能，应急预案作为评估决策工作的核心，并没有得到足够的重视。在海洋渔业突发事件类型增多和复杂程度加大的背景下，一旦发生重大或不明的突发事件，需要专业的统计分析人员发挥评估作用，相关领导从全局出发发挥决策作用，应急预案发挥职责界定、快速响应和部门协调作用，此时，执行型系统的实用性就会大打折扣，难以满足实际需要。

第二，多数系统在公众沟通方面有明显的欠缺。我国宪法中的人民主权原则及对公民基本自由和政治权利的规定，为民众的知情权提供了坚实的法律依据，近年来，随着公众法律意识的增强，其对突发事件知情权的诉求越发强烈。与此同时，青岛市海洋渔业部门网站作为海洋渔业应急管理工作中政府与公众网上沟通的重要平台，当前仍在使用人工手段发布突发事件信息，会不可避免地出现信息迟报、漏报、错报等情况，以 2010 年 12 月 12 日为例，国家海洋预报台于 8 时发布警报，预计 12 日上午至 13 日中午渤海湾将出现风暴增水，而青岛市海洋与渔业局官方网站直到 15 日才发布相关信息，此时事件已经结束。① 同时，部分网站缺少公众留言功能，政府和公众之间缺乏网上互动渠道。

第三，各系统间功能重叠和互通互联程度低，加剧了海洋渔业部门间的争权诿责。在我国海洋管理领域，由海监、渔政、海警、海关、海事各部门共同管理所造成的"五龙闹海"现象由来已久，按方案出台前的海洋管理体制，海洋渔业应急管理工作的任务分散在部门中，职能越位、职责交叉等现象比比皆是，由此造成各部门系统的功能重叠；同时，由于各部门间缺乏

---

① 国务院：《国家突发公共事件总体应急预案》，新华社：http://www.xinhuanet.com。

协调统一的运行机制，各系统的互联互通程度也较低。因此，各部门在工作中难以进行有效的资源共享、集中管理和统一协作，而这又加剧了部门间的职责交叉、争权诿责等不良现象。

三 青岛市决策型系统建设的重要性

考虑到我国正在进行的政府工作能力建设、服务型政府建设和行政体制改革，结合现有系统存在的诸多问题，青岛市决策型系统建设的重要性主要有以下几点。

第一，决策型系统建设是提高政府工作能力的必然要求。加强政府工作能力建设是贯彻落实十八大精神的重要举措，是保障和改善民生的重要内容。当前，海洋渔业应急管理部门作为海洋渔业生产安全和相关民众生命财产安全的保障部门，其工作能力建设的重心是提高对重大或不明突发事件的决策能力。在决策型系统建设中，吸取了现有系统在处理此类事件过程中的教训，结合类似系统建设的成功经验，将以应急预案为核心的评估决策子系统作为系统的关键部分进行重点设计，以实现对事件信息的快速、准确、有效的评估决策，切合海洋渔业应急管理工作对系统决策能力的要求。

第二，决策型系统建设是建设服务型政府的必然要求。《国家突发公共事件总体应急预案》明确规定，"突发事件的信息发布应当及时、准确、客观、全面。要在事件发生的第一时间向社会发布简要信息，随后发布初步核实情况、政府应对措施和公众防范措施"，① 而公众沟通作为我国建设服务型政府的重要内容，应在海洋渔业应急管理系统的建设中得到足够重视。决策型系统将公众沟通系统作为三个应用子系统之一，在海洋渔业部门网站建设新型的突发事件信息发布平台，突发事件信息、决策信息、指令信息等通过电子政务平台的传送，将按预先定义的格式自动发布在平台上，缩短了发布时间，提高了应急管理工作的效率，满足了公众的知情权；平台还设计有公众留言功能，接收来自公众的反馈信息和相关诉求，形成政府和公众的网

---

① 青岛市海洋与渔业局：《关于风暴潮、海浪警报的通知》，http://ocean.qingdao.gov.cn。

上互动机制，协助政府发现风险源，调动相关资源，有利于事件的及时解决。

第三，决策型系统建设是推进行政体制改革的必然要求。随着党的十八大报告的提出，尤其是在《国务院机构改革与职能转变方案》出台后，"大部制"改革的进程不断加快，旧有的海洋渔业管理体系正被逐渐打破，"五龙闹海"问题有望得到彻底解决。"大部制"改革对整合海洋渔业应急管理部门、构建集中统一的海洋渔业应急管理体系提出了现实的要求，也为决策型系统的建设提供了难得的契机。在决策型系统中，现有系统将被整合为指挥调度子系统，负责评估决策子系统所发出的决策信息的执行，双方各司其职，构建起统一、畅通的海洋渔业应急业务流程，系统建成后将对集中统一的海洋渔业应急管理体系提供有力的支持，进而促进改革的持续深入。

四　青岛市决策型系统的基本设计

根据对决策型系统建设的背景和重要性的分析，进行了系统的基本设计。

（一）决策型系统的设计原则

决策型系统的设计在符合普通信息系统的设计原则的基础上，应着重考虑海洋渔业应急管理工作的特点。基于对系统处理能力及所处理事件的性质的要求，设计中应强调三点原则。

第一，重点突出。评估决策功能是决策型系统的核心功能，决定着系统关键的决策能力，因此，应建设评估决策子系统作为决策型系统的核心子系统。其中，应急预案作为子系统的核心，保证决策工作正确高效的推进；相关领导作为子系统的决策者，把握决策工作的整体方向，果断进行决策；统计分析人员和专家作为子系统的辅助者，保障信息来源的可靠性和决策的专业性。三者的设计应针对各自的特点和作用进行：一是应建设完善的预案库，并在事件结束后及时更新，同时在评估决策系统内设置应急预案的查询、启动、执行、结束等相关模块，完整、有效地发挥应急预案的功能；二是应考虑相关领导的决策需要，设计直观、快捷的决策功能；三是应借助先进的统计分析工具建设统计分析功能，同时建设完备的专家库。

第二，易集成性。出于系统整合的需要，系统设计应完善地支持新旧系统间功能、数据的集成，从而使决策型系统能够提供较高的工作效率。具体设计中，应利用中间件技术，提供多样的接口支撑丰富的组网方式，全面支持需要整合的现有系统的工作环境。

第三，较强的安全性。海洋渔业应急管理工作事关民众的生命财产健康安全，对和谐社会建设意义重大，系统必须充分考虑安全方面的设计，保证系统 365 天 24 小时全天候运行，具体设计中，应提供自动报警、自动备份、恢复、限制访问量等功能，并尽量降低维护次数。

（二）青岛市海洋渔业应急管理系统的体系架构

考虑到《国务院机构改革与职能转变方案》新近公布，还未对新国家海洋局的职能、机构、人员制定"三定"规定，新的海洋渔业应急管理体系尚未成型，因此根据现有体制进行系统设计并不合适。基于对方案和已有体系改革研究成果的理解，青岛市海洋渔业应急管理体系适于作如下改进。

青岛市海洋渔业应急管理体系应由市海洋渔业应急指挥中心（一级）、区域海洋渔业应急指挥中心（二级）、基层海洋渔业应急指挥中心（三级）组成，按级别成隶属关系。各级指挥中心作为其所辖区域海洋渔业应急管理的核心机构（指挥中心设在各级海洋渔业应急管理领导小组办公室内，小组办公室设在各级海洋渔业应急管理部门或相关办事处内），综合统筹各级海洋渔业应急管理部门和公安、消防、卫生等联动部门。通过电子政务平台，各级指挥中心实现系统互联，从而形成信息共享、应急协同、覆盖全市的海洋渔业应急管理体系。依据所设计的青岛市海洋渔业应急管理体系，系统的体系架构设计如图 1 所示，虚箭头表示系统的信息流方向，实箭头表示指令流方向。

（三）决策型系统的业务流程

依据系统的体系架构，二级、三级指挥中心所应对的突发事件大都规模较小，应对难度较低，其系统所需求的功能以监测预警、指挥调度为主，同

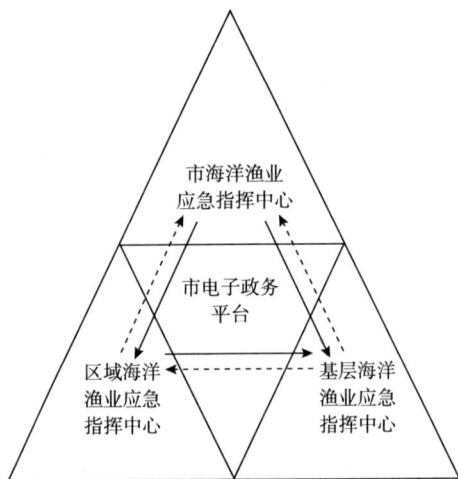

图1 青岛市海洋渔业应急管理体系的架构设计

时出于经济性的考虑，区域和基层海洋渔业部门现有的执行型系统能够基本满足需求，因此暂不考虑在市级以下部门建设决策型系统；而一级指挥中心所处理的海洋渔业突发事件通常具有规模大、成因复杂、应对难度高的特点，需求的功能以评估决策为主，因此适于建设决策型系统，其主要使用人员为青岛市海洋渔业应急指挥中心的领导。

根据一级指挥中心的功能需求，针对重大或不明的海洋渔业突发事件，决策型系统的业务流程设计如下。

（1）风险的监测和预警

根据《国家突发公共事件总体应急预案》规定，突发事件依据可能造成的危害程度、紧急程度和发展势态分为四级：Ⅰ级（特别严重）、Ⅱ级（严重）、Ⅲ级（较重）、Ⅳ级（一般）。[①] 青岛市三级指挥中心管理的监测预警设备在获取事件信息后，对规模、发展势态等较为明朗的事件，若为Ⅲ级和Ⅳ级类型，三级指挥中心应独立解决；若为Ⅱ级，报告二级指挥中心解决；若为Ⅰ级或规模、发展势态不明朗的类型，应在第一时间直接报告一级指挥中心解决。若在解决进程中发现新的情况或工作难以继续，也应逐级上

[①] 孙云谭：《中国海洋应急管理研究》，博士学位论文，中国海洋大学渔业经济与管理系，2010。

报解决。

（2）事件信息的接收和评估决策

一级指挥中心设置值班室，负责接收海洋渔业突发事件信息。除了下级指挥中心的上报，事件接收的方式还有：第一，上级部门的指示；第二，周边省市海洋渔业部门的转报；第三，知情者通过网站、电话等方式的上报；第四，指挥中心统计分析部门的工作人员及相关专家通过综合分析现有数据，提前预测出可能发生的突发事件。[①] 系统接报后，值班人员需要准确、清晰地确认事件详细信息，并将突发事件信息上报给指挥中心的统计分析部门和相关领导进行处理。统计分析部门的工作人员接收信息后，比较历史数据、过往案例等，迅速对其性质、类型、发展倾向等进行专业的统计分析，以图形、表格等直观的形式整理成报告，上报给指挥中心的领导。指挥中心的领导根据报告，参考现场情况，在专家的协助下，决定是否启动相应应急预案进行应对。

（3）指挥调度

应急预案启动后，指挥中心的领导统一指挥，发布调度指令，下级指挥中心根据应急预案和指令，派出由相关部门人员、车辆、船只、飞机等组成的事件处理小组（携带通信设备）到达现场，采取相应的应急措施，并将现场的语音、视频等信息通过通信设备传回指挥中心，形成有效互动，完善的解决突发事件。

（4）事件后期处理

事件处理完毕后，统计分析部门的工作人员将事件基本信息、起因、对策、处理结果、分析信息等汇总到海洋渔业数据中心，为未来类似突发事件的趋势分析做好准备；同时，在通过比较发现事件中应急预案的实际执行过程与原始要求的差异后，更新应急预案。

自突发事件发生到处理完毕，事件发生、评估决策、指挥调度、事件结果等全部信息都将同步公布在突发事件信息平台上，同时将知情者的重要信息反馈给领导参考。系统的主要业务流程如图2所示，虚箭头表示系统的信息流方向，实箭头表示指令流方向。

---

① 朱坚真、李珠江：《海洋与渔业应急管理》，海洋出版社，2007。

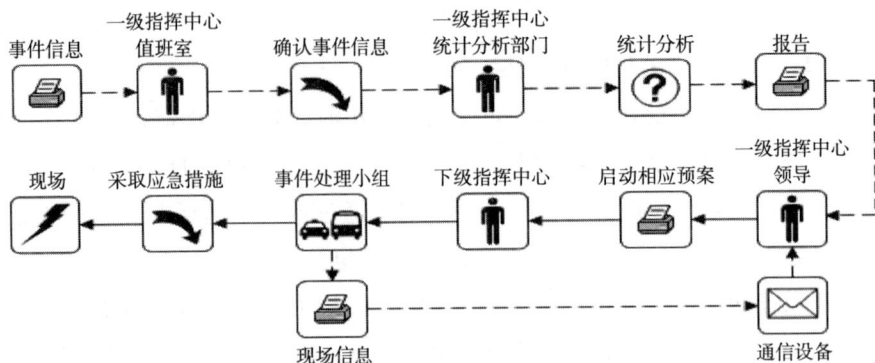

图2 青岛市海洋渔业应急管理体系的业务流程

依据系统的业务流程，将决策型系统划分为评估决策、指挥调度和公众沟通三大应用子系统。系统以海洋渔业数据中心为数据库，利用现有的市电子政务平台实现各级、各子系统间数据信息、事件信息的报送和指令信息的下达。各应用子系统和海洋渔业数据中心的功能设计如下。

评估决策系统接收来自上级部门系统的指令信息、下级和周边部门系统的事件信息及海洋渔业数据中心的数据信息，借助统计分析工具分析信息并获得直观的事件报告，在预案库、专家库和资源库的协助下输出决策信息，传送到指挥调度系统和公众沟通系统。事后，将事件汇总信息和应急预案更新信息传送到海洋渔业数据中心。

指挥调度系统接收来自评估决策系统的决策信息，借助大屏幕指挥系统、无线指挥系统等输出指令信息，传送到下级和周边部门系统及公众沟通系统。

公众沟通系统接收来自评估决策系统、指挥调度系统的各类信息，依据已定义好的相关格式自动发布于突发事件信息平台，同时输出公众留言信息，传送到评估决策系统。

海洋渔业数据中心的建设应以预案库、专家库和资源库为主，负责对各类应急预案、案例、部门信息、专家信息、政策法规、地图等的收集、加工和存储，输出相关数据信息，传送到评估决策系统。事后，接收来自评估决策系统的事件汇总信息和应急预案更新信息。系统的组成和工作流程如图3所示，虚箭头表示系统的信息流方向，实箭头表示指令流方向。

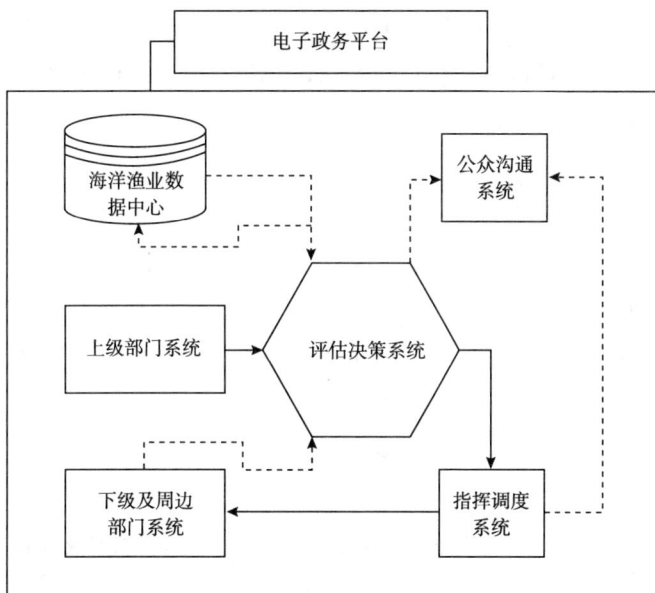

图 3 海洋渔业系统的组成和工作流程

五 决策型系统建设应具备的条件和面临的困难

信息系统建设是一项投资大、标准高的工程，涉及资源、技术、人员等各个方面，决策者的支持、资金的支持、成熟的开发团队等条件缺一不可，否则很可能会导致项目偏离、拖延、停工甚至失败。

决策型系统的设计在符合普通信息系统的设计原则的基础上，还应着重考虑海洋渔业应急管理工作的特点。基于对改革措施推行、现有系统整合和建设人员素质的考虑，系统建设还应具备的条件有三点：第一，有效推进海洋渔业部门改革，建立规范的海洋渔业应急管理体系，没有管理体系为基础，不可能建成有效的信息系统；第二，有效地整合利用现有系统，益处有两点，一是节省大量系统建设、人员培训费用，减轻国家负担；二是避免各级海洋渔业应急管理相关人员因对新系统的生疏而延误工作；第三，具备海洋渔业应急管理专业知识的人员参与系统建设，以在系统建设团队中发挥自身的优势，从用户的角度出发，保证系统建设的正确方向。

但是，我们应该清醒地看到，以上的条件都伴随着一定的困难：第一，

"五龙闹海"现象是长期以来各方势力博弈的结果，短期内难以得到根本性解决，体系更新下将依旧存在尾大不掉的隐患，改革措施难以有效推行；第二，部分现有系统因其设计思想、技术手段的落后已经难以支撑当前及未来的工作需要，如若保留，很有可能成为未来工作中的定时炸弹；第三，我国当前具备海洋渔业应急管理专业知识的系统建设人员极少，致使系统建设容易偏离设计的原则和思想，其根本原因是我国高校未设置相关的专业和课程，导致类似的系统建设人员大都缺乏背景知识。这些困难显然阻碍了决策型系统的建设。针对这些困难，相关人员还需进行进一步的研究和改善。

参考文献

陈海亮：《广东省海洋与渔业信息化建设研究》，《海洋信息化建设》2010 年第 4 期。

黄立文、宫福忠、文元桥：《内河综合海事应急管理系统的设计与实现》，《交通信息与安全》2009 年第 2 期。

刘志东、马龙：《应急指挥信息系统设计》，电子工业出版社，2009。

罗伯特·希斯著，王成译《危机管理》，中信出版社，2001。

孙云谭：《中国海洋应急管理研究》，博士学位论文，中国海洋大学渔业经济与管理系，2010。

朱坚真、李珠江：《海洋与渔业应急管理》，海洋出版社，2007。

中德社会政策比较

Social Policy in a Market Economy

ORR Wolfgang Strehl *

1 Introduction

The primary question of the paper is why does a market economy need a social policy? A truly market economist – for example like Milton Freedman but many more as well – would always deny that a social policy in a market economy is needed. The market itself is the most social institution. The market is social. The market testifies justice, when the market is free. However, it is nowadays out of any question, that policy is needed, especially a social policy. Policy seems to be a system requirement. *Social* means that it is for the general public, only for the ones who needed it. Only indigent people should benefit from that. And what "need" means is subject to political decision. There is no market decision rule for that problem.

Germany for example spends nearly half of its annual budget for *social* topics, such as unemployment insurance, health insurance, old age insurance and many more. Billions of Euros are annually spent for (so called) social purposes.

---

* Prof. Dr. ORR Wolfgang, Berlin School of Economics and Law.

But what is the theoretical base for that? That policy is deciding alike does not necessarily mean that there is a theory, saying, you have to do that in a special way. So this paper tries to trace back the roots of social policy in theoretical perspective.

2 The pre–classical economy

It always seems good to start arguing with old Greek thinkers. It was not economy that was striking their minds a lot. Economic thinking was part of *political economy*. Politics was predominant. Economy only had to help politics. But the social problem was completely in their sight. They thought about and argued about the people "that are left behind". Both the social system and the election system had been class–system. There have been different classes down to the slaves, that rightless people. The social system was a class system as well. There are people who work for the society, and those who work for their personal property.

But the economic thinking showed that these people are necessary. They are necessary for the reproduction of the society. They are needed for lower works Such as handycraft and agriculture. So any helps for them will help the class system to survive. The principle, for giving them any kind of aid had been the *subsidiarity principle*. It was the firm belief of classical thinkers that too much help would make people lazy. So the aid those people received was the aid by which they could help themselves. Nobody knew how much money to be spent for this aid.

There was no real theoretical foundation for social aid. There was always the political struggle for how much money should be spent for these social affairs. And the struggle went on until the days of the 18th century, the days of Adam Smith. But the *subsidiarity principle* gave the base for any social aid throughout the history; and provided the base for the Christian social aid, up to the time of the classical economist, namely Adam Smith, David Ricardo and their followers.

Economy had been under the reign of ethics. Ethical standards provided the world with what economy "had to do". Economy had been a derivative of political, ethical standards. If somebody owns more than what he needed, he had to spend for the needed people. This had been the credo of the Christianity.

But this is not the theoretical base for a social policy. It was a very common base for charity, in the 17th up to the 19th century.

3 The Classical Economy

The *pure economic theoretical thinking* started in the middle of the 18th century. Adam Smith was the first one to show that a stand – alone market economy will finally show the most of welfare for the majority of a nation. In his most famous book, *The Wealth of Nation* (1773), he quoted that a market economy is all that is needed. The market was introduced as a major paradigm into the economic world – in any world. The market, a fictitious place where people exchange whatever they want to exchange, guarantees the welfare of the nation. But it must be a free market which is free from any outside interference, especially power in any form. The moral philosopher Adam Smith was always *combating*. And as there is more than one nation in this world, exchange between nations guarantees the maximum welfare in all nations of the world, finally worldwide, if there is free trade. David Ricardo quoted that a worldwide division of labor guarantees the maximum of welfare for the whole world. This was and still is the theoretical foundation of globalization.

But it had been a necessary base of classical thinking, that goods exchanged are *equal.* That needed a measure for finding out what is meant by "equal"。 The measure had been the *labor incorporated* (objective measure of value). The used resource labor had been the measure for the exchange of (equal) goods. If the same quantity of labor is needed to produce one table or two stools, the exchange rate is one table against two stools. And the market will eliminate everybody who cannot match that exchange rate. To be more efficient the division of labor was introduced. In a team (that is a modern term) that is well organized less labor is needed so the exchange rate will sink, goods becoming "cheaper". The

233

production process became the center of economic research.

The market is the "invisible hand", the scepter that guarantees maximum welfare. That leads to a very simple market model figure.

However, Adam Smith's objective value measurement could only be guaranteed by the long range "price". He was sure, that in the long run this measure must be fulfilled. But in the short term prices can vary around that long run prices. Personal wishes, attitudes can lead to prices different from these long run prices, for supply and demand can be unequal by that. That would in our modern terminology lead to a crisis.

In his book *The Theory of Moral Sentiments* (1759), written and published prior to the Wealth of Nations, he analyzed the human behavior and started with a sentence that even the old Greek thinkers could have written: "How selfish soever man may be supposed, there are evidently some principles in his nature, which interest him in the fortune of others, and render their happiness necessary to him, though he derives nothing from it, except the pleasure of seeing it" (6th edition, London 1790). This could be the center of *utility* thinking as well. And in fact it is.

4　The Neoclassical Economy

The progress from classical to neoclassical economy can roughly be described by the elimination of anything like ethics. Standards and problems like that are no longer part of the economic thinking. Anything WHY somebody is doing something is given from outside the economy, is a data. This marks the turn from objective value measurement to a subjective measurement of value, based only in the preferences of the individuals.

A few things only that neoclassical economist changed from the classical economic thinking, but these things are fundamental to create a new economy.

The price is only influenced by general demand. And demand is influenced by attitudes of individuals. And economists, according to the utilitarian philosophers thought – until nowadays only had to sum up individual behaviors, given in the terms of demand, and the result is the maximum of welfare in a nation. The price is a resulting variable from demand and supply and is a measure for the scarcity of goods. The price is constituted by the relation between endless individual needs and the quantity of goods delivered.

And of course the theory must have some fundamental assumptions of the human behavior. These are very close to the classical basics. One is *more is better than less*. Another one is the *economic principle* that is said to be economic thinking "par excellence": to reach a given goal with a minimum of input, or turn a given set of input to a maximum of result. The economic principle marks the center of economic reasoning and constitutes the identity of economy.

That finally pointed out that economic thinking is "reduced" to an input output – thinking. Anything WHY somebody is doing something is no longer inherent in economic theory. Economic theory is *simply* a decision – helping technique. Not WHY somebody is doing something but HOW he is doing that. And to do it properly and correctly, means nothing else but keeping the standards of economic theory. So the economic theory could never be wrong, only the treating of economic techniques had been wrong.

The market model changed slightly. The driver of economic behavior became the preferences of individuals. And key variable became the price.

To show that this kind of economy guarantees the highest welfare, they just took over the basic standards of the classical economy: the market paradigm with perfect competition and free floating prices.

But this kind of theory has a big problem: in a well – organized market – one that shows perfect competition (many suppliers and many demanders) – price equals marginal costs. But where is the profit? Is profit just a consequence of market imperfection?

The theory gives no answer to the question where the surplus comes from?

Neoclassical theory is not a profit – theory. But profit is the measure for profitability, seems to be the key factor for economic actions.

Instead of that the interest of neoclassical theory is to prove, that a social system based on individualism guarantees a maximum of welfare for most of the people (utilitarianism).

And individualism means freedom of the individual and the political theory for that is called liberalism.

The basic neo – classical figure is the homo oeconomicus (economic man). A figure who is always acting rationally, according to the economic principle, is maximizing his personal utility. Furthermore, he has no preferences, he is a quantity adjuster. He always takes care of his budget restrictions. And of course: he has complete information.

Economic theory must be a (political?) decision theory. The theory must fix what must be done. Different kinds of policies have been derived from the neo – classical thinking. Competition policy for competition is a must for any neo – classical economist. And competition means, you have to take care, that the markets are free (market policy!) for the price has to do its job: to bring into accordance supply and demand. Competition needs a couple of assumptions: spirit of competition, declining prices, improving quality – only the fittest survive (social Darwinism) – and others. Then individual preferences are like *invisible hands* that eliminate inefficient suppliers. But that only can work when the economy is free from superfluous state's regulation.

But any decision theory needs a decision criterion. For a neoclassical based economic policy Vilfredo Pareto expressed it that way: Optimality is given, if it is impossible to make any one person better off without making at least one individual worse off. This point is defined by the optimal allocation of resources and the optimal distribution of income. It is impossible, to make it better off – in the meaning of Pareto.

This is the decision criterion for any neo – classically based economic policy.

But anyone should keep in mind the base of neo – classical economic reasoning: the homo oeconomicus. A selfish individual, always acting according to its own welfare, and only doing what he thoughts is the best for himself. And of course, he has complete information. He knows everything, not only the actual consequence of his decision but all the future consequences as well. This is not only for him but also for anybody everywhere.

Ethically it is grounded in the individualism like it is formulated by the founders of this philosophical theory: J. Bentham, J. St. Mill. But this kind of thinking traces back to the old Greek times.

Utilitarianism is a philosophy about actions to be right or wrong. And the morally best action would be one that improves the overall happiness, giving happiness to the greatest possible number of individuals. Or in the words of Bentham: The greatest good for the greatest number. That includes all future consequences of the human behavior.

Let's do a short but simple thought experiment to make clear the implication of the Pareto optimality. Let there be 10 personal computers and only two persons A and B. Let A own all the 10 personal computers, B should have none. This is of course a Pareto optimal situation: To give a computer to B, you have to take one off from A.

You have to keep in mind, that neo – classic is a static theory. No time exists in there. Dynamic for a neo – classical thinker is a sequence of static situations. Not the time between two static points is what a neo – classical thinker is interested in; he is only interested in the different points when according to J. B. Says a market is cleared. For every supply is seeking its demand.

But there are at least three assumptions for the Pareto efficiency: No public goods allowed, externalities are not existing and the presence of perfect competition.

We already defined perfect competition. Externalities are defined as costs or benefits that affect an individual in its individual situation in a positive or negative way. Positive means that this individual is not carrying the cost but enjoy the benefits. Negative means that this individual is hindered to reach its personal welfare maximum, because the (negative) externalities did not allow that individual to decide only for their own personal pleasure.

237

So it is easy to see, why any theory based on individualism must consequently demand the absence of externalities. The individual cannot fulfil its preferences.

But externalities are very important for any kind of politics. Because another definition of externalities runs like this: social costs are higher than the individual costs. For the causer of externality (for example noise) does not incur these externalities in his economic accounting (cost accounting) so that the community has to prevent individuals from that noise, the community has to carry the costs. So politics aimed to avoiding externalities or in case they can't be avoided, the causer to carry the costs (Pigou – Tax!). To point that out clearly: externalities that are compensated via the market are no externalities any longer. For they are reflected in the price. Externalities are never compensated via the market because if they are, they are no longer externalities.

Much more important finally is the demand of absence of any kind of public good.

Goods can be classified under different kind of aspects. The important dividing for us here is like mentioned above; we have to divide goods into economic goods and free goods. Free goods (air, sunlight) should not be produced; you can use them as they are. They will never have any price, for you need no resources to provide the world with them. Nobody is interested in producing them, selling them, because they are free for use. There is no incentive for anybody to put resources in that. And the incentive is making money. You can name that making profit.

Economic goods must be produced. They are not in the world itself. Economic goods always are a transformation. For that you need resources to bring them out. Whether this is an airplane or something to eat likes a piece of meat or milk or something like that. You have to spend resources (labor for example) to bring them into the world. That is why economic goods must be produced. And that is why the economic principle can work. You have an input (resources) and an output (goods to be produced). And the measure for being economically: the profit. The more you make, the better you are.

Economic goods are divided into *private* goods and *public* goods. Private goods always have a price, consumption is competitive – by buying them you gain property rights. Private goods belong to an individual. And the individual can do with that good whatever the individual wants to do.

That is the difference to public goods. They are not free in the meaning of the definition of free goods. Public goods must be produced; you need resources to make them. But they do not have a market in the final use. The use is free. But you have to pay for them. Not directly by using them but via tax.

One very important difference between a public good and a private good is: private goods always have a market, that's why they show a price. Public goods never have a market, that's why they never show a price. Private goods promise you a profit, the difference between what you paid for the resources needed and the price you can realize in a market (earnings minus operating expense) .

But public goods are not free of money. From their nature (street – light, national safety, streets and so on) the single person would show the free – rider – position because the person cannot be excluded from the use of that good. The traffic lights shine for everybody, and the national safety is for anybody's safety. Streets are for general use. They are part of infrastructure, a structure provided by the community for everybody's use, financed by the public budget. From the benefits of a private good somebody can be excluded, not from the benefit of a public good. So: public goods do not promise any kind of profit. No market, no price, no profit.

You have to keep in mind that a public good have no market. But market is the only place where a price can be found. And by that a market takes care for the optimal allocation of resources via the price. And if there is no market, there is no price – no optimal allocation of resources. It is a big problem for public goods and for merit goods as well.

A big critic of the neo – classical theory had been Mr John Maynard Keynes. But not really, for he still believes in the basics of market economy. The only aspect that he adds was the possibility of a crisis. The neo – classic had been

239

and still is a crisis – free area. If every offer is finding its demand（J. B. Say）, then markets are always cleared and the maximum of welfare is achieved. No space left for a crisis.

So Keynes added time to the neo – classical theory and found out that there could be frictions from one static equilibrium to the next one. And frictions imply unemployment. That leads to sinking loans and maybe the demand cannot clear the markets. So it will turn down like a spiral staircase. And that is the job of the state: by deficit spending to work anti – cyclical: To spend money in a going – down phase and save money in an up – going – turn.

The frictions stem from the fact that people give money an inherent value. It is unbelievable for the pre – classic thinkers who did not allow to lean money against interest rate. Keynes was a broker, a speculator. He was always working with money. For the neo – classical theorists, money was just an intermediary. It is easier to change goods against money rather than good against good. But when individuals keep back the money for expectations like to get more money later on, frictions can happen, disequilibrium occurs.

Keynes had been the first to give the state（government）an original place in an economy. But it was not the job of a normal individual; it was in contrast the real opposite of this. Because the state should spend money when individual does not spend money, to improve demand and via the multiplicator start a new up – going – phase. That mean, that the state should exactly act in opposition to the individuals. The state has somewhat a maintaining function for the capitalistic system. The state has to repair what is the result of individual actions.

Even the neo – classic theory nowadays expects the state to do something like that. There is only a difference with the tools. With Keynes the most important tool had been the budget. Finally to spend money the state doesn't have. With Milton Friedman the most important variable is the quantity of money running around. And that is to govern by the interest rate.

But that is a struggle that is not that important for us here. Because finally both would agree, that a special social policy is not needed. Friedman would think so, because he has been a purely neo – classical thinker that believed in the power of a market economy. Any state's intervention would have been a horror to him. After the so called Chile Putsch of Pinochet, Friedman was called (the Chicago Boys!) and the problems of the Chilean economy are still at hand.

5   A social market economy

But an enhanced economic model in modern times looks like that:

Germany subsequently followell *liberal philosophers* after World War II (v. Hayek, Müller – Armack, W. Eucken) and fixed in its constitution that Germany has a *Social Market Economy System.* That is not necessarily a Market Economy in the common sense.

Liberalism is a heterogeneous philosophy. The already mentioned M. Friedman is called a neo – liberal economist; The Austrian and German School are named Ordoliberalism. But the difference is that classical (neo –) liberalism firmly believes in the efficiency and effectivity of a market economy. No state's intervention is needed; in contrast, state's intervention would be disruptive. And the German and the Austrian School of Liberalism (Ordoliberalism) thinks that a market economy will not guarantee the most possible welfare but state's regulation is needed to serve welfare or at least to avoid and limit personal poverty. In the German constitution is fixed that every German has the right to live a life with social security and that everybody must be able to benefits from the social standards of the country. In the Ordo liberalism the state's role is out of question. But all refer to the same base: liberalism.

6   Public Administration

The Neo – Liberalism has been and still is the base of New Public Management (NPM) . In the NPM state's functions are revised. The state ought to do as less as possible, reduce itself to an absolute minimum. A free market

241

secures the best possible result. So the NPM reduces the state to an economic figure. What is good for successful private companies must be good for the public administration as well. Ronald Reagan, President of the United States of America, and Margaret Thatcher, Prime Minister of the United Kingdom, were the most famous known key – figures. Both fought against the extensive state that the world has seen in the post – war period. And both wanted to free the market. Margaret Thatcher fought against trade unions because they are limitations to the labor market. And her name stands for any possible privatization, in order to reduce governmental activities.

The credo of the NPM was revision of state's activities, privatization, and deregulation.

In Germany NPM became the New Steering Model (NStM). The difference to the NPM is primary the internal orientation. The NStM is seeking to use industrial engineering techniques in the public administration.

From the beginning of the 20th century we can talk of an autonomous industrial engineering. Here we name F. W. Taylor as the kick – off of industrial engineering because he was the first to think about the efficiency and effectivity of a production process. Although A. Smith introduced the division of labor as positive for the result of a production process, we would give Taylor the favour that he consequently started to think in terms of economy: input and output thinking. He is named to be the founder of scientific management.

But all kinds of input – output thinking need resources or goals to achieve. And the measure for operating effectiveness is finally the profit. But the state provides the community with public goods; the state is non – competing with private companies. So what should be the guideline for public activities?

If you think of the administration as being a simple company, you have to have in mind, what are the essentials for a private company? Private property, interest of special proprietor group, follows their private goals. Of course the company must fulfil the financial equilibrium, money – in and money – out must be in accordance in a medium range. But does the public administration really behave in the interest of a special proprietor group? Is there any proprietor group? Do the state and therefore the public administration belong to anybody?

Not in the meaning of the Ordoliberalism. The state is neutral: politics not, public administration yes.

Public administration finally lacks a concise goal system to make fruitfully use of industrial engineering technics.

Consequently private companies must follow the profit goal, the more profit the better. That preserves a company from being unfriendly taken over by another company. Every private company can go bankrupt. Not the public administration. The main task of the public administration is to decide according to common welfare. No private company has to do that. While a private company is trying to maximize their profit the public administration tries to maximize the common welfare. And the common welfare is not determined. It is subject to political decision.

That's why we have to talk about the last kind of goods: merit goods, introduced by R. Musgrave thinking about Public Finance. They can either be provided by private companies or public companies or administration. But it is political conviction, that more of them should be consumed. Public education, health – care or cultural institutions are objects of merit goods. The state is heavily subsidizing merit goods. Because it is the firm belief of politicians that citizens should make extensive use of them. For what any reason. So the ordoliberal state implemented compulsory schooling and tries its best to improve the number of young people with a bachelor degree. The ordo liberal state subsidizes theatres, operas and museums. The ordoliberal state is doing everything what he thought best to be for the community. And that is subject to general elections.

The decision rule for all that is not given by a market. If one thinks that the politician is maximizing the number of votes you can easily see the economic impact.

A theatre, an opera or a museum may be forced under the reign of economy, but its final base is the public task that is not subject to economy. Because if it would be subject to economic reasoning maybe it would be eliminated, stopped, suppressed. There is no market for public education. There are private schools, private universities – but their role is just a marginal one. Education is viewed to be a public task in Germany's social market economy. In Germany they privatized parts of what used to be public: water supply, waste water collection, garbage collection.

7　Conclusion

We wanted to show that there is not really a base in economic theory for a social policy. Economic theory is to prove that a stand – alone market economy (free from *superfluous* state's regulation) is the best possible social system. The market is always the best " regulator". The market is justice. Although this was never been proven in mankind history, the theory could not be wrong. Only men make mistakes that lead to poverty and social differentiation.

Although the liberal economic philosophy is the background for all activities to reform public administration, the problems still are at hand. In that way we still miss a special industrial engineering for the public administration. Neither can economic theory establish the necessity of social policy nor can the industrial engineering justify the activities of the public administration. Economic theory can show you the consequences of a social policy, if all the actors act rational in the meaning of the theory. Just like private industrial engineering tools can be useful in the private economy. But it is still not sure that they would help the public administration doing its job.

References

Smith, Adam (1759), The Theory of Moral Sentiments.

Smith, Adam (1776), The Wealth of Nations.

Ricardo, David (1817), Principles of Political Economy and Taxation.

Keynes, Maynard (1930), John Treatise on Money.

Eucken, Walter (1940), Die *Grundlagen der Nationalökonomie*.

Musgrave, Richard (1959), The Theory of Public Finance: A Study in Public Economy.

Traditional Paths to the German Social State[*]

Hans Paul Prümm[**]

1 Introduction

It is quite necessary to remember that what today is a matter of course was long times far from being self – evident – such as the social state. I recall in this respect the almost proverbial set of Margaret Thatcher (1925 – 2013) in 1987 "There is no such thing like society" by what she made ridiculous social cohesions. The consequence can be read at Robert Nozick (1938 – 2002) arguing for a minimal state "limited to the narrow functions of protection against force, theft, fraud, enforcement of contracts, and so on." These two quotations show the necessity to survey paths to social state; because it was a long way to the today's German social state.

This essay is primarily not to be understood as mediating historical facts but quite as socially – didactic contribution demonstrating for readers the importance of the idea of social state or – as formulated by article (art.) 23 paragraph

---

[*] An extended German version will be published in the May – version of Verwaltungsrundschau.

[**] Prof. Dr. Hans Paul Prümm, Berlin School of Economics and Law.

(para.) 1 sentence 1 German Basic Law (Grundgesetz [GG]) – the "social principles" .

Since a legal doctrine is "neither autonomous nor completely self – sufficient" its term can ultimately only "understood and explained 'metalegaly' , namely by history of politics. "

One can search and discuss political and historical elements along certain social tasks – training and employment promotion, social assistance, social security insurance, tax policy, or socialization providers of social services – charitable organizations, in general management integrated governmental departments, or social security insurance agencies or – and so we go on here – selected social ideas contributing to the social state.

The attempt to emphasize the cultural tradition of social elements of German history, always a part of European history, is to understand as contrast to the corresponding radical market trends in Germany and especially with regard to the other U. S. American way of life and: The small – written "social state" may not be a weak state; strengthening its position in social – political discussion is the main concern of this historical – cultural essay.

2 Concept of social state

The "social (s) state" appears in the Basic Law at two places: art. 20 para. 1 and art. 28 para. 1 GG. The constitution does not define this concept.

It therefore makes sense to orient themselves to the major German institution in constitutional matters, the Federal Constitutional Court (FCC) . This didn't define the social state but sees it, however, as "a guiding principle of all government measures... to 'social justice' . " The FCC interprets the social state auxiliary readiness of state, however relativized also in accordance with the economic performance of society and state:

"Given its (scil. 'social state', H. P. P.) broad and vague meaning an obligation to grant certain social benefits cannot be deduced. It is merely

247

mandatory that the social state shall establish the minimum conditions for a dignified life of its citizens. . . . In addition, the legislature is open to a wide range of discretion".

What matters in detail to the corresponding social state tasks is controversial but one cannot cut down the social state on the fields of Social Security Code (Sozialgesetzbuch, SGB):

- SGB I General
- SGB II Basic provision for jobseekers
- SGB III Employment Promotion
- SGB IV Common provisions for social security insurance
- SGB V Statutory health insurance
- Book VI Statutory pension insurance
- SGB VII Statutory accident insurance
- SGB VIII Children and youth welfare Law
- SGB IX Rehabilitation and participation of disabled people
- SGB X Social administration procedures and social data protection
- SGB XI Long term care insurance
- SGB XII Social assistance

Rather, social state includes the areas of health and safety, training, tenant protection, economic and financial governance, social security and tax reforms – here it should be noted that in the period 1980 to 2010 the burden of employees through taxes and social contributions of 28.8% to 33% increased, while the burden of income fell from 19.2% to 12.1% – land reform, asset accumulation, infrastructure planning, socialization, or even just social justice "translated" by Frank Nullmeier by "distributive justice".

Thus, since first social state involves more than welfare state and secondly the quasi – official translation of GG by the German Federal Ministry of Justice uses the term "social state" instead "welfare state" we prefer here the social – state – concept.

3 Paths to the social state

The creation and development of the state, its goals, tasks, and control instruments, especially the law, are cultural achievements of a society always historically caused also. These historical sources of the social state should be investigated. Since no comprehensive research can be presented here, selections are necessary illustrated in the headings of this chapter. The separated paths in reality are not as clearly separable as suggested by the here approach; however, the study calls for distinction.

The historic quarry offers critics of the respective circumstances as well as ways and instruments for optimizing the criticized circumstances.

3.1 Religious paths

The most important religious source for development of German history with respect to social behavior is still Christianity; after all, in the year 2013, began the official celebration of the "Day of German Unity" with an ecumenical service. Very important texts are the Beatitudes of Jesus in the Sermon on the Mount:

- Blessed are the poor in spirit: for theirs is the kingdom of heaven.
- Blessed are those who mourn: for they shall be comforted.
- Blessed are the gentle: for they shall inherit the earth.
- Blessed are those who hunger and thirst after righteousness: for they shall be filled.
- Blessed are the merciful for they shall obtain mercy.
- Blessed are the pure in heart: for they shall see God.
- Blessed are the peacemakers: for they shall be called children of God.
- Blessed are those who have been persecuted for righteousness' sake: for theirs is the Kingdom of Heaven.

And the announcement of the last judgement by Jesus:

249

Come, blessed of my Father, inherit the kingdom prepared for you from the foundation of the world: for

- I was hungry, and you gave me to eat.
- I was thirsty, and you gave me drink.
- I was a stranger, and you took me in.
- I was naked, and you clothed me.
- I was sick, and you visited me.
- I was in prison, and you came unto me.

These tenets are taken up again and again in the course of church history. 325 the Council of Nicaea requires all Christians to help the poor, strangers and the sick – as a result a Confessionale of the late Middle Ages declares the withholding of wages an outrageous sin:

Particularly well known are the stories of St. Martin of Tours (316 – 397) who as a Roman soldier divided in a cold winter his warm cloak with sword and gave one half a beggar as well as of Francis of Assisi (1181 – 1226) whose monks were required to take the vow of poverty and look after the poor.

In the Middle Ages and the early modern period, the church was actually the only institution looking after the poor giving alms. In proportion as the Church could no longer bear this burden alone, she was supported by the municipal welfare, and the state welfare.

The first war arranged in 1530 by the "Reichspolizeiverordnung" (National Police Order), the latter was prescribed as a state duty but neither as individual legal right nor as option of lawsuit – a consequence of the alms concept. As example, § 1, Title 19, Part II General Law for the Prussian States of 1794 should be cited:

"The state is well placed to provide for the food and resources of those citizens who do not obtain their own living and cannot get the same from other individuals who are required to support them. "

Although a similar individual legal right has been introduced under the Weimar Constitution it could not be sued for the courts. Only under social state of

GG the individual right to social assistance became enforceable. One can present this relationship by this graph:

- Under Basis Law individual right to social support can be suited
- Under Weimar Constitution right to social support was introduced

251

- In Prussia social support became state's duty
- At the beginning of Modern Period social support became municipal duty
- Concil of Nicea declared almsgiving to Christian duty
- Jesus beatifies the almsgiver

Regardless of the alms distribution the churches also have taken care of the education of children and youth long before the state did it. A particularly striking example is the Franckesche Stiftungen (Francke's Foundations) in Halle where especially orphans were trained academically and professionally since 1695.

For a long time churches believed in God – given justice of the given distribution of goods. Only with the emergence of the social question in the 19th century meant the Catholic bishop of Mainz, Wilhelm Emmanuel Freiherr von Ketteler, Wilhelm (1811 – 1877): "This whole business income now falls exclusively to the capital, while the workers do not have the least share. This distribution of the excessive profits, however, does not seem to conform to the natural justice..." Similar critic was expressed by the Protestant minister Johann Hinrich Wichern (1808 – 1881).

An important element of "public welfare" in sense of art. 74 para. 1 nr. 7 GG is the principle of subsidiarity as expressed in art. 4 para. 2 SGB VIII:

"As far as appropriate facilities, services, and events from recognized institutions of youth welfare services are operated or created in time public youth welfare shall refrain from own measures."

This principle is primarily due to encyclical Quadragesimo, published 1931 by Pope Pius XI:

"Just as it is gravely wrong to take from individuals what they can accomplish by their own initiative and industry and give it to the community, so also it is an injustice and at the same time a grave evil and disturbance of right order to assign to a greater and higher association what lesser and subordinate organizations can do. For every social activity ought of its very nature to furnish help to the members of the body social, and never destroy and absorb them."

As a result of this approach there are in Germany strong civic welfare organizations from the Catholic Caritas, the Evangelical Diakonia, and the Central Welfare Office of Jews in Germany to the policy – oriented Arbeiterwohlfahrt (Workers'Welfare) and Volkssolidarität (National Solidarity), the politically neutral German Red Cross and the reservoir of smaller organizations, Paritätischer Wohlfahrtsverband (Joint Welfare Association).

Regardless of the trend to secularization of German society one should be aware that the religious arguments should be considered in secular discourse; what Jürgen Habermas pointed out in the last years.

3. 2   Philosophical paths

For a long time philosophy was "ancilla theologae" and not really developed independent concepts. Only with the – gradual – separation of the two sciences the political and social philosophy and the state and constitutional doctrine developed new concepts. The most comprehensive conceptions we find in the utopias of Thomas More (1478 – 1535), Francis Bacon (1561 – 1626), and Tommaso Campanella (1568 – 1639), dealing not only with social critics but also with social perspectives of a life free from hunger and thirst, and thus demonstrate the wishes of many people for a life free from want.

Of course, there have been philosophers in Germany clear opponent of the welfare, the best known is Friedrich Nietzsche. In his poem "To the Mistral" in the appendix to "The Gay Science" it is said:

Those who come must move as quickly as the wind, we'll have no sickly, Crippled, withered, in our crew;

Off with hypocrites and preachers, Proper folk and prosy teachers, Sweep them from our heaven blue.

Sweep away all sad grimaces, Whirl the dust into the faces Of the dismal sick and cold!

Hunt them from our breezy places.

Adam Smith (1723 – 1790) is usually classified as an economic theorist, however, dealt not only with economic issues; he also dedicated to the education problem and thus quite social state positions:

"The education of the common people requires, perhaps, in a civilized and commercial society, the attention of the public, more than that of people of some rank and fortune. People of some rank and fortune are generally eighteen or nineteen years of age before they enter upon that particular business, profession, or trade, by which they propose to distinguish themselves in the world. They have, before that, full time to acquire, or at least to fit themselves for afterwards acquiring, every accomplishment which can recommend them to the public esteem, or render them worthy of it. Their parents or guardians are generally sufficiently anxious that they should be so accomplished, and are in most cases, willing enough to lay out the expense which is necessary for that purpose. If they are not always properly educated, it is seldom from the want of expense laid out upon their education, but from the improper application of that expense. It is seldom from the want of masters, but from the negligence and incapacity of the masters who are to be had, and from the difficulty, or rather from the impossibility, which there is, in the present state of things, of finding any better. The employments, too, in which people of some rank or fortune spend the greater part of their lives, are not, like those of the common people, simple and uniform. They are almost all of them extremely complicated, and such as exercise the head more than the hands. The understandings of those who are engaged in such employments, can seldom grow torpid for want of exercise. The employments of people of some rank and fortune, besides, are seldom such as harass them from morning to night. They generally have a good deal of leisure, during which they may perfect themselves in every branch, either of useful or ornamental knowledge, of which they may have laid the foundation, or for which they may have acquired some taste in the earlier part of life.

It is otherwise with the common people. They have little time to spare for education. Their parents can scarce afford to maintain them, even in infancy. As soon as they are able to work, they must apply to some trade, by which they can earn their subsistence. That trade, too, is generally so simple and uniform, as to give little exercise to the understanding; while, at the same time, their labour is both so constant and so severe, that it leaves them little leisure and less inclination to apply to, or even to think of any thing else.

But though the common people cannot, in any civilized society, be so well instructed as people of some rank and fortune; the most essential parts of education, however, to read, write, and account, can be acquired at so early a period of life, that the greater part, even of those who are to be bred to the lowest occupations, have time to acquire them before they can be employed in those occupations. For a very small expense, the public can facilitate, can encourage and can even impose upon almost the whole body of the people, the necessity of acquiring those most essential parts of education.

The public can facilitate this acquisition, by establishing in every parish or district a little school, where children maybe taught for a reward so moderate, that even a common labourer may afford it; the master being partly, but not wholly, paid by the public; because, if he was wholly, or even principally, paid by it, he would soon learn to neglect his business. In Scotland, the establishment of such parish schools has taught almost the whole common people to read, and a very great proportion of them to write and account. In England, the establishment of charity schools has had an effect of the same kind, though not so universally, because the establishment is not so universal. If, in those little schools, the books by which the children are taught to read, were a little more instructive than they commonly are; and if, instead of a little smattering in Latin, which the children of the common people are sometimes taught there, and which can scarce ever be of any use to them, they were instructed in the elementary parts of geometry and mechanics; the literary education of this rank of people would, perhaps, be as complete as can be. There is scarce a common trade, which does not afford some opportunities of applying to it the principles of geometry and mechanics, and which would not, therefore, gradually exercise and improve the common people in those principles, the necessary introduction to the most sublime, as well as to the most useful sciences.

The public can encourage the acquisition of those most essential parts of education, by giving small premiums, and little badges of distinction, to the children of the common people who excel in them.

The public can impose upon almost the whole body of the people the necessity of acquiring the most essential parts of education, by obliging every man to undergo an examination or probation in them, before he can obtain the freedom in any corporation, or be allowed to set up any trade, either in a village or town corporate."

As one of the first German philosophers, Johann Gottlieb Fichte (1762 – 1814) formulated in contrast to Wilhelm von Humboldt (1767 – 1835): "It is the absolute duty of the state to guarantee its citizens their working life and to ensure share of leisure." That involves not only an employment policy but also working time limits – as today expressed in the Sunday and holiday laws of the German Länder (states).

Hermann Heller (1891 – 1933) is the inventor of the "social state". In his seminal essay "Rule of Law or Dictatorship" he created the concept of "social state governed by the rule of law"; a legal system that does not permit the "anarchist frenzy of our capitalist production" but obliged the state to secure "our culture" by shaping the economy.

3.3   Economic paths

The here discussed economic – social elements are only understood by the concept of the free market formulated by Adam Smith:

"As every individual, therefore, endeavours as much as he can, both to employ his capital in the support of domestic industry, and so to direct that industry that its produce maybe of the greatest value; every individual necessarily labours to render the annual revenue of the society as great as he can. He generally, indeed, neither intends to promote the public interest, nor knows how much he is promoting it. By preferring the support of domestic to that of foreign industry, he intends only his own security; and by directing that industry in such a manner as its produce may be of the greatest value, he intends only his own gain; and he is in this, as in many other cases, led by an invisible hand to promote an end which was no part of his intention. Nor is it always the worse for the society that it was no part of it. By pursuing his own interest, he frequently promotes that of the society more effectually than when he really intends to promote it. I have never known much good done by those who affected to trade for the public good. It is an affectation, indeed, not very common among merchants, and very few words need be employed in dissuading them from it. "

This concept Wilhelm von Humboldt (1767 – 1835) described for Germany as follows:

"The State should abstain from all care for the positive welfare of the citizens and go no farther than protect their security against itself and even against foreign enemies; for no other ends he may restrict citizen's freedom. "

Although this model in Germany was never implemented in pure form, however, led it to the creation of the intellectual construct of "Nachwächterstaat" (Night – watchman state) by Ferdinand Lassalle (1825 – 1864):

"This is a night – watchman idea, gentlemen, a night watchman – idea because the state can only be thought as image of a night – watchman himself whose entire function is to prevent robbery and burglary. "

This warning by Lassalle was also a call for government economic policy.

It is very interesting that the theory of Karl Max (1818 – 1863) did not play a positive role in formulation of social statehood because Parliamentary Council understood social state as a open political concept.

At the interface between economics and politics, the founding of the "Verein für Socialpolitik" (Social Policy Association) in 1873 must be mentioned. Here gathered primarily economic and social scientists to act out their scientific expertise in the policy area against the laissez – faire of the German Manchester School on the one hand and on the other hand against the socialist revolutionary ideas of the socialism.

3.4   Political paths

Under this point we subsume steps into the direction of social state, as we have outlined above, at least for a short period. For a long time there were hardly any rebellions in Germany. Only in connection with the Reformation, initiated mainly – but not exclusively – by Martin Luther (1483 – 1546), it is about the Twelve Articles of the Swabian peasantry from the year 1525:

1. Every municipality shall have the right to elect and remove a preacher if he behaves improperly. The preacher shall preach the gospel simply, straight and clearly without any human amendment, for, it is written, that we can only come to God by true belief.

2. The preachers shall be paid from the great tithe. A potential surplus shall be used to pay for the poor and the war tax. The small tithe shall be dismissed, for it has been trumped – up by humans, for the Lord, our master, has created the cattle free for mankind.

3. It has been practice so far, that we have been held as villein, which is pitiful, given that Christ redeemed all of us with his precious bloodshed, the shepherd as well as the highest, no one excluded. Therefore, it is devised by the scripture, that we are and that we want to be free.

4. It is unfraternal and not in accordance with the word of God that the simple man does not have the right to catch game, fowls, and fish. For, when God our master created man, he gave him power over all animals, the bird in the air and the fish in the water.

5. The high gentlemen have taken sole possession of the woods. If the poor man needs something, he has to buy it for double money. Therefore, all the woods that were not bought (relates to former community woods, which many rulers had simply appropriated) shall be given back to the municipality so that anybody can satisfy his needs for timber and firewood thereof.

6. One shall have understanding (pretty much reduce) with regard to the corvee which keeps increasing from day to day to how our parents served in

accordance with exclusively the word of God.

7. The nobility shall not raise the peasant's corvee in excess of what was established at bestowal. (Raising corvee without any agreement was not unusual.)

8. Many properties can not support the levies (lease fees). Honest men shall inspect these properties and shall determine the levy upon their discretion so that the peasant shall not do his work in vain, for every person is worth his pay.

9. New rules are ever made for the great outcry "große Frevel" (a fine that had to be paid to the court). One does not punish with regards to the subject but at discretion (raising fines and arbitrary punishment was common). It is our opinion that we shall be punished by old, written penalty with regards to what was done and not to favour.

10. Several have appropriated meadows and acres (community land that was at the disposition of all members), that belong to the municipality. Those we want back to our common hands.

11. The "Todfall" (a sort of inheritance tax) shall be abolished altogether and never again shall widows and orphans be robbed contrary to God and honour.

12. It is our decision and final opinion that if one or several of the articles mentioned herein were not in accordance with the word of God, those we shall refrain from if it is explained to us on the basis of the scripture. If several articles were already granted to us and it emerged afterwards that they were ill, they shall be dead and null. Likewise, we want to have reserved that if even more articles arc found in the writ that were against God and a grievance to though neighbour.

Here one can see a number of social – state elements, such as use of taxes for "social welfare" (2), opening up opportunities even to provide for the livelihood (4 and 5), reduction of mandatory manual work and services (6 and 7), socially beneficial contributions (8) and pooling of agricultural land (10).

A landmark for Germany was the French Revolution under the slogan "Liberty, Equality, Fraternity". It attacked not only the foundations of the three levels system: Cleric – Nobles – Citizens / Farmers, but in 1793 formulated at art. 21 Jacobin Constitution the constitutional duty of society to support the unemployed:

"Society owes subsistence to unfortunate citizens, either by procuring work for or by providing the means of existence for those unable to work. "

Here, an anti – religious movement has replaced the religious motivated alms by a secular "sacred duty".

An important political step for the financial security of workers for the situations in which they were unable to work, not only for Germany but because their model effect for many other countries too, the Bismarckian social security insurances:

- 1883: Health Insurance
- 1884: Accident Insurance
- 1889: Disability and Old – Age Insurance; the last granted the workers a pension from the 71st years but the average life expectancy was 40 years at that time.

These social security insurances – and that justifies their classification under the political aspect – sprang not only from the point of concern for the workers, however, particularly should keep down Social Democracy. Following the motto "carrot and stick" Otto von Bismarck in 1878 initiated the "Law against the Public Danger of Social Democratic Endeavours". In this context Otto von Bismarck said:

"As early as February of this year, we can express our conviction that the healing of social damage will be sought not only through the repression of social democratic excesses but equally on the positive promotion of the welfare of workers. "

The statutory social security insurance system was further expanded:

- 1927 Unemployment Insurance
- 1995 Long term care Insurance

Although since the mid – 19th century trade unions – such as the printers' association in 1849 – were founded, they became a serious political power only in 1892 due to concentration to "General Commission of Trade Unions of Germany". The unions reached through agitations, strikes, and collective bargaining to improve working conditions; such as the introduction of the eight – hour day.

3. 5   Artistic paths

3. 5. 1   Literature

Since the welfare state also means redistribution it is thus not irrelevant that in many parts of Germany – but not only here – the desire to take the rich and give to the poor, repeatedly found expression in stories of "just" bandits. The most famous of these "noble robbers" is Robin Hood. But be reminded of the German "socialist bandits", the Rhenish Schinderhannes or the Bavarian Hiesel. Here ventilated the idea of redistribution of unjust material properties. At first glance, the treatment of this robber concept in the context of social state traditions seems contrary to the subject because bands of robbers and states are diametrically opposite. However, Aurelius Augustine (354 – 430) connected the two institutions asking: "Justice being taken away, then, what are kingdoms but great robberies?"

In other literary genres we find social state elements too: For example in Christoph Martin Wieland's (1733 – 1813) educational novel "The Golden Mirror", where it says:

"After Salameks opinion the biggest and best of all the sultans was the one... who gives the poor at least one tenth of its income."

or Heinrich Heine (1797 – 1856) "Germany. A Winter's Tale", where he calls for redistribution:

"A new song, a better song,

O friends, I speak to thee!

Here upon Earth we shall full soon

A heavenly realm decree.

Joyful we on earth shall be

And we shall starve no more;

The rotten belly shall not feed

On the fruits of industry. "

A very good description of relationship between freedom of hunger and human dignity delivers Friedrich Schiller (1759 – 1805) in an epigram:

"No more of that, I pray you. To eat, to live give him. Have you covered the nakedness the dignity is by itself. "

In the European area are probably the two most important novels "Oliver Twist" by Charles Dickens (1812 – 1870) with his still poignant description of (criminal) child labor and "Germinal" by Emile Zola (1840 – 1902), where the harsh working conditions of the miners are described. For Germany, "The Weavers" by Gerhart Hauptmann (1862 – 1946) delivered a precise description of the revolt of the Silesian weavers in 1844 against poor working conditions and low wages; the stage play caused the German emperor Wilhelm II (1859 – 1941) to leave his box during the premiere.

3.5.2　Fine Arts

Fine Arts have been devoted to the aspect of Caritas very early. Here "Seven Works of Mercy" by von Barend van Orley (1491 – 1542) is shown:

Jesus outlines the seven mercies as the gateway to heaven:

(1) Hungry dine.

(2) Give the thirsty to drink.

(3) Clothing the naked.

(4) Take strangers.

(5) Visit sick.

(6) Visit prisoners.

(7) Burying the dead.

The picture illustrates vividly, for the illiterates too, what to do for entering the heaven. That this relationship was a quite intentional it can be seen by the fact that the image of Barend van Orley was commissioned by the urban welfare Antwerp.

A special position in our context takes the "Allegory of Good and Bad Government" by Ambrogio Lorenzetti (1290 – 1348) in the town hall of Siena.

In this allegory justice is equated with the public interest which ultimately derives from God.

However, over a long period critical representations of the social conditions in the fine Arts remain the exception. Known in Europe were the engravings of William Hogarth (1697 – 1764) showing the social ills in England, such as the "Beer Street at Gin Lane":

263

Another painter should be mentioned: Francisco José de Goya y Lucientes (1746 – 1828) painting the unbearable conditions in a madhouse:

At latest with the emergence of the social question, suffering person, whether from hunger, housing shortages, or his hard work, became subject of fine art which was understood more and more as medium to accuse the social grievances and, thus, to contribute to the strengthening of the social state principle. For examples may be mentioned the "Silesian Weavers" by Käthe Kollwitz (1867 – 1945):

and the "Weavers" by Max Liebermann (1847 – 1935):

which shows the hard working conditions.

More and more artificial photographers as Hermann Drawe (1867 – 1925) and Emil Kläger (1880 – 1936) or Heinrich Zille (1858 – 1925) recorded and accused in Vienna respective Berlin the misery of the poor: I quote the slide

"Homless at the fire" of Drawe/ Kläger

and Zille's photograph

"Wooden collectors pulling handcart"

3.5.3 Music

The concept music means in our context instrumental and vocal music. Especially the last item was an appropriate mean promoting social – state ideas: Folksongs often accuse tension between the rich and the poor. But for a long time music served mainly the praise of God and the rulers. Only with the peasant wars in the 15th century, the first songs accusing the social conditions were sung. These were complaints of farmers and craftsmen about the poor working conditions; e. g. the farmer song from 1500 "The Farmers Have United and Get by Force". Since the 18th century similar lamentations were sung by workers; e. g.

"The Blind Miner" .

At the same time so called workers fight songs were published. One of the most popular songs is the Internationale, written in 1871 by Eugène Pottier (1816 – 1887) and composed 1888 by Pierre De Geyter (1848 – 1932) . It starts:

"Stand up, damned of the Earth Stand up, prisoners of starvation!"

and combines critics (starvation) and a political tool (stand up) for changing the criticized circumstances.

However, social critics we find in the high – culture music too. A very prominent example is the 1928 premiered " Three Penny Opera" texted by Bertold Brecht (1898 – 1956) and composed by Kurt Weill (1900 – 1950), a remake of John Gay's (1685 – 1732) "The Beggar Opera" .

4   Summary and Outlook

The paper shows that social state is not a product of legal considerations and processes only; however, there are many sources of social state: religious, philosophical, economic, political, and artistic approaches.

The division shown here between different cultural traces is, of course, a scientific construct. In reality, there are interrelations (1) between and (2) within the different approaches to social state. For example (1) the St. Martin – story is a religious approach as well as a part of category fine Arts, and (2) celebration of, just bandits we can categorize in literature as well in folksongs.

In 1958 the FCC declared that social state includes " progress to social justice" . That means the obligation to care of the social needs on the one hand and on the other hand to develop a more socially just society.

The " social state" appears in the German Basic Law in lowercase letters only: " sozialer Bundesstaat" (social federal state) and, sozialer Rechtsstaat (social state governed by the rule of law) . However, it may not be a small weak but a strong Social State protecting and promoting the social justice.

Because social state is embedded in connection with other state principles, especially the democratic principle, "progress of social justice" can be driven forward ultimately in a democratic manner only. The decision – making authority lies neither in the hands of elite in the sense of Joseph A. Schumpeter (1883 – 1950) nor in den hands of a bureaucracy in the sense of Max Weber. For strengthening the social state arguments in the democratic discourse it is necessary to recall the social marks in the history.

Reference

An extended German version will be published in the May – version of Verwaltungsrundschau.

FCC, decision of 17. 08. 1956 – 1 BvB 2/51 – BVerGE 5, 85 (198); translation H. P. P.

FCC, decision of 29. 05. 1990 – 1 BvL 20, 26, 184 und 4/86 – E 82, 60 (80); translation H. P. P.

Ernst Hillebrand: Das Soziale und das Demokratische: Baustellen einer Sozialdemokratie für das 21. Jahrhundert, in: Christian Kellermann/ Henning Meyer (eds.): Die Gute Gesellschaft. Soziale und demokratische Politik im 21. Jahrhundert, 2013, p. 265 (270).

Frank Nullmeier: Politische Theorie des Sozialstaats, 2001, p. 362.

Federal Ministry of Justice, under http: //www. gesetze – im – internet. de/englisch_ gg/ [26. 01. 2014].

Cf. the problem under 4. too.

Cf. Werner Hofmann: Ideengeschichte der sozialen Bewegung des 19. und 20. Jahrhunderts, 5. ed. , 1974, p. 22.

Cf. T S Eliot: Christianity and Culture: The Idea of a Christian Society and Notes towards the Definition of Culture (1948), 1960, p. 200: "An individual European may not believe that the Christian faith is true, and yet what he says, and makes, and does will all spring out of his heritage of Christian culture and depend upon that culture for its meaning. . . I do not believe that culture of Europe could survive the complete disappearance of the Christian faith."

Matthew 5, 3 – 10, quoted after The World English Bible (WEB), available under http: //ebible. org/ [26. 01. 2014].

Matthew 25, 34 – 36, fn. Fehler: Referenz nicht gefunden.

http: //digital. staatsbibliothek – berlin. de/dms/werkansicht/? PPN = PPN731634993 &

PHYSID = PHYS_ 0001 [26.01.2014]; the quoted text can be read in column three, first bloc.

To St. Martin closer Sebastian Ristow: Sankt Martin – ein Römer der Spätantike, in: Christoph Stiegemann/ Martin Kroker/ Wolfgang Walter (eds.): Credo. Christianisierung Europas im Mittelalter. Band I Essays, S. p. 182.

Cf. Michael Mollat: Die Armen im Mittelalter, 1984.

Under http://www.smixx.de/ra/Links _ F – R/Reichspolizeiordnung _ 1530. pdf [26.01.2014].

Allgemeines Landrecht für die Preußischen Staaten von 1794, 2. ed. , 1994, p. 669; translation H. P. P.

Federal Administration Court (FAC), decision of 24.06.1954 – V C 78/54 – , NJW 1954, 1541 (headnote): "As far as the law obliges the agency to social assistance the citizen has corresponding individual rights. " Translation H. P. P.

See closer Hoger Zaunstöck/ Thomas Müller – Bahlke/ Claus Veltmann (ed.): Die Welt verändern. August Hermann Francke – Ein Lebenswerk um 1700. Katalog zur Jahresausstellung der Franckeschen Stiftungen vom 24. März bis 21. Juli 2013, 2013.

Freiherr von Ketteler: Die Arbeiterfrage und das Christentum (1884) quoted according Jürgen Boeckh/ Ernst – Ulrich Huster/ Benjamin Benz: Sozialpolitik in Deutschland, 3. ed. , 2011, p. 43.

Johann Hinrich Wichern: Die Innere Mission der deutschen Evangelischen Kirche (1849), qouted according Werner Pöls (ed.): Deutsche Sozialgeschichte. Dokumente und Skizzen, Band I: 1815 – 1870, 2. ed. , 1976, p. 283.

Pius XI, Quadragesimo anno (1931), under http://www.vatican.va/index.htm [16.01.2014].

Jürgen Habermas: Vorpolitische Grundlagen des Rechtsstaates, in: The same/ Joseph Ratzinger: Dialektik der Säkularisierung. Über Vernunft und Religion, 2005, p. 15 (34 f) .

Printed at Heinisch (ed.): Der utopische Staat. Morus Utopia. Campanella Sonnenstaat. Bacon Neu – Atlantis, 1960.

Quoted accordinghttp://ia700500.us.archive.org/23/items/completenietasch10nietuoft/ completenietasch10nietuoft_ djvu. txt.

Adam Smith: The Wealth of Nations (1776), 2003, Book V Chapter I Part III Article 2d.

Johann Gottlieben Fichte: Das System der Rechtslehre (1812), in: The Same:

Ausgewählte Politische Schriften, 1977, p. 217 (271).

Hermann Heller: Rechtsstaat oder Diktatur (1929), in: The same: Gesammelte Schriften, 1971, Zweiter Band 3, p. 443 (461 f. 2).

Adam Smith, fn. Fehler: Referenz nicht gefunden, Book 4, Chapter II.

Wilhelm von Humboldt: Ideen zu einem Versuch, die Grenzen der Wirksamkeit des Staats zu bestimmen (1792), 1967, p. 52; translation H. P. P.

Ferdinand Lassalle: Arbeiterprogramm (1862), in: The same: Reden und Schriften. Aus der Arbeiteragitation 1862 – 1864, 1970 p. 22 (55).

Hermann Hartwich: Sozialstaatspostulat und gesellschaftlicher status quo, 1970, does not list Marx in the index.

Self – description of Verein für Socialpolitik, underhttp: //www. socialpolitik. org/ vfs. php? mode = informationen&lang = 1 [26. 01. 2014].

http: //en. wikipedia. org/wiki/Twelve_ Articles [26. 01. 2014].

See under http: //www. college. columbia. edu/core/sites/core/files/text/Preface% 20to% 20the% 20Constitution% 20of% 201793. pdf [26. 01. 2014].

Albert Soboul: Die große französische Revolution. Ein Abriß ihrer Geschichte, 2. ed. , 1973, p. 310: Dechristianisation.

Otto Stegmann: Die Invaliditäts – und Altersrente. Recht und Pflichten der Arbeitnehmer, sowie der Arbeitgeber auf Grund der einschlägigen Bestimmungen des Gesetzes vom 22. Juni 1889, 4. Aufl. 1890, p. 13.

M. Luy: Lebenserwartung in Deutschland, unter: http: //www. lebenserwartung. info/ index – Dateien/ledeu. htm [26. 01. 2014].

Quoted according Lothar F. Neumann/ Klaus Schaper: Die Sozialordnung der Bundesrepublik Deutschland, 5. Aufl. , 2008. p. 28; translation H. P. P.

Brockhaus. Die Enzyklopädie in 24 Bänden, 20. ed. , 2001, keyword Gewerkschaften.

Cf. Eric J. Hobsbawm: Primitive Rebels: Studies in Archaic Forms of Social Movement in the 19th and 20th Centuries, 1959.

Manfred Franke (ed.): Schinderhannes. Kriminalgeschichte, voller Abenteuer und Wunder doch streng der Wahrheit getreu 1802, 1977.

Ludwig Tieck: Der Bayersche Hiesel (1791), 2005.

Aurelius Augustinus: City of God (425), http: //www. newadvent. org/fathers/ index. html [26. 01. 2014], Book IV Chapter 4.

Christoph Martin Wieland: Der Goldene Spiegel oder Die Könige von Scheschian. Eine wahre Geschichte aus dem Scheschianischen übersetzt (1772), undated, p. 110 f. ; translation H. P. P.

Heinrich Heine: Deutschland ein Wintermärchen (1844), in: The same: Sämtliche Werke in zwölf Bänden, undated, Zweiter Band, p. 119 (124); translation http: // en. wikipedia. org/wiki/Germany. _ A_ Winter% 27s_ Tale [26. 01. 2014] .

Friedrich Schiller: Epigramme (1782 – 1788), in: The same: Sämtliche Werke Band I, 2004, p. 243 (248); translation H. P. P.

Taken from http: //de. wahooart. com/@ @ /8XZSP4 – Bernaert – Van – Orley – Das – J% C3% BCngste – Gericht [26. 01. 2014] .

The last mercy is not mentioned by Matthew, fn. Fehler: Referenz nicht gefunden; lassen Sie ein Dokument übersetzenes wurde wegen der Pestepidemien im Mittelalter kanone

It was canonized because the plague in medieval Europe: Patrick de Rynck, Die Kunst Bilder zu lesen. Die Alten Meister entschlüsseln und verstehen 1, 2005, p. 150: Barend van Orley. Jüngstes Gericht.

Patrick De Rynck, Fn. Fehler: Referenz nicht gefunden.

Taken from Wikepedia. The free Encyclopedia [26. 01. 2014] ; see closer Stephan Albrecht: Gemeinwohl, in: Uwe Fleckner/ Martin Warnke/ Hendrik Ziegler (eds.): Handbuch der politischen Ikonographie, Band I: Abdankung bis Huldigung, 2011, p. 401.

Taken from Wikepedia. The free Encyclopedia [26. 01. 2014] . These engravings were so popular that the German philosopher Christoph Lichtenberg annotated the German editions.

Taken from Wikepedia. The free Encyclopedia [26. 01. 2014] .

Taken from Deutsches Historisches Museum [26. 01. 2014] .

Taken from Zeno. org. Meine Bibliothek [26. 01. 2014] .

See closer Isabelle Lindermann: Bilder des "anderen" Wien; Hermann Drawes und Emil Klägers Lichtbildvortrag Durch die Wiener Quartiere des Elends und Verbrechens, in: Agnes Husslein – Arco/Thomas Köhler/Ralf Burmeister/Alexander Klee/Annelie Lütgens (eds.): Wien – Berlin. Kunst zweier Metropolen, 2013, p. 98.

http: //www. google. de/imgres? sa = X&biw = 1280&bih = 929&tbm = isch&tbnid = uKDxvLOkSFez7M% 3A&imgrefurl = http% 3A% 2F% 2Fwww. adulteducation. at% 2Fde% 2Fhistoriografie% 2Fausstellung% 2F449% 2F&docid = L4hjX7uO3qYo _ M&imgurl = http% 3A% 2F% 2Ffiles. adulteducation. at% 2Fonlinehistoriografie% 2FB – 11 _ Obdachloser – beim –

Feuer – sitzend_ 72 dpi. jpg&w = 278&h = 220&ei = hmzhUuysCcLQtQal – oCYBw&zoom = 1&iact = rc&dur = 1680&page = 1&start = 0&ndsp = 36&ved = 0CKIBEK0DMBc〔26. 01. 2014〕.

http：//pixcluster2. freshworx. de/pix736261/k_ Bildo_ o65147. jpg〔26. 01. 2014〕.

Es wollt ein Bauer früh aufstehn. . . 222 Volklieder. ed. by, Zupfgeigenhansel "/ Thomas Friz/ Erich Schmeckenbecher, 2. Ed. , 1978, p. 55.

Cf. Wolfgang Steinitz：Deutsche Volkslieder demokratischen Charakters aus sechs Jahrhunderten. Band I und Band II reprinted und zusammengebunden, 1979, Band I, p. XX.

See the text at Wolfgang Steinitz, Fn. Fehler：Referenz nicht gefunden, Band I, p. 14.

See the text at Wolfgang Steinitz, Fn. Fehler：Referenz nicht gefunden, Band I, p. 278 f.

See to these functions of history 3.

Hear under http：//www. youtube. com/watch? v = 6 – lXRHZ2fTY〔26. 01. 2014〕.

Hear under http：//www. youtube. com/watch? v = Pt9RJR6xc48〔26. 01. 2014〕.

Cf. El Grecco（1541 – 1614）：St. Martin and the Beggarr, under http：// en. wikipedia. org/wiki/File：El_ Greco_ –_ San_ Mart% C3% ADn_ y_ el_ mendigo. jpg〔26. 01. 2014〕.

See the texts in respect with Schinderhannes and Hiesel at Wolfgang Steinitz, Fn. Fehler：Referenz nicht gefunden, Band I, p. 102 ff.

Joseph A. Schumpeter, Kapitalismus, Sozialismus und Demokratie, （1950）, 1972, S. 461 f.

Max Weber：Wirtschaft und Gesellschaft. Grundriss der verstehenden Soziologie （posthumously, 1921）, 5. Aufl. , 1972. p. 126 ff.

The Present German Social Policy and Its Impacts on Families

Dörte Busch [*]

1 Introduction

Germany operates as social state as well as social market economy, Article 20 (1) of the German Constitution. In addition Germany has to observe the European Union Law and is embedded into the European Social Charter and the European Charter of Fundamental Rights to achieve the objectives social protection and inclusion. All programs concerning social security introduced by the German state are based on that legal framework. An effective social policy is characterized by the way it gives all members of society an equal way of getting access to the social life and thereby encourages social mobility and social inclusion and helps combating poverty.

For 80% of German people, the family is of central importance and enjoys a high value in society. Since 2005 social policy with the focus on families has been

---

* Prof. Dr. Dörte Busch, Berlin School of Economics and Law.

one of the political key areas and the government agreed to take measures to improve family life.

2 The Situation in Germany

Germany has approximately 80 million inhabitants including 12. 9 million children under the age of 18. In 2011 a total of 8. 1 million families with minor children lived in Germany. Marriage is the most commonly encountered family form with a share of 5. 7 million married couples. The number of unmarried cohabiting couples with children has further increased during the last 15 years（743 thousand couples）. The 3rd family form is represented by 1. 6 million lone parents.

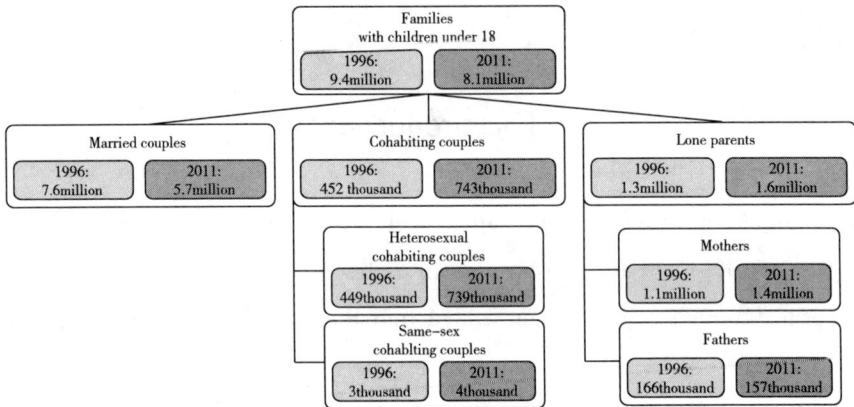

Figure 1

The state provides subsidies to help individuals as lone parents and the smaller groupings in society including families. In 2010 the system consisted of 156 different subsidies with a volume of 200 billion Euro much more than in other countries representing 2. 07% of the German GDP in 2009. It is noticeably less compared with the OECD average of 2. 61% . More than 70% of the subsidies consist of tax advantages and cash benefits whereas in Sweden and Denmark it takes only 42% . Other countries, however, invest more directly in structures such as child care and day schools. The total public expenditure amounts 146000 Euro per child up to 18 years. The OECD average is just under 124000 Euros. In consequence, Germany is spending a lot of money annually for social protection concerning families. Germany takes an international top position on family support without positively affecting the number of births. The effectiveness is not convincing.

This is also illustrated by the weighted index of social justice of 6. 89 in OECD Countries in 2011. Germany is next to the OECD average of 6. 55.

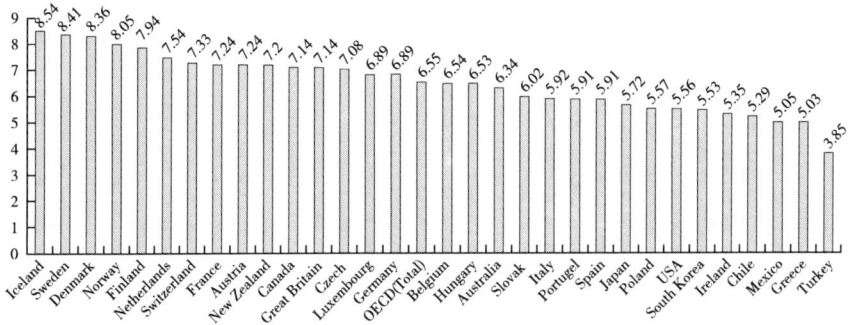

Figure 2

Germany also faces the problem of children living in poverty. Roughly 16% of the children in Germany are living in poverty in according to the definition of the OECD. The at – risk – of – poverty rate has remained nearly constantly the last years.

The situation in Germany is characterized by some other key data influencing the family policy that are comparable with Chinese situation in general. In 2011 the total fertility rate amounts to 1. 4 in Germany, 1. 7 in China and is not enough to maintain the population of the countries. Both countries stand below the replacement level. The average age in Germany is 45. 70 years close to Japan. That of Chinese people is 36. 30 years (2012) . The difference is 9. 4 years or 20% from the German target. But both countries are facing the demographic problem causing huge challenges with the social security system. According to statistical data the average age in Germany is increasing.

3 Social Policy, Measures, Impacts

Additional to the aspect of sustainability the federal government has identified specific targets in quality of life, inter – generational equity, social cohesion and international responsibilities.

General principle of the federal family policy is the promotion of the freedom of choice: families should be able to live the way they want to live themselves.

The conditions for families have been optimized during the last years with a clear focus on work – life – balance and better education of children. The state implemented a wide range of measures as the following:

1. Parental benefit, 2007

The parental benefit was introduced in 2007. It is not only a modification of the former existing child care benefit which is based on the breadwinner model, as it represents a new concept which justifies the change of terms. Regularly, parents give up their occupation after the birth of a child and take parental leave for a certain time. In 95% of all cases women take parental leave, while men increase their work commitment.

The parental benefit is intended to provide effective and sustainable economic security for families' right after the birth of a child. It has three aims:

● Parental benefit shall avoid the interruption in income flows (function of substitution income),

● Parental benefit shall offer a genuine choice to share child care between father and mother and

● Parental benefit shall promote the economic independence of both parents and shall appropriately compensate the opportunity costs.

It is guaranteed to all parents: employees in the broadest sense, civil servants, self – employed and unemployed parents, as well as students and apprentices. Basically the parental benefit is paid for twelve months. Two partner months are paid additionally, on condition that the other parent takes parental leave, too. In this case, parents can freely split the fourteen – month period between them. It is also possible to spread the full parental benefit budget over a period of up to twenty eight months. Parents get paid in order to compensate the loss for staying home and care for their babies. Parental benefit is designed as an income substitution benefit. Employees, who interrupt their occupational life or reduce their weekly working hours (max. 30 hours), receive an in – come – related parental benefit amounting up to 67% of the averaged income earned before the birth of the child (during the previous twelve months) to a maximum of 1800 per month. Low – income earner (less than 1000 per month) receive an increased benefit up to 100% of their previous income. Due to the substitution function, parental benefit is paid to part – time workers in relation to the real loss of income. The whole income is credited against the parental benefit.

The parental benefit is an effective social benefit becoming more and more favorable for young families.

Up to now the state has spent 30 billion Euro. It avoids negative short time impacts of the former long lasting benefit and long term disadvantages for women. According to the duration of parental leave, the possibility of finding employment in the labour market and career chances grades and the poverty risk significantly declines. Fathers take approximately 3 months parental leave. It is not a long period but it helps in understanding family work and to leave traditional roles of men and women behind. In fact it supports a cultural change in family life towards equality of women and men.

2. Care leave, 2008

Since 2008 Germany has a care leave system similar to the parental leave program. It is an important innovative measure the social policy has taken. It considers the needs of an aging society. The goal is to set up a family care for older people instead of placing them in professional care in a nursing home. On the other hand it serves the work – life – balance, too. It is not a monetary benefit.

Until 2012 employees were entitled to unpaid leave from work or part time work for a period of up to six months with a guaranty of returning to the working place under certain conditions. The care leave was not as effective as intended due to the short period of six month. Empirically two years seem to be an optimal duration which the state introduced in 2012 and a system of an income – working time – compensation, too. But the care leave is not a legal right any longer. The effectiveness of the new care leave depends on the negotiation between employers and employees. Under the perspective of collective labor law the care leave can also be part of union agreements and is also a good field of internal agreements. Since then no evaluation has been available.

3. Educational package for needy children, 2011

As mentioned before it's one of the most important political goals of the Federal Government to improve the prospects of disadvantaged groups for social and economic participation. One of the policies in that name is still education. It was the main task of the state in that respect to secure the quantitative and qualitative improvement of the educational system.

Educational policy is in anyway a social policy. In Germany you have to take into account the different legal competences under the German Basic Law which generally makes the policy complicated on the federal level. The Federal State has only a small corridor taking measures in this field namely on the basis of the Social Code Book VIII (Kinder – und Jugendhilfe) referring to child care. Since the last few years the Federal State has emphasized the education in the early childhood (children at the age of 3 until starting school).

The German society model refers to the subsidiarity principle. Everybody in need gets help from the state to secure the sociocultural subsistence minimum including inclusion in society. That is the basic concept up to now. It serves the principles of equal opportunities as one of the main functions of the social security system.

Under these guidelines the German state introduced an educational package in 2011 to fulfill the requirements set up by the Federal Constitutional Court concerning the inclusion of children. The subsistence minimum applies to children as well as to adults according to their special needs. This program is only for 2.5 million needy children of low – income families and mainly covers needs concerning education and inclusion in society.

This package consists of benefits as of transportation to and from school, lunch in a care center, school or after school care center, cultural, sports and leisure activities, learning support, school materials and support for day trips and class outings.

The concept is good but the administration of the benefits is much too complicated and not sufficiently transparent to parents.

4. Extension of the legal right to childcare, 2008 – 2013

Both, national and federal governments have planned the expanding childcare to facilitate access to education, help prevent social inequality during schooling, have a preventive effect and improve the chances for better social inclusion. The childcare expansion is the top priority for the federal government.

To invest in the infrastructure is recommended best by all experts as most effective measure to support young families. Much has already been achieved in raising the number of day – care places for children. Since 2013 the program has met the nationwide needs in general; 750000 day – care places has cost about 5. 4 billion. As of August 2013, every one – year – old child has the legal right to a day – care place. The additional 30000 day – care places were financed by the Federal State.

In addition, the Federal Ministry for Family Affairs has issued a supportive 10 – point program in May 2012 which allows further strengthening of the child day – care and a better promotion of in – house childcare. Furthermore, additional professionals must be found and qualified for childcare.

5. Betreuungsgeld ("child – care benefit") , 2013

The most controversial benefit favored by the Federal Government came into force in August 2013. The government takes a general principle as a basis applying to all parents: the freedom of choice between bringing – up their children themselves or using professional day – care. Betreuungsgeld "as child – care benefit" is a monthly payment for parents who do not trust their children to professional day – care. The amount of 100 will be raised up to 140 in August 2014. This child – care benefit is meant to honour the parental work.

The problem of setting a false incentive is obvious for most experts. The concept promotes the breadwinner model and does not stay abreast of changes in our society. On the other hand the government takes measures (e. g. new day – care places) to integrate more women in the labour market. The policy is contradictory.

Especially for low – income families it is attractive to take the money instead of using the professional day – care. Often children with a migrant background need the early education in day – care centers as a base for getting a successful start in school. It is also known that only more and higher cash benefits (e. g. child benefit of current 184 monthly) are not as effective as other policy measures (see above) and not what young families wish as a support.

4　Challenge：family forms

In Germany family ranks extraordinarily. It stands under the constitutional protection in Article 6 of Basic Law of the Federal Republic of Germany. In the last few years Germany is facing another challenge concerning the family.

The "family" is rapidly changing. In our society nowadays are occurring many types of families. The complete social system is still based on the classical family: that used to be a married couple (father, mother) and of course two children, a boy and a girl at best. This traditional and long kept upright picture of the ideal family is no longer at hand. Today the family shows new structures and forms that could be seen in many different facets. That process can also be observed in China. The Chinese development leads to new functions of the family and means also a challenge for social security because the modern Chinese household becomes smaller and the family's function of future security is weakening.

In Germany more and more children live in so – called patchwork families Which are these made up from the remnants of divorced families (in 2011 10% – 14% of all couples) . 9% of all families are unmarried cohabiting couples with children. During the last 15 years the number has almost doubled. Also an increase of 6% up to 20% in the number of lone parents was observed.

Basically, in this context the Federal Government acts to support lone parents who have the highest risk of poverty and to establish the equality of same – gender unions under the Law on civil partnership (Lebenspartnerschaftsgesetz) of the Federal Republic of Germany. The legal frame of same – gender unions refer to the common family term and, in fact, they live with children in only 4000 household (0. 05% of families) .

The German population increasingly accepts other parent – child communities as a family. In 2012 nearly three – quarters of the population say it for a non – married couple with children, 58% for lone parents and 42% for same – gender unions with children. But for the federal family policy it is not a reason to change the legal frame and coordinate all family subsidies for ensuring equal opportunities for all parents.

As a family I see:

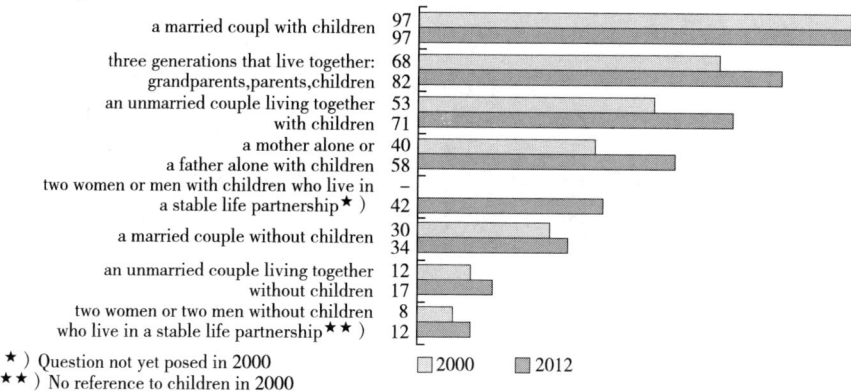

a married coupl with children	97 97
three generations that live together: grandparents,parents,children	68 82
an unmarried couple living together with children	53 71
a mother alone or a father alone with children	40 58
two women or men with children who live in a stable life partnership★)	– 42
a married couple without children	30 34
an unmarried couple living together without children	12 17
two women or two men without children who live in a stable life partnership★★)	8 12

★) Question not yet posed in 2000
★★) No reference to children in 2000

☐ 2000   ▦ 2012

Based on the population of the Federal Republic of Germany aged 16 and older
Source:Allensbacher Archlv,Monltor Familienleben 2012.IfD–Umfrage 7000.

Figure 3

5　Conclusion

Family policy and families have changed over the past thirty years. Nonetheless it must be the goal of a government to follow a sustainability strategy. But the question is: how is the goal to achieve? The general task of the policy is to hand out guidelines for the population. But the discrepancy between reality and politics cannot endlessly grow. Politics has to reflect and to refer to changes in society.

For the future it is essential to develop a consistent family – based system of social subsidies, which takes precisely into account the family situation. This includes e. g. to rethink the large number of social subsidies and completely includes the unmarried cohabiting couples as family form for ensuring equal rights. Thereorganisation is one important measure as well as improving the infrastructure for family life, e. g. a better quality of day – care, a better work – life – balance in enterprises. To be able to finance this, it means a shift of as constitutionally protected marriage out of the family.

The concepts for this development still need to be generated and a lot of research waits for being done on this topic in the near future.

Reference

The German Federal Government's 4th Report on Poverty and Wealth, Berlin 2013, page II. See Special Eurobarometer 321, Poverty and Social Exclusion, Bruessels 2010.

Family Report 2012, page 14.

Starting Point was the Coalition Agreement concluded by the parties CDU, CSU and SPD "Working together for Germany – With courage and compassion" on 11 November 2005.

Family Report 2012, page 14.

Federal Ministry of Family, Seniors, Women and Youth (BMFSFJ), Statement 16 January 2013; BMFSFJ, Bestandsaufnahme der familienbezogenen Leistungen und Maßnahmen des Staates im Jahr 2010, http://www. bmsfsj. de (all websites visited on 20 February 2014).

http://www. oecd. org; Frankfurter Allgemeine Zeitung, number 141, 21 June 2013, page 13.

OECD, Comparative Child Well – being across the OECD, 2005, page 35.

The German Federal Government's 4th Report on Poverty and Wealth, Berlin 2013, page VII.

Worldbank, Fertility rate, total (births per woman) 2009 - 2011, http: // data. worldbank.

org/indicator/SP. DYN. TFRT. IN; see the changing of family structures in China Tan Jung et. al. , China's Social Development, 2010, page 28 ff.

http: //www. statista. com.

National Sustainable Development Strategy 2012 Progress Report.

Politischer Bericht zur Gesamtevaluation der ehe – und familienbezogenen Leistungen, 2013, page 6.

Bundeselterngeld – und Elternzeitgesetz, BEEG, BGBl. 2006 I page 2748, into fore 1 July 2007.

Federal Ministry of Family, Seniors, Women and Youth, Seventh Family Report, 2005, http: //www. bmfsfj. de.

Sozialbericht 2013, page 210.

http: //www. bmfsfj. de.

BMFSFJ, Vaterschaft und Elternzeit, 2012; see also the regular report on parentel benefit, http: //www. bmsfsj. de.

Pflegezeitgesetz, 28 May 2008, BGBl. I page 874, into fore 1 July 2008.

Familienpflegezeitgesetz, 6 December 2011, BGBl. I page 2564, into force 1 January 2012.

Federal Ministry of Labour and Social Affairs, The Educational Package – A New Start for Taking Part, Berlin 2013.

Bundesverfassungsgericht (BVerfG) 9. Februar 2010 – 1 BvL 1/09, Neue Juristische Wochenschrift (NJW) 2010, 505.

National Social Report 2012, page 12.

http: //www. bmsfsj. de.

Tagesbetreuungsausbaugesetz (TAG) 27. Dezember 2004, BGBl. I page 3852, into force: 1 January 2005; Kinderförderungsgesetz, 10. Dezember 2008, BGBl. I page 2403, into force: 16 December 2008; . Gesetz zur zusätzlichen Förderung von Kindern unter drei Jahren in Tageseinrichtungen und in Kindertagespflege, 15. Februar 2013; into force: 21 February 2013, BGBl. I page 250, http: //www. bmsfsj. de; NSC 2012, page 12.

Betreuungsgeldgesetz 15. Februar 2013, BGBl. I page 254, into force 1 August 2013.

Tang Jun et. al. , China's Social Development, 2010, page 28 ff. , 37.

Family Report 2012, page 14.

Statistisches Bundesamt 2012, Mikrozensus 2011: Familien und Haushalte; Politischer Bericht zur Gesamtevaluation der ehe – und familienbezogenen Leistungen, 2013, page 2 – 3.

Allensbacher Archiv, Monitor Familienleben 2012, IfD Umfrage 7000.

See the first step in this direction: Politischer Bericht zur Gesamtevaluation der ehe – und familienbezogenen Leistungen, 2013.

Hospital Alliances and Healthcare Supply Networks – A German Perspective

Jochen Breinlinger – O'Reilly [*]

In recent years the number of cases in German hospitals has been rising constantly whereas the number of beds has been falling steadily (Destatis, 2011) . In addition to this the number of hospitals from all three different types of hospital owners (public, private, and charity based hospitals) is falling as well. As a reaction to this development there are many hospitals, which already formed alliances.

There is the example of the biggest hospital alliance (Association of Communal/Regional Large Hospitals) , which is introduced with special regard to the hospital chain Vivantes owned by the State of Berlin.

Furthermore, there will be a description of the management of alliances and different dimensions of networking/network formation in healthcare. The last part will explain the interchange and interconnectivity within a hospital alliance.

Association of Communal/Regional Large Hospitals (AKG) and Managing Alliances

Since 1997 the AKG is an interest group consisting of 21 large hospitals in

* Prof. Dr. Jochen Breinlinger – O'Reilly Berlin School of Economics and Law.

Germany with a total revenue of 7. 2 billion Euro. At present the association represents about 33000 beds, 1. 5 million patients and 96000 members of staff. It is herewith acting for about 7% of the overall German hospital market (www. kommunale – grosskrankenhaeuser. de).

For managing alliances, be it hospital alliances or different types of commercial alliances, there are different degrees of integration and dependency. An alliance with the lowest degree of integration and dependency is a so called "informal cooperation". It is followed by a "formal cooperation" once the level of integration and dependency are equally higher. On a medium level the kind of alliance would be based on a "contractual joint venture", which would turn into an "equity joint ownership", if the intensity of integration and dependency would reach the next level. The highest form of managing an alliance is done by means of "mergers and acquisitions", which represents the highest degree of integration and dependency (Busacker and Clarke, 2001).

Another approach to systematize the forming of a healthcare network can be explained by using the following three dimensions: 1) Width of indication, 2) Network density and 3) Depth of integration. The width of indication includes indication – specific, subject – specific, and process – specific healthcare fields as well as an overall healthcare supply. The depth of integration contains inpatient and outpatient care, ambulant nursing service, rehabilitation, transportation, pharmaceuticals, remedies, and auxiliary means. In essence it can be said that the higher the depth of integration, the higher the network density (Schreyögg, 2009).

Structure and Interconnectivity of a Hospital Alliance

The structure of a hospital alliance involves several different actors with different tasksand interests. On a horizontal level, a hospital can form a regional or supra – regional cooperation with other hospitals of the same brand image and performance profile, which supports and strengthens the negotiation power and could also help to support the guarantee and quality promise. On a vertical level, a hospital is connected to the general practitioners and medical specialists, who maintain high regional and supra – regional acceptance. As a result the number of patients being treated is growing. On a lateral level, a hospital also has the option to establish ties to medical devices companies. The possible outcome from this kind of collaboration could be an innovation – friendly hospital with the latest status of medical technology enhanced by quality leadership.

With the lot of these partners, a hospital can establish medical service centers and integrate healthcare and therefore will be well positioned for partnership with payers/health insurances. The result could help to increase the number of patients, to decrease the costs, and increase the quality of care and the ability to innovate. All in all, it helps to ensure the popularity and the positive image (Töpfer and Großekatthöfer, 2006).

Conclusion: Pros and Cons for Hospital Alliances and Healthcare Supply Networks

Hospital alliances and healthcare supply networks exist within a triangle of different actors/interest groups/stakeholders, which include the public and private health insurers, the consumers (patients, insured persons), and the providers (outpatient, inpatient). Given that hospital alliances have to deal with these different actors in the health system, there are advantages and disadvantages, which can have to be described. Firstly, the synergies in the using of facilities and technologies have to be named. Secondly, the ability and flexibility to refer patients and employees is increased. Furthermore, there is a positive impact on the qualification and continuous education of experts and staff. Lastly, the overcoming of sectoral boundaries within the system can clearly be seen as an advantage. Although the inflexibility of monopolistic structures, large entities can result in disadvantages, this would call for political intervention.

Quality Assurance in the Healthcare Sector: A Comparative Analysis of ISO and KTQ in Germany

Frank Diebel [*]

The need for certification of health facilities existed for many years. In Germany, for example, about ten years ago, the "voluntary" certification process of the German Cooperation for Transparency and Quality in Healthcare (KTQ) was initially developed for the hospital sector that now also provides specifics for medical practices and medical centers, rehabilitation facilities, inpatient and outpatient care facilities, hospices, alternative forms of housing in the healthcare sector, and emergency services. In addition to JCI, the KTQ process was long considered the only certification procedure that was specifically tailored to the hospital sector. It was deliberately designed "by practitioners for practitioners" and, over a decade, it represented the most common certification standard in the German hospital sector. However, many healthcare facilities also apply the cross – industry applicable ISO standard DIN EN ISO 9001: 2008. Because of its international recognition, it has always played a major role in the market for

* Prof. Dr. Frank Diebel, Berlin School of Economics and Law.

certification procedures and, thus, it is renowned for its high prevalence in the industrial sector as well as in many service sectors. But the application of the ISO – Norm in the health sector is demanding. The technically abstract written ISO 9001 standard that is originated from the manufacturing industry is often difficult to be understood by health practitioners. For a hospital employee, therefore, it is often very challenging to imagine how to translate it into health facilities. The demand for a specific ISO standard for the healthcare sector arose accordingly. In December 2012, the DIN EN 15224 was published to fulfill this demand. This specific norm is considered to represent the translation of the ISO 9001 to facilities of the healthcare sector. [1]

In the following parts, the basic elements of the certification procedures for healthcare facilities of the Cooperation for Transparency and Quality in Healthcare (KTQ) and the International Standardization Organization (ISO) will be compared. The main criteria for the comparison are their health focus, their catalogues, their approaches as well as their strengths and weaknesses.

1 Design of the KTQ Certification Procedure

According to the German Law, all providers in the system of statutory health insurance must be committed to the principle of quality assurance. The Fifth Book of the German Social Code (SGB V) regulates the basic requirements for quality assurance. Amongst others, they include the statutory obligation to establish an internal quality management and to participate in activities of cross – institutional external quality assurance (§ 135a SGB V) . Thus, in 2012, there were 2017 hospitals in Germany, of which 70 percent had a certifiable internal quality management system. [2] The current market leader for external hospital certification in

---

[1]   Bamberg, Christian et al. DIN EN 15224 – spezifische Norm für das Gesundheitswesen. Qualitätsmanagement im Gesundheitswesen, http: //www. tuev – media. de/leseprob/lp_ 90714. pdf (visited on Dec. 11th, 2013), pp. 1 –3.

[2]   Federal Statistical Office, http: //www. destatis. de (visited on December 10th, 2013) .

Germany is the Cooperation for Transparency and Quality in Healthcare. Currently, 516 German hospitals are certified according to the KTQ certification model. [1]

The KTQ model has a strict patient orientation. The patient is at the focus of its certification procedure in every step of the internal and external assessment procedure. In this context, the KTQ catalogue is divided into six categories: patient orientation, employee orientation, safety, information and communication, leadership, and quality management. These six categories "form the central elements to describe the patient's requirements... [and] are especially important to patients, relatives, accompanying persons and also to the employees of a facility". [2]

The KTQ model offers five types of certification procedures (manuals): for hospitals, medical practices and medical service centers, hospices, rehabilitation facilities, and emergency rescue service facilities. For those it offers various certification options: single facility certification, group certification, network certification, and certification of single health units within facilities. For instance, with the certification option "group certification" it is possible to certify different locations that provide the same type of care within a healthcare alliance, while the option "network certification" offers the possibility to certify healthcare facilities of different types at different locations. All methods are based on the KTQ model and include the above mentioned six categories that follow the PDCA – cycle (Plan – Do – Check – Act).

The PDCA approach of KTQ requires that the health facilities set in motion a process of continuous improvement, but it provides neither a norm or standard to be followed nor a clinical process orientation. It is topic – oriented, instead. Even though the KTQ model provides a specific certification model for healthcare providers being accepted in Germany, it is not recognized on the international stage, not even within the European Union.

---

① Cooperation for Transparency and Quality in Healthcare, http://www. ktq. de (visited on Dec. 11th, 2013).

② KTQ Manual Hospital, 2009, p. 10.

2　Design of the ISO Certification Procedure

In recent years, more and mone German clinics and clinic consortia plan to move to the ISO model. Some main arguments for the widespread intention to move refer to higher development potential. Because of its international recognition, transparency, and comparability, its more process – oriented approach and the use of synergies with other service areas of hospitals, the decision makers find the development potential. The development of the ISO norm DIN EN 15224: 2012 is supposed to support this intention.

The aim of DIN EN 15224: 2012 is to provide a specific process – oriented quality management norm for institutions of the healthcare sector that is state of the art, generally accepted, internationally recognized, and taking legal requirements into account. The main chapters of the ISO standard DIN EN 15224: 2012 stay identical to the DIN EN ISO 9001: 2008. The eight principles of a "learning organization", for instance, remain unchanged: customer focus (the patient being the key costumer), leadership, involvement of personnel, process orientation, system – oriented management approach, continuous improvement, decision – making based on facts, and mutually beneficial supplier relationships. In this way, the idea of ISO 9001 of an integrated and process – oriented organization is adopted. The DIN EN 15224 norm provides three types of processes that are now explicitly emphasized: clinical processes, research, and education. The clinical processes with their core services of patient care including all activities, professional groups and institutions of service delivery are now the focus of this standard. [1]

Based on the comprehensive WHO definition of "health", the standard has

---

[1]　Sens, Brigitte. DIN EN 15224: 2012 – eine neue Zertifizierungsnorm für Qualitätsmanagementsysteme in Gesundheitseinrichtungen. Interdisciplinary Contributions to Hospital Management: Medicine, Patient Safety and Economics, http: //www. clinotel – journal. de/article – id – 011. html (May 25th, 2013), p. 4.

a clear patient focus and describes requirements for efficacy, safety and availability of healthcare services. As a basis for a high quality and safety in healthcare, eleven quality characteristics are defined: adequateness, availability, continuity and consistency, punctuality and accessibility, effectivity, efficiency and equality of healthcare, evidence – and knowledge – based healthcare, personalized care, inclusion of the patient, and patient safety.

3 Conclusion

Compared with the KTQ model that offers four certification options, ISO offers a single facility certification only. However, ISO does not need specialized certification procedures (manuals), Hospitals, medical practices and medical service centers, hospices, rehabilitation facilities, and emergency rescue service facilities like the KTQ model. Instead, the DIN EN 15224: 2012 manual provides a norm for all health facilities in one.

The specific design of a guide for the interpretation of the DIN EN 15224 for the purpose of the audit is still on its way. It remains to be seen whether this new healthcare specific standard will prevail in Germany compared to the KTQ model. At least it seems to represent a good basis for suggestions to an integrated quality and risk management as well as a good opportunity to modernize the performance of processes in terms of whether they are adequately aligned with the benefits of the patient and patient safety. [1]

---

[1] Sens, Brigitte. DIN EN 15224: 2012 – eine neue Zertifizierungsnorm für Qualitätsmanagementsysteme in Gesundheitseinrichtungen. Interdisciplinary Contributions to Hospital Management: Medicine, Patient Safety and Economics, http: //www. clinotel – journal. de/article – id – 011. html (May 25th, 2013), p. 7.

中德社会改革与整体社会政策协调

Perspectives on the Disequilibrium of Public Financial Capacity among Cities* in X Province, Western China

Xing Qiangguo**

Abstract   Disequilibrium of public financial capacity is an extrusive phenomenon in Western China cities, and this is a key topic involving basic public services. The report here cites that phenomenon in Sichuan Province as a case that includes 18 cities[1]. Statistic description shows that there are great gaps among cities in X Province in Western China, and there is an up – trend in the disequilibrium of public financial capacity.

Keywords   Disequilibrium; Public Financial Capacity; Basic Public Service; Western China cities; X Province

---

*   Here the cities are defined as the cities in prefecture – level or sub – provincial level. Cities in China are divided in descending order as county level, prefecture level, sub – provincial level, municipality level administratively. Of course, cities in China also can be divided in terms of population scale, most prefecture – level cities have middle – scale population from 50 thousand to 200 thousand; population at sub – provincial level is equal to or above 2 millions.

**   Prof. Dr. Xing Qiangguo, Southwestern University of Finance and Economics.

①   Prefecture autonomous regions are not included because the absence of data.

1 Introduction

Since the implement ation of Western Development policy, cities' economy in X Province has been growing significantly over the years. And continuing economic growth has close relationship with basic public services. And on the other hand, there are extrusive differences among cities in western China. One of the differences is about public financial capacity[①], which is of great importance to basic public service. This report relies on descriptive statistics to demonstrate the problem, and bring out intuitive thinking on the causes and impacts of the disequilibrium of public finance capacity.

2 Issues

As public financial capacity closely involves with basic public services in Western China cities, disequilibrium of public financial capacity is a big concern in public service. This report uses the data of 18 cities of X Province in Western China to illustrate this topic. There are four issues in this report: measurement, current situation, future trend, and implication of the disequilibrium.

The first issue: How to measure the disequilibrium of public financial capacity? Local budget income per capita (LBIP) is applied to measurement of public financial capacity. Reasons are listed belon: a city is a relatively independent financial unit; LBIP is a uniform and objective measurement for all cities; LBIP is the average measurement in terms of per capita which compares cities of different scale.

The second issue: What is the current situation of LBIP? Descriptive statistics is applied in this report.

The third issue: What would be the future trend of LBIP? Intuitive thinking is applied in this report, based on descriptive statistics.

---

① Public financial capacity is measured in terms of local public budget income per capita.

3 Description

The following 3 figures are sorted out from Statistical Yearbook of China. And it is easy to see the disequilibrium of local budget income per capita in major cities of X Province in Western China. And similar pattern can be found in other provinces in Western China, the case is a reference for other cities in Western China provinces. There are 4 figures to demonstrate the phenomena of disequilibrium.

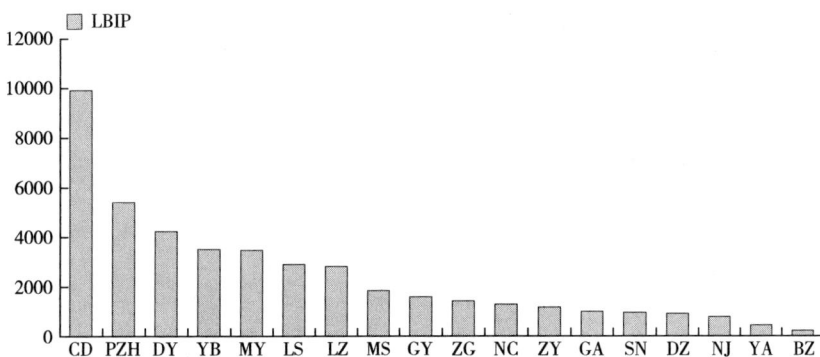

Fig. 1   Cross section _ LBIP, X Province, 2011

Figure 1 describes the current situation of the disequilibrium of public financial capacity in 2011 (2012 data is not available).

Figure 2 demonstrates the current trend of the disequilibrium of 2002 – 2011 period. It is easy to observe that the gaps have been becoming wider over the years.

Figure 3 demonstrates the standard deviation of LBIP in 2002 – 2011 period. It is easy to observe that the differences have been monotonely increasing in the 10 – year interval.

4   Implications

Two conclusions can be drawn from the statistic description. (1) There are

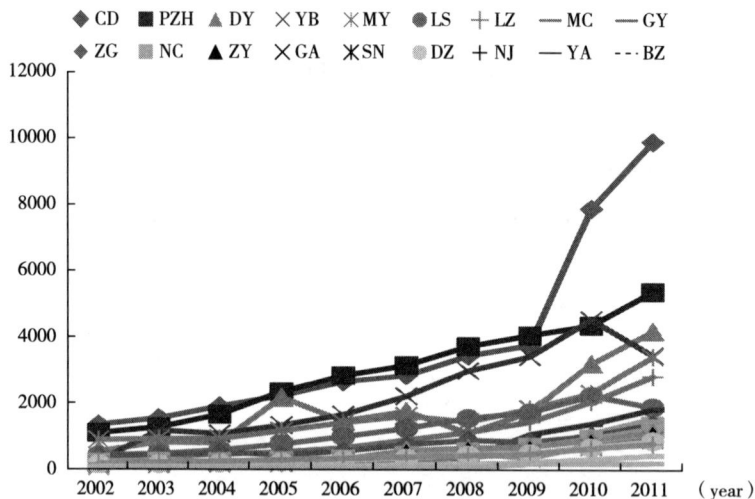

Fig. 2　Panel Data _ LBIP，X Province，2002 – 2011

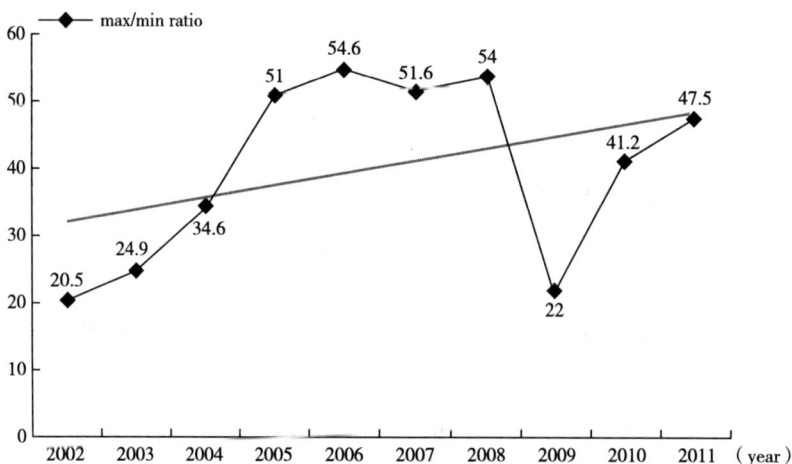

Fig. 3　Standard Deviation of LBIP，X Province，2002 – 2011

alarming gaps of LBIP among cities in X province，which implies great gaps of public financial capacity among these cities（2011）.（2）There is a trend of increase in LBIP of X Province，which implies the gaps has a up – trend in the 2002 – 2011 period.

Two tentative extensions from the above conclusions：（1）Western China cities have similar economic conditions，so the above conclusions are good

298

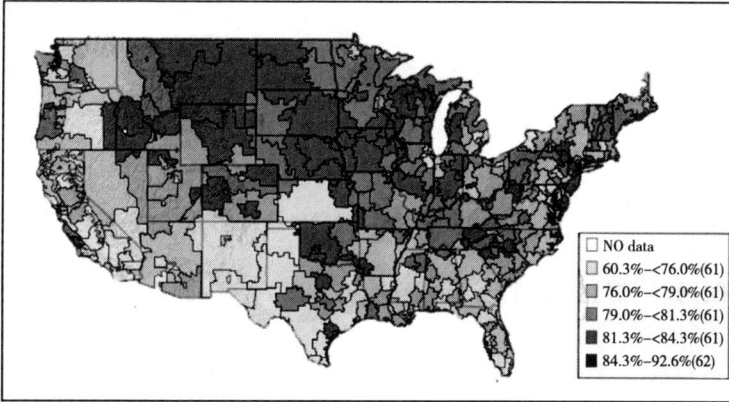

Fig. 4   the max/min ratios of LBIP in 2002 – 2011 period. It is easy to observe that,
the ratio is amazing, and it keeps the high ratio,
and even higher, with a zigzag pattern.

references for other cities in a province or another in Western China. (2) The disequilibrium will continue in the near future, because of the cities' inertia of economic pattern in the coming years.

It is sensible to raise this question: the disequilibrium will a constitute challenge to basic public services. Practice today tells us that there are significant differences in a variety of public service fields in Western China cities. Medical coverage ratio is a case in point, and different cities have different coverage ratio, and the gaps are great.

Suppose the medical coverage ratio is not a special case, instead of a uniform issue in public service, how can we assure the basic public service? What is the meaning of basic public services. We need meditation and research.

The Effect of Unemployment Insurance Cross – industry Subsidies on Employment

Yun Li[*]

Abstract   This paper studies the short run employment effect of U. S. unemployment insurance policies. I build simulated instruments for the state UI policy measures to avoid endogeneity issue of policy measures derived from administrative data. I find the effect of UI taxes and benefits to employment goes away when I add state year interaction to the regressions to account for the fact that states change their tax schedules annually if necessary to balance UI trust fund. I then regress state average UI measures on lagged state unemployment rate and find clear evidence for policy endogeneity in state UI programs.

Keywords   Unemployment Insurance; Subsidy; Employment; Simulated Instruments; Policy Endogeneity

1   Introduction

The Unemployment Insurance (UI) system in the United States provides

---

*   Dr. Yun Li, Southwestern University of Finance and Economics.

temporary relief to those who become involuntarily unemployed through no fault of their own. It is an important social insurance that covers 97% of all salary and wage workers. On the other hand, the UI system creates a by – product that is in most cases undesirable – a subsidy from the firms and industries of stable employment to those that have volatile changes in their employment levels. Munts and Asher (1980) and Anderson and Meyer (1993) present evidence of cross – industry UI subsidies. Usually construction industry is the most consistent subsidy receiver while service industry is the most consistent subsidy provider. Because the UI system in the U. S. operates through federal – state joint programs, there are striking differences in the size of UI subsidies across states due to the varying degrees of experience – rating of state UI tax schedules and different industrial compositions of the states.

Theoretically the potential availability of such subsidies provides an incentive for employers to use temporary layoffs to weather seasonal and cyclical fluctuations in product demand (see Feldstein 1976; Baily 1977; Card and Levine 1994) . The incentive has become smaller after UI benefits became taxable, first for high – income individuals starting in 1979, then for most recipients in 1982, finally for all UI recipients in 1987. To the extent that UI subsidies still exist, it is possible that it can help some employers of higher layoff risk stay in business a little longer than they could without the subsidy. But at the industry level, are the subsidies large enough to create a distortionary effect on industrial development? Would the cross – industry subsidies created by the UI system lead to shrinkages of our more stable industries, and expansions of the more volatile industries? In this study I look for evidence to answer this question.

Earlier empirical work in this area has either used endogenous policy measures calculated from administrative data on payroll or UI taxes paid, or just used state level measures such as minimum taxes, maximum taxes and state average subsidies derived from maximum benefits and averageing taxes. I build simulation programs to calculate state average UI taxes, benefits, and subsidies per worker by industry that capture variations in state UI laws and regulations. I run a national multiyear data set through the simulators to make sure that my simulated UI measurements are not entangled by variations arise from changing economic environment or the endogenous reactions of local businesses to state UI policy. Using the simulated instruments I test the effect of UI policy on industry employment using Quarterly Census of Employment and Wages (QCEW) data from all 50 states and DC for each year during the 1990 – 2000 period.

I regress log industry employment on the simulated instruments for UI average taxes, benefits, or subsidies per worker by industry, including state dummies, year dummies, industry dummies, interaction terms between state and industry, and between year and industry. I find that benefits have a positive effect on employment, while taxes have a negative effect on employment. Since subsides are just benefits minus taxes, I found positive employment effect of subsides when I use the subsidies instrument instead of taxes and benefits instruments. But after adding state year interaction terms in my regressions I find no significant effect of UI policy measurements on employment. The effects of UI vanished after I count for the fact that states change their policies in each's own timing depending on state specific economic environment and each state's own UI trust fund balance. I argue that this indicates the policy or legislative endogeneity problem which arises when state policies are influenced by economic and political conditions within the state. In the case of UI policies, states have to adjust tax and benefit schedules to keep their UI trust funds balanced. In a bad year when unemployment is high, states have to adopt less favorable tax schedules and hold on to benefit increases. When the economy is doing well and fewer people are on UI payments states lower taxes and have more room to increase benefits. When I account for such endogenous policy changes by adding state year interaction term, the positive effect of benefits and negative effect of taxes on employment nearly reduce to zero.

To further investigate the policy endogeneity issue in state UI programs, I regress state average UI taxes, benefits, and subsidies per worker on lagged state unemployment rate (in year $t - 1$) and find strong positive effect of state unemployment rate of year $t - 1$ on state average taxes in year t. The effect is statistically significant. State unemployment rate of year $t - 1$ has a small and insignificant effect on state average benefits in year t.

The rest of the paper is organized as follows: next section presents a brief description of the UI system in the United States and describes how subsidies are generated. Section III is a brief literature review. Section IV presents the empirical strategy of this study. Section V discusses the results. Section VI provides evidence for policy endogeneity in state UI programs, and section VII concludes. I also include an appendix on the construction of simulated instruments for UI measurements at the end.

2　Unemployment Insurance Subsidies

The idea of publicly provided unemployment insurance was originated by the state of Wisconsin in 1932. Starting from 1935, the Social Security Act has effectively encouraged all states to run their own UI programs. Under the provision of the Federal Unemployment Tax Act (FUTA), a federal payroll tax is levied on covered employers, with 90% of the tax deductible given that the employers pay state UI taxes timely under an approved state UI program. Initially the federal tax rate was 1% on the total annual wages of a worker, with the effective tax rate being 0.1% after the 90% credit. In 1940 the federal tax was changed to 3% (0.3% effective tax rate after credit) on the federal UI taxable wage base, which was the first \$3000 annual wages of a worker at that time. Since then both the federal tax rate and the federal taxable wage base have been increased over time. The current federal tax rate is 6.2%, with 5.4% deductible making the effective tax rate 0.8%. The federal taxable wage base was increased several times over the years, and has stayed at \$7000 since 1983.

All state laws currently set a maximum UI tax rate of 5.4% or higher on state taxable wages. In 2011, 40 states and DC set their maximum UI tax rates above 5.4%; with 9 states at or above 10%, and the highest maximum UI tax rate being 13.5576%, set by the state of Pennsylvania. Taxable wage bases also vary dramatically across states. In 2011 only 3 states, Arizona, California, and Florida keep their taxable wage base at \$ 7000[①], the same as the federal taxable wage base. All other states and DC have state taxable wage bases above that level. 13 states set a taxable wage base above \$ 20000 in 2011, with the highest being \$ 37300 in the state of Washington.

The states deposit the tax contributions in state UI trust funds, from which all regular benefits and 50% of extended benefits are paid out. [②]The federal FUTA tax revenues fund the other 50% of extended benefits and also pay for the administrative costs of state UI programs. The regular benefits usually last between 26 to 30 weeks, while the extended benefits are available during periods of high unemployment for another 13 weeks after the regular benefits are exhausted. [③]State laws specify the eligibility conditions, formula for the calculation of weekly benefit amounts (WBA), and the maximum benefits available based on the unemployed worker's work and earnings history in the base period, usually the past four to five quarters before unemployment starts, up to a state maximum amount. The UI benefits an unemployed worker receives do not depend on her employer's layoff experience. States usually adjust the WBA and the maximum amount of total benefits an individual can receive annually to account for inflation or index them to state average wage.

All states experience – rate the covered employers – the tax rate levied on each employer depends on the history of its tax contributions and benefits charged. The experience – ratings are not complete though. Most states have a nonzero minimum tax rate, while all states have a maximum tax rate, ranging from 5.4% to low double digit rates, varying over time. Under such tax schedules, the narrower is

---

① This is a change from 7 states in 2007.

② With the exception being the current economic downturn started in 2008. The American Recovery and Reinvestment Act of 2009 began temporary 100% Federal funding of Extended Benefits. The Tax Relief, Unemployment Insurance Reauthorization, and Job Creation Act of 2010 (P. L. 111 – 312) extended 100% Federal funding of Extended Benefits to January 4, 2012.

③ 99 weeks total is the current maximum.

the range of the tax rates, the more incomplete is the experience – rating. Also, most of the employers that pay the minimum tax rate are charged a higher "premium" than their risks of layoff entail, while most of those paying the maximum tax rate get a free ride for additional benefits charged after the tax rate they pay reaches the maximum. Additionally, state tax schedules between the minimum and the maximum rates usually step up, rather than increasing linearly. Most states also collect additional taxes to fund employment services and training programs and to cover noncharged and inefficiently charged benefits. [1]All states have provisions to keep the state UI trust fund solvent. Some states have a set of tax schedules, ranging from the least favorable to the most favorable, that are automatically adjusted annually depending on the state UI trust fund balance. Others have different levels of subsidiary tax rates, in many cases called the solvency tax rates, triggered when the state trust fund balance dips below certain levels. These additional taxes are usually not experience – rated.

The incompleteness of experience – rating, together with the across – the – board administrative and subsidiary taxes creates UI subsidies across firms and industries of different layoff experiences, and years of varying economic conditions. The cross – state variations and over time changes in the generosity of UI benefits and the varying degrees of incompleteness of the experience – rating of the state UI tax schedules provide excellent identification tools in estimating the effect of UI policies on labor market outcomes.

3 Literature Review

Earlier empirical work on the effect of UI subsidies on employment at industry level has been scarce and far between. Deere (1991) looks at the effect of

---

[1] Noncharged benefits are those charged to a general account rather than an individual employer account. Ineffectively charged benefits include those charged to inactive and terminated accounts and those charged to an employer's experience rating account after the previously charged benefits to the account were sufficient to qualify the employer for the maximum contribution rate.

incomplete experience rating on industry employment shares in a state/year from 1962 to 1969. The UI policy measures he uses are state minimum UI tax per worker, state maximum UI tax per worker, and state average subsidy per worker, defined as the present discounted value of the difference between state maximum UI benefits per worker, adjusted for their nontaxability as they were not taxable before 1979, and the average UI taxes per worker. The regressions he runs were stratified by industry, with industry employment share in a state/year as the dependent variable and the UI measurements mentioned above as the explanatory variables. He finds that an increase in the state average subsidy increases the employment share of construction industry while decreases employment shares in mining and services industry. He finds small and statistically insignificant effect of UI on the employment shares of other industries.

There is a policy endogeneity issue that his work does not deal with. Construction industry, being a very cyclical one, may very likely have a smaller employment share in a state at the time when the economy is in a downturn for that state. If the state average subsidy is also lower when the economy is doing poorly because states have to raise taxes to balance their UI trust funds in bad economic environment, then his method would show a positive correlation between lower state average subsidy and lower employment share of the construction industry which is not necessarily a causal relationship. Running stratified regressions by industry does not allow the possibility of controlling for state specific time effect, which may correlate with or even lead to the change of state average subsidy and industry employment shares simultaneously. Although not very convincing, Deere's paper was the first empirical work aiming at measuring the effect of UI subsidies on industrial composition of a state.

Anderson and Meyer (1997) estimate the effect of UI tax rate on earnings and employment using CWBH data from 1978 to 1984, which are UI administrative records from eight states with data including firm level quarterly payroll, employment, and UI taxes paid. They use first difference model to estimate the effect of effective UI tax rate on earnings and employment. They use

2SLS to control for heteroskedasticity in error terms, and also include state, year, quarter fixed effects. They do not control for industry fixed effect or include interactions between industry, state and year. They calculate the firm level effective UI tax rate by dividing taxes paid by earnings. They also calculate market level tax rate by grouping firms using SIC code and then taking averages. They experiment with different market definitions using 2 - digit, 3 - digit and 4 - digit SIC codes. On firm level, they find negative earnings effect between - 0. 194 (when market level tax rate is included in the regression) to - 0. 260 (when market level tax rate is not included) . They find positive but statistically insignificant employment effect. They conclude that at the firm level, only a small portion of the taxes can be shifted to wages, and the employment effect is close to zero.

At the industry level, they find negative earnings effect of market average tax rate, between - 0. 810 to - 0. 911 depending on the aggregation level of market. They find close to zero employment effect using the 4 - digit industry definition; larger (0. 912 with a s. d. of 0. 815) but statistically insignificant employment effect using the 3 - digit industry definition, and sharply larger (3. 111 with a s. d. of 1. 043) and statistically significant employment effect using the 2 - digit industry definition. This positive effect of tax rate on employment obviously contradicts the negative (close to - 1) effect on earnings, but they do not explore this further in their study.

There are a few concerns about their method. First, their tax rate variables are derived from administrative data on taxes paid, which are endogenous with employment and earnings. Firms' decisions on employment and wages obviously may lead to changes in their tax rates, not just the other way around. They use the average earnings from two periods when calculating the change of tax rate, but this does not take away that endogeneity completely. Second, dividing the tax paid by the average reported earnings creates a division bias, which leads to a negative bias of the earnings regressions and a positive bias of the employment regressions (See Borjas, 1980) . Estimating a first difference model instead of a level model does not fix this division bias problem. The large positive effect of tax rate on

307

employment in the regressions for 2 - digit industries may be a result of such bias. If that is the case, then there is reason to worry about the potential negative bias in the earnings estimates. Third, as mentioned earlier, they control for state, year and quarter fixed effects and interactions, but do not control for industry fixed effect, nor do they include industry in any interaction terms. Although their regressions are at first differences, some industry effect should persist for several reasons. Different industries should react to changes in tax rate differently. An industry that is paying very high effective tax rates may not react to a 1% change in their tax rate the same as an industry that is paying very low tax rate. Besides the UI taxes, there are other transaction costs of adjusting employment level or compensation packages which vary dramatically across industries, causing them to react to changes of tax rate differently. Also business cycles influence the industries differently. For example, the construction industry may be hit by bad economic conditions and have a higher layoff rate, a higher tax rate and lower earnings while the services industry not impacted immediately can have relatively small or no change in their employment level, tax rate and earnings during the same period. Without controlling for industry effect, it's hard to rule out spurious correlations between changes of tax rate and changes of earnings and employment level.

4　Data and Specification

A. Employment Data

To analyze the effect of UI policies on employment at the industry level I need data on employment and measurements of UI policies by state, year and industry. I obtain employment data from Quarterly Census of Employment and Wages (QCEW). The QCEW is a cooperative program involving the Bureau of Labor Statistics (BLS) of the Department of Labor (DOL) and the State Employment Security Agencies (SESAs). It derives its data from quarterly tax reports submitted to the SESAs by employers subject to state UI laws and from federal agencies subject to the Unemployment Compensation for Federal Employees (UCFE) program. This includes 99. 7% of all wage and salary civilian employment. It publishes a quarterly count of employment and wages for these jobs, available at county, MSA, state and national levels by industry. In 2001 the QCEW data went through an industry coding change. Before 2001, the QCEW data were coded according to the Standard Industrial Classification (SIC) system. Starting from 2001, the QCEW data have been coded according to the North American Industry Classification System (NAICS) . For consistency of over – time comparison, I use QCEW data for the period of 1990 to 2000. I look at employment by 9 major industries at state level. I derive the annual employment numbers by averaging the quarterly employment numbers.

B. Simulated instruments for UI policy measures

The key explanatory variables are measurements of average UI taxes, benefits, or subsidies per worker by industry for each state and year. Because the administrative data on UI taxes paid and benefits received are endogenous to the underlying economic conditions such as the state industrial composition and level of employment that generate the tax contributions and the demand for benefits at the first place, it is better to construct instrumental variables for UI policy measurements that capture the cross – state and over time variations in UI laws and regulations, such as the incompleteness of experience – rating of UI tax schedules and the generosity of benefits, but do not reflect the endogenous underlying economic conditions. I build detailed simulation programs of the UI tax and benefit system of each state for every year during the 1990 – 2000 period, then apply these simulation programs to a multiyear national sample from the Current Population Survey (CPS) March Supplement data.

The CPS March Supplement is an Annual Demographic Survey that is the primary source of detailed information on income and work experience in the United States. The information that the CPS March Supplement data collect includes workers' annual earnings, industry of longest job held, weeks of unemployment and receipt of unemployment compensation in the prior year. Like

QCEW did in 2000, the CPS changed industry coding system in 2003. Before 2003, the CPS data were coded according to the SIC system, while starting from 2003, the CPS data have been coded according to the NAICS system. One major difference between NAICS and SIC is the newly recognized information industry under NAICS. Another difference is the expansion of service industry in NAICS. Under SIC system the firms providing services to an industry are coded as part of that industry, while under NAICS the service providers are coded as part of the service industry. Because the changes in industry coding, and also due to the fact that there are more variations in UI laws before 2000 than after, I focus my study on the the period of 1990 to 2000.

To make sure that the input data I run through the simulated programs are exogenous to state UI laws and free from the influence of business cycles I pool multiyear CPS March Supplement data to create a simulated sample. I utilize CPS March Supplement data from 1991 – 2002, which have information on interviewees' labor force experience in 1990 – 2001. I keep in my sample workers between the age of 25 to 55, in private sector and in jobs that are subject to state UI laws – employed wage earners or the incorporated self – employed. I then assign the full twelve year national sample to each year and state, inflating or deflating the nominal earnings by the Consumer Price Index (CPI) to reflect earnings in each year's dollars. I run this pooled sample through the UI tax and benefit simulation programs to calculate the UI taxes payable and benefit received (when applicable) for each worker as if this simulated sample lived in each of those states and years. I calculate the industry average UI taxes and benefits per worker by dividing the total taxes paid and benefit received in an industry by the number of workers in that industry. This way I construct the instruments of industry average UI taxes and benefits that capture the clean structural differences and over time changes in state UI policy.

Appendix A provides a detailed discussion on the construction of the simulated instruments. I also run tests of correlation between the instruments and the reported UI measures at state level. The instruments have strong correlation with the reported UI measures, with R^2 being or close to 0. 90. Table A1, A2 describe the raw input data for the simulation programs, Table A3 describes the outputs of these simulation programs, and Table A4 shows the results of the tests of correlation between the simulated instruments and the reported UI measurements at state level.

C. Regression Specifications

To analyze the impact of UI subsidies on industry employment level I run regressions of reduced form employment equations with log annual average employment in an industry – state – year as the dependent variable and average UI subsidy per worker to an industry – state – year as the dependent variable. I also include state, year, industry dummies and add the interaction terms:

$$Log \ (Employment_{i,s,t}) \ = \alpha + \beta * Subsidies_{i,s,t} + state \ dummies_s +$$
$$year \ dummies_t + industry \ dummies_i + state_s * \ industry_i +$$
$$year_t * \ industry_i + state_s * \ year_t + \varepsilon_{i,s,t}$$

Log (Employment$_{i,s,t}$) is the log annual average employment in industry i, state s, and year t. Subsidies$_{i,s,t}$ is the average subsidies received per worker in industry i, state s, and year t. State dummies$_s$ is a set of dummy variables for all states and DC, year dummies$_t$ is a set of year dummies for each year in 1990 – 2000, industry dummies$_i$ is a set of dummies for 9 major industries, state$_s$ * industry$_i$ is a set of interaction terms between each state and every industry, year$_t$ * industry$_i$ is a set of interaction terms between each year and every industry, state$_s$ * year$_t$ is a set of interaction terms between each state and every year. I use robust, clustered by state standard errors to count for within state correlations in the error term and weigh the regressions with industry employment level in 1990 in one set of the regressions.

The state dummies control for fixed differences in employment levels across states due to variations in population size and other state specific economic conditions. The industry dummies control for fixed differences in employment levels across industries. The year dummies control for the changes in the aggregate employment level over the years. The state industry interaction terms control for state specific industry sizes that may correlate with the level of average UI subsidies to that industry. Larger industries have more lobbying power and may influence the UI tax policy in a way that lead to higher subsides. The year industry interactions control for changes in industry specific economic conditions over time. I also include the state year interactions to control for changes in employment levels due to state specific time effects that may correlate with changes in UI subsidies. All states have to adjust their tax schedules to balance their state UI trust funds. Some states have automatic adjustment system while others make annual changes in their tax schedule when necessary. An increase in subsidy can be a result of lower tax rates due to continuing economic boost. It could also be possible at the onset of an economic downturn, when benefits charged increase due to higher unemployment rate and UI benefit receipt but the tax schedules haven't get increased yet. By including the state year interactions I control for the sporadic correlation between the average UI subsidy and employment levels that both correlate with the overall state economic condition in a specific year.

To see clearly the effects of UI taxes and benefits on industry employment levels I run another set of regressions using simulated instruments for industry average UI taxes and benefits per worker.

$$Log\ (Employment_{i,s,t})\ =\ \alpha + \beta_1 * taxes_{i,s,t} + \beta_2 * benefits_{i,s,t} +$$
$$state\ dummies_s + year\ dummies_t + industry\ dummies_i + state_s * industry_i +$$
$$year_t * industry_i + state_s * year_t + \varepsilon_{i,s,t}$$

$Taxes_{i,s,t}$ is the average taxes payable per worker in industry i, state s, and year t, $benefits_{i,s,t}$ is the average benefits received per worker in industry i, state s, and year t. I include the same dummy variables and interaction terms in the regression.

5　Results

Table 1 is a summary of the data. Benefits, taxes, and subsides are simulated instruments for average UI measurements per worker by industry in a state/year, in 1990 dollars. I do not normalize the taxes to make state UI system "balanced" each year since in practice they are not balanced annually. In earlier empirical work, for example, Anderson and Meyer (1993), normalizing of the taxes is done by first finding the ratio of total taxes to total benefits in a state/ year, then dividing the industry specific taxes amount by the state tax – to – benefit ratio in that year. Normalizing basically adds the state year effect into the taxes variable and makes the two inseparable. I keep my taxes variable not normalized so that I can clearly analyze the effect of taxes, separately from the state year effect. The employment and wages data are from QCEW. Employment is the annual average level derived from quarterly data, and average wages are derived from total annual wages divided by annual average employment. For the industries that have zero employment in 1990, I drop them from the data for the whole period. I have total 4537 observations.

Table 2 reports regression results of log annual average employment of an industry at the state level on industry average UI benefits and taxes or subsidies per worker for that state/year. All regressions include state, year and industry dummies. Model (1) and model (4) also include state industry interactions to capture different industrial compositions across states. I see consistent results no matter I used the benefits and taxes instruments, or the subsidy instrument. The result of model (1) shows that the effect of benefits on employment is 0. 00124, with a clustered (by state) standard error of 0. 00085. Meaning on average, an increase of average benefits per worker by $ 97. 25, a standard deviation, will lead to approximately a 12. 06% increase in the industry employment level. The effect of taxes on employment is negative: – 0. 00032, with a clustered (by state) standard error of 0. 00011. Meaning on average, an increase of average taxes per worker in an industry by $ 201. 36, a standard deviation, will lead to approximately a 6. 44% drop in employment level in the industry. The result of model (4) shows positive employment effect of subsidies: 0. 00033, clustered (by state) standard error of 0. 00012. Meaning that on average, an increase of average subsidies per worker in an industry by $153.45, a standard deviation, will lead to an increase of industry employment by 5.06%. Those are quite large and statistically significant effects, but I have not controlled for year industry effect and state year effect yet.

In model (2) and (5) I add year industry interactions to account for that fact that business cycles affect industries differently. The results do not change much from model (1) and (4). In model (2) the positive effect of benefits increases to 0.00156, while the negative effect of taxes reduces in magnitude to −0.00029, but they are still quite close to the results of model (1). Model (5) shows similar positive effect of subsidies on employment, 0.00030. Adding year industry interaction terms does not change the result much.

I then add the state year interactions in model (3) and model (6) to account for the fact that states change their UI tax schedules at each state's own timing depending mostly on the UI trust fund balance. So some states may raise UI taxes (thus lower subsidies) across the board in a year while other states might leave the tax schedules unchanged or even have them lowered. Model (3) and model (6) show the results after I add this state year interaction term to the regressions. The effects of UI measures become much smaller comparing to the earlier models. After accounting for the political economic impact captured by the state year interaction term, the coefficient for benefits becomes 0.00029, with a clustered robust standard error of 0.00052. It become very small, about 1/5 of the effect shown in model (2), and is statistically insignificant. The coefficient of taxes also becomes smaller in magnitude, and is statistically insignificant too. The same happens to the coefficient of subsidies in model (6): it becomes 0.00007, with a clustered robust standard error of 0.00009, which means on average, an increase of subsidies by a standard deviation ($153.45) will lead to a 1.07% increase in employment level. Before adding the state year interactions, the effect of an increase in subsidies by a standard deviation on employment level is 5.06%, about 5 times in magnitude. Also after accounting for state year interactions the effect of subsidies on employment becomes statistically insignificant. The same happens to Model (3) where the effect of benefits and taxes on employment level become much smaller when the political economic variations across states over years are accounted for.

While Anderson and Meyer (1997) find close to zero employment effect using the 4 - digit industry definition; they find positive but statistically insignificant employment effect using the 3 - digit industry definition, and sharply larger and statistically significant employment effect using the 2 - digit industry definition. To interpret their result from the 2 - digit industry data literally, a 1% increase in effective tax rate leads to a 3.1% increase in industry employment. This positive effect of tax rate on employment contradicts the negative (close to - 1) effect on earnings they find using the 2 - digit industry definition. They acknowledge the sharp differences of employment effects across industry definitions, but do not investigate further in their study. It is possible that since they derive the effective tax rate variable by dividing the taxes paid by the average reported earnings, they create a division bias. Their earnings equation is negatively biased, and employment equation is positively biased as a result (See Borjas, 1980 for a detailed discussion of division bias).

To check the robustness of my regression results, I then weigh the regressions by state - industry employment level in 1990 and report the results in Table 3. The benefits coefficients in table 3 become much smaller than those in table 2, indicating that the positive effect of benefits on employment in table 2 come mostly from the smaller industries. When I do stratified regressions by industry, I confirm that fact. After accounting for all fixed effects and interactions, I find a negative effect of benefits on employment, and a close to zero effect of taxes on employment in the weighted regressions. Subsidies regressions have relatively comparable results from the weighted regressions and the unweighted regressions. Before accounting for state year interactions, the coefficient of subsidies is 0.00025, indicating an increase of subsidies by a standard deviation would lead to a 3.84% increase in employment. After adding the interaction, the effect is not just reduced, it actually becomes negative, although with a much larger standard error so I consider it close to zero: -0.00003 with a clustered robust standard error of 0.00010.

6　Evidence of Policy Endogeneity

My results show that accounting for state specific year effect changes the results dramatically, indicating the possible existence of policy endogeneity issue in UI state laws and regulations. Since I build simulation programs for state UI policies and run simulated multiyear national sample through the simulators, I have already eliminated all endogeneity problems in the UI measures, except for policy endogeneity which arises when states change the UI laws and regulations as a response to the state specific economic conditions. Although this has been suspected (see Besley and Case 2000, and Kubik and Moran 2001), little work has been done to address it. Earlier empirical work looking at the effect of UI on employment has simply assumed the policy endogeneity away. With the simulated instruments for state UI policy measures, I am able to test the policy endogeneity hypothesis and provide some evidence in this area.

I run regressions with UI policy measures in year t as dependent variables and state unemployment rate in year $t-1$ as the explanatory variable. I control for state and year fixed effects, and use clustered robust standard errors to count for within state correlations in the error term.

$$UI\ policy\ measure_{s,t} = \alpha + \beta * Unemployment\ rate_{s,t-1} + state\ dummies_s + year\ dummies_t + \varepsilon_{s,t}$$

Table 4 presents the summaries of my data. During the 1990 – 2000 period, the state unemployment rates ranged from 1.709% to 11.349%, with an average of 5.054%. The simulated state average UI taxes per worker ranged from a minimum of \$120.62 to a maximum of \$598.84 in 1990 dollar, and the simulated state average benefits per worker ranged from \$88.92 to \$176.03 in 1990 dollar. The regression results are provided in Table 5. Model (1) looks at the effect of lagged unemployment rate on state average taxes per worker. I find a very strong positive effect here. The coefficient is 1017. 35 with a standard error of 292. 13. That means a one standard deviation increase of state unemployment rate of year $t - 1$ leads to an increase of state average taxes per worker in year t by $ 17. 39, which is 7% on average. Model (2) looks at the effect of lagged state unemployment rate on state average benefits per worker. I find a small positive relationship: 34. 63 with a clustered robust standard error of 36. 05, not significant in any way. Model (3) tests the effect of lagged state unemployment rate on state average subsidies per worker. Subsidies are simply benefits minus taxes. I find a strong negative effect: - 982. 71 with a clustered robust standard error of 284. 14. Higher unemployment rates lead to significantly lower subsidies in the year after.

Remember the policy measures I use are simulated instruments from a multiyear national data, which only capture the state policy structure, and are free from changes in economic conditions over years and across states. States do not change their UI benefit schedule much over time, except for adjusting for inflation. But they do adjust their tax schedules often, annually if necessary, to keep their UI trust funds solvent. Table 5 provides some evidence to this policy endogeneity.

7　Conclusion

My results provide some evidence that political economic conditions may have driven the results of earlier work. Due to data or methodology restrictions – regressions stratified by industry so that no state year interactions are possible, endogenous tax variables, normalization of tax variables making separation of political economic impact impossible, division bias caused by using tax rate instead of tax amount, etc. – their results although go pretty well with theory predictions, may possibly be driven empirically by the fact that the states that suffer from high unemployment tend to have lower subsidies to industries due to higher tax rates necessary to balance the stat UI trust fund. After accounting for this policy endogeneity by adding the state year interaction term, I show that UI subsidies have a very small (and on average negative) effect on employment level. Consider that the average UI benefits and taxes per worker are only about 1% of average annual wage, these UI policy measures may too small to create an change of industrial composition, although intra – industry movement may be possible and not measured in my study.

Appendix A   On the Construction of Simulated Instruments for UI Taxes, Benefits, and Subsidies

This appendix explains the construction of instrumental variables for industry average UI taxes, benefits and subsidies per worker in a state/year. The simulated instruments are constructed in three steps. First, I write detailed computer programs that model state UI laws and regulations of all 50 states and the District of Columbia for each year during the 1990 – 2000 period. Then in the second step, I take a national multiyear sample, and assign it to each state/year. I run this sample through the computer simulation programs to calculate the taxes payable and benefits received for each individual as if they had "lived" in each state/year. I then calculate the industry average taxes and benefits by dividing the total amount of taxes (benefits) by the number of observations in each industry. The industry average subsides are then calculated as benefits minus taxes. By using the same simulated sample for each state/year, I obtain clean variations that arise from cross – sectional differences and over time changes in state UI laws and regulations only. This method of constructing simulated instrument is illustrated in Gruber (1997) and Currie and Gruber (1996).

Tax simulator

The tax simulator models state laws and regulations on a covered worker's UI taxes payable in a year, given her annual wages, the industry of the longest job she held during the year, and the state she lived in. I write computer programs for each year during the 1990 – 2000 period, covering workers in all 50 states and DC. The detailed formulas for calculating UI taxes payable vary by state and change over time, but they all have the following components: the worker's annual wages up to the state taxable wage base, the experience – rated part of UI taxes, additional state UI taxes that are not experience – rated, and federal taxes after deduction. The formula for calculating the annual UI taxes payable for a worker is:

*UI Taxes payable = Min (taxable wage base, annual wage) * experience – rated tax rate + Additional state taxes + Federal taxes after deduction*

As I mentioned before, the amount of UI taxes payable from a covered worker depends on the tax rate charged on her employer. Since I am interested in the effect of UI policy at the industry level, the more relevant UI tax rates for my purpose are the industry average tax rates, rather than the tax rates levied on individual firms. To get industry average tax rates, I simulate the experience – rating process states go through when they decide on the individual firms' tax rates: experience – rate the industries using their unemployment history. Again to avoid endogeneity, I use multiyear national unemployment rates by industry, rather than the industrial unemployment rates at the state/year level. I use Current Population Survey (CPS) basic monthly data from 1989 – 2001 to calculate the average national unemployment rates by industry during this period.

CPS is a monthly survey of about 50000 households conducted by the Bureau of the Census for the Bureau of Labor Statistics. It has been conducted for over 50 years, and is the primary source of information on the labor force characteristics of the U. S. population. CPS used the SIC codes to define industries up to the year 2002, and switched to use the NAICS codes from 2003 and onward. The major changes in the industry coding of CPS data include the introduction of information industry and the expanded service industry under the NAICS system. I define industries using the SIC codes for 1989 – 2001, and have 9 major industries.

With each industry's national unemployment " experience " – average national unemployment rate during 1989 – 2001, I experience – rate the industries

319

by assigning the industry with the lowest (best) unemployment experience the minimum experience – rated tax rate in any given state in a year, assigning the industry with the highest (worst) unemployment experience the maximum experience – rated tax rate in any given state in a year, and linearly assign the experience – rated tax rates to the industries that lie in between the two ends of the range of tax rates depending on their own unemployment experiences. If I use $Unexp_i$ for the unemployment experience of industry i, *Lowest Unexp* for the lowest industry unemployment experience among all industries, *Range of Unexp* for the difference between the highest and lowest unemployment experiences among all industries, and *Range of tax rates$_{s,t}$* for the range of tax rates in state s, year t, then the experience – rated tax rate for industry i in state s and year t can calculated as follows:

$$\textit{Experience – rated Tax rate}_{i,s,t} = \textit{Minimum tax rate}_{s,t} + (\textit{Unexp}_i -$$
$$\textit{Lowest Unexp}) * (\textit{Range of tax rates}_{s,t}) / \textit{Range of Unexp}$$

To gather information on accurate state tax rate schedules, state taxable wage bases and administrative and other subsidiary taxes over the years, I start with the Department of Labor (DOL) website. It has documents and tables on UI financing and benefits at state level updated annually or biannually in the Unemployment Insurance Section, under *State Law Information*. For additional details when necessary, especially for earlier years, I rely on *State Unemployment Insurance Reporters* compiled every year by the Commerce Clearing House (CCH), available online through *Intelliconnect* and *State by State Guide to Human Resources Law*. These resources together provide accurate information on taxable wage base, minimum tax rate, maximum tax rate, administrative and other subsidiary taxes in a state in a given year during 1990 – 2000 for the construction of my UI tax simulator.

The data I run through the tax simulation program is a pooled multiyear national data set from CPS March Supplement data from 1991 – 2002. I limit the observations to individuals from age 25 to 55 years old, who worked in the private sector, and who were wage – earners or the incorporated self – employed. I use 2 – digit SIC codes and divide them into 9 major industries. Table A1 describes this data set. I have total 492581 observations. These individuals were from all 50 states and DC, with an average age of 38, and on average they worked 47 weeks in year prior to interview. Their annual average wages were $30851.

I run this multiyear national sample through the UI tax simulator of each state/ year, calculate every worker's UI tax payable under each state's UI program, get the total taxes paid by industry, then divide that amount by the total number of observations in the industry to get the average taxes payable per worker by industry in a state/year. I do this both with and without using the personal weights for March supplement data and get very similar results.

Benefit simulator

I build the state UI benefit simulation program exactly as the state laws specify, including the eligibility test, the weekly benefit amount (WBA) formula, and the maximum benefits calculation. Eligibility is usually conditioning on base period earnings and/or weeks worked in the base period, which is usually the four or five quarters prior to the quarter when unemployment happens. The WBA formula varies across states and over time, but usually is between 50% or 60% of average weekly earnings of the whole base period, or of the quarter of highest earrings in the base period, up to the maximum WBA specified by the state law. Some states also provide additional benefits for dependent children. The total benefits an unemployed worker receives is then calculated as:

$$Total\ Benefits\ =\ WBA\ *\ Duration\ on\ Unemployment\ Compensation$$

The maximum duration of unemployment compensation varies across states, but is usually 26 weeks for regular benefits, and can go as long as 30 weeks for several states. Total benefits are also subject to a state maximum amount, and is usually no more than 1/3 to 1/2 of the benefit receiver's total earnings in the base period.

I again run a simulated multiyear national sample through the UI benefit

321

simulation program. This sample comes from CPS March Supplement from 1990 – 2002. CPS March Supplement data have a question on whether the interviewee has received any UI benefit in the prior year. For the individuals who reported that they have received UI benefits, I then calculate the amount of benefits they would be eligible for if they had "lived" in each state/year during 1990 – 2000. This simulated data is smaller than the data I run through the tax simulation program because to calculate an individual's UI benefit received in year t, I need to locate her in CPS March data in two consecutive years – I need to see her in year $t+1$'s data saying that she received unemployment compensation in year t, and also see her report year $t-1$'s earnings which is considered the base period earnings and is needed for eligibility test, WBA calculation, and maximum benefits calculation. I merge CPS March Supplement data of two consecutive years during 1990 – 2002 following the strict criteria outlined in Madrian and Lefgren, 2000. Except for year 1995's data that can not be merged with year 1994's data due to a complete change of interviewees that happened in 1995, the match rates between other two consecutive years are between 19% to 30%. I limit the observations to individuals from age 25 to 55 years old in the year of UI benefit receipt (or nonreceipt), who worked in the private sector, and who Ire wage – earners or the incorporated self – employed. I use 2 – digit SIC codes and divide them into 9 major industries. I then pool the merged data together and make it a multiyear national data set. I assign it to each state and year during 1990 – 2000 to calculate the UI benefit received under each state's UI program as if this identical sample of individuals had "lived" in each state/year. The merit of using a multiyear national sample is to avoid confusing variations that arise in the sample itself, such as unemployment rates and industrial composition that vary over time and cross – sectionally, so that I capture the structural differences and over time changes in state UI benefit laws and regulations only. Table A2 describes this simulated sample that I run through the benefit simulator. I have total 145068 observations, that are from all 50 states and DC, worked in all 9 industries, and made on average $ 25, 939 in annual earnings in 1990 dollars. Among them 6. 33% , or 9185 individuals reported that they had received UI compensation in the prior year.

To calculate an individual's eligibility for and the amount of UI benefit received in year t, I need to know her earnings in the base period, which I use her annual wages in year $t-1$ as a proxy. As mentioned above, I merge CPS March Supplement data of two consecutive years to follow the individual over two years so that I have information on both her UI benefit receipt, and her earnings in the year before unemployment.

For the duration of UI benefit received, I use the duration of average national unemployment spells of the industry she worked in as a proxy, as I are interested in the average benefits at the industry level. I calculate the national average duration (weeks) of unemployment for each industry using CPS basic monthly data from 1990 to 2002. Since regular unemployment benefits usually last 26 weeks at most, I top code the individual unemployment duration by 26 weeks. Then I calculate the total benefits an individual gets by multiplying the WBA by industry average duration of unemployment, subject to a personal maximum depending on the individual's base period earnings, and a state maximum amount. To summarize, the steps in calculating an individual's UI benefits received in a given state/year are:

1. Identify potential UI benefit receivers by the CPS question on UI benefit receipt.

2. For a given state/year, run the eligibility test for state UI benefits. On average about 97% of the reported UI benefit receivers pass the eligibility tests.

3. Calculate the WBA for those individuals who satisfy step 1 and 2.

4. Calculate the total benefit amount for an individual by multiplying WBA by industry average duration of unemployment subject to a maximum amount depending on the individual's base period earnings. This amount is also subject to the state maximum benefits for an individual.

With this information I then calculate the industry average benefits per worker by dividing the total benefits received in an industry by the total observations in the industry.

Subsidies

I subtract the average taxes per worker from average benefits per worker in an industry to get the instrument for average UI subsidies per worker by industry. Since I use national sample of multiple years, my simulated instruments capture variations in UI laws and regulations across states and over time, and do not reflect the different economic conditions or state characteristics. The usage of simulated instruments is an important improvement over earlier work which relied on administrative data of reported taxes paid which is endogenous to the economic conditions such as state employment level and wages. It is also better than just using the state minimum and maximum taxes and average subsidy as policy measurements which only capture the range of tax rates, and leave out other sources of variations in cross – industry subsidies. Table A3 describes the simulated instruments for average UI benefits, taxes, and subsides per worker by industry during each year in 1990 – 2000.

Test of Correlation between the Simulated instruments and the reported UI measures

After generating the simulated instruments for UI benefits, taxes, and subsidies, I regress reported UI measures on these simulated instruments to find out how ill they correlate. I use state level information on total UI taxes paid, total regular benefits provided, and number of covered employment in each state in Social Security Bulletin (SSB) published every year. I calculate the average UI taxes paid and benefits received per worker at the state level for each state/year during 1990 – 2000 using the tables in SSB. I then calculate the simulated average taxes and benefits per worker at state level using the outputs from my UI tax and benefit simulators. I regress the reported measures on my simulated instruments, including state dummies and year dummies in my regressions. The results are reported in Table A4. After dropping 7 observations due to SSB data input errors that led to extremely low average taxes or extremely high average benefits I have 554 observations altogether. Both the simulated benefits instrument and the simulated taxes instrument correlate with reported measures very closely, with the adjusted R^2 being 0. 9007 and 0. 8773. The simulated instrument for subsidies derived from the benefits and taxes instruments also correlates with the imputed reported subsidies measure pretty ill, with the adjusted R^2 being 0. 3474.

Table 1   Descriptive Statistics of the Data Set

	Mean	Std. Dev.	Min	Max
	(1)	(2)	(3)	(4)
Benefits	143. 66	97. 25	43. 76	520. 05
Taxes	276. 83	201. 36	41. 37	1513. 10
Subsidies	- 133. 17	153. 45	- 1040. 63	87. 73
Employment	234809	383547	48	4549657
Average Wages	25035. 45	8519. 55	9572. 81	109010. 90
Log (Employment)	11. 3856	1. 5764	3. 8712	15. 3306
Log (Average Wages)	10. 0681	0. 3557	9. 1667	11. 5992

Notes: data on industry average at state level, 1990 – 2000. Industries with zero employment are dropped. Industries that had zero employment at state level in 1990 are dropped for that state in subsequent years (4537 observations).

Table 2   The Effect of Average UI Measures Per Worker on Employment, 1990 – 2000 Data Unweighted IV Regression Results

	(1)	(2)	(3)	(4)	(5)	(6)
Benefits	0. 00124	0. 00156	0. 00029			
	(0. 00085)	(0. 00097)	(0. 00052)			
Taxes	- 0. 00032	- 0. 00029	- 0. 00007			
	(0. 00011)	(0. 00013)	(0. 00009)			
Subsidies				0. 00033	0. 00030	0. 00007
				(0. 00012)	(0. 00014)	(0. 00009)
State * industry Effect	Yes	Yes	Yes	Yes	Yes	Yes
Year * industry Effect	No	Yes	Yes	No	Yes	Yes
State * year Effect	No	No	Yes	No	No	Yes
N	4537	4537	4537	4537	4537	4537

Notes: the dependent variable is the log of of employment in an industry at the state level. All regressions also include state dummies, year dummies, and industry dummies. Clustered robust standard errors are in parentheses.

**Table 3　The Effect of Average UI Measures Per Worker on Employment,
1990 – 2000 Data Weighted IV Regression Results**

	(1)	(2)	(3)	(4)	(5)	(6)
Benefits	– 0.00113	0.00015	– 0.00093			
	(0.00061)	(0.00053)	(0.00060)			
Taxes	– 0.00021	– 0.00025	0.00001			
	(0.00009)	(0.00010)	(0.00010)			
Subsidies				0.00019	0.00025	– 0.00003
				(0.00009)	(0.00010)	(0.00010)
State * industry Effect	Yes	Yes	Yes	Yes	Yes	Yes
Year * industry Effect	No	Yes	Yes	No	Yes	Yes
State * year Effect	No	No	Yes	No	No	Yes
N	4537	4537	4537	4537	4537	4537

Notes: the dependent variable is the log of employment in an industry at the state level. The regressions are weighted by the number of employees in the industry at the state level in 1990. All regressions also include state dummies, year dummies, and industry dummies. Clustered robust standard errors are in parentheses.

Table 4　Descriptive Statistics of the Data Set for Policy Endogeneity Test

	Mean	Std. Dev.	Min	Max
	(1)	(2)	(3)	(4)
State Average Taxes Per Worker	247.04	87.57	120.62	598.84
State Average Benefits Per Worker	123.97	18.71	88.92	176.03
State Average Subsidies Per Worker	– 123.07	78.12	– 464.03	7.09
State Unemployment Rate, $t - 1$	5.054%	1.709%	1.709%	11.349%

Notes: summaries of simulated IVs for state average UI taxes, benefits, and subsides per worker for each year during 1990 – 2000 in 1990 dollars, and lagged ($t - 1$) state annual unemployment rates calculated using CPS basic monthly data 1990 – 2000 by the authors (561 observations).

Table 5　The Effect of State Unemployment Rate of Year $t-1$ on State Average UI Measures Per Worker, 1990 – 2000 Data

	(1)	(2)	(3)
	Taxes	Benefits	Subsidies
Unemployment rate of $t-1$	1017. 35	34. 63	-982. 71
	(292. 13)	(36. 05)	(284. 14)
Year effect	Yes	Yes	Yes
State effect	Yes	Yes	Yes
N	561	561	561

Notes: the dependent variables are the state average UI taxes, benefits, and subsidies per worker. All regressions also include state dummies and year dummies. Clustered robust standard errors are in parentheses.

Table A1　Descriptive Statistics of the Raw Input Data for the Tax Simulation Program

	Mean	Std. Dev.	Min	Max
	(1)	(2)	(3)	(4)
Year of Survey	1997	3. 59	1991	2002
State	28	15. 36	1	56
Age	39	8. 35	26	56
Weeks Worked	47. 65	10. 44	1	52
Annual Wages	30850. 82	33036. 77	1. 00	576372. 00
Industry	6. 43	2. 32	1	9

Notes: Data from CPS March Supplement 1991 – 2002 on prior year's labor market experience. Total 492581 observations.

Table A2　Descriptive Statistics of the Raw Input Data for the Benefit Simulation Program

	Mean	Std. Dev.	Min	Max
	(1)	(2)	(3)	(4)
Year	1996	3. 59	1990	2002
State	28	15. 36	1	56
Age	39	8. 29	26	56
UC Receipt	0. 0633	0. 2435	0	1
Weeks Worked	47. 87	10. 31	1	52
Annual Wages	25938. 51	26231. 97	1. 00	388886. 00
Industry	6	2. 30	1	9

Notes: Data from CPS March Supplement 1991 – 2002 on prior year's labor market experience. Total 145068 observations.

Table A3　Descriptive Statistics of the Simulated Instruments

	Mean	Std. Dev.	Min	Max
	(1)	(2)	(3)	(4)
Benefits	144. 33	26. 08	91. 54	231. 93
Taxes	285. 82	100. 73	158. 27	678. 11
Subsidies	− 141. 48	89. 10	− 469. 49	9. 35

Note: summary of simulated annual average UI benefits, taxes, subsidies at the state level in all states and DC during 1990 – 2000, 561 observations.

Table A4　Test of Correlation between Reported UI Measures and Instruments, 1990 – 2000 Data

	(1)	(2)	(3)
	Benefits	Taxes	Subsidies
instrument for Benefits	1. 73986		
	(0. 75266)		
instrument for Taxes		0. 53369	
		(0. 06717)	
instrument for Subsidies			0. 50422
			(0. 12896)
State dummies	Yes	Yes	Yes
Year dummies	Yes	Yes	Yes
N	554	554	554
Adjusted R^2	0. 9117	0. 8909	0. 4194

Note: The dependent variables are the reported average UI measures per worker at state level, calculated by the authors. Data source: Social Security Bulletin 1990 – 2000. The independent variables are the simulated IVs for UI measures at state level, generated by the authors. I dropped 7 state/year observations due to SSB data input errors that lead to extremely low average taxes or high average benefits in the reported data. I have total 554 state/year observations. Clustered robust standard errors in parentheses.

References

Anderson, Patricia M. and Meyer, Bruce D. , 1993. "The Unemployment Insurance Payroll Tax and Interindustry and Interfirm Subsidies. " *Tax Policy and the Economy* 7: 111 – 144.

Anderson, Patricia M. and Meyer, Bruce D. , 1997. "The Effects of Firm Specific Taxes and Government Mandates with an Application to the U. S. Unemployment Insurance Program. " *Journal of Public Economics* 65: 119 – 145.

Baily, Martin Neil, 1977. "On the Theory of Layoffs and Unemployment" . *Econometrica* 45: 1043 – 1064.

Besley, Timothy and Case, Anne, 2000. " Unnatural Experiments? Estimating the Incidence of Endogenous Policies. " *The Economic Journal* 110: F672 – F694.

Borjas, George J. , 1980. "The Relationship Between Wages and Weekly Hours of Work: The Role of Division Bias. " *The Journal of Human Resources*, vol. 15, no. 3: 409 – 423.

Card, David and Levine, Phillip B. , 1994. "Unemployment Insurance Taxes and the Cyclical and Seasonal Properties of Unemployment. " *Journal of Public Economics* 53: 1 – 29.

Currie, Janet and Gruber, Jonathan, 1996. "Saving Babies: The Efficacy and Cost of Recent Expansions of Medicaid Eligibility for Pregnant Women. " *Journal of Political Economy*, vol. 104, no. 6: 1263 – 1296.

Deere, Donald R. , 1991. "Unemployment Insurance and Employment. " *Journal of Labor Economics*: vol. 9, no. 4: 307 – 324.

Feldstein, Martin, 1976. "Temporary Layoffs in the Theory of Unemployment. " *Journal of Political Economy*, vol. 84, no. 5: 937 – 957.

Gruber, Jonathan, 1997. " The Consumption Smoothing Benefits of Unemployment Insurance. " *The American Economic Review*, vol. 87, no. 1: 192 – 205.

Kubik, Jeffrey D. and Moran, John R. , " Can Policy Changes Be Treated as Natural Experiments? Evidence from State Excise Taxes, 2001. " *Center for Policy Research*. Paper 118.

Madrian, Brigitte C. , Lefgren, Lars John, 2000. " An Approach to Longitudinally Matching Current Population Survey (CPS) Respondents. " *Journal of Economic and Social Measurements*, vol. 26: 31 – 62.

Munts, Raymond C. , Asher, Ephraim, 1980. " Cross – Subsidies Among Industries from 1969 to 1978. " *Unemployment Compensation: Studies and Research*, vol 2: 277 – 298. Washington, DC: National Commission on Unemployment Compensation.

Social Security Administration. Social Security Bulletin, Unemployment Insurance, Summary Data on State Programs, 1990 – 2000.

State by State Guide to Human Resources Law, 1990 – 2000. Buckley IV, John F. , Carmell, William A. , Gray, Peter S. , Green, Ronald M. , et al. Wolters Klulr Law &

Business.

U. S. Department of Labor, Employment and Training Administration. UI State Laws. 1990 – 2000.

http://www. ows. doleta. gov/unemploy/statelaws. asp.

Unemployment Insurance Reporter, Federal and All States, 1990 – 2000. Commerce Clearing House (CCH). Available online through *Intelliconnect*.

Hospital Treatment Rates and Spillover Effects: Does Ownership Matter?

Badi H. Baltagi   Yin – Fang Yen [*]

Abstract   This paper studies the effect of hospital ownership on treatment rates allowing for spatial correlation among hospitals. Competition among hospitals and knowledge spillovers generate significant externalities which we try to capture using the spatial Durbin model. Using a panel of 2342 hospitals in the 48 continental states observed over the period from 2005 to 2008, we find significant spatial correlation of medical service treatment rates among hospitals. We also get mixed results on the effect of hospital ownership on treatment rates that depends upon the market structure where the hospital is located and which varies by treatment type.

1 Introduction

The quality and cost effectiveness of the health care system in the U. S. are two of the major concerns of the Affordable Care Act (ACA) . According to

*   Badi H. Baltagi, Yin – Fang Yen, Department of Economics and Center for Policy Research
    Syracuse University, Southwestern University of Finance and Economics.

World Health Organization (WHO), the total health expenditure of the U. S. accounted for 17. 9% of the national GDP in 2010, which was the highest in the world. Despite spending this high expenditure on health, the health outcomes were not significantly better than those of other countries. In this paper we focus on ownership of the hospitals and their treatment rates. We distinguish between three types of hospital ownership: For – profit, not – for – profit, and government owned hospitals. There is an extensive literature focusing on hospital ownership, see for example Sloan (2000), McClellan and Staiger (2000), Sloan et al. (2001), Kessler and McClellan (2002), Horwitz and Nichols (2009), Bayindir (2012), to mention a few. A brief review of the different ownership theories and the empirical evidence is given in section 2. The empirical studies have mixed results. Both not – for – profit and government hospitals enjoy tax exemptions and financial advantages. They may have the luxury of using their profits to finance less profitable services. Sloan (2000) finds that not – for – profit hospitals provide better overall quality to the community. Bayindir (2012) suggests that not – for – profit hospitals are more likely to treat uninsured patients and patients with public health insurance than for – profits hospitals. Some studies indicate that for – profits are profit – seeking and have more financial incentives to provide better treatment and attract patients, while other studies suggest that there is no difference in quality between not – for – profits and for – profits hospitals. On the demand side, Jung, Feldman, and Scanlon (2011) find that hospitals with better reputation and higher quality of health care tend to increase patients' willingness to revisit. Moscone, Tosetti, and Vittadini (2012) suggest that information from neighbors along with patients' previous experience and hospital characteristics play important roles in their choice of hospitals in Italy. Porell and Adams (1995) survey the literature and report that patients are more likely to choose hospitals with better health outcomes. The health care market is based on the interactions between hospitals and patients. We explore how this market generates externalities among hospitals. In particular, we study how the treatment rates of one hospital may be affected by the treatment rates and competition from other neighboring hospitals.

The competition level of the market may be affected by the distance between hospitals, the hospital's reputation and the quality of hospitals[1]. Tay (2003) suggests that patients have a tradeoff between the quality of the hospital and the distance to other hospitals[2]. Hospitals improve their quality to attract patients from other neighborhoods[3]. Horwitz and Nichols (2009) find that not – for – profit hospitals are more likely to provide relatively profitable services in a market with a higher proportion of for – profit admissions. Government hospitals are the least likely to offer profitable services and the most likely to offer unprofitable services.

Knowledge spillovers may also contribute to externalities of health care. "A large medical literature has documented the important role of social networks in physician adoption of new technologies, suggesting that knowledge externalities are the source of the productivity spillovers. " See Chandra and Staiger (2007, p. 133) . Physicians may learn from each other and possibly transfer to another hospital, especially when a new technology or equipment is introduced. Hence, it is important to take into account the possible spillovers from one hospital to its neighboring hospitals.

These spilloverscreate a spatial correlation of quality, which is presented in Figure 1. The maps present the geographic distribution of the summary Hospital Compare quality scores by hospital referral region[4] (HRR) in the United States

---

①   We do not argue that price of medical services is negligible, but most patients have insurance (Tay, 2003) . Insurance companies cover a major part of medical expense. Moreover, patients who are aged 65 and above are most likely covered by Medicare. The out – of – pocket payments from patients are relatively low (Sloan, 2000) . Porell and Adams (1995) indicate that studies do not find significant price effects when they use gross charges as the price measure.

②   While almost half of acute myocardial infarction (AMI, or heart attack) patients are admitted to the closest hospital from home, more than 50% of the patients are willing to travel four to five miles further on average for better quality health care.

③   However, using mortality rates, other empirical studies show mixed results of the effects of the competition on quality (see Gaynor, 2006) .

④   Dartmouth Atlas defines the hospital referral regions by the regional market of health care. Patients are able to transfer or be referred to another hospital for major cardiovascular surgical procedures and for neurosurgery in the same HRR. One HRR can cross different counties and states.

in 2005 （The Dartmouth Atlas of Health Care）. The scores indicate the average percentages of heart attack, heart failure, and pneumonia clinical processes that are given to patients in the HRR. Figure 1a shows the spatial patterns of the overall score. The treatment rates are above 90% in many HRRs in the middle and north eastern United States. One may argue that these HRRs are wealthier urban areas. Therefore, their overall medical quality is higher than the national average. The geographic clusters suggest heterogeneity of health care across the country. However, we also find geographic clusters of high treatment rates in some less wealthy HRRs, such as those in North Carolina. This confirms the results by Skinner （2012） that demographic variables cannot fully explain the geographic variations in health care. The clusters may also indicate that the medical quality of one HRR is correlated with that of its neighboring HRRs. Focusing on the treatment rates by illness condition, we find the geographic patterns of heart attack and heart failure treatments in Figures 1b and 1c to be similar to that of the overall treatments. The geographic pattern of pneumonia treatments in Figure 1d is slightly different from heart disease treatments, but a spatial correlation persists.

When examining the interaction among hospitals, most studies utilize the Herfindahl – Hirschman Index （HHI） or similar market share variables as measures of competition level or market structure. While these indices are good measures of the aggregate competition level of the market, they do not take distances between hospitals into consideration. A market with three hospitals close to each other is considered to have the same competition as one with three hospitals spread out.

In this paper, we utilize spatial Durbin model of hospital treatment rates. This spatial model is able to identify the intensity of geographic correlations. Other studies using spatial analysis in health care include Mobley et al. （2006） who studied elderly access to primary care services. They use the spatial lag model, which includes the spatial lagged dependent variable to model spillovers. They find a strong and positive spatial correlation for hospital treatments. However, they do not consider hospital ownership as an aspect of quality disparity.

In addition to spillover effects, the spatial Durbin model allows us to examine whether the market structure affects the treatment rates. The market of medical services is composed of hospitals with different characteristics, such as ownership and size. As suggested by Horwitz and Nichols (2009), hospitals have different treatment decisions based on the market structure they are facing. We cannot assume the spillover effects are the same for all types of markets. Operational strategies of hospitals may not only differ by the type of ownership but may also respond to the type of ownership of neighbors.

We use clinical process treatment rates from Hospital Compare as our dependent variable. Compared to other measures, like the mortality rate or the length of hospital stays, the process treatment rates are less noisy and reflect real hospital medical services. Our study finds strong and positive spillover effects among hospitals for heart attack patients. The spillover effects are even stronger for less acute illness conditions like heart failure and pneumonia. We find some evidence that not – for – profit hospitals provide better medical services than government and for – profit hospitals, but the treatments also differ by the market structure. Hospitals in a market with stronger intensity of not – for – profit hospitals are more likely to provide medications at discharge but less likely to perform percutaneous coronary intervention (PCI) in time. Moreover, the treatment rates of hospitals decrease if they are surrounded by large hospitals. The overall effect depends on the characteristics of the hospital, the spillover effects, and the market structure.

2   Literature Review

Unlike most of the industries that are composed of for – profit firms, about 60% of the non – federal hospitals in the United States were not – for – profit and only 20% were for – profit in 2010. As Horwitz and Nichols (2009, p. 925) summarize in their Table 1, there are four theories of not – for – profit hospitals: (1) maximizing own output (Newhouse, 1970): not – for – profits are profit – seeking and maximize profitable services as for – profits do. They will offer more health care until profits are driven to zero; (2) maximizing the community output (Lee and Weisbrod, 1977): the goal of not – for – profits is to benefit the whole community and to maximize market output including unprofitable services; (3) for – profit in disguise (Pauly and Redisch, 1973): nonprofits would be essentially identical to for – profit hospitals in equilibrium, with economic profits counted as costs (salaries or perquisites accruing to staff physicians); and (4) a mixture of (1) and (2) (Hirth, 1997): not – for – profits behave depending on the competition level of the market. They are profit – seeking when facing competition.

The empirical studies have mixed results. Tax exemptions allow not – for – profit and government hospitals to provide better quality to the community or more medical care to uninsured patients (Sloan, 2000; Bayindir, 2012). Clement et al. (2002) note that for – profit hospitals provide less charity care than not – for – profits. Sloan et al. (2001) find that for – profit hospitals are more likely to use high – tech procedures with higher costs, while Kessler and McClellan (2002) find that areas with for – profit hospitals have lower hospital expenditures, but virtually the same patient health outcomes. They conclude that for – profit hospitals have important spillover benefits for medical productivity. Geweke, Gowrisankaran, and Town (2003) use a Bayesian model to estimate hospital quality in Los Angeles County. Focusing on elderly pneumonia patients, they find that there is not a definitive difference in mortality rates by hospital ownership. This is in line with the results of Sloan et al. (2001) and Sloan and Taylor (1999). These studies find weak evidence that the mortality rate of Medicare patients and the probability of readmission differ by hospital ownership.

However, when competition and market structure are taken into consideration, several studies suggest that the first or the last theory has more support. Horwitz and Nichols (2009) find not – for – profit hospitals are more likely to provide profitable services in a high for – profit market (15% of for – profit admissions or higher). The spillovers of medical services provided make not – for – profit hospitals behave more like for – profits in a high for – profit market. The role of hospital ownership is less important when the competition level increases. Not – for – profits compete with for – profit hospitals by providing better quality of health care (Sloan, 2000) . McClellan and Staiger (2000) also suggest that the growing difference in mortality rates of the elderly AMI patients between for – profit and not – for – profit hospitals may be attributed to various factors, including location. The treatment decisions may depend on the competition level of the market hospitals are located in.

Besides competition, knowledge spillovers among physicians could also cause spatial correlations. Physicians are more likely to practice intensive treatments in a market with advanced medical technologies. Chandra and Staiger (2007) find that spillovers of technology increase the treatment rate in the market. Cardiac catheterization rate of AMI patients is higher in a market with a higher propensity for intensive treatments. Physicians learn practice skills from other physicians, and possibly transfer these skills to other hospitals due to job movement or due to these physicians working at multiple hospitals. About 40% of physicians with inpatient duty work at more than one hospital (Fisher et al. , 2007) . This mobility increases the probability of exchanging knowledge among physicians. Therefore, interactions and spatial correlations of treatments among hospitals should not be neglected when we examine hospital treatment rates.

Mobley et al. (2006) study this geographic correlation of health care in the U. S. They use Admissions for Ambulatory Care Sensitive Conditions (ACSCs) among elderly patients in the late 1990s as the preventive care utilization measure. ACSCs are preventable admissions and therefore can be an indicator of *poor quality*. They use a spatial lag model with both maximum likelihood and two stage least squares methods. They find strong and positive spatial correlations. More ACSCs in neighboring hospitals are associated with an increase in ACSCs for the hospital itself. The utilization rates are not significantly different between the elderly living in poor rural areas and those living in urban areas.

3　Data and Methodology

We model hospital treatment rates using the spatial Durbin panel model given by

$$y_t = \lambda W y_t + H_t \gamma_1 + X_t \beta + W H_t \gamma_2 + \varepsilon_8 + \tau_t + u_t \quad t = 1, 2, \ldots, T$$

$$u_{it} + \mu_t + v_{it} \quad i = 1, 2, \ldots, N$$

where y_t is an (Nx1) vector of treatment rates for N hospitals at time t. W is an (NxN) spatial weight matrix, whose diagonal elements are zero and whose off diagonal elements are the normalized inverse distance from hospital i to hospital j. This weight matrix is row – normalized, i. e., the elements in each row sum to one, $\sum_1^N w_{ij} = 1$. $W y_t$ is the spatial lagged dependent variable, which presents the weighted average treatment rates of neighboring hospitals. λ thus measures the spillover effect of hospital treatment rates. H_t is an (Nxk) matrix of hospital characteristics, and X_t is an (Nxc) matrix of county demographic variables where hospital i is located. ε_s and τ_t are state and year fixed effects. u_t is an (Nx1) vector of error component disturbances. As the second equation shows, the typical element of u_{it} is the hospital random effect μ_t and a remainder classical disturbance v_{it}. μ_t is assumed to be i. i. d. $(0, \sigma_\mu^2)$ and v_{it} is assumed to be i. i. d. $(0, \sigma_v^2)$. μ_i and v_{it} are independent of each other and the regressors H_t and X_t.

Our panel data consists of all hospitals in the 48 continental states that reported their treatment rates every year from 2005 to 2008. Neighboring hospitals are those within a 30 miles radius. Thirty miles may seem arbitrary, but Horwitz and Nichols (2007) indicate that 90% of the discharges are from a mean radius of 21. 5 miles of non – rural hospitals, compared to 25. 2 miles for rural hospitals. Therefore, 30 miles seems reasonable to cover the potential market.

Our dependent variables are the treatment ratesfrom Hospital Compare of the Centers for Medicare and Medicaid Services. This data set was released in 2004. The treatment rates are the percentages of the eligible adult patients who were actually given seven clinical processes of care for heart attack treatments[1]. Instead of examining the spillover effects on each of the seven AMI clinical processes separately, we combine them into four categories: (1) overall treatment rate; (2) giving aspirin and/or beta blockers at arrival; (3) prescribing aspirin/beta blockers/angiotensin converting enzyme (ACE) inhibitors at discharge; and (4) giving percutaneous coronary intervention (PCI) within 120 minutes of arrival[2]. The first category refers to the average of all treatments offered to AMI patients. The medications are similar in the second and third categories, but the timing of prescriptions indicates different treatment purposes. The second category indicates timely treatments that can relieve the conditions. The third category implies preventive treatments to reduce the probability of readmissions. These three categories are obtained using a weighted average where the weights are the number of cases in each process. PCI is a coronary angioplasty. It is a relatively high intensity treatment, which requires skilled staff and equipment.

A heart attack is a very acute condition, and patients need immediate medical care. They are most likely to be taken to hospitals in distinct local markets[3]. This precludes patients from travelling long distances to seek care and in turn being less likely to select the hospital they like. In addition, hospitals need to treat patients who check in to the emergency room, regardless of their insurance type. Focusing on heart attack processes allow us to reduce the selection issue between patients and hospitals. As Chandra and Staiger (2007, p. 117) put it: "markets for heart attack treatment are geographically distinct... mobility is limited, and it is possible to observe production in many distinct local markets."

There are several advantages of using Hospital Compare as our quality

---

[1] Hospital Compare includes 17 clinic processes of care in total for heart attack, heart failure, and pneumonia.

[2] Smoking consultation is also included in the overall treatment receiving rate.

[3] Even if patients travel four to five miles for better treatments as suggested by Tay (2003), these hospitals may still be within one market according to our definition of neighborhood.

measures. First, the processes reflect the real medical services that are delivered to patients in a timely manner. Even though using health outcomes, such as mortality rate, as quality measures can cover unobservable factors, they could be noisy due to relatively low mortality probability (McClellan and Staiger, 2000). The processes in Hospital Compare are timely and effective for patients. Many of the processes for AMI patients are recommended in the ACC/AHA Guidelines for the Management of Patients with Acute Myocardial Infarction (1999). Second, most of these processes are not intensive or require advanced technologies. Hospitals should be able to provide the treatments regardless of the size and the specialization of the hospital. We acknowledge that these are the basic treatments, which can be achieved easily. One hospital with lower treatment rates may not guarantee a worse overall quality. It may focus on other medical and non – medical services that are not included in the data, such as open heart surgery. However, these non – intensive treatments, such as giving beta blockers, serve as a marker of the quality of non – intensive medical management in a hospital, see Chandra and Staiger (2007, p. 118). Heidenreich and McClellan (2001) and Rogers et al. (2000) find that giving aspirin/beta blockers/ACE inhibitors is the major reason for increasing survival rate following AMI. Third, these measures only include patients who are appropriate for the treatments. One limitation of our data is that it is at the hospital level. Without patient – level data, we have no information about the characteristics and illness severity of patients.

Data for the hospital characteristics are taken from the AHA Guide and Provider of Services File, which includes: indicators of not – for – profit hospitals, for – profit hospitals, teaching hospitals[1], and locating in an MSA; number of beds; number of nurses per bed; and HHI. Herfindahl – Hirschman Index (HHI) is the sum of squares of each hospital's market share based on the

---

[1] Teaching hospitals include hospitals with Council of Teaching Hospitals designation, hospitals approved to participate in residency and/or internship training by the Accreditation Council for Graduate Medical Education, and those with medical school affiliation reported to the American Medical Association.

number of beds within its neighborhood. HHI is an indicator of market concentration/competition. A larger index indicates a lower concentration of the health care market. The market may be dominated by one large hospital and few small hospitals. The spatial lagged hospital characteristics, WH_t, include indicators of for – profit, not – for – profit, and teaching hospitals; number of beds; and number of nurses per bed. γ_2 represents the spillover effects of neighboring hospitals' characteristics.

The characteristics of potential patients are controlled by county demographic variables, which are from the American Community Survey of the U. S. Census Bureau. This data set includes only counties with a population of 65000 and above in 2005 and 2006. Therefore, hospitals in our data are located in relatively more urbanized areas. We control for percentages of never married individuals age 15 and above, high school dropouts, high school graduates, male, Hispanic, black, and elderly (age 65 and above); median earnings; and population density per square mile. One may argue the disparity of health care quality is due to geographic heterogeneity. Patients receive better treatment because they are located in an area with better medical care resources. These county demographic variables are good proxies for geographical heterogeneity.

Table 1 presents the descriptive statistics of our data. The treatment rates of the four heart attack treatment categories have large means and small minimum values. This suggests that the distributions of treatment rates are skewed. Out of 2342 hospitals in our sample, 18. 5% are for – profit, 68. 7% are non – profit hospitals. The proportion of non – profit hospitals is slightly higher than the national average but closer to that in the non – rural areas (Horwitz and Nichols, 2007) . Of these hospitals, 41. 2% have teaching status and 89. 4% are located in MSAs. The average number of beds is 263 and the average number of nurses per bed is 1. 1. The average (median earnings) is $ 33790 and the average population density is 2230 individuals per square mile. Among the potential patients, 30. 9% are never – married, 44% have at most a high school degree, 12. 5% are elderly, 14. 5% are Hispanic and 12. 5% are black.

4 Empirical Results

We estimate our spatial Durbin panel data model using the generalized moments (GM) estimator[1]with random effects. See LeSage and Pace (2009) for a nice introduction of the spatial Durbin model and Kapoor, Kelejian and Prucha (2007) for details on the GM methodology. Also, Mutl and Pfaffermayr (2010) for an extension of the GM methodology to the spatial lag model and Debarsy (2012) for the spatial Durbin model. See also Elhorst (2003) for maximum likelihood estimation of spatial lag panel models, and Lee and Yu (2010) and Baltagi (2011) for recent surveys of spatial panels.

Table 2 presents the spillover effects of the heart attack treatment rates using a GM estimator. Some of the diagnostics performed include testing the joint significance of the state dummies as well as the time dummies. These were jointly significant for all models considered. Similarly, the hospital random effects are significant for all models. The first two columns show the GM estimation of the overall heart attack treatment rate. Without controlling for the market structure in the first column, we find that not – for – profit hospitals provide better health care to heart attack patients than government hospitals. Surprisingly, the treatments in for – profit hospitals are not significantly different from government hospitals. The number of beds, the number of nurses per bed, and being a teaching hospital are all positively associated with hospital quality. These are in line with the studies of Keeler et al. (1992) and Geweke, Gowrisankaran, and Town (2003) . Yuan et al.

---

[1] We use the full set of moment conditions, see Millo and Piras (2012) for details. We also estimate the model using maximum likelihood estimation (MLE) using XSMLE: Stata module for spatial panel data model estimation, see Belotti, Hughes, and Mortari (2013) . The MLE results were similar to those using the GM estimator except for smaller estimates of lambda. However, all the lambda estimates were statistically significant at the 1% significance level. These results are available upon request from the authors.

(2000) also find that teaching not – for profit hospitals have lower mortality rates and infer that they provide over – all better quality of care. Aiken et al. (2002) reports that a higher patient – per – nurse ratio increases the mortality rate of AMI. We find little evidence that demographic variables affect hospital treatments. Hospitals provide better quality in an area with a higher never – married population, and lower quality in an area with more blacks and higher population density.

The estimate of lambda indicates the magnitude of spillover effects among hospitals. For the overall treatment rate in column (1), the spatial correlation coefficient estimate is 0. 414 without the measures of market structure. This suggests that when the average heart attack treatment rate of neighboring hospitals increases by 1% , the hospital's treatment rate also increases by 0. 414% . This effect is large and close to the results found by Mobley et al. (2006) .

After adding the market structure variables in column (2), the estimation results are similar to those in column (1) . However, the effects of blacks and population density are no longer significant. The lambda estimate increases to 0. 5. Ownership of neighboring hospitals does not impact its own quality, while the effect of its own not – for – profit status becomes weaker. Hospitals provide fewer treatments in a market with teaching hospitals and larger neighboring hospitals. The significance of market structure variables suggest that ignoring these may generate biased results. In addition, these results suggest that the treatment decisions of hospitals may be associated with a higher quality of neighbors rather than the distribution of hospital ownership in the market. Larger hospitals provide more health care, but when a hospital is close to larger hospitals, its treatment rates are lower. Columns (3) to (8) decompose the overall treatment into more specific heart attack treatments. Focusing on the estimation with market structure variables, we find weak evidence that for – profit hospitals provide fewer medications to patients after they arrive than government hospitals. Not – for – profit hospitals have a higher PCI treatment rate than government hospitals. We find that number of beds, number of nurses per bed, and teaching status are positively associated with the medication treatment rates at both arrival and discharge, but not with PCI. The number of nurses per bed has relatively strong effects, but the number of beds is not significant. Teaching hospitals are more likely to give medications to heart attack patients. This is in line with the suggestion of Sloan (2000) that major teaching hospitals have better quality and non – teaching government hospitals have the worst outcome for elderly patients. What is interesting is that teaching status is negatively associated with the PCI treatment rate. This could be because teaching hospitals have longer waiting time to perform PCI than other hospitals (Nallamothu et al., 2005).

Hospitals provide more medications but fewer PCI treatments in areas with a more never – married population. The percentage of high school graduates has a negative relationship with medications at discharge and PCI. Hospitals give more medications at discharge in an area with an older population and a higher population density.

The lambda estimates range from 0. 4 to 0. 48. Focusing on estimation with market structure, a 1% increase in average treatment rate of each category in neighboring hospitals is associated with an increase of 0. 45%, 0. 48%, and 0. 41%, respectively, in the hospital's own treatment rate. The spillover effect of PCI is relatively smaller than other treatments. This may be due to a technology specialty, and proficiency of doctors and nurses. However, the strong and positive spatial correlation of PCI confirms the results of Chandra and Staiger (2007). Hospitals are more likely to perform these treatments in a market with a high propensity of intensive treatments.

Except for the number of beds, market structure has different impacts on each treatment category. With not – for – profit hospitals in the market, a hospital is more likely to prescribe medications at discharge but less likely to perform PCI. All the treatments decrease when there are larger hospitals nearby. Interestingly, a hospital prescribes fewer medications at discharge when there are teaching hospitals in its neighborhood.

5　Spillover Effects on Other Illness Conditions

Hospital Compare also includes four processes of heart failure and six processes of pneumonia[1]. These two illness conditions are less acute in the sense that patients have more likelihood to travel further for treatments, or for preferred physicians, or for insurance reasons. Hence, we expect the effects of competition among hospitals and the geographic heterogeneity to be stronger. We combine these treatments for each illness condition and apply the previous spatial panel Durbin model to the average treatment rates of heart failure and pneumonia.

The GM estimation results are presented in Table 3. The first two columns are the estimation of heart failure treatments and the latter two columns are for pneumonia treatments. Focusing on the estimation with market structure, the results in column (2) suggest that not – for – profit hospitals provide more treatments than government hospitals. Both the number of beds and the number of nurses per bed increase the treatment rates of heart failure patients. The lambda estimate indicates that when neighboring hospitals increase their heart failure treatment rate by 1% on average, it increases its own hospital treatment rate by around 0. 67% . Similar to heart attack treatments, larger hospitals in the neighborhood decrease the treatment rates of own hospital.

Column (4) suggests that both for – profit and not – for – profit hospitals provide more pneumonia treatments than government hospitals. Teaching hospitals, however, are less likely to provide these pneumonia treatments. Hospitals also provide fewer treatments to areas with high minority populations. The lambda

---

[1]　The processes of heart failure includes an evaluation of the left ventricular systolic function, ACE inhibitor, discharge instructions, and smoking cessation advice during a hospital stay. The processes of pneumonia include giving initial antibiotic within 4 hours of arrival, screening for pneumococcal vaccination status, giving oxygenation, performing blood culture prior to the first hospital dose of antibiotics, giving smoking cessation advice, and giving appropriate initial antibiotics to immune – competent patients with pneumonia during the first 24 hours after arrival.

estimate indicates that when neighboring hospitals increase their pneumonia treatment rates by 1% on average, it increases its own hospital treatment rate by around 0. 56% . Hospitals have lower treatment rates when they have for – profit, not – for – profit and teaching hospitals in their neighborhoods.

6　Discussion

Our results suggest that not – for – profit hospitals provide better quality, especially for cardiac treatments. McClellan and Staiger (2000) also suggest that not – for – profit hospitals treat elderly patients with heart diseases slightly better than for – profits. One of the possible explanations is that for – profit hospitals are more aggressive on cost control. Eggleston and Shen (2011) find that the mortality rate for elderly heart attack patients is higher in for – profit hospitals, because they have more restrictive budget constraints. McKay and Deily (2008) also suggest that reductions in costs are associated with adverse consequences on health outcomes. In addition, not – for – profit hospitals enjoy tax exemptions. They are able to transfer the profit to services that are beneficial to patients. If the not – for – profit hospitals provide better services due to tax exemption, charitable obligations may benefit heart attack patients.

However, the effect of ownership depends on treatments and market structure. The results on PCI treatments suggest that not – for – profit hospitals provide better quality of heart attack treatments in an inter – sectoral market. When a market has only for – profit or only not – for – profit hospitals, there is no significant effect or the effects are traded off. However, when a not – for – profit hospital is located in a high for – profit market, the PCI treatment rate is significantly higher. According to the study of Horwitz and Nichols (2009), PCI is a relatively profitable service. This result is in line with their study that not – for – profits provide more profitable services in a high for – profit market. We also do not find strong evidence that hospitals provide different quality by ownership on heart attack treatments other than PCI. Not – for – profit hospitals

346

provide better heart failure treatment regardless of the ownership composition in the market. Ownership of neighboring hospitals offset the high pneumonia treatment rates of for – profit and not – for – profit hospitals. Therefore, our results on hospital ownership are mixed.

Our results support the competition hypothesis. Hospitals have lower treatment rates when they compete with hospitals of better quality. Competition may generate both positive and negative externalities at the same time. Hospitals compete by providing better quality, while improving quality can be very costly (Morey et al. , 1992) . Fournier and Mitchell (1992) and Robinson and Luft (1985) suggest that the level of competition is associated with increasing cost. The overall effect could be in line with studies of Propper, Burgess, and Green (2004) that competitions lower hospital quality[1]. Also, when a hospital has a larger neighbor, there is a higher probability of empty beds which is costly (Gaynor and Anderson, 1995) . Hospitals with more beds have diseconomy of scale. The cost may increase with increasing beds (Keeler, Melnick, and Zwanziger, 1999) . Hospitals may offer fewer treatments for financial reasons.

As expected, we also find that the spillover effect is stronger for less acute illness treatments than heart attack treatments. Less acute illnesses allow patients to travel further, making the competition among hospitals to increase. Positive externalities from competition and knowledge spillover improve medical services in the whole market.

Our results corroborate similar findings for France by Gobillon and Milcent (2012) . These authors find that local composition of ownership and demographic variables have limited effects on spatial disparity of innovative treatments in France. They also find strong spillover effects and suggest that regional unobservable factors account for 20% of spatial disparities.

----

[1] There are other studies that suggest competitions improve cost – effectiveness and generate economy of scale (Dranove, Shanley, and Simon, 1992; Kessler and McClellan, 2000, Zwanziger and Melnick, 1988) . In addition, Bloom et al. (2010) find that competition increases management quality of the public hospitals in the UK.

Since the overall effect depends upon the characteristics of the hospital itself, spillovers and market structure, this may explain why Gaynor (2006) suggests a mixed result for the effect of competition on hospital quality. Vickers and Yarrow (1988) also conclude that the competition level in the market could be a more important determinant of performance than type of ownership.

7　Conclusion

Our study employs a spatial Durbin panel data model to control for geographic correlation of treatments among hospitals. Our results suggest strong and positive spillover effects among hospitals. Our results should be tempered by the fact that we included basic treatments which were limited by data availability. Some hospitals may perform other effective treatments which are not available in our data set. In addition we only focused on three illness conditions. Some hospitals may provide better quality care treatments for other illness conditions not reported in our data set.

Our results on hospital ownership are mixed. While we find some evidence that hospitals have different operation strategies by ownership, this also depends on the market structure where the hospital is located. One thing that policy makers should not ignore is the effect of spillovers which we found to be strong and significant.

References

Aiken, Linda H. , Sean P. Clarke, Douglas M. Sloane, et al. 2002. "Hospital Nurse Staffing and Patient Mortality, Nurse Burnout, and Job Dissatisfaction." *The Journal of the American Medical Association* 288 (16): 1987 – 1993.

Baltagi, Badi H. 2011. "*Spatial Panels,*" Chapter 15 in *The Handbook of Empirical Economics and Finance*, Aman Ullah and David E. A. Giles, editors, Chapman and Hall, pp. 435 – 454.

Bayindir, Esra Eren. 2012. "Hospital Ownership Type and Treatment Choices." *Journal of Health Economics* 31: 359 – 370.

Bloom, Nicholas, Carol Propper, Stephan Seiler, and John Van Reenen. 2010. "The Impact of Competition on Management Quality: Evidence from Public Hospitals. " National Bureau of Economic Research (NBER) Working Paper No. 16032.

Belotti F. , Hughes G. , and Piano Mortari A. 2013. XSMLE: Stata module for spatial panel data models estimation, Statistical Software Components S457610, Boston College Department of Economics.

Chandra, Amitabh, and Douglas O. Staiger. 2007. "Productivity Spillovers in Health Care: Evidence from the Treatment of Heart Attacks. " *Journal of Political Economy* 115 (1): 103 – 140.

Clement, Jan P. , Kenneth R. White, and Vivian Valdmanis. 2002. "Charity Care: Do Not – For – Profits Influence For – Profits?" *Medical Care Research and Review* 57 (1): 59 – 78.

Debarsy, Nicolas. 2012. "The Mundlak Approach in the Spatial Durbin Panel Data Model. " *Spatial Economic Analysis* 7: 109 – 131.

Dranove, David, Mark Shanley, and Carol Simon. 1992. "Is Hospital Competition Wasteful?" *The RAND Journal of Economics* 23 (2): 247 – 262.

Eggleston, Karen, and Yu – Chu Shen. 2011. "Soft Budget Constraints and Ownership: Empirical Evidence from US Hospitals. " *Economics Letters* 110: 7 – 11.

Elhorst, J. Paul. 2003. "Specification and Estimation of Spatial Panel Data Models. " *International Regional Science Review* 26 (3): 244 – 268.

Fisher, Elliott S. , Douglas O. Staiger, Julie P. W. Bynum, and Daniel J. Gottlieb. 2007. "Creating Accountable Care Organizations: The Extended Hospital Medical Staff. " *Health Affairs* 26 (1): 44 – 57.

Fournier, Gary M. , and Jean M. Mitchell. 1992. "Hospital Costs and Competition for Services: A Multiproduct Analysis. " *The Review of Economics and Statistics* 74 (4): 627 – 634.

Gaynor, Martin. 2006. "What Do We Know About Competition and Quality In Health Care Markets?" National Bureau of Economic Research (NBER) Working Paper No. 12301.

Gaynor, Martin, and Gerard F. Anderson. 1995. "Uncertain Demand, the Structure of Hospital Costs, and the Cost of Empty Hospital Beds. " *Journal of Health Economics* 14: 291 – 317.

Geweke, John, Gautam Gowrisankaran, and Robert J. Town. 2003. "Bayesian Inference for Hospital Quality in a Selection Model. " *Econometrica* 71 (4): 1215 – 1238.

Gobillon, Laurent, and Carine Milcent. 2012. " Spatial Disparities in Hospital

Performance. " Forthcoming in: *Journal of Economic Geography*.

Heidenreich, Paul A. , and Mark McClellan. 2001. "Trends in Treatment and Outcomes for Acute Myocardial Infarction: 1975 – 1995. " *The American Journal of Medicine* 110 (3): 165 – 174.

Hirth, Richard A. 1997. "Competition between For – Profit and Not – For – Profit Health Care Providers: Can It Help Achieve Social Goals. " *Medical Care Research and Review* 54: 414 – 438.

Horwitz, Jill R. , and Austin Nichols. 2007. "What Do Nonprofits Maximize? Nonprofit Hospital Service Provision and Market Ownership Mix. " National Bureau of Economic Research (NBER) Working Paper No. 13246.

Horwitz, Jill R. , and Austin Nichols. 2009. "Hospital Ownership and Medical Services: Market Mix, Spillover Effects, and Nonprofit Objectives. " *Journal of Health Economics* 28: 924 – 937.

Jung, Kyoungrae, Roger Feldman, and Dennis Scanlon. 2011. "Where Would You Go For Your Next Hospitalization?" *Journal of Health Economics* 30: 832 – 841.

Kapoor, M. , Kelejian, H. H. , Prucha, I. R. 2007. "Panel Data Models with Spatially Correlated Error Components. " *Journal of Econometrics* 140 (1): 97 – 130.

Keeler, Daniel P. and Mark B. McCleallan. 2000. "Is Hospital Competition Socially Wasteful?" *The Quarterly Journal of Economics* 115 (2): 577 – 615.

Keeler, Emmett B. , Glenn Melnick, and Jack Zwanziger. 1999. "The Changing Effects of Competition on Non – Profit and For – Profit Hospital Pricing Behavior" . *Journal of Health Economics* 18: 69 – 86.

Keeler, Emmett B. , Lisa V. Rubenstein; Katherine L. Kahn, et al. 1992. "Hospital Characteristics and Quality of Care. " *The Journal of the American Medical Association* 268 (13): 1709 – 1714.

Kessler, Daniel P. , and Mark B. McClellan. 2002. "The Effects of Hospital Ownership on Medical Productivity. " *The RAND Journal of Economics* 33: 488 – 506.

Lee, A. James, and Burton Allen Weisbrod. 1977. "Collective Goods and the Voluntary Sector: The Case of the Hospital Industry. " In: Burton Allen Weisbrod, editor. *The Voluntary Nonprofit Sector.* Lexington Books, Lexington, MA.

Lee, Lung – fei, and Jihai Yu. 2010. "Some Recent Developments in Spatial Panel Data Models. " *Regional Science and Urban Economics* 40: 255 – 271.

LeSage, J. , and Pace, R. K. , 2009. An Introduction to Spatial Econometrics. CRC

Press, Taylor & Francis Group, Boca Raton, London, New York.

McClellan, Mark, and Douglas Staiger. 2000. "Comparing Hospital Quality at For - Profit and Not - For - Profit Hospitals. " In: David M. Cutler, editor. *The changing hospital industry: comparing not – for – profit and for – profit institutions*. Chicago: The University of Chicago Press.

McKay, Niccie L. , and Mary E. Deily. 2008. "Cost Inefficiency and Hospital Health Outcomes. " *Health Economics* 17: 833 – 848.

Millo, Giovanni, and Gianfranco Piras. 2012. "Splm: Spatial Panel Data Models in R. " *Journal of Statistical Software* 47 (1): 1 – 38.

Mobley, Lee R. , Elisabeth Root, Luc Anselin, et al. 2006. "Spatial Analysis of Elderly Access to Primary Care Services. " *International Journal of Health Geographics*: 5 – 19.

Morey, Richard C. , David J. Fine, Stephen W. Loree, et al. 1992. "The Trade - Off between Hospital Cost and Quality of Care: An Exploratory Empirical Analysis. " *Medical Care* 30 (8): 677 – 698.

Moscone, Francesco, Elisa Tosetti, and Giorgio Vittadini. 2012. "Social Interaction in Patients' Hospital Choice: Evidences from Italy. " *Journal of the Royal Statistical Society* 175 (2): 453 – 472.

Mutl, J. and M. Pfaffermayr. 2010. "The Hausman Test in a Cliff and Ord Panel Model. " *Econometrics Journal*, 10: 1 – 30.

Nallamothu, Brahmajee K et al. 2005. "Times to Treatment in Transfer Patients Undergoing Primary Percutaneous Coronary Intervention in the United States. " *Circulation* 111: 761 – 767.

Newhouse, Joseph P. 1970. "Toward a Theory of Not - For - Profit Institutions: An Economic Model of a Hospital. " *The American Economic Review* 60: 64 – 74.

Pauly, Mark, and Michael Redisch. 1973. " The Not - For - Profit Hospital as Physicians' Cooperative. " *The American Economic Review* 63: 87 – 99.

Porell, Frank W. , and E. Kathleen Adams. 1995. "Hospital Choice Models: A Review and Assessment of Their Utility for Policy Impact Analysis. " *Medical Care Research and Review* 52 (2): 158 – 195.

Propper, Carol, Simon Burgess, and Katherine Green. 2004. " Does Competition Between Hospitals Improve the Quality of Care? Hospital Death Rate and the NHS Internal Market. " *Journal of Public Economics* 88: 1247 – 1272.

Robinson, James C., and Harold S. Luft. 1985. "The Impact of Hospital Market Structure on Patient Volume, Average Length of Stay, and the Cost of Care." *Journal of Health Economics* 4: 333 – 356.

Rogers, William J., John G. Canto, Costas T. Lambrew, et al. 2000. "Temporal Trends in the Treatment of Over 1.5 Million Patients with Myocardial Infarction in the U.S. from 1990 through 1999." *Journal of the American College of Cardiology* 36 (7): 2056 – 2063.

Ryan, Thomas J., Elliott M. Antman, Neil H. Brooks, et al. 1999. "1999 Update: ACC/AHA Guidelines for the Management of Patients with Acute Myocardial Infarction: Executive Summary and Recommendations: A Report of the American College of Cardiology/American Heart Association Task Force on Practice Guidelines." *Circulation* 100: 1016 – 1030.

Skinner, Jonathan. 2012. "Causes and Consequences of Regional Variations in Health Care." in Thomas G. McGuire, Mark V. Pauly, and Pedro P. Baros, editors. *Handbook of Health Economics Vol.* 2. Elsevier Science B. V.

Sloan, Frank A. 2000. "Not – For – Profit Ownership and Hospital Behavior." in Culyer, A. J. and Newhouse, J. P., editors. *Handbook of Health Economics.* Elsevier Science B. V.

Sloan, Frank A., Gabriel A. Picone, Donald H. Taylor Jr., Shin – Yi Chou. 2001. "Hospital Ownership and Cost and Quality of Care: Is There a Dime's Worth of Difference?" *Journal of Health Economics* 20: 1 – 21.

Sloan, Frank A., and Donald H. Taylor. 1999. "Does Ownership Affect the Cost of Medicare?" In: Rettenmaier, A. J., Saving, T. R., editors. *Medicare Reform: Issues and Answers.* University of Chicago Press, Chicago, IL: 99 – 129.

Tay, Abigail. 2003. "Assessing Competition in Hospital Care Markets: The Importance of Accounting for Quality Differentiation." *The RAND Journal of Economics* 34 (4): 786 – 814.

The Dartmouth Atlas of Health Care. Available atwww. dartmouthatlas. org. Last accessed Februery 2013.

Vickers, John, and George K. Yarrow. 1988. "Privatization: An Economics Analysis." MIT Press, Cambridge, MA.

Yuan, Zhong, Gregory S. Cooper, Douglas Einstadter, et al. 2000. "The Association between Hospital Type and Mortality and Length of Stay: A Study of 16.9 Million Hospitalized Medicare Beneficiaries." *Medical Care* 38 (2): 231 – 245.

Zwanziger, Jack, and Glenn A. Melnick. 1988. "The Effects of Hospital Competition and the Medicare PPS Program on Hospitals Cost Behavior in California. " *Journal of Health Economics* 7: 301 – 320.

Figure 1　Geographic Distribution of the Summary Hospital Compare Quality Score in Hospital Referral Regions

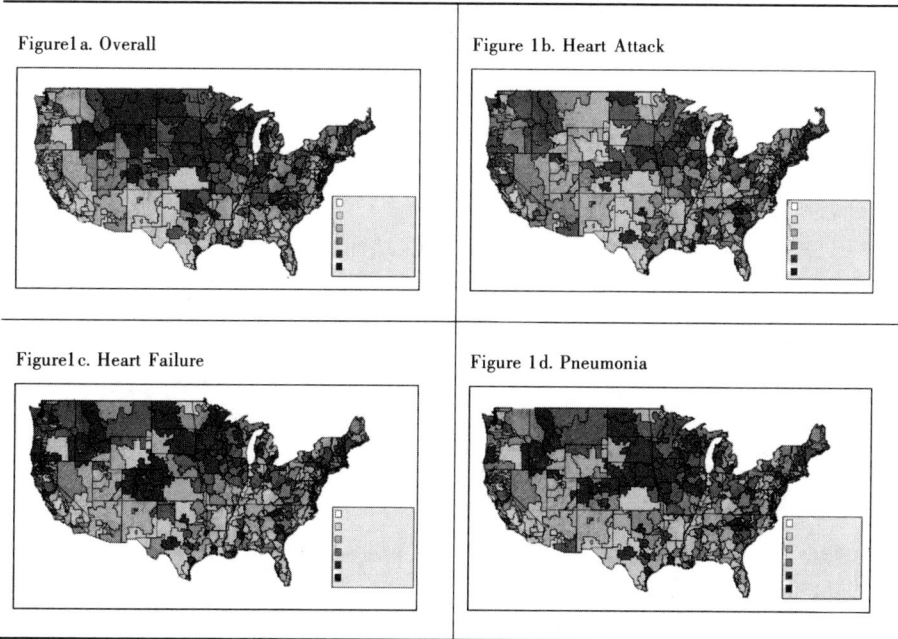

Figure 1 a. Overall

Figure 1 b. Heart Attack

Figure 1 c. Heart Failure

Figure 1 d. Pneumonia

Source: The Dartmouth Atlas of Health Care （The Dartmouth Institute for Health Policy and Clinical Practice） .

Table 1　Descriptive Statistics

	Mean	Std. Dev.	Min	Max
Dependent Variables:				
Heart Attack Treatments:				
Overall	0. 921	0. 065	0. 257	1
Medication at arrival	0. 934	0. 063	0. 28	1
Medication at discharge	0. 917	0. 086	0	1
PCI	0. 627	0. 197	0	1
Heart Failure Overall Treatments:	0. 797	0. 129	0. 05	1
Pneumonia Overall Treatments:	0. 835	0. 082	0. 447	1

Continued

	Mean	Std. Dev.	Min	Max
Independent Variables:				
For – profit	0. 185	0. 389	0	1
Not – for – profit	0. 687	0. 464	0	1
Number of beds (in 100's)	2. 632	2. 103	0. 04	22. 07
Nurses per bed	1. 102	0. 522	0. 2	7. 04
Teaching Status	0. 412	0. 49	0	1
Located in an MSA	0. 894	0. 308	0	1
HHI	0. 137	0. 172	0. 001	0. 971
% never married	0. 309	0. 06	0. 166	0. 557
% HS dropouts	0. 151	0. 059	0. 018	0. 418
% HS grads	0. 29	0. 067	0. 116	0. 55
Median earnings (in 10000's)	3. 379	0. 061	1. 741	6. 09
% male	0. 49	0. 011	0. 445	0. 58
% Hispanic	0. 145	0. 159	0	0. 951
% black	0. 126	0. 129	0	0. 668
% elderly	0. 125	0. 033	0. 046	0. 335
Population density (in 10000's)	0. 223	0. 668	0. 001	0. 716

Table 2　Estimates of Spillover Effects and Hospital Characteristics on Heart Attack Treatments

Treatment	Overall		Medication at arrival		Medication at discharge		PCI	
	(1)	(2)	(3)	(4)	(5)	(6)	(7)	(8)
For – profit	− 0. 005	− 0. 005	− 0. 008**	− 0. 007*	− 0. 008	− 0. 007	0. 010	0. 013
	(0. 004)	(0. 004)	(0. 004)	(0. 004)	(0. 005)	(0. 005)	(0. 018)	(0. 018)
Not – for – profit	0. 007**	0. 006*	0. 003	0. 003	0. 005	0. 003	0. 058***	0. 058***
	(0. 003)	(0. 003)	(0. 003)	(0. 003)	(0. 004)	(0. 004)	(0. 016)	(0. 016)
Number of beds	0. 004***	0. 005***	0. 004***	0. 004***	0. 007***	0. 007***	0. 003	0. 002
	(0. 001)	(0. 001)	(0. 001)	(0. 001)	(0. 001)	(0. 001)	(0. 002)	(0. 002)
Nurses per bed	0. 008***	0. 008***	0. 008***	0. 008***	0. 008***	0. 008***	0. 038***	0. 036***
	(0. 002)	(0. 002)	(0. 002)	(0. 002)	(0. 003)	(0. 003)	(0. 009)	(0. 009)
Teaching Status	0. 011***	0. 013***	0. 011***	0. 013***	0. 018***	0. 020***	− 0. 019*	− 0. 019*

Continued

Treatment	Overall		Medication at arrival		Medication at discharge		PCI	
	(1)	(2)	(3)	(4)	(5)	(6)	(7)	(8)
	(0.002)	(0.002)	(0.002)	(0.002)	(0.003)	(0.003)	(0.010)	(0.010)
Located in an MSA	0.003	0.005	0.001	0.003	0.006	0.008	0.030	0.031
	(0.005)	(0.005)	(0.004)	(0.004)	(0.006)	(0.006)	(0.033)	(0.033)
HHI	− 0.010	− 0.010	− 0.011	− 0.012	− 0.013	− 0.012	− 0.009	− 0.001
	(0.009)	(0.010)	(0.009)	(0.009)	(0.012)	(0.013)	(0.050)	(0.050)
% never married	0.061**	0.064**	0.051*	0.053*	0.076**	0.077**	− 0.286*	− 0.280*
	(0.028)	(0.029)	(0.028)	(0.028)	(0.038)	(0.039)	(0.153)	(0.153)
% HS dropouts	− 0.037	− 0.033	− 0.030	− 0.032	− 0.060*	− 0.045	− 0.080	− 0.118
	(0.032)	(0.032)	(0.031)	(0.031)	(0.044)	(0.044)	(0.175)	(0.176)
% HS grads	− 0.015	− 0.019	− 0.018	− 0.022	− 0.054	− 0.057*	− 0.256*	− 0.236*
	(0.025)	(0.025)	(0.025)	(0.025)	(0.034)	(0.034)	(0.133)	(0.133)
Median earnings	0.003	0.004	0.003	0.004	0.001	0.004	− 0.010	− 0.010
	(0.003)	(0.003)	(0.003)	(0.003)	(0.004)	(0.004)	(0.017)	(0.017)
% male	0.013	− 0.026	0.094	0.064	0.035	− 0.026	0.606	0.688
	(0.111)	(0.112)	(0.111)	(0.112)	(0.151)	(0.154)	(0.640)	(0.639)
% Hispanic	− 0.016	− 0.003	− 0.004	0.005	− 0.031*	− 0.010	− 0.069	− 0.068
	(0.014)	(0.014)	(0.013)	(0.013)	(0.018)	(0.019)	(0.075)	(0.075)
% black	− 0.029*	− 0.019	− 0.018	− 0.009	− 0.031	− 0.018	− 0.134*	− 0.119
	(0.015)	(0.015)	(0.015)	(0.015)	(0.020)	(0.021)	(0.081)	(0.008)
% elderly	0.071	0.078	0.078	0.083	0.122*	0.132*	− 0.010	− 0.091
	(0.052)	(0.053)	(0.050)	(0.051)	(0.070)	(0.070)	(0.271)	(0.271)
Population density	− 0.004**	− 0.004	− 0.003*	− 0.003	− 0.006**	− 0.005*	− 0.008	− 0.007
	(0.002)	(0.002)	(0.002)	(0.002)	(0.003)	(0.003)	(0.011)	(0.011)
Spatial (λ)	0.414***	0.500***	0.424***	0.452***	0.350***	0.476***	0.401***	0.414***
	(0.067)	(0.076)	(0.071)	(0.079)	(0.068)	(0.080)	(0.087)	(0.082)
Market Structure:								
For − profit		− 0.001		− 0.0004		0.005		− 0.001
		(0.007)		(0.007)		(0.010)		(0.028)
Not − for − profit		0.007		0.007		0.015*		− 0.056**
		(0.006)		(0.006)		(0.008)		(0.024)
Number of beds		− 0.004***		− 0.003***		− 0.005***		− 0.007**

355

Continued

Treatment	Overall		Medication at arrival		Medication at discharge		PCI	
	(1)	(2)	(3)	(4)	(5)	(6)	(7)	(8)
		(0.001)		(0.001)		(0.002)		(0.003)
Nurses per bed		0.003		0.005		0.004		− 0.022
		(0.004)		(0.004)		(0.005)		(0.016)
Teaching Status		− 0.008**		− 0.005		− 0.011**		0.020
		(0.004)		(0.004)		(0.005)		(0.015)
State fixed effect?	Yes	Yes	Yes	Yes	Yes	Yes	Yes	Yes
Year fixed effect?	Yes	Yes	Yes	Yes	Yes	Yes	Yes	Yes
F – test for state fixed effects	3.33***	2.92***	3.68***	3.11***	3.50***	3.10***	3.37***	3.42***
F – test for year fixed effects	63***	62***	77***	77***	90***	89***	21***	22***
Number of hospitals	2094	2094	2094	2094	2094	2094	941	941
Observations	8376	8376	8376	8376	8376	8376	3764	3764

Standard errors are in parentheses.

* Significant at 10%.

** Significant at 5%.

*** Significant at 1%.

Table 3 Estimates of Spillover Effects and Hospital Characteristics on Heart Failure and Pneumonia Treatments

Treatment	Heart Failure		Pneumonia	
	(1)	(2)	(3)	(4)
For – profit	0.002	0.003	0.011***	0.010***
	(0.007)	(0.007)	(0.004)	(0.004)
Not – for – profit	0.024***	0.024***	0.020***	0.020***
	(0.006)	(0.006)	(0.003)	(0.003)
Number of beds	0.005***	0.005***	− 0.001	− 0.001
	(0.001)	(0.001)	(0.001)	(0.001)
Nurses per bed	0.011***	0.010***	0.000	0.000
	(0.004)	(0.004)	(0.002)	(0.002)

Continued

Treatment	Heart Failure		Pneumonia	
	(1)	(2)	(3)	(4)
Teaching Status	0. 002	0. 004	-0. 008 ***	-0. 007 ***
	(0. 004)	(0. 004)	(0. 002)	(0. 002)
Located in an MSA	0. 006	0. 009	-0. 001	0. 001
	(0. 009)	(0. 009)	(0. 004)	(0. 004)
HHI	-0. 025	-0. 026	-0. 010	-0. 012
	(0. 018)	(0. 018)	(0. 008)	(0. 009)
% never married	-0. 047	-0. 036	-0. 003	0. 001
	(0. 055)	(0. 056)	(0. 027)	(0. 027)
% HS dropouts	-0. 030	-0. 036	0. 007	0. 004
	(0. 059)	(0. 060)	(0. 029)	(0. 029)
% HS grads	0. 004	-0. 008	0. 015	0. 012
	(0. 048)	(0. 049)	(0. 024)	(0. 024)
Median earnings	0. 002	0. 002	0. 004	0. 004
	(0. 006)	(0. 006)	(0. 003)	(0. 003)
% male	-0. 310	-0. 354 *	-0. 046	-0. 057
	(0. 210)	(0. 212)	(0. 105)	(0. 105)
% Hispanic	0. 013	0. 023	-0. 022 *	-0. 025 *
	(0. 025)	(0. 026)	(0. 013)	(0. 013)
% black	-0. 011	0. 002	-0. 028 *	-0. 031 **
	(0. 029)	(0. 030)	(0. 014)	(0. 015)
% elderly	0. 039	0. 039	-0. 002	-0. 003
	(0. 101)	(0. 102)	(0. 049)	(0. 051)
Population density	-0. 002	-0. 002	-0. 002	-0. 002
	(0. 004)	(0. 004)	(0. 002)	(0. 002)
Spatial (λ)	0. 694 ***	0. 669 ***	0. 777 ***	0. 555 ***
	(0. 078)	(0. 077)	(0. 073)	(0. 067)
Market Structure:				
For - profit		-0. 015		-0. 017 **
		(0. 014)		(0. 007)
Not - for - profit		-0. 010		-0. 013 **

Continued

Treatment	Heart Failure		Pneumonia	
	(1)	(2)	(3)	(4)
		(0.012)		(0.006)
Number of beds		−0.006**		−0.001
		(0.002)		(0.001)
Nurses per bed		0.001		−0.001
		(0.007)		(0.003)
Teaching Status		−0.007		−0.006*
		(0.007)		(0.004)
State fixed effect?	Yes	Yes	Yes	Yes
Year fixed effect?	Yes	Yes	Yes	Yes
F − test statistic for state fixed effects	5.74***	5.39***	8.72***	8.20***
F − test statistic for year fixed effects	244.7***	244***	634***	636***
Number of hospitals	2192	2192	2134	2134
Observations	8768	8768	8536	8536

Standard errors are in parentheses.

* Significant at 10%.

** Significant at 5%.

*** Significant at 1%.

358

附　录

2013 中德公共管理国际研讨会开幕式纪要

2013 年 9 月 24 日上午 8 点到 8 点 30 分，2013 中德公共管理国际研讨会开幕式在西南财经大学光华校区住友苑两楼会议室举行，开幕式由西南财经大学公共管理学院院长唐兴霖教授主持。

西南财经大学张宗益校长首先致欢迎辞。张校长代表学校对出席本次会议的各位嘉宾表示热烈欢迎，也向本届研讨会的顺利开幕表示热烈祝贺。张校长指出，在西南财经大学举办的第八届中德公共管理国际研讨会，要一起探讨中国和德国公共管理理论与实践当中的重要问题。中德公共管理国际研讨会是我们学校与德国柏林经济与政法大学一起共同举办的，创始于 2006 年，现在已经是中德两国学者研讨公共管理理论与实践的重要学术平台。这个平台虽然始建于 2006 年，但实际上我们学校与德国柏林经济与政法大学合作可以追溯到 1986 年。这 27 年以来，我们学校与柏林经济与政法大学的合作领域不断拓宽，而且是在持续地发展。应该说，两个学校的合作是富有远见而且卓有成效的。西南财经大学在这个过程当中也得到了相当大的发展。张校长指出，目前而言，无论是中国还是欧美国家，经济建设都面临许多共同的问题，在交通、教育、社区发展、就业、民生、医疗等方面，都存在许多问题需要共同来探讨。张校长期待本届研讨会能够围绕一些新问题新挑战展开深入对话，取得新的突破。最后，张校长祝第八届中德公共管理国际研讨会圆满成功！

德国成都领事馆副领事马晏子先生致辞。马晏子先生说："今天非常高兴能在这里参加第八届中德公共管理国际研讨会，和大家一起探讨有关社会管理与公共管理方面的问题，因为现在在中国这是个非常重要的问题。上个月德国开始的议会选举已经得到了各界人士的关注。而之所以会引起如此多的关注，主要是因为德国社会的发展对整个欧洲的发展都有相当大的影响。在欧洲，西班牙、希腊等国家都属于福利过高的国家，由此也引发了相当多的社会问题。政府的很多决策决定了各个国家经济的发展及购买力，整个社会的变迁和发展变成了非常重要的问题。在德国，两党之间的变动也往往影响整个社会的发展，与此同时，整个民族的发展也决定了社会的发展。中国还存在一些社会问题，如老龄化问题，这些问题都需要采用科学的方法去分析和解决。因此我非常希望通过这次会议与大家一同深入探讨这些社会问题。西南财经大学与德国柏林经济与政法大学的此次合作就提供了很好的平台来讨论这些问题。我在此预祝大会的成功！"

德国柏林经济与政法大学公共管理学院院长 Busch 教授致辞。Busch 院长说："我非常高兴今天能来参加此次会议，同时也非常感谢西南财经大学对我们的邀请。我也代表德国柏林经济与政法大学的校长祝贺此次会议顺利召开。Busch 院长说，这次大会代表了中德两国和中德两校间长久以来的友谊，我们非常珍惜这份友谊，同时希望我们的合作能够更好地发展下去。中国和德国作为两个大国，彼此间有很多相似的地方，也都正在经历着整个社会的变革。在我们的社会管理中，也都面临着很多相似的问题。包括刚才提到的有关人口老龄化的问题，以及很多关于贫困人口的问题。所以希望我们所有专家能够在一起共同探讨这些问题，也非常高兴有许多来自其他学校的专家来到这里与我们一同讨论。通过这次大会，希望我们可以在未来更好地合作与研究。我也在此预祝大会成功，希望大家都能够有很好的探讨与交流！"

广西民族大学副校长李珍刚教授致辞。李珍刚教授说："我很高兴能够在西南财经大学参加第八届中德公共管理国际研讨会。我代表各地前来参加本次盛会的专家教授，对此次会议的召开表示热烈的祝贺，对西南财经大学及公共管理学院的盛意邀请和周到安排表示由衷的谢意。"李珍刚教授认为这次会议以社会改革和社会政策为主题很有意义。中共十八大指出，要在改善民生和创新管理中加强社会建设，社会领域的改革和建设需要科学有效的社会政策加以规范、引导。在我国，社会改革和社会政策是相互影响，相辅相成的。社会改革和社会政策的理论相互印证，相互支撑。理论是行动的先导，无论是社会改革还是社会政策，我们国家目前都处于探索阶段，还有许多薄弱环节乃至空白亟待探讨，因此迫切需要科学理论加以探索和指导。可以说，在实践上社会改革和社会政策应处于我国社会发展的前沿地带，理论上，社会改革和社会政策研究正上升为我国社会科学的先驱。在社会改革和社会政策领域，国外特别像德国这样发达的国家，已经有了一百多年的发展历史，积累了丰富的经验教训，提出了诸多富有影响的相关结论，成了人类文明的重要组成部分，值得我们学习和进步。这次国际学术会议汇聚了中德两国的学术专家，为大量探讨社会改革和社会政策提供了良好的交流平台。李珍刚教授说："我和唐兴霖院长说，西南财大是学术集市，我们是赶集来了。相信在西南财经大学提供的这个国际学术集市和学术交流平台上，各位专家能够积极交流，相信在座各位都会取得很大的收获。同时，这次研讨会所形成的成果也必将对我国社会改革、社会改革的推进和社会政策的创新，以及我国社会建设的科学化、社会发展的现代化提供积极的推动作用。最后，预祝这次国际学术研讨会取得圆满成功！"

2013 中德公共管理国际研讨会闭幕式纪要

2013 年 9 月 24 日 17 点 15 分到 17 点 30 分，2013 中德公共管理国际研讨会闭幕式在西南财经大学光华校区住友苑二楼会议室举行，闭幕式由西南财经大学公共管理学院分党委书记章群教授主持。

西南财经大学副校长尹庆双教授总结发言。尹庆双教授说由西南财经大学和柏林经济与政法大学联合举办、西南财经大学公共管理学院承办的"第八届中德公共管理国际研讨会"即将进入尾声。这次与会的 60 多名专家就共同感兴趣的社会改革与社会政策问题进行了激烈的、饶有兴趣的讨论，各位的精彩演讲及思想火花已经展现在大家面前，并留在了西南财经大学。我们学校和德国柏林经济与政法大学的合作已经 27 年了，开始于 1986 年。合作的方式涵盖了教学、科研、教师和学生交换、国际研讨会、联合培养研究生及在各自的刊物上发表对方文章等项目。尹庆双教授说，记得我们中德公共管理国际研讨会的开始在 2006 年，是当时我和 Kulke 教授在柏林敲定的。在双方合作过程中，除了中德公共管理国际研讨会以外，双方还经常一起相互交流并交换留学生。我觉得这是非常有意义的一个项目。在此我要代表学校，感谢在座的三位德国教授。如果说西南财经大学和德国柏林经济与政法大学的合作是一个长跑的话，那么这三位是前三棒。第一棒，是我们项目的开拓者 Kulke 教授。Kulke 教授即将退休，对此我表达两层意思。第一，感谢他长期以来对这个合作项目的支持，对此我表达敬意。第二，我们友谊长存。要感谢的第二位教授，是 Breinlinger 教授，他是第二棒。他把公共卫生管理引入了公共管理学科，引入了与西南财经大学的合作项目中。要感谢的第三位教授是 Busch 院长，她在双方留学生交换项目当中，开拓了一个新的领域。非常感谢这三位优秀教授对我们长期合作所作出的努力，希望未来我们双方学校能够有更多的合作机会！

德国柏林经济与政法大学公共管理学院院长 Busch 教授总结发言。Busch 教授说："非常有幸能够参加这次国际研讨会，同时也很感谢刚刚尹校长所讲对我们工作的认可。这次研讨会不仅仅是西南财经大学和我们学校共同探讨和研究学术的平台，更是促进中德两国之间相互沟通，共同学习的一个机会。今天各位学者的演讲都非常精彩，相信在座的各位都有非常大的收获。同时，希望往后每届的研讨也都会像今天一样精彩。我也期待在今后能够和西南财经大学有更多更好的合作机会，盼望下次与大家见面！"

西南财经大学公共管理学院院长唐兴霖教授总结发言。唐兴霖教授说，首先非常感谢尹校长和 Busch 院长的总结发言，同时也感谢今天各位学者在研讨会上作的精彩演讲。唐兴霖教授说，这次研讨会有两个"没有想到"：一是没有想到研讨会的时间过得这么快，好像刚刚开始就结束了，二是没有想到学校、各兄弟院校、社会媒体这么支持这次研讨会。这次研讨会主要围绕"社会改革和社会政策"主题展开，在研究和比较中德两国社会改革和社会政策现状的同时，探讨了解决社会问题的方法路径，以及公共管理研究发展的新方向。虽然研讨会仅仅持续了一天，但大家在此交流、沟通、分享、研讨，不同的观点得到了碰撞与融合，形成了更为成熟的思想沉淀。唐兴霖教授说，非常高兴有今天这样的机会，能够和柏林经济与政法大学的优秀学者有这样面对面的交流，同时期待在未来双方学校能够有更多更好的合作项目和机会。唐兴霖教授说，建议明年在德国举办的"第九届中德公共管理国际研讨会"主题为"社会创新与公共服务"。唐兴霖院长再次感谢各位学者莅临西南财大，期待今后每年的此时此刻，我们都能相聚一堂，共襄盛举！最后唐兴霖院长宣布第八届中德公共管理国际研讨会顺利闭幕！

图书在版编目（CIP）数据

走向社会治理的公共管理：2013 第八届中德公共管理国际研讨会
论文集／尹庆双，唐兴霖主编 .—北京：社会科学文献出版社，2014.6
ISBN 978 - 7 - 5097 - 6036 - 9

Ⅰ.①走…　Ⅱ.①尹…②唐…　Ⅲ.①公共管理 - 研究 - 中国 - 文集
②公共管理 - 研究 - 德国 - 文集　Ⅳ.①D63 - 53②D751.63 - 53

中国版本图书馆 CIP 数据核字（2014）第 106480 号

走向社会治理的公共管理

——2013 第八届中德公共管理国际研讨会论文集

主　　编／尹庆双　唐兴霖

出 版 人／谢寿光
出 版 者／社会科学文献出版社
地　　址／北京市西城区北三环中路甲 29 号院 3 号楼华龙大厦
邮政编码／100029

责任部门／社会政法分社　（010）59367156　　　责任编辑／李　响
电子信箱／shekebu@ ssap. cn　　　　　　　　责任校对／王翠荣
项目统筹／曹义恒　　　　　　　　　　　　　责任印制／岳　阳
经　　销／社会科学文献出版社市场营销中心　（010）59367081　59367089
读者服务／读者服务中心　（010）59367028

印　　装／三河市尚艺印装有限公司
开　　本／787mm×1092mm　1/16　　　　　印　　张／23.25
版　　次／2014 年 6 月第 1 版　　　　　　　彩插印张／0.5
印　　次／2014 年 6 月第 1 次印刷　　　　　字　　数／377 千字
书　　号／ISBN 978 - 7 - 5097 - 6036 - 9
定　　价／88.00 元